American
Military
Thought

The American Heritage Series

The American Heritage Series

UNDER THE GENERAL EDITORSHIP OF
LEONARD W. LEVY AND ALFRED YOUNG

American Military Thought

Edited by
WALTER MILLIS

Center for the
Study of Democratic Institutions

THE BOBBS-MERRILL COMPANY, INC.
A Subsidiary of Howard W. Sams & Co., Inc.
PUBLISHERS • INDIANAPOLIS • NEW YORK • KANSAS CITY

American
Military
Thought

The American Heritage Series

Foreword

THIS VOLUME IS THE FIRST ANTHOLOGY OF ITS KIND, THE FIRST TO collect the original materials that demonstrate how Americans "have tended to think about war, military policy, and the military factor in their free society." Of obvious value to specialists, it should interest all students of American history, for whom it can open a subject they can no longer afford to neglect. And for all who believe that "war is too important to be left to the generals," the book can provide perspective on the perilous dilemmas that confront the United States.

The aim of the anthology is to assemble the most important documents for American military history up to 1945 and to suggest no more than the broad outlines of "the military revolution" since then. There have been very few theorists of American military policy. The country's leading military figures have usually not been military philosophers, and the country in general has not given serious thought to military problems until quite recently. The documents reflect these realities. Here are selections from several of America's few influential professional military thinkers: Henry W. Halleck, Emory Upton, and Alfred Thayer Mahan. Here are the state papers of presidents and other leading political figures that reflect the national consensus on military thought, from Washington and Hamilton to Kennedy and McNamara. And here, especially, are little-known official reports of the Secretaries of War and of the Navy, military commissions and chiefs of staff.

Walter Millis brings to this task the perspective not of a historian of battle tactics but of a historian and journalist long interested in the political, social, and economic implications of military policy. His book, *Arms and Men,* is the pathfinding synthesis of the subject. His works on the origins of America's War with Spain, World War I, and World War II reflect the same broad interests, as does his writing in recent years on the search for alternatives to war in the nuclear age.

This book is one of a series of which the aim is to provide the essential primary sources of the American experience, especially of American thought. The series, when completed, will constitute a documentary library of American history, filling a need long felt among scholars, students, librarians, and general readers for authoritative collections of original materials. Some volumes will illuminate the thought of significant individuals, such as James Madison or Louis Brandeis; some will deal with movements, such as that of the Antifederalists or the Populists; others will be organized around special themes, such as Puritan political thought, or American Catholic thought on social questions. Many volumes will take up the large number of subjects traditionally studied in American history for which, surprisingly, there are no documentary anthologies; others will pioneer in introducing contemporary subjects of increasing importance to scholars. The series aspires to maintain the high standards demanded of contemporary editing, providing authentic texts, intelligently and unobtrusively edited. It will also have the distinction of presenting pieces of substantial length which give the full character and flavor of the original. The series will be the most comprehensive and authoritative of its kind.

LEONARD W. LEVY
ALFRED YOUNG

Contents

Introduction

ASSEMBLING A DOCUMENTATION OF AMERICAN MILITARY THOUGHT is a task that raises difficulties of subject matter, source, and definition, as well as of selection. American military men, until quite recently, have not generally been given to philosophical reflection on their profession. We have produced no Clausewitzes and not many who rank with the leading European theorists of war. When "The Makers of Modern Strategy," a conspectus of military thought, was published (under the editorship of Edward Mead Earle) during World War II, only two of the thirty-four men individually studied were Americans—Alexander Hamilton and Alfred Thayer Mahan. American soldiers, to say nothing of the civilians, have produced an immense literature on war, but overwhelmingly it deals with either military history or military techniques—tactics, weaponry, logistics—neither subject being quite what is ordinarily implied by "military thought." In their memoirs and papers, our outstanding military figures have, as a rule, confined themselves to the narration of the triumphs over which they presided rather than to the thoughtful analysis of the implications. William Tecumseh Sherman, for example, probably our most brilliant and perceptive soldier down to the World War II era, left no formal statement of his theories of war or of his strategic insights, which were to influence many commanders in the twentieth century.

Another difficulty is that American military thinking has usually proceeded in controversy—in the earlier days over weaponry and tactics, later over organization and command, more recently over basic strategic concepts. It is not easy to document three centuries of controversy; to do so fairly, one would have to present all sides of innumerable arguments. The solution here adopted has been to try to find documents that represent such measure of consensus as was from time to time achieved. It is for this reason that many of the papers here collected are not by professional soldiers or seamen; they are statements by Presidents, civilian secretaries or boards, and acts of Congress, authoritatively summarizing the outcome of much military debate. To most or all of these documents military men made large contribution. The series of annual reports of the Secretary of War, for example, through which Elihu Root achieved the reorganization of the Army after the Spanish-American War, were produced only with the advice and help of the abler soldiers, and are legitimate examples of military thought even if they were written by a Wall Street lawyer with no military experience whatever until President McKinley asked him to take over the War Department.

It has seemed necessary, indeed, to adopt a broad definition of "American military thought." It is here taken to include the way in which not only American professional soldiers but also Americans generally have tended to think about war, military policy, and the military factor in their free society. This definition, broad as it is, at the same time excludes many types of material. There is no attempt to report on the British and Continental writers whose influence was always dominant in American thinking. The concern is not with military history, as such, or, for the most part, with military technology. During the long security of the nineteenth century, when all basic issues of national policy and national strategy seemed settled for good, military thought turned largely on technical problems—the design of weapons, tactics, regimental organization, the introduction of steam and armor into naval warfare—and while argument could be lively, these issues are of little present relevance. Only as the rapid development of military technology began, from the turn of this century on, to shape policy and strategy, do the techniques of war become an increasingly significant element in the literature.

Many other aspects of American military thought will not be documented in a volume of this character. The pacifist movement of the 1840's and the military responses to it; the perennial questions of civil-military relations; the several "great debates" between the isolationist and the interventionist views of international affairs; the socioeconomic problems involved in the development of a massive war industry; the complex strategic issues presented in the course of waging two world wars; the problems of disarmament and international organization—each of these has had prominent place in American thinking about war and military policy, but it is quite impracticable to pursue them all in what is designed not as history but as documentation. Actually, most of these issues are reflected, in one way or another, in the papers here assembled; they are intended to give a general view.

These basic documents indicate how American military thought, as it is here broadly defined, has been shaped and has developed from colonial times until today. They are grouped into six parts, representing the six major phases through which American military history has progressed.

I. The Formative Period: To 1816

Until the time of the Revolution there was little that would today be recognized as military thought in America, or anywhere else, for that matter. War, like poverty and pestilence, was too much a part of mankind's common lot to awake much attention in itself; while the military institutions of the British colonies in North America grew naturally out of their circumstances, with little need for theory. Most of the colonies began perforce as quasi-military communities, compelled to defend themselves not only against nature and the Indians but also against rival European colonial enterprises. The people were generally armed—as was not the case in the Europe they had left behind—and skilled in the use of their weapons. They appointed their military captains as well as their governors. War was for them very directly a matter of a common defense, although against strictly local perils; and not until they found themselves involved in the imperial wars of the eighteenth century did war begin to take on a larger meaning. Two traditions that have colored American military thought ever since are rooted in these colonial origins. One is that war is primarily a matter of defense, and of local defense as far as possible; the other is that every able-bodied male is directly obligated to defend the group.

The (at times contradictory) influence of both traditions appears over and over again in subsequent history. It was even detectable as late as 1940–1941, when Franklin Roosevelt sought to meet the problems of general war in Europe with a local, Western Hemisphere defense, while at the same time accepting peacetime conscription, never before imposed, as a means of making it good. The ideas implicit in these policies were set forth in 1641 in "The Massachusetts Body of Liberties":

> No man shall be compelled to go out of the limits of this plantation upon any offensive wars which this Commonwealth or any of our friends or confederates shall voluntarily undertake. But only upon such vindictive and defensive wars in our own behalf or the behalf of our friends and confederates as shall be enterprised by the counsel and consent of a court general, or by authority derived from the same.

The document defined the principal officers of the colony as "our governor, deputy governor, assistants, treasurer, general of our wars. And our admiral at sea." All were to be elected annually by "the freemen of this plantation." This was a terse statement of the principles, including popular and civilian control of the military and of war policy, that, inherited from colonial times, have ruled for three centuries in American military thought.[1]

It was the French and Indian War of the eighteenth century that compelled elaboration of the simple, earlier military concepts. These wars involved more than mere local defense against Indians and competing colonies; they were reflections of great European power struggles, in which the colonials were finding themselves increasingly entangled. The colonial militias might be

[1] William H. Whitmore (ed.), *The Colonial Laws of Massachusetts Reprinted from the Edition of 1672* (Boston: Rockwell and Churchill, 1890), pp. 35, 47.

adequate as defense against Indian raids, but hardly against Indian raids fomented and supported by one great European power as incident to its struggle with another. Nor was the question any longer one of mere frontier defense. The settled seaboard communities, which had long ago lost their military and pioneer character, found their interests involved along with those of the backwoodsmen. The colonials loyally provided volunteer (not militia) forces for distant service in support of the regular British battalions sent out to prosecute the war. They even organized full-time, paid regular forces of their own, like the Virginia Regiment with which Colonel George Washington sought to protect the frontier after Braddock's defeat. The colonials were finding themselves compelled to think more seriously than before about the basic problems of war and defense in the increasingly complex world of eighteenth-century empire.

The novelty, as well as the urgency, of these military issues is illustrated by Benjamin Franklin's *Plain Truth* of 1747 (Document 1). This was an appeal to the citizens of Philadelphia to form a volunteer militia—the colonial government had refused to establish one—primarily for defense against the French and Spanish privateers who had appeared on the Delaware. As the argument makes clear, the situation in Pennsylvania, dominated by the Quaker influence, was a peculiar one: a similar appeal would not have been necessary in New York or Massachusetts. The pamphlet remains, however, an interesting example of the older ways of thinking about war and defense as well as of the new concepts that events were beginning to impose. Franklin's dictum that "the Way to Secure Peace is to be prepared for war" was doubtless not the first appearance of this ancient precept in American military thought, but it is an early example of an argument that has echoed through the literature ever since.

Victory in the Seven Years' War brought with it a complex train of issues concerning the colonies' relations with the home empire. Most of them turned at bottom on the military problem. They involved questions of war and defense, of defense financing, of the locus of military power and command within the British imperial system, of the impact of the king's standing armies on the liberties of the people. In the controversies that followed, the thoughtful were impressed by the significance of military and defense factors in the organization of a free society. But no solutions could be found within the creaking framework of eighteenth-century British politics and administration, and the result was the American Revolution.

It seems reasonable to say that the liberty for which the Americans struck in 1775 was a liberty not so much from the minor oppressions of George III and his ministers as from the restraints, exactions, and tyrannies being imposed upon them by the European great-power war system itself—that "system of war and expence," as Thomas Paine was to call it (Document 6), which he thought inherent in monarchical government. At all events, the Americans' declaration of independence from the British military system compelled them to create a military system of their own, both to fight the Revolution through to victory and to erect a viable nation upon the result. The war and the early postwar years, including the severe shock of Shays's Rebellion, forced them into a lot of serious thinking about the place of war, military power, and military institutions in the free society they were endeavoring to establish. Washington's comments and advice have been quoted ever since they were uttered (Documents 2, 3). The Constitution is a military as well as a political charter (Document 4). In its military clauses, in the glosses upon them by Hamilton, James Madison, and John Jay in *The Federalist* (Document 5), in the early military legislation, one finds the foundation documents that have influenced American military thinking down to our own day.

The actual military establishment with which the infant republic began its career was almost non-existent—a standing army reduced to the lowest limits of a frontier police, a few small naval vessels left over from the Revolution, and little that was serviceable in the way of coastal fortification. But the renewal of general war in Europe in 1793 was soon to force us into ideas about enlarged military requirements. It brought home the fact that in freeing ourselves from the exactions of the British military system, we had divorced ourselves from its protections as well. Our maritime commerce could no longer look to the Royal Navy for defense; we would now have to supply our own. And the depredations of the Algerine corsairs against our shipping in the Mediterranean led to the frigate bill of 1794, the real foundation of American naval power. But piracy was the least of the perils with which the new general war in Europe confronted us. We were now neutrals, as we had not been before, caught amid the tramplings of giants. Armed force might be necessary to secure respect for our neutral rights at sea, if not for our neutrality itself. Washington put the idea very clearly in his final annual message in 1796 (Document 8). We must have some substantial naval power, not on a scale to rival the big British, French, and Spanish navies, but sufficient to inspire caution on both warring sides, lest it be thrown as a makeweight to the support of one. The situation was growing so serious that the Adams administration proposed a ten thousand-man army, to be commanded by General Washington. At the same time, it set up a separate Navy Department (up to that time naval affairs had been under the jurisdiction of Henry Knox, the Secretary of War); and in 1798 the first Secretary of the Navy, Benjamin Stoddert, recommended a maximum program of naval expansion, up to the limits of shipyard and manning capacity. He proposed for the first time (Document 9) the building of seventy-four-gun ships of the line—more effective expressions of naval power than even the heavy frigates could ever be. Military thought was enlarging its horizons. In the same year, however, crisis reached its climax in the Quasi-War with the French Directory, which was fought at sea without need either for Stoddert's 74's or the ten thousand–man army. But we continued to struggle with the problems of maintaining both our neutral rights at sea and our neutral position itself through a series of political, diplomatic, and military incidents—the Alien and Sedition Acts of 1798, the Barbary War, Thomas Jefferson's experiments with embargo and nonintercourse, the *Chesapeake* affair of 1807—until a complex train of circumstances brought us finally to the War of 1812.

The indifferent success of our volunteer-and-militia armies in

that conflict, the failure of our cruising frigates to protect either
our commerce or our coasts, the ease with which the British
sacked Washington and raided in Chesapeake Bay, and the negotiated and unsatisfactory peace might have suggested that our
military institutions were defective and the military thinking that
had formed them inadequate. Yet the achievements of Oliver
Hazard Perry and Thomas Macdonough on the Great Lakes and
Andrew Jackson's resounding victory at New Orleans—after the
peace treaty had been signed—confirmed the popular confidence
in the American military system. The experience left lasting
strands in American military thought. It established our independence of the European great-power war system. European
militarism and navalism were none of our affair. The most we had
to fear from beyond the Atlantic moat—and it is curious how long
this idea was to survive—were possible raiding expeditions bent
on the plunder of our rich coastal cities. The only other military
perils that were thought to concern us were those that might conceivably arise within the Western Hemisphere, where great armed
forces were unnecessary to defend an already predominant power
position. Another general war in Europe might involve us once
more in all the difficulties of the Napoleonic period, but such a
possibility was remote. Prudence of course required the maintenance of a military system, but under these fortunate circumstances it need be only a very modest one. As usually happens, we
had emerged from the War of 1812 with considerably larger
peacetime military establishments than we had before thought
necessary; but our basic military institutions had seemed, on the
whole, to work well, and the experiences of the Napoleonic era
had suggested no change in the underlying principles as they had
been worked out by the authors of the Constitution. And now
some forty years of world war and convulsion were over. The long
period of isolated security was beginning.

II. Isolated Security: 1817–1861

The coming of peace necessitated the rescaling of the military
defenses and the readjustment of military thinking to what ap-

peared to be the long-term requirements. At the outset they seemed considerable. A large and, for the first time, continuing program of naval building was promptly authorized. With the capital's recent fate vividly in mind, the massive Fortress Monroe at Old Point Comfort was begun in 1817; while the Bernard-Elliott-Totten board of engineers provided in their reports (Document 13) not only a considered rationale for seacoast fortification but also an extensive construction program. For some years the Regular Army was to be maintained at the relatively large strength of ten thousand men. And it was in 1816 that the Military Academy at West Point was reorganized (with the appointment of Sylvanus Thayer as superintendent) into an effective center of military thought and education, thus giving us for the first time the foundation for a professional officer corps.

Speaking in the House in the same year, the gaunt young South Carolina Congressman John C. Calhoun sought to pitch the nation's military thinking to a high level of preparedness (Document 10). Arguing for a Navy as powerful as we could build and man, he warned that however peaceful the scene might be at the moment, there would be wars in the future. Long and "bloody" wars with Britain, he prophesied, were not only probable, they were "certain." But the Rush-Bagot Agreement of 1817, in effect neutralizing the Great Lakes frontier, hardly sustained him; and Congress was growing increasingly reluctant to spend money on contingencies so remote. It was slow to fill the authorized naval and fortification programs with appropriations. James Monroe's first inaugural address (Document 11) reflects more accurately than Calhoun's warnings the state of American thought on war and defense policy at this time.

Calhoun went on to become Monroe's Secretary of War and to continue his efforts to strengthen and improve the Army, but in 1820 an economy-minded Congress peremptorily ordered him to submit a plan for reducing the Army to no more than six thousand officers and men. This gave rise to Calhoun's celebrated proposal for an "expansible army" (Document 12), the first serious attempt to meet in a systematic way the problem of maintaining in time of peace a military structure capable of dealing in an emergency with the necessities of war. If, he argued, the legislators insisted on reducing the Army to this minimal level, they should do so with a plan for making rapid and effective expansion possible in crisis. In the end, Congress reduced the Army without adopting the essential features of the plan. But it was long to remain a landmark in the development of American military thought. Half a century later, when Army organization was again under study, Sherman, with all the experience of the Civil War behind him, could still cite Calhoun as having said almost all that need be said on the subject (Document 21).

Through the ensuing decades the basic patterns of American military thought and policy remained unchanged. They were set forth from time to time in Presidential statements, as in John Quincy Adams' second annual message (Document 14) or the messages (Document 15) of Andrew Jackson, our second military President. They were exemplified in the varying defense measures adopted in accordance with changing circumstances and technology. They were implicit in the work of the abler and more thoughtful young professional soldiers now beginning to appear from West Point.

In all, the underlying assumptions are the same. In all, American military policy is regarded as purely prudential and defensive. It occurred to no one that we could have aggressive aims or intent. It was unquestioned that the Navy would provide the first line of this defense. Peacetime requirements upon it would be small—no more than to police the seas in the suppression of the slave trade or in support of our merchantmen and whalers in distant seas. But in a possible emergency, the Navy should have a reserve capacity to act in order to discourage blockade of the seaports and protect the coastal cities against pillage. The Navy should be backed by effective coastal fortifications to keep its yards and bases secure and to assist it in defending the cities against bombardment. The Army's role, in this concept, would be filled in time of peace by a very small regular force, no larger than was necessary to supply a frontier police and skeleton garrisons for the coastal forts and to keep alive a knowledge of the military arts and techniques. In the event of emergency the Army would serve as a trained nucleus around which citizen-volunteer armies could be formed in whatever numbers might be necessary. The state militias, in which universal service was obligatory, would provide a pool of at least partially trained recruits; while the militia organizations themselves could be used on the call of the Presdent for local defense. The whole system would, of course, be under the strict control of the civil authority, vested in the President as commander-in-chief and in Congress as holder of the purse strings.

This was the broad pattern that ruled American military thinking almost without question from the end of the Napoleonic wars down to the turn of the century. The sufficiency of the institutions in which we embodied this pattern might come into question from time to time, and some of the basic assumptions might even occasionally be challenged. Thus the Board of Navy Commissioners, proposing in 1836 (Document 16) a sweeping building-program to include no less than fifteen line-of-battle ships, were advancing an almost Mahanite concept of sea power that scarcely accorded with the conventional ideas of the Navy's modest defensive role. In the following year, in fact, the government launched the *U.S.S. Pennsylvania*, 120 guns, one of the most powerful sailing warships ever built. But technology was drastically altering the course of naval thought. The *Pennsylvania* was an anachronism when she was launched; the great sailing battle-fleet was not built and basic naval policy remained as before.

West Point encouraged its graduates to study the mounting military literature of the Napoleonic era and several, like Henry Wager Halleck and George B. McClellan, found opportunity to see the European military systems at first hand. The lessons they drew from this, however, were perforce of mainly tactical and technical application. And there was no opportunity to practice grand strategy in the miserable, muddy guerrilla warfare of the Florida jungles or to reflect upon the larger issues of military policy. All the old problems of the undisciplined militia and of

command divided between federal and state authority recurred
in the Seminole War, but except for the professional soldiers involved few paid much attention to them. And the Florida wars,
like the Western Indian fighting, were after all mere police operations that seemed scarcely to affect the great questions of war,
peace, and defense in a free society.

When these questions were posed, as they were increasingly
because of the rise of the peace societies in the 1840's, they were
discussed—in that era of peace and profound security—in a doctrinaire and theoretical way by soldiers no less than by pacifists
and clergymen. Even as the Mexican War was impending, there
was little tendency to relate the discussion to the immediate realities of international politics. When a young Boston lawyer,
Charles S. Sumner, shocked his Fourth of July audience in 1845
with an impassioned demonstration that armies and navies were
of "no use" and that there could not be "in our age any peace
that is not honorable, any war that is not dishonorable,"[2] he may
have had the Oregon and Texas questions in mind but he did not
mention them in his theoretic and moralistic argument. In 1846,
just as the Mexican War was beginning, Halleck published *Elements of Military Art and Science* (Document 17), which was to
remain until the Civil War as the leading American text on the
subject. It is noteworthy that Halleck felt it necessary to begin
with a long introductory rebuttal of the pacifist clergy; he defended just and unavoidable wars in terms as doctrinaire as their
own. The rest of the book is a scholarly but still generalized discussion, mainly on military organization and techniques. Even
the section on "military polity," while related more directly to
American defense issues, is wholly theoretical; and the Mexican
War is scarcely mentioned except for the prefatory statement that
the work might be "useful to a class of officers now likely to be
called into military service."

The Mexican War, like its predecessors, did little to change
the general tenor of American military thought. Almost entirely

[2] Charles S. Sumner, *The True Grandeur of Nations* (Boston: American
Peace Society, 1845), pp. 7, 54.

a land war, it suggested no alteration in naval policy; and, on the whole, a brilliant success, it gave rise to no demands for military reform. Some technical improvements, such as the enlargement of the field artillery component, survived for a time. In other ways technological change was asserting its imperatives. The smoothbore shoulder arm, for example, was giving way to the rifled musket. Seacoast fortification was resumed on a large scale in the 1840's, utilizing the new Dahlgren and, later on, Rodman heavy guns. The planners were happily ignorant of the fact that the chief military result would be to provide the Confederacy with the walls and batteries behind which it was to defy the Union a few years later. By 1850 the introduction of steam propulsion had made it impossible to go on building sail battleships like the *Pennsylvania,* and in 1853 the Pierce administration brought in a program (Document 18) for building a number of the wooden-screw sloops now appearing in foreign navies. Pierce supported the proposal, it would seem, less for military than for domestic political reasons. Tacitly directed against British naval power in the Caribbean Sea, the proposal would divert the rising flames of sectional conflict; while the Southerners voted for the ships as possibly facilitating the acquisition of new slave states in Cuba and the Antilles. The steam sloops were a reflection of technological change and internal politics rather than of national defense policy.

As the sectional struggle intensified during the 1850's neither side gave much thought to its possible military implications. And even if the war had been more clearly foreseen, it would have been manifestly impossible, in a democratic political system, to provide a national military policy capable of dealing with a civil conflict. North and South alike went into the fratricidal war with the military ideas and institutions that had served the national military interest well enough since 1789, but were inapplicable to this massive crisis. The war to which these institutions now gave rise was to be unprecedented in scope and savagery. Waged on both sides by able and professionally trained commanders leading great armies of initially raw, citizen soldiers, it was to impose a toll of "blood, sweat, and tears" beyond anything that anyone had dreamt of. It signalized several revolutionary advances in military technology; and it left a profound impression on American military thought and on American ways of thinking about war in general.

III. Isolated Security: 1862–1898

Yet the influence of the Civil War is not easily documented. The nation's basic reaction was, quite simply, one of "Never again." As a civil war, moreover, this seemed to have been a non-recurrent tragedy. At enormous cost the Union had been preserved, but this issue had been settled once for all. As late as 1885, Ulysses S. Grant, our foremost soldier, observed in concluding his memoirs that "there can scarcely be a possible chance of a conflict, such as the last one, occurring among our own people again"; and he saw no comparable perils on the world horizon. His valedictory advice was quite like Jackson's (Document 15) a half century before: rely on a strong Navy backed by seacoast fortifications—the Army needed no special changes. The war, he said, had been "a fearful lesson." But what it should teach us was not to revise our military institutions; it was "the necessity of avoiding wars in the future."[3]

The war of course generated an enormous literature, but it was overwhelmingly concerned with recording the great events just past rather than with theorizing about their future implications. Sherman, for example, concluded his own memoirs, published in 1875, with no more than a few minor and mainly technical suggestions, such as the importance of the new rail transport and the superiority of volunteer over conscripted troops or bounty men. Yet Sherman was probably our most forceful and original military thinker; he was a significant forerunner of the strategic and total warfare that was to be brought to such grim perfection in the twentieth century, and the influence of his methods was lasting,

[3] Ulysses S. Grant, *Personal Memoirs of U. S. Grant*, II (New York: The Century Company, 1885), pp. 388, 391.

although somewhat difficult to document. His correspondence with Grant in which the famous march through Georgia was conceived, planned, and launched (Document 19) at least gives much of the quality and tenor of Sherman's approach to war.

But no one, including Sherman himself, applied the lessons of the war to possible future conflicts that few imagined could occur. The Grand Army of the Republic was demobilized; most of the great Civil War Navy was sold off, while the armor-clads and cruising ships that were retained were allowed to deteriorate into technological obsolescence. The coastal forts were repaired and maintained in their Civil War state, already almost wholly useless against new developments in artillery and armor. Once the French were out of Mexico and the occupation requirements in the South had been met, the regular Army was reduced to a frontier police of about twenty-five thousand men, at which level it remained until 1898. The unworkable state-militia system continued to provide the only reserves. When in the 1880's there was renewed interest in the National Guard, it was stimulated more by the need for keeping domestic order in face of the rising industrial strife of the period than by the requirements of national defense. In the late 1870's Congress, again motivated, as in Calhoun's time, mainly by economy, established a Joint Committee to look into Army organization. Headed by Rhode Island's Senator Ambrose E. Burnside, the bewhiskered general who had presided over the Union disaster at Fredericksburg in 1862, its report (Document 21) had little practical effect; although with its supporting papers by Sherman, Winfield Scott, Hancock, McClellan, and others, it supplies a useful conspectus of military attitudes at the time.

Yet if military policy was static, military thinking—influenced by the Civil War, by the new technology, and by the startling success of the German professional soldiers in the Franco-Prussian War of 1870–1871—was not. Again, as in the 1830's, some of our abler officers were sent abroad to study and report on the great European military systems and the industrial supports behind them. Sherman founded the modern structure of military higher education by establishing the School of Application for Infantry and Cavalry at Leavenworth, Kansas, in 1881; three years later, Rear Admiral Stephen B. Luce carried military education an important step forward by establishing the naval War College at Newport, Rhode Island. Out of these intellectual stirrings would emerge the two most influential military thinkers of the pre-1914 era—Emory Upton and Alfred Thayer Mahan.

Their combined effect was greatly to enlarge the dimensions of American military thought. Upton was a protégé of Sherman's, who sent him around the world in the mid 1870's to study the great-power military systems and their colonial adjuncts. Returning, he began work on *The Military Policy of the United States* (Document 22), which was virtually complete in 1880. The book was not formally published until 1904 but the manuscript was circulated among the leading soldiers of the day, and its influence is traceable from 1880 on.

Upton was breaking new ground; he himself said he was advancing into "a field thus far unoccupied." If his essential argument—that the United States had never had a proper military policy and in all our wars had wasted enormous amounts of life and money for lack of foresight and preparation—sounds obvious today, it is because this pioneer work impressed itself so deeply on Upton's professional and popular successors. Many of the ideas that were to become commonplace in later discussion, for example, defense measures used as a preventive or "deterrent" and defense appropriations as a form of "insurance," if not original with Upton, were at least introduced by his forceful presentation into the main stream of American military thinking. Upton would probably not himself have recognized the fully militarized "garrison state" to which his ideas might logically lead; even Elihu Root, in his introduction to the published book, noted that Upton may have been too little aware of the political limitations on military policy. But it was Upton's arguments that really prepared the way for the mass conscript armies of 1917–1918; here were the beginnings of our entry upon the stage of global military power.

At the time of his death in 1881, however, Upton was virtually unknown beyond a small circle of professional military men. What really began the American military revival in the 1880's was neither fresh thinking nor any change in the international situation; it was primarily the now total obsoleteness of the Navy and the coastal fortifications. It was folly to continue indefinitely repairing the wooden screw sloops of the Civil War era, when they could be only helpless victims of the new cruisers appearing abroad. In 1883 we began the construction of three small, unprotected steel cruisers (still carrying full sail rig) as replacements for the wooden steam sloops. As President Chester A. Arthur's annual message of 1883 (Document 23) made plain, this represented no departure from established policy. It was simply updating it to accord with the new technology. But if the old ships were obsolete, so were the forts supporting them. The Cleveland administration not only pushed forward with naval replacement, but also turned its attention to the coast defenses. A board of officers under the Secretary of War, William C. Endicott, brought in a somewhat breath-taking program (Document 24) for their rehabilitation, discussing the whole problem in terms that are illuminative of the state of military thinking at the time. Meanwhile, the Gun-Foundry Board, another group of officers and engineers, had toured the European armament works to return with recommendations for establishing a heavy armaments industry under mixed government and private ownership to supply the heavy ordnance and armor plate the new ships and forts would require.

Amid this considerable activity of military thought, our most influential military theorist, Alfred Thayer Mahan, began the work at the War College in Newport that was to make him famous. He was soon to find powerful allies in his advocacy of the new doctrines of "sea power." Cleveland's Democratic administration had carried forward the replacement of the wooden cruising fleet; but Benjamin Harrison and the Republicans who came to power in 1889 were ready, for a variety of reasons, to explore wider horizons. The new Secretary of the Navy, Benjamin F.

Tracy, in his first annual report (Document 26) boldly brought in a program for the construction of seagoing battleships, avowedly to enable us in time to "rank with" the major European sea powers. Mahan advised Tracy and probably helped him write the report.

Mahan's famous *The Influence of Sea Power on History, 1660–1783* (Document 25) was published in the following year, 1890, and powerfully affected the debates over the battleship building-program. Congress was reluctant to accept what it sensed was a significant change in basic naval policy—though it was not so represented by its advocates—and in the end reduced the Tracy program to only three battleships. Tracy, it was later said, had been "far in advance of the country."[4] But the enlarged ideas of naval policy had taken root, and the battleship building went on. On the eve of the Spanish-American War, a fourth ship had been completed and five more were under construction. The basis had been laid on which the United States was soon to be raised to the rank of a major sea power.

IV. The United States as a World Power: 1899–1922

By the winter of 1897–1898, as the Cuban problem was visibly developing toward what might be our first foreign war since the Mexican War, the United States had done something toward modernizing the antiquated weapons systems of the Civil War era. It had improved military education and training and, though far from sufficiently, even National Guard training; it had acquired larger ideas of the potential of sea power. But the basic patterns of American military thinking were what they had always been. War was a remote danger. Our military policy itself was purely prudential and defensive. In any real emergency, "a million men would spring to arms overnight"—an idea expressed by William Jennings Bryan, although one which must have been shared by many less imaginative and more sober politicians—but

[4] John D. Long, *The New American Navy*, I (New York: The Outlook Company, 1903) p. 53.

emergencies of this kind would be of others' doing. The idea that the United States would ever raise major expeditionary forces to exert its military power on the world stage scarcely occurred to anyone. Yet in April 1898, this was what we suddenly found ourselves doing. The impact on American military thinking of this experience, and of the near collapse of our military system which resulted, was immediate.

In his annual report of December 1899 (Document 27), the newly appointed Secretary of War, Elihu Root, felt it necessary to declare that "the real object of having an army is to provide for war." It was clear that this seemingly obvious principle had not been applied in the design of the army with which we went to war with Spain. Reflecting the views of the abler soldiers who advised him, Root saw that the Army needed almost everything—better military education and an improved system of officer selection and promotion; a command and planning organization based on the general-staff system; a reorganization of the bureau system for procurement, administration, and supply; a mobilizable reserve, to be obtained, if not by the supersession of the states' part-time armies, at least by their consolidation into an effective and Federally controlled reserve component.

It was also apparent that the Army needed modern weapons and equipment. These were provided in the excellent Springfield shoulder rifle and model 1902 three-inch field gun, which were not outmoded until the mid 1930's. Root opened a lot of windows upon the musty air of conventional military thinking. But he was to be less than wholly successful with his basic reforms. A decade later the political and intraservice controversies to which they gave rise were still acute; his contribution, however, remains essential to any account of the development of military thought in the United States.

The Navy had also revealed deficiencies as a fighting machine, but they were much less glaring than those of the Army. With its new concepts of sea power, what the Navy seemed chiefly to require was not fresh thinking or reorganization but more ships, as well as an Isthmian canal to permit their deployment in either ocean on the global stage the war had opened to us. Theodore Roosevelt succeeded to the Presidency in 1901. In his first annual message, in December (Document 28), he was already calling for the "completion" of a big battle-fleet, commensurate with our newly acquired overseas responsibilities. Except, conceivably, for the defense of the Philippines against Japan, the practical utility of such a fleet in the existing state of international politics was not too clear. But under the Mahanite teaching the possession of sea power was more important than any particular objective to which it might be applied. In many further books and papers, Admiral Mahan provided the philosophical foundations sustaining the big-battleship building programs of the McKinley and Roosevelt eras. By 1903 the Navy General Board—which served some of the planning functions of a general staff—had formally taken as its policy the provision of a fleet "equal or superior to that of any probable enemy." In this, the "any probable" was already coming to mean "any possible" enemy. Indulging in a form of long-range prophecy that has seldom succeeded in military planning, the board decided that this would require "a fleet of 48 battleships, with the attendant lesser units, ready for action by 1920."[5] Congress and the public failed to share such visions; but Roosevelt continued to demand big building programs, and when he left office in 1909 the United States, almost without intending it, stood as the world's second greatest naval power.

The sea-power doctrines of Mahan and Roosevelt had tended to bring us back, as it were, into direct and competitive contact with the great European military powers. President William Howard Taft, a man of peace and a lawyer who believed in arbitral and judicial processes in international affairs, cut the building program to one battleship a year and thus allowed the Anglo-German naval race, to which American navalism was largely irrelevant anyway, to sweep past us. Nor was he responsive to the efforts of his Chief of Staff, Leonard Wood, to build

[5] This conclusion was not made public until the General Board cited it ten years later (Document 31). See *Annual Reports of the Navy Department, 1913*, p. 33.

on the beginnings that Elihu Root had made with the Army. For Army thinking, no less than that of the Navy, tended to bring the country back into the great-power war system from which we had declared our emancipation in 1816. Not only had Root been less than wholly successful in reforming the Army into an instrument capable of "providing for war," but the war he had envisaged had been something on the order of the Spanish-American or the Boer War. No one, at the turn of the century, had any idea of imitating the huge, fully trained and equipped conscript armies that the European powers and Japan were creating. Yet almost imperceptibly American military thought now began to take these as its model.

Increasingly, the lessons of the Civil War—our first total conflict, which it had been assumed could never recur—were restudied. Upton's *The Military Policy of the United States,* finally published in 1904, was widely read. Military thought turned increasingly to a war, not with a decrepit Spain, but with some hypothetical first-class power. The Russo-Japanese War of 1904–1905 gave professionals an inkling, at least, of what this might imply. As early as 1908, Wood, who after his services in Cuba and the Philippines was already perhaps our leading soldier, had launched a tireless campaign for "preparedness" (Document 29). Preparedness, stemming basically from Upton's ideas, not only stressed the paucity of our military resources and the continued inefficiency of Army organization; it also related our military institutions directly to the European military complex, which was even then building toward the catastrophe of 1914. We had to be prepared against greater perils than we had previously been aware of. Not only were there the new overseas commitments to defend; worse than that, modern overseas transport made it at least theoretically possible for the Europeans or the Japanese, possessing great conscript armies, suddenly to land very large forces in the Western Hemisphere. The American military establishment might still be only prudential, as before; but the merest prudence now required us to maintain a system capable of fielding fully trained and equipped armies as rapidly as such foreign forces could be brought to the undefended beaches beyond the coastal forts.

This was a considerable raising of the sights; and in the untroubled atmosphere of 1910, when Wood became Chief of Staff, it was not an appealing notion. In December of that year President Taft publicly rebuked his new chief by observing that the defenses were entirely adequate since there was not then "the slightest prospect of war in any part of the world in which the United States could conceivably have a part."[6] But Wood was undeterred; he set out, as one of his biographers observes, "to destroy the illusion of isolation,"[7] and in the end was brilliantly to succeed. The argument that the United States must be prepared to meet the worst that might, even theoretically, be brought against it from beyond the seas laid the psychological and planning foundations that were to enable us a few years later to throw an army of two million men into Europe. By 1912 Wood had advanced military thinking so far that the General Staff report, in August of that year, on "The Organization of the Land Forces of the United States" (Document 30) could declare that "it is our most important military problem to devise means for preparing great armies of citizen soldiers to meet the emergency of modern war." American military thought had been moved out of the parochial concepts of the past and placed in a global setting.

Congress and the country, however, resisted these large new concepts; and if Taft had been cool to military and naval expansion, his successor, Woodrow Wilson, was almost totally uninterested. When the Navy General Board again asked, in 1913, for four new battleships it was severely cut down by the new Secretary of the Navy, Josephus Daniels; and though Wood was to remain as Chief of Staff until the summer of 1914, the President paid no attention to his demands for an enlarged Army, an organized reserve, and a populace universally trained to arms. Wilson

[6] Herman Hagedorn, *Leonard Wood*, II (New York: Harper & Brothers, 1931), p. 104.

[7] Isaac F. Marcosson, *Leonard Wood* (New York: John Lane Company, 1917), p. 63.

had almost no concept of the role of military power in the stormy world through which he was so soon to be called upon to guide American destinies. Until the staggering impact of the Great War of 1914, popular and, to some extent, even professional military thought in America remained much as Root and Roosevelt had left it.

The outbreak of general war in Europe of course changed everything. Almost from the outset we found ourselves involved in much the same problems of neutrality that we had encountered in the Napoleonic period. Almost from the beginning some believed we should aggressively throw our power, so vastly greater now than it had been in those earlier days, into the scales to secure what seemed to us the ends of peace and justice; whereas others believed that in a world so filled with violence we should retire into our continental fortress, hoarding our strength in order to play a commanding military role in whatever situation might emerge at the war's end. In these several strands of thought there were certain contradictions, but all converged on the same point: the preparedness for which General Wood had so long been laboring. By 1915 there was little agreement in the United States as to just what it was that we should prepare for, but the idea that we must be prepared had taken a powerful hold on the public, as well as the professional, imagination.

It was translated into formal policy in two documents: the War Department General Staff report on "A Proper Military Policy for the United States" of September (Document 32) and the Navy General Board reports of October and November 1915 (Document 33). These provided the basis for the massive programs of military and naval expansion adopted in the summer of 1916, and must be taken as representative of the best military thought that could be brought to bear on the problem of defense as it then stood. What is suggestive today is not so much the inadequacy of these programs as their irrelevance to the actual crisis that was to engulf us only a few months later.

Both the Army and the Navy programs were pitched for the long range; their effects could not be felt until four or five years later, when the European war would presumably be over. The War Department plan, moreover, was drastically modified. The General Staff had proposed, in effect, to supersede the National Guard with a "Continental Army" of part-time citizen soldiers under wholly federal control. This, Congress rejected, preferring instead to raise the National Guard—in numbers, equipment, training, and federal responsibility—into a force comparable to what the Continental Army would have been. It did not work in practice, as the Continental Army probably would not have worked either.

The President's signature on the 1916 Defense Act was barely dry when the mobilization on the Mexican border, incident to Pershing's pursuit of Pancho Villa, put the law to the test. In his report at the end of the year, the Chief of Staff, Hugh Scott, described the failure of the volunteer principle, for the regulars as well as for the National Guard, and frankly called for conscription (Document 34). The nation would never have acceded then. But in the following April we declared war on Germany. Both of the 1916 programs, with much of the military reasoning that had produced them, were swept away; the Navy suspended its battleship building to concentrate on the destroyers and merchant ships demanded by the U-boat war; whereas the Army, with the nation enthusiastically behind it, turned to raising a conscript mass-army to be shipped to France.

Ultimately, the war was won; the great wartime forces were, as usual, demobilized; and military thought again tried to apply the lessons to an obscure future. The results, as embodied in the 1919 report of the wartime Chief of Staff, Peyton C. March (Document 35), and in the 1920 Defense Act, which it outlined, today seem less than impressive. The Defense Act essentially represented a plan to repeat, more efficiently and with less time-lag, the great feat of 1918 in raising and equipping a conscript mass-army on the 1918 pattern. It took little account of the great technological changes foreshadowed by the appearance of the airplane, the tank, telephonic and radio communications, and motorized field transport. It did not ask whether a 1918-type army would be relevant through the coming years to an international situation that World War I had so profoundly transformed. To the Congress and the people it was not to seem so for the 1920 plan was never supplied with the appropriations necessary to make it effective; and when major war again impended, it was to find us about as badly unprepared as we had been in 1916.

Naval thinking was even less affected than that of the Army by the vast changes that had been wrought in the world. The Navy's first postwar plan was simply to resume construction of the big battleship and battle-cruiser programs authorized in 1916. From this folly—as it must seem today—it was rescued by the civil authority. Charles Evans Hughes, Warren Harding's Secretary of State, negotiated the Washington Naval Treaty (Document 36), which redefined American naval policy in terms more consonant with the actualities of the postwar international system. Many naval officers were bitterly opposed to the sacrifice of the magnificent new ships that this entailed; but Hughes had the support of the Naval high command, and the treaty system must stand as exemplifying the best naval thought in the early 1920's. At all events, the Defense Act of 1920 and the Washington Naval Treaty of 1922 completed the postwar reorientation of American military ideas and institutions. Between them, they reestablished the traditional isolationist, prudential, and defensive attitudes toward the military problem in the free society. Though the United States was now among the greatest of the great powers, the nation as a whole largely lost interest in military affairs. A new period had begun.

V. World Power: 1923–1947

Throughout the interwar period, military thought in the United States was dominated, almost to the exclusion of every other consideration, by the great controversies over "air power." The military airplane was by no means the only challenge presented by the new technology to the old patterns, but it was the most obvious, the most disruptive, and the most difficult to reconcile with the traditional thinking embodied in the 1920 Defense

Act. It made over tactics in both land and naval warfare; by eras-
ing the ancient and convenient division between armies and
navies, it raised formidable problems of organization, command,
and procurement; and it introduced new, revolutionary, and, as
yet largely untried, strategic doctrines that in turn raised basic
issues of military and national policy. From the end of the war
down to the late 1930's hardly a year went by without some
board or Congressional committee discussing the problems of air
policy; and their reports show how widely they were compelled,
in doing so, to range over the whole field of military and defense
thinking.

Beneath this general air of controversy, military thought, particularly in the Navy, was able to make considerable technical
advances. Our Navy took the lead among the powers in the development of ship-borne aviation and naval air tactics, as well as
of other techniques, such as resupply at sea and assault over defended beaches, that were to be of vital importance in World
War II. The Army Air Service (later the Army Air Corps) developed new types of airplanes at least comparable to those appearing abroad; helped establish a small but efficient aviation
industry and a commercial air-transport system; and elaborated
strategic and tactical doctrines of its own. Its near obsession with
the goal of "independent air power" perhaps unduly warped both
the doctrines and the equipment design, but they did provide a
valuable foundation for the great wartime air effort.

The Army as a whole, with no popular support except for its
air component, and denied the men and money that the 1920 act
had intended it to have, did what it could within the limits of its
meager appropriations. It improved its command and training
techniques and continued to develop its system of military higher
education. It tried, at least, to keep up with foreign progress in
armor, motorized field transport, and artillery. But the command
and training systems perforce remained largely on paper—to
maintain its force of reserve officers, for example, it had to substitute correspondence courses for field training—its combat units
were progressively skeletonized out of existence; and it could

produce only a few prototypes of the new tanks and weapons. When World War II broke out in 1939, months after Hitler had rolled his armored divisions into Czechoslovakia, the Army had some reasonably good tank models, but no effective armored formations whatever; and even its air component, despite having absorbed so much of the available resources, had, as its Commanding General Hap Arnold later said, "plans but no planes."

Much of the story can be read in one or another of the documents here presented. It was not until 1933 that a board of officers under Major General Hugh Drum worked out a reasonable compromise of the air-power controversy. Its essentials were accepted by a mainly civilian board under Newton D. Baker, the wartime Secretary of War, in the following year (Document 38). This report, if it did not end the air-power controversy, at least set forth an air policy that was to be followed thereafter and was to prove more or less satisfactory to most of the parties concerned.

The Baker Board, like its predecessors, had addressed its problem in the old, theoretical way, in terms of some possible but at the time quite unforeseeable future "emergency." But by 1934 the lineaments of probable emergency were already appearing on the horizon. The Japanese had opened their "China Incident" in Manchuria in 1931; Hitler came to power in Germany in 1933; both of these powers had announced their withdrawal from the League of Nations; and Mussolini had for years been trying to drill a martial ardor into his people. It was becoming increasingly imperative to relate American military thinking more directly to the perils visibly gathering on the international scene. In 1934 the Vinson-Trammel Act authorized new naval construction up to the full treaty ratios. This was in large part an antidepression rather than a military measure. But in 1936 the naval-treaty system itself, which had been tottering for some time, collapsed with Japan's withdrawal; and naval building was intensified. In their annual reports for 1937, the Secretary of War and the Army Chief of Staff sounded an early note of alarm, both as to the threatening state of the world and the deficient condition of the Army. In October of the same year President Franklin Roosevelt made his celebrated "quarantine" speech. The suggestion was not pursued; but some may have asked what military forces we possessed to enforce a quarantine, should one be authorized on an aggressor state.

In 1938, the year of the Munich Conference, Congress authorized an overall 20 per cent increase in naval tonnage; while the Army reports of the same year (Document 39) outlined a serious program of Army reconstruction. The Army-Navy Joint Board (predecessor of the Joint Chiefs of Staff) began in 1938 to overhaul Pacific war plans now recognized obsolete.[8] The Army General Staff, realizing that its mobilization plans, based on the unfulfilled 1920 Defense Act, were completely unrealistic and outdated, worked out a new "Protective Mobilization Plan," representing the best that military thought could do in the face of the new conditions.

The documentation (Document 39) plainly shows both the lamentable condition into which the Army had fallen during the depression years and the professional soldiers' response to this problem. The P.M.P. is significant in military thought in that it covered the whole spectrum of military power, industrial as well as specifically military; and it provided at least the basic framework of American military planning down to the Lend-Lease Act of 1940 if not to the bombing of Pearl Harbor. At the same time, at its inception it represented less a professional estimate of what the world crisis demanded than a guess as to what was the best that could be done, given the current mood of Congress and the country, with the exiguous military resources then available or likely to be forthcoming. The 1938 reports were, naturally, to expatiate upon how much had been effected to place the country in a satisfactory military position. But as had happened after the adoption of the defense measures of 1916, events were soon to demonstrate the total inadequacy of such planning as the P.M.P. reflected and of the military posture that it had envisaged. The

[8] Mark S. Watson, *Chief of Staff: Pre-war Plans and Preparations* (Department of the Army, 1950), p. 92.

professional soldiers, seamen, and airmen were unperceptive about many of the demands the new war would make; a great deal of cherished theory had to be revised in its course, but one cannot blame the military professionals for want either of intelligence or of flexibility in addressing the appalling new problems.

It is possible only briefly to outline American military thought through the tremendous years of World War II. Until December 1941, both professional and popular military thinking was badly confused by the uncertainties of the international situation, the complications of domestic politics, and the elusiveness of Franklin Roosevelt's adroit but sometimes obscure statesmanship. There were obstructive inconsistencies between the policies of "all aid to Britain" and of building our own hemispheric defense; between hemisphere defense and the restraint of Japan in Asia; between the claims of independent air power and those of the ground army; between the need for raising a great military force and the repeated promise that "your sons are not going to be sent into any foreign wars." After the bombing of Pearl Harbor, however, military thought, in one sense, was abruptly simplified. Suddenly there was but one goal—victory over Germany and Japan—and but one avenue to its achievement—securing the maximum amount of men, machines, raw materials, and ideas, anything that would contribute. Within this context, plan and policy of course had to deal with many difficult and subtle issues of strategy, allocation, politics, and propaganda. The merely technical problems concerning strategy, weapons development, resources, transportation, military industry, and military management were overwhelming in their complexity; but it was, in the last analysis, events rather than policy that imposed the answers. From 1941 to 1945 it was "a condition, not a theory" that confronted the American people. Only when the war was over could theory and foresight resume their accustomed authority.

Once more military thought faced an unpredictable future, but one complicated now by a military revolution more fundamental and far-reaching than that wrought by the airplane a generation before. It was the revolution announced by the atomic bombs detonated over Japan and, less clearly realized at the time, the Germans' successful development of the long-range ballistic missile. At the end of World War II, both the American people and their military professionals were far more sophisticated than they had been in 1918; but it was still to take them years to grasp the implications of what had happened, not all of which are clear even today. The position of professional military thinking as the war ended is well exemplified in the final reports of the three service chiefs of staff, published at the end of 1945. Fleet Admiral Ernest J. King, the Chief of Naval Operations, had little to say as to further policy; but both the Chief of Staff, George C. Marshall, and H. H. Arnold, Commanding General of the Army Air Force, went at length into the problems of the new era as they saw them (Document 40). General Marshall was perhaps looking more into a past that was then irrecoverable, and General Arnold into a future that was in many ways to dispute his confident predictions; but this was how the problem seemed to our ablest military thinkers at the end of 1945.

It left two great, unanswered questions: what to do about the military application of atomic energy, and how to reorganize the nation's military arm into an effective instrument of diplomacy and policy in the new, and very strange, world that the war had created. Both issues were well stated in President Harry/S. Truman's annual message of January 1947 (Document 41). Though closely related, they were, initially, pursued almost independently. The Atomic Energy Act of 1946 and the abortive Baruch Plan, presented in the following year to the United Nations, were worked out almost without reference to the issues of service unification; and the National Security Act of 1947, which set up our present military system (Document 42), shows few evidences of the nuclear revolution. But with the Atomic Energy Act and the National Security Act the immediate postwar questions were temporarily resolved. This was the position at which American military thought had arrived as we faced a future more complex, more uncertain, and perhaps more dangerous than ever.

VI. The Military Revolution: Since 1948

In the aftermath of World War I American military thought was embalmed in the 1922 Naval Treaty and the 1920 Defense Act. The perilous and tumultuously changing international situation after 1947 permitted of no such process. In the two decades since the end of World War II Americans have thought and argued over military and defense problems more intensively than in any other period of their history. The 1947 National Security Act was to undergo the first of its numerous amendments within two years of its adoption; while the Soviet achievement of a nuclear capability at the same time moved the nuclear weaponry into the center of our strategic thinking. The cold war, the Korean War, the wars in southeast Asia, the development of the ballistic missile and the invasion of space, the rise of the new nations out of the collapse of the old European colonial empires, and the Communist revolution in Cuba—all were to focus a fearful attention on the political, economic, and technological problems of war and peace unprecedented in our experience. Matters once left largely to the general staffs, the war colleges, or the Congressional military committees have become the stuff of most civil politics and diplomacy. Whole schools of civilian scholars and scientists, many of them combat veterans of the wars to which they now devote their attention, have sprung up beside the professional soldiers to study the basic issues of military policy and technology; while the professional soldiers, in turn, have been compelled to broaden their views over wide fields of the physical and social sciences, not formerly regarded as within their competence. Of the resultant sea of intellectual activity only the main currents and cross-currents can be documented in this volume. The political, strategic, and technological arguments of the past twenty years are far too complex to follow in detail.

The two major problems engaging American military thought in 1947 were: (1) the reconciliation of the ancient war system to the fact of nuclear energy; and (2) the reorganization of the total defense structure—including its political and economic, as well as its purely military, aspects—into an effective instrument of national security and well-being. Initially, the two problems were pursued more or less independently. Only in quite recent years has the massive intellectual effort devoted to them appeared to be coalescing into a more or less consistent body of military-political theory, far from complete as yet, but representing what may fairly be called the position of American military thought today.

The process has led, on the one hand, to the nuclear stalemate and the modern concept of deterrence as the only rational goal of intelligible military policy. It has also led, on the other hand, to the huge, unified, and overwhelmingly powerful Department of Defense, under strict civilian control, but intimately related to almost every aspect of the nation's political, economic, and social life. From Benjamin Franklin, calling on his fellow-townsmen in 1747 to form a voluntary militia, to Robert S. McNamara (Document 47), describing over two centuries later the massive military machine over which he presides as Secretary of Defense, there stretches a continuous, unbroken thread of American military thinking, which this volume has sought to document.

Chronology

1754–1763	French and Indian War
1775–1783	American Revolution
1789	Ratification of the Constitution
1794	Congress authorizes six heavy frigates, the foundation of the post-Revolutionary Navy.
1798	Establishment of a separate Navy Department
1798	Quasi-War with France
1812–1815	War of 1812
1835	Beginning of the introduction of steam power into the Navy
1846–1848	Mexican War
1861–1865	Civil War
1883	Congress authorizes three steel cruisers, signalizing a military revival, which also led to rebuilding the coastal forts and to improvements in the Army and National Guard.
1890	Congress authorizes modern, seagoing battleships.
1898	Spanish-American War, accompanied by the annexation of Hawaii and resulting in the acquisition of Puerto Rico, Guam, and the Philippines
1899–1902	Philippine Insurrection
1901	Beginning of Army reform under Elihu Root
1904–1914	Construction of the Panama Canal
1907–1909	Voyage of the American battle fleet around the world
1908	Army contracts for its first airplane.
1914	Outbreak of World War I
1916	Agitation for preparedness, resulting in the adoption of the Defense Act of 1916 and the 1916 naval building program

1916	Mobilization of the Army and National Guard on the Mexican border
1917–1919	War with Germany and the signing of the Treaty of Versailles
1920	National Defense Act of 1920, establishing a permanent organization of the Army
1922	Treaty of Washington, imposing naval limitation on the United States, Great Britain, and Japan and, in some respects, on France and Italy
1935	Establishment of the General Headquarters Air Force, providing the Army with a semiautonomous air arm
1939	Outbreak of World War II
1940	Selective Service Act, the first peacetime conscription
1941	Bombing of Pearl Harbor; the United States enters the war.
1945	End of the war in Europe in May and in the Pacific in September
1945	The United States detonates the first atomic bomb and employs the weapon against Hiroshima and Nagasaki.
1947	National Security Act, establishing an independent Department of the Air Force and a Secretary of Defense, and making other institutional changes from which the present national security organization and Department of Defense developed
1949	Soviet Union detonates its first atomic bomb.
1950–1953	Korean War
1952	United States detonates the first thermonuclear, or megaton, bomb.
1957	Soviet Union orbits the first artificial satellite, and announces an intercontinental ballistic missile. Development of the long-range guided missile as a major carrier of nuclear weapons dates from about this time.

1960   *U.S.S. George Washington,* a nuclear-powered sub-
            marine, makes the first successful underwater
            launch of an intermediate-range guided missile
            capable of carrying a nuclear warhead.

1962   Crisis over the Soviet introduction of missiles into
            Cuba

Selected Bibliography

As far as I know, no other books deal precisely with this field, and no appropriate bibliographies for it exist. It has been necessary to quarry the documents themselves from a wide variety of quite unrelated sources; these are all fully identified in the text, and it would serve no useful purpose to list them again here. If, on the other hand, one attempts to point to other sources in which fragments of relevant material may be found, one is involved with virtually the whole body of American writing on military history, biography, and policy. The titles given below do not constitute a bibliography of the subject. This is simply a selected list of books that, for one reason or another, seem particularly useful in the further study of American military thought.

Bennett, Frank M. *The Steam Navy of the United States.* Pittsburgh: W. T. Nicholson, 1896.

Bernardo, C. Joseph, and Bacon, Eugene H. *American Military Policy; Its Development Since 1775.* Harrisburg: The Military Service Publishing Company, 1955.

Earle, Edward Mead, ed. *Makers of Modern Strategy.* Princeton: Princeton University Press, 1943.

Ekirch, Arthur E., Jr. *The Civilian and the Military.* New York: Oxford University Press, 1956.

Gillie, Mildred Harmer. *Forging the Thunderbolt.* Harrisburg: The Military Service Publishing Company, 1947.

Hagedorn, Herman. *Leonard Wood.* New York: Harper & Brothers, 1931.

Huntington, Samuel P. *The Soldier and the State.* Cambridge: Harvard University Press, 1957.

Janowitz, Morris. *The Professional Soldier.* Glencoe: The Free Press, 1960.

Kahn, Herman. *On Thermonuclear War*. Princeton: Princeton University Press, 1960.

Millis, Walter. *Arms and Men: A Study in American Military History*. New York: G. P. Putnam's Sons, 1956.

Millis, Walter, *et al. Arms and the State*. New York: Twentieth Century Fund, 1958.

Morison, Samuel Eliot. *The Two-Ocean War*. Boston: Little, Brown, 1963.

Palmer, John McAuley. *America in Arms*. New Haven: Yale University Press, 1941.

Puleston, W. D. *Mahan: The Life and Work of Captain Alfred Thayer Mahan*. New Haven: Yale University Press, 1939.

Raymond, Jack. *Power at the Pentagon*. New York: Harper & Row, 1964.

Ropp, Theodore. *War in the Modern World*. Durham: Duke University Press, 1959.

Spaulding, Oliver Lyman. *The United States Army in War and Peace*. New York: G. P. Putnam's Sons, 1937.

Sprout, Harold and Margaret. *The Rise of American Naval Power*. Princeton: Princeton University Press, 1939.

Watson, Mark S. *Chief of Staff: Prewar Plans and Preparations*. Washington: Government Printing Office, 1950.

Editor's Note

THE TEXTS HERE GIVEN HAVE BEEN REPRODUCED EITHER FROM THE
books and public documents in which they first appeared or, in
the case of the earlier authors, from standard compilations of
their writings. Aside from the correction of a very few obvious
typographical errors, no changes have been introduced, the original spelling, capitalization and punctuation being allowed to
stand without the designation *sic*. Where an excerpt begins in
the middle of a sentence, the first word is capitalized. Original
footnotes have been eliminated from the texts except in a few
instances where they seemed necessary for clarity or completeness.
All other textual footnotes have been introduced by the editor,
and are so indicated.

Heavy excision was unavoidable in most of the documents. But
the essential meaning has always been preserved by deleting only
detail unnecessary to the argument. In one or two cases con-
nective matter has been supplied by the editor, and indicated by
brackets. In every case, ellipses show where material has been
omitted. Ellipses at the end of one paragraph and indented at the
start of the next indicate that one paragraph or more has been
deleted.

PART ONE

The Formative
Period: To 1816

1. Benjamin Franklin Calls for a Volunteer Militia

FRANKLIN'S *Plain Truth,* PUBLISHED IN 1747 OVER THE SIGNATURE "A Tradesman of Philadelphia," was a call for the formation of a volunteer "military association," primarily to protect the city against the depredations of French and Dutch privateers who had appeared in the Delaware Bay and River. At the time, Pennsylvania, geographically protected and under Quaker influence, had no militia. Franklin would not have had to make his argument in the other colonies, but it stands as a good illustration of the way in which problems of war and defense were regarded in the mid-eighteenth century, when the imperial wars of the European great powers were beginning seriously to involve the colonials.

. . . War, at this Time, rages over a great Part of the known World; our News-Papers are Weekly filled with fresh Accounts of the Destruction it every where occasions. Pennsylvania, indeed, situate in the Center of the Colonies, has hitherto enjoy'd profound Repose; and tho' our Nation is engag'd in a bloody War, with two great and powerful Kingdoms, yet, defended, in a great Degree, from the French on the one Hand by the Northern Provinces, and from the Spaniards on the other by the Southern, at no small Expence to each, our People have, till lately, slept securely in their Habitations.

From Leonard W. Larrabee (ed.), *The Papers of Benjamin Franklin,* III (New Haven: Yale University Press, 1961), pp. 191–204. Reprinted by permission of the publisher.

There is no British Colony excepting this, but has made some Kind of Provision for its Defence; many of them have therefore never been attempted by an Enemy; and others that were attack'd, have generally defended themselves with Success. The Length and Difficulty of our Bay and River has been thought so effectual a Security to us, that hitherto no Means have been entered into that might discourage an Attempt upon us, or prevent its succeeding.

But whatever Security this might have been while both Country and City were poor, and the Advantage to be expected scarce worth the Hazard of an Attempt, it is now doubted whether we can any longer safely depend upon it. Our Wealth, of late Years much encreas'd, is one strong Temptation, our defenceless State another, to induce an Enemy to attack us; while the Acquaintance they have lately gained with our Bay and River, by Means of the Prisoners and Flags of Truce they have had among us; by Spies which they almost every where maintain, and perhaps from Traitors among ourselves; with the Facility of getting Pilots to conduct them; and the known Absence of Ships of War, during the greatest Part of the Year, from both Virginia and New-York, ever since the War began, render the Appearance of Success to the Enemy far more promising, and therefore highly encrease our DANGER. . . .

. . . And is our *Country*, any more than our City, altogether free from Danger? Perhaps not. We have, 'tis true, had a long Peace with the Indians: But it is a long Peace indeed, as well as a long Lane, that has no Ending. The French know the Power and Importance of the Six Nations, and spare no Artifice, Pains or Expence, to gain them to their Interest. By their Priests they have converted many to their Religion, and these have openly espoused their Cause. The rest appear irresolute which Part to take; no Persuasions, tho' enforced with costly Presents, having yet been able to engage them generally on our Side, tho' we had numerous Forces on their Borders, ready to second and support them. What then may be expected, now those Forces are, by Orders from the Crown, to be disbanded; when our boasted Expedition is laid aside, thro' want (as it may appear to them) either of Strength or Courage; when they see that the French, and their Indians, boldly, and with Impunity, ravage the Frontiers of New-York, and scalp the Inhabitants; when those few Indians that engaged with us against the French, are left exposed to their Resentment: When they consider these Things, is there no Danger that, thro' Disgust at our Usage, joined with Fear of the French Power, and greater Confidence in their Promises and Protection than in ours, they may be wholly gained over by our Enemies, and join in the War against us? If such should be the Case, which God forbid, how soon may the Mischief spread to our Frontier Counties? And what may we expect to be the Consequence, but deserting of Plantations, Ruin, Bloodshed and Confusion!

Perhaps some in the City, Towns and Plantations near the River, may say to themselves, *An Indian War on the Frontiers will not affect us; the Enemy will never come near our Habitations; let those concern'd take Care of themselves.* And others who live in the Country, when they are told of the Danger the City is in from Attempts by Sea, may say, *What is that to us? The Enemy will be satisfied with the Plunder of the Town, and never think it worth his while to visit our Plantations: Let the Town take care of itself.* These are not mere Suppositions, for I have heard some talk in this strange Manner. But are these the Sentiments of true Pennsylvanians, of Fellow-Countrymen, or even of Men that have common Sense or Goodness? Is not the whole Province one Body, united by living under the same Laws, and enjoying the same Priviledges? . . . When New-England, a distant Colony, involv'd itself in a grievous Debt to reduce Cape-Breton, we freely gave *Four Thousand Pounds* for *their* Relief. And at another Time, remembering that Great Britain, still more distant, groan'd under heavy Taxes in Supporting the War, we threw in our Mite to their Assistance, by a free Gift of *Three Thousand Pounds:* And shall Country and Town join in helping Strangers (as those comparatively are) and yet refuse to assist each other?

But whatever different Opinions we have of our Security in other Respects, our TRADE, all seem to agree, is in Danger of being ruin'd in another Year. The great Success of our Enemies, in two different Cruizes this last Summer in our Bay, must give them the greatest Encouragement to repeat more frequently their Visits, the Profit being almost certain, and the Risque next to nothing. Will not the first Effect of this be, an Enhauncing of the Price of all foreign Goods to the Tradesman and Farmer, who use or consume them? For the Rate of Insurance will increase in Proportion to the Hazard of Importing them; and in the same Proportion will the Price of those Goods increase. If the Price of the Tradesman's Work and the Farmer's Produce would encrease equally with the Price of foreign Commodities, the Damage would not be so great: But the direct contrary must happen. For the same Hazard, or Rate of Insurance, that raises the Price of what is imported, must be deducted out of, and lower the Price of what is exported. Without this Addition and Deduction, as long as the Enemy cruize at our Capes, and take those Vessels that attempt to *go out*, as well as those that endeavour to *come in*, none can afford to trade, and Business must be soon at a Stand. And will not the Consequences be, A discouraging of many of the Vessels that us'd to come from other Places to purchase our Produce, and thereby a Turning of the Trade to Ports that can be entered with less Danger, and capable of furnishing them with the same Commodities, as New-York, &c? A Lessening of Business to every Shopkeeper, together with Multitudes of bad Debts; the high Rate of Goods discouraging the Buyers, and the low Rates of their Labour and Produce rendering them unable to pay for what they had bought: Loss of Employment to the Tradesman, and bad Pay for what little he does: And lastly, Loss of many Inhabitants, who will retire to other Provinces not subject to the like Inconveniencies; whence a Lowering of the Value of Lands, Lots, and Houses.

The Enemy, no doubt, have been told, That the People of Pennsylvania are Quakers, and against all Defence, from a Principle of Conscience; this, tho' true of a Part, and that a small Part only of the Inhabitants, is commonly said of the Whole; and what may make it look probable to Strangers, is, that in Fact, nothing is done by any Part of the People towards their Defence. But to refuse Defending one's self or one's Country, is so unusual a Thing among Mankind, that possibly they may not believe it, till by Experience they find, they can come higher and higher up our River, seize our Vessels, land and plunder our Plantations and Villages, and retire with their Booty unmolested. Will not this confirm the Report, and give them the greatest Encouragement to strike one bold Stroke for the City, and for the whole Plunder of the River?

It is said by some, that the Expence of a Vessel to guard our Trade, would be very heavy, greater than perhaps all the Enemy can be supposed to take from us at Sea would amount to; and that it would be cheaper for the Government to open an Insurance-Office, and pay all Losses. But is this right Reasoning? I think not: For what the Enemy takes is clear Loss to us, and Gain to him; encreasing his Riches and Strength as much as it diminishes ours, so making the Difference double; whereas the Money paid our own Tradesmen for Building and Fitting out a Vessel of Defence, remains in the Country, and circulates among us; what is paid to the Officers and Seamen that navigate her, is also spent ashore, and soon gets into other Hands; the Farmer receives the Money for her Provisions; and on the whole, nothing is clearly lost to the Country but her Wear and Tear, or so much as she sells for at the End of the War less than her first Cost. This Loss, and a trifling one it is, is all the Inconvenience; But how many and how great are the Conveniencies and Advantages! And should the Enemy, thro' our Supineness and Neglect to provide for the Defence both of our Trade and Country, be encouraged to attempt this City, and after plundering us of our Goods, either *burn it,* or put it to Ransom; how great would that Loss be! Besides the Confusion, Terror, and Distress, so many Hundreds of Families would be involv'd in!

The Thought of this latter Circumstance so much affects me, that I cannot forbear expatiating somewhat more upon it. You have, my dear Countrymen, and Fellow Citizens, Riches to tempt a considerable Force to unite and attack you, but are under no

Ties or Engagements to unite for your Defence. Hence, on the first Alarm, *Terror* will spread over All; and as no Man can with Certainty depend that another will stand by him, beyond Doubt very many will seek Safety by a speedy Flight. Those that are reputed rich, will flee, thro' Fear of Torture, to make them produce more than they are able. The Man that has a Wife and Children, will find them hanging on his Neck, beseeching him with Tears to quit the City, and save his Life, to guide and protect them in that Time of general Desolation and Ruin. All will run into Confusion, amidst Cries and Lamentations, and the Hurry and Disorder of Departers, carrying away their Effects. The Few that remain will be unable to resist. *Sacking* the City will be the first, and *Burning* it, in all Probability, the last Act of the Enemy. . . .

'Tis true, with very little Notice, the Rich may shift for themselves. The Means of speedy Flight are ready in their Hands; and with some previous Care to lodge Money and Effects in distant and secure Places, tho' they should lose much, yet enough may be left them, and to spare. But most unhappily circumstanced indeed are we, the middling People, the Tradesmen, Shopkeepers, and Farmers of this Province and City! We cannot all fly with our Families; and if we could, how shall we subsist? No; we and they, and what little we have gained by hard Labour and Industry, must bear the Brunt: The Weight of Contributions, extorted by the Enemy (as it is of Taxes among ourselves) must be surely borne by us. Nor can it be avoided as we stand at present; for tho' we are numerous, we are quite defenceless, having neither Forts, Arms, Union, nor Discipline. And tho' it were true, that our Trade might be protected at no great Expence, and our Country and our City easily defended, if proper Measures were but taken; yet who shall take these Measures? Who shall pay that Expence? On whom may we fix our Eyes with the least Expectation that they will do any one Thing for our Security? Should we address that wealthy and powerful Body of People, who have ever since the War governed our Elections, and filled almost every Seat in our Assembly? . . . They have already been by great Numbers of the

People petitioned in vain. Our late Governor did for Years sollicit, request, and even threaten them in vain. The Council have since twice remonstrated to them in vain. Their religious Prepossessions are unchangeable, their Obstinacy invincible. Is there then the least Hope remaining, that from that Quarter any Thing should arise for our Security?

And is our Prospect better, if we turn our Eyes to the Strength of the *opposite Party,* those Great and rich Men, Merchants and others, who are ever railing at Quakers for doing what their Principles seem to require, and what in Charity we ought to believe they think their Duty, but take no one Step themselves for the Publick Safety? . . . *Rage* at the Disappointment of their little Schemes for Power, gnaws their Souls, and fills them with such cordial Hatred to their Opponents, that every Proposal, by the Execution of which *those* may receive Benefit as well as themselves, is rejected with Indignation. *What,* say they, *shall we lay out our Money to protect the Trade of Quakers? Shall we fight to defend Quakers? No; Let the Trade perish, and the City burn; let what will happen, we shall never lift a Finger to prevent it.* Yet the Quakers have *Conscience* to plead for their Resolution not to fight, which these Gentlemen have not. . . .

Thus unfortunately are we circumstanc'd at this Time, my dear Countrymen and Fellow-Citizens; we, I mean, the middling People, the Farmers, Shopkeepers and Tradesmen of this City and Country. Thro' the Dissensions of our Leaders, thro' *mistaken Principles* of *Religion,* join'd with a Love of Worldly Power, on the one Hand; thro' *Pride, Envy* and *implacable Resentment* on the other; our Lives, our Families and little Fortunes, dear to us as any Great Man's can be to him, are to remain continually expos'd to Destruction, from an enterprizing, cruel, now well-inform'd, and by Success encourag'd Enemy. . . . Our Case indeed is dangerously bad; but perhaps there is yet a Remedy, if we have but the Prudence and the Spirit to apply it.

If this now flourishing City, and greatly improving Colony, is destroy'd and ruin'd, it will not be for want of Numbers of Inhabitants able to bear Arms in its Defence. 'Tis computed that we have at least (exclusive of the Quakers) 60,000 Fighting Men, acquainted with Fire-Arms, many of them Hunters and Marksmen, hardy and bold. All we want is Order, Discipline, and a few Cannon. At present we are like the separate Filaments of Flax before the Thread is form'd, without Strength because without Connection; but UNION would make us strong and even formidable: Tho' the *Great* should neither help nor join us; tho' they should even oppose our Uniting, from some mean Views of their own, yet, if we resolve upon it, and it please GOD to inspire us with the necessary Prudence and Vigour, it *may* be effected. . . . Were this Union form'd, were we once united, thoroughly arm'd and disciplin'd, was every Thing in our Power done for our Security, as far as human Means and Foresight could provide, we might then, *with more Propriety,* humbly ask the Assistance of Heaven, and a Blessing on our lawful Endeavours. The very Fame of our Strength and Readiness would be a Means of Discouraging our Enemies; for 'tis a wise and true Saying, that *One Sword often keeps another in the Scabbard.* The Way to secure Peace is to be prepared for War. They that are on their Guard, and appear ready to receive their Adversaries, are in much less Danger of being attack'd, than the supine, secure and negligent. We have yet a Winter before us, which may afford a good and almost sufficient Opportunity for this, if we seize and improve it with a becoming Vigour. And if the Hints contained in this Paper are so happy as to meet with a suitable Disposition of Mind in his Countrymen and Fellow Citizens, the Writer of it will, in a few Days, lay before them a Form of an ASSOCIATION for the Purposes herein mentioned, together with a practicable Scheme for raising the Money necessary for the Defence of our Trade, City, and Country, without laying a Burthen on any Man.

May the GOD *of* WISDOM, STRENGTH *and* POWER, *the Lord of the Armies of Israel, inspire us with Prudence in this Time of* DANGER; *take away from us all the Seeds of Contention and Division, and unite the Hearts and Counsels of all of us, of whatever* SECT *or* NATION, *in one Bond of Peace, Brotherly Love, and generous Publick Spirit; May he give us Strength and Resolution to amend our Lives, and remove from among us every Thing that is displeasing to him; afford us his most gracious Protection, confound the Designs of our Enemies, and give* PEACE *in all our Borders, is the sincere Prayer of*

A TRADESMAN of Philadelphia.

2. George Washington Remakes a Citizen Army in Wartime

WASHINGTON WAS OF COURSE A COMMANDING FIGURE IN THE EARLY formulation of American military thinking; from his time until our own, his letters and papers have been studied as guides to sound military policy. One of the best known is his letter to the president of the Continental Congress written from Harlem Heights, New York, in September 1776, when he was once more facing the problem of dissolving one army and raising a new one to carry through the long pull that the Revolution promised to be.

To The President of Congress

Colonel Morris's, on the Heights of Harlem,
September 24, 1776.

Sir: From the hours allotted to Sleep, I will borrow a few Moments to convey my thoughts on sundry important matters to Congress. I shall offer them, with that sincerity which ought to characterize a man of candour; and with the freedom which may be used in giving useful information, without incurring the imputation of presumption.

We are now as it were, upon the eve of another dissolution of our Army; the remembrance of the difficulties which happened upon that occasion last year, the consequences which might have followed the change, if proper advantages had been taken by the Enemy; added to a knowledge of the present temper and Sit-

From John C. Fitzpatrick (ed.), *The Writings of George Washington*, 6 (Washington, D.C.: Government Printing Office, 1932), pp. 106–116.

uation of the Troops, reflect but a very gloomy prospect upon the appearance of things now, and satisfie me, beyond the possibility of doubt, that unless some speedy, and effectual measures are adopted by Congress, our cause will be lost.

It is in vain to expect, that any (or more than a trifling) part of this Army will again engage in the Service on the encouragement offered by Congress. When Men find that their Townsmen and Companions are receiving 20, 30, and more Dollars, for a few Months Service, (which is truely the case) it cannot be expected; without using compulsion; and to force them into the Service would answer no valuable purpose. When Men are irritated, and the Passions inflamed, they fly hastely and chearfully to Arms; but after the first emotions are over, to expect, among such People, as compose the bulk of an Army, that they are influenced by any other principles than those of Interest, is to look for what never did, and I fear never will happen; the Congress will deceive themselves therefore if they expect it.

A Soldier reasoned with upon the goodness of the cause he is engaged in, and the inestimable rights he is contending for, hears you with patience, and acknowledges the truth of your observations, but adds, that it is of no more Importance to him than others. The Officer makes you the same reply, with this further remark, that his pay will not support him, and he cannot ruin himself and Family to serve his Country, when every Member of the community is equally Interested and benefitted by his Labours. The few therefore, who act upon Principles of disinterestedness, are, comparatively speaking, no more than a drop in the Ocean. It becomes evidently clear then, that as this Contest is not likely to be the Work of a day; as the War must be carried on systematically, and to do it, you must have good Officers, there are, in my Judgment, no other possible means to obtain them but by establishing your Army upon a permanent footing; and giving your Officers good pay; this will induce Gentlemen, and Men of Character to engage; and till the bulk of your Officers are composed of such persons as are actuated by Principles of honour, and a spirit of enterprize, you have little to expect from them.— They ought to have such allowances as will enable them to live like, and support the Characters of Gentlemen; and not be driven by a scanty pittance to the low, and dirty arts which many of them practice, to filch the Public of more than the difference of pay would amount to upon an ample allowe. besides, something is due to the Man who puts his life in his hands, hazards his health, and forsakes the Sweets of domestic enjoyments. Why a Captn. in the Continental Service should receive no more than 5/. Curry [5 *s*. currency] per day, for performing the same duties that an officer of the same Rank in the British Service receives 10/. Sterlg. for, I never could conceive; especially when the latter is provided with every necessary he requires, upon the best terms, and the former can scarce procure them, at any Rate. There is nothing that gives a Man consequence, and renders him fit for Command, like a support that renders him Independant of every body but the State he Serves.

With respect to the Men, nothing but a good bounty can obtain them upon a permanent establishment; and for no shorter time than the continuance of the War, ought they to be engaged; as Facts incontestibly prove, that the difficulty, and cost of Inlistments, increase with time. When the Army was first raised at Cambridge, I am persuaded the Men might have been got without a bounty for the War: after this, they began to see that the Contest was not likely to end so speedily as was immagined, and to feel their consequence, by remarking, that to get the Militia In, in the course of last year, many Towns were induced to give them a bounty. Foreseeing the Evils resulting from this, and the destructive consequences which unavoidably would follow short Inlistments, I took the Liberty in a long Letter, written by myself (date not now recollected, as my Letter Book is not here) to recommend the Inlistments for and during the War; assigning such Reasons for it, as experience has since convinced me were well founded. At that time twenty Dollars would, I am persuaded, have engaged the Men for this term. But it will not do to look back, and if the present opportunity is slip'd, I am perswaded that twelve months more will Increase our difficulties fourfold. I shall therefore take the freedom of giving it as my opinion, that a good Bounty be immediately offered, aided by the proffer of at least 100, or 150 Acres of Land and a suit of Cloaths and Blankt, to each non-Comd. [noncommissioned] Officer and Soldier; as I have good authority for saying, that however high the Men's pay may appear, it is barely sufficient in the present scarcity and dearness of all kinds of goods, to keep them in Cloaths, much less afford support to their Families. If this encouragement then is given to the Men, and such Pay allowed the Officers as will induce Gentlemen of Character and liberal Sentiments to engage; and proper care and precaution are used in the nomination (having more regard to the Characters of Persons, than the Number of Men they can Inlist) we should in a little time have an Army able to cope with any that can be opposed to it, as there are excellent Materials to form one out of: but while the only merit an Officer possesses is his ability to raise Men; while those Men consider, and treat him as an equal; and (in the Character of an Officer) regard him no more than a broomstick, being mixed together as one common herd; no order, nor no discipline can prevail; nor will the Officer ever meet with that respect which is essentially necessary to due subordination.

To place any dependance upon Militia, is, assuredly, resting upon a broken staff. Men just dragged from the tender Scenes of domestick life; unaccustomed to the din of Arms; totally unacquainted with every kind of Military skill, which being followed by a want of confidence in themselves, when opposed to Troops regularly train'd, disciplined, and appointed, superior in knowledge, and superior in Arms, makes them timid, and ready to fly from their own shadows. Besides, the sudden change in their manner of living, (particularly in the lodging) brings on sickness in many; impatience in all, and such an unconquerable desire of returning to their respective homes that it not only produces shameful, and scandalous Desertions among themselves, but infuses the like spirit in others. Again, Men accustomed to unbounded freedom, and no controul, cannot brook the Restraint which is indispensably necessary to the good order and Government of an Army; without which, licentiousness, and every kind of disorder triumpantly reign. To bring Men to a proper degree of Subordination, is not the work of a day, a Month or even a year;

and unhappily for us, and the cause we are Engaged in, the little discipline I have been labouring to establish in the Army under my immediate Command, is in a manner done away by having such a mixture of Troops as have been called together within these few Months.

Relaxed, and unfit, as our Rules and Regulations of War are, for the Government of an Army, the Militia (those properly so called, for of these we have two sorts, the Six Months Men and those sent in as a temporary aid) do not think themselves subject to 'em, and therefore take liberties, which the Soldier is punished for; this creates jealousy; jealousy begets dissatisfaction, and these by degrees ripen into Mutiny; keeping the whole Army in a confused, and disordered State; rendering the time of those who wish to see regularity and good Order prevail more unhappy than Words can describe. Besides this, such repeated changes take place, that all arrangement is set at nought, and the constant fluctuation of things, deranges every plan, as fast as adopted.

These Sir, Congress may be assured, are but a small part of the Inconveniences which might be enumerated and attributed to Militia; but there is one that merits particular attention, and that is the expence. Certain I am, that it would be cheaper to keep 50, or 100,000 Men in constant pay than to depend upon half the number, and supply the other half occasionally by Militia. The time the latter is in pay before and after they are in Camp, assembling and Marching; the waste of Ammunition; the consumption of Stores, which in spite of every Resolution, and requisition of Congress they must be furnished with, or sent home, added to other incidental expences consequent upon their coming, and conduct in Camp, surpasses all Idea, and destroys every kind of regularity and oeconomy which you could establish among fixed and Settled Troops; and will, in my opinion prove (if the scheme is adhered to) the Ruin of our Cause.

The Jealousies of a standing Army, and the Evils to be apprehended from one, are remote; and in my judgment, situated and circumstanced as we are, not at all to be dreaded; but the consequence of wanting one, according to my Ideas, formed from the present view of things, is certain, and inevitable Ruin; for if I was called upon to declare upon Oath, whether the Militia have been most serviceable or hurtful upon the whole; I should subscribe to the latter. I do not mean by this however to arraign the Conduct of Congress, in so doing I should equally condemn my own measures, (if I did not my judgment); but experience, which is the best criterion to work by, so fully, clearly, and decisively reprobates the practice of trusting to Militia, that no Man who regards order, regularity, and oeconomy; or who has any regard for his own honour, Character, or peace of Mind, will risk them upon this Issue.

No less attention should be paid to the choice of Surgeons than other Officers of the Army; they should undergo a regular examination; and if not appointed by the Director Genl. and Surgeons of the Hospital, they ought to be subordinate to, and governed by his directions; the Regimental Surgeons I am speaking of, many of whom are very great Rascals, countenancing the Men in sham Complaints to exempt them from duty, and often receiving Bribes to Certifie Indispositions, with a view to procure discharges or Furloughs; but independant of these practices, while they are considered as unconnected with the Genl. Hospital there will be nothing but continual Complaints of each other: The Director of the Hospital charging them with enormity in their drafts for the Sick; and they him, for denying such things as are necessary. In short, there is a constant bickering among them, which tends greatly to the Injury of the Sick; and will always subsist till the Regimental Surgeons are made to look up to the Director Genl. of the Hospital as a Superior. Whether this is the case in regular Armies, or not, I cannot undertake to say; but certain I am there is a necessity for it in this, or the Sick will suffer; the Regimental Surgeons are aiming, I am persuaded, to break up the Genl. Hospital, and have, in numberless Instances, drawn for Medicines, Stores &ca. in the most profuse and extravagant manner, for private purposes.

Another matter highly worthy of attention, is, that other Rules and Regulation's may be adopted for the Government of the Army than those now in existence, otherwise the Army, but for the name, might as well be disbanded. For the most attrocious offences, (one or two Instances only excepted) a Man receives no more than 39 Lashes; and these perhaps (thro' the collusion of the Officer who is to see it inflicted), are given in such a manner as to become rather a matter of sport than punishment; but when inflicted as they ought, many hardend fellows who have been the Subjects, have declared that for a bottle of Rum they would undergo a Second operation; it is evident therefore that this punishment is inadequate to many Crimes it is assigned to, as a proof of it, thirty and 40 Soldiers will desert at a time; and of late, a practice prevails, (as you will see by my Letter of the 22d) of the most alarming nature; and which will, if it cannot be checked, prove fatal both to the Country and Army; I mean the infamous practice of Plundering, for under the Idea of Tory property, or property which may fall into the hands of the Enemy, no Man is secure in his effects, and scarcely in his Person; for in order to get at them, we have several Instances of People being frightend out of their Houses under pretence of those Houses being ordered to be burnt, and this is done with a view of seizing the Goods; nay, in order that the villany may be more effectually concealed, some Houses have actually been burnt to cover the theft.

I have with some others, used my utmost endeavours to stop this horrid practice, but under the present lust after plunder, and want of Laws to punish Offenders, I might almost as well attempt to remove Mount Atlas.—I have ordered instant corporal Punishment upon every Man who passes our Lines, or is seen with Plunder, that the Offenders might be punished for disobedience of Orders; and Inclose you the proceedings of a Court Martial held upon an Officer, who with a Party of Men had robbed a House a little beyond our Lines of a Number of valuable Goods; among which (to shew that nothing escapes) were four large Pier looking Glasses, Women's Cloaths, and other Articles which one would think, could be of no Earthly use to him. He was met by a Major of Brigade who ordered him to return the Goods, as taken contrary to Genl. Orders, which he not only peremptorily refused to do, but drew up his Party and swore he would defend them at the hazard of his Life; on which I ordered him to be arrested, and tryed for Plundering, Disobedience of Orders, and Mutiny; for the Result, I refer to the Proceedings of the Court; whose judgment appeared so exceedingly extraordinary, that I ordered a Reconsideration of the matter, upon which, and with the Assistance of fresh evidence, they made Shift to Cashier him.

I adduce this Instance to give some Idea to Congress of the Currt. [current] Sentiments and general run of the Officers which compose the present Army; and to shew how exceedingly necessary it is to be careful in the choice of the New Sett, even if it should take double the time to compleat the Levies. An Army formed of good Officers moves like Clock-Work; but there is no Situation upon Earth, less enviable, nor more distressing, than that Person's who is at the head of Troops, who are regardless of Order and discipline; and who are unprovided with almost every necessary. In a word the difficulties which have forever surrounded me since I have been in the Service, and kept my Mind constantly upon the stretch; The Wounds which my Feelings as an Officer have received by a thousand things which have happened, contrary to my expectation and Wishes; the effect of my own Conduct, and present appearance of things, so little pleasing to myself, as to render it a matter of no Surprize (to me) if I should stand capitally censured by Congress; added to a consciousness of my inability to govern an Army composed of such discordant parts, and under such a variety of intricate and perplexing circumstances; induces not only a belief, but a thorough conviction in my Mind, that it will be impossible unless there is a thorough change in our Military Systems for me to conduct matters in such a manner, as to give satisfaction to the Publick which is all the recompence I aim at, or ever wished for. . . .

3. Washington Recommends a Permanent Military Establishment

CORNWALLIS SURRENDERED AT YORKTOWN IN OCTOBER 1781. By THE spring of 1783 the peace commissioners were in Europe, the Army had been concentrated at Newburgh, New York, on the Hudson River, and the Revolutionary War was visibly running down. The

Army itself was beginning to evaporate; but the problem of a permanent military establishment obviously remained. Alexander Hamilton,
in his capacity as chairman of the Committee on the Peace Establishment of the Continental Congress, wrote to ask Washington's views.
The considered reply of May 1783 is a good illustration of our best
military thought as the Revolution ended.

Sentiments on a Peace Establishment

A Peace Establishment for the United States of America may
in my opinion be classed under four different heads Vizt:
First. A regular and standing force, for Garrisoning West Point
and such other Posts upon our Northern, Western, and Southern
Frontiers, as shall be deemed necessary to awe the Indians, pro-
tect our Trade, prevent the encroachment of our Neighbours of
Canada and the Florida's, and guard us at least from surprizes;
Also for security of our Magazines.
Secondly. A well organized Militia; upon a Plan that will per-
vade all the States, and introduce similarity in their Establish-
ment Manoeuvres, Exercises and Arms.
Thirdly. Establishing Arsenals of all kinds of Military Stores.
Fourthly. Accademies, one or more for the Instruction of the
Art Military; particularly those Branches of it which respect En-
gineering and Artillery, which are highly essential, and the knowledge of which, is most difficult to obtain. Also Manufactories [fac-
tories] of some kinds of Military Stores.
Upon each of these, and in the order in which they stand, I
shall give my sentiments as concisely as I can, and with that freedom which the Committee have authorized.
Altho' a *large* standing Army in time of Peace hath ever been
considered dangerous to the liberties of a Country, yet a few
Troops, under certain circumstances, are not only safe, but indispensably necessary. Fortunately for us our relative situation requires but few. The same circumstances which so effectually
retarded, and in the end conspired to defeat the attempts of Brit-

From *The Writings of Washington,* 26, pp. 374–377, 380–398.

ain to subdue us, will now powerfully tend to render us secure. Our *distance* from the European States in a great degree frees us of apprehension, from their numerous regular forces and the Insults and dangers which are to be dreaded from their Ambition.

But, if our danger from those powers was more imminent, yet we are too poor to maintain a standing Army adequate to our defence, and was our Country more populous and rich, still it could not be done without great oppression of the people. Besides, as soon as we are able to raise funds more than adequate to the discharge of the Debts incurred by the Revolution, it may become a Question worthy of consideration, whether the surplus should not be applied in preparations for building and equipping a Navy, without which, in case of War we could neither protect our Commerce, nor yield that Assistance to each other, which, on such an extent of Sea-Coast, our mutual Safety would require.

Fortifications on the Sea Board may be considered in two points of view, first as part of the general defence, and next, as securities to Dock Yards, and Arsenals for Ship Building, neither of which shall I take into this plan; because the first would be difficult, if not, under our circumstances, impracticable; at any rate amazingly expensive. The other, because it is a matter out of my line, and to which I am by no means competent, as it requires a consideration of many circumstances, to which I have never paid attention.

The Troops requisite for the Post of West Point, for the Magazines, and for our Northern, Western and Southern Frontiers, ought, in my opinion, to amount to 2631 Officers of all denominations included; besides the Corps of Invalids.[1] If this number should be thought large, I would only observe; that the British Force in Canada is now powerful, and, by report, will be increased; that the frontier is very extensive; that the Tribes of Indians within our Territory are numerous, soured and jealous; that Communications must be established with the exterior Posts; And, that it may be policy and oeconomy, to appear respectable in the Eyes of the Indians, at the Commencement of our National Inter-

[1] Men passed to inactive or police duties for reasons of partial disability [Ed.].

course and Traffic with them. In a word, that it is better to reduce our force hereafter, by degrees, than to have it to increase after some unfortunate disasters may have happened to the Garrisons; discouraging to us, and an inducement to the Enemy to attempt a repetition of them.

Besides these Considerations, we are not to forget, that altho' by the Treaty, half the Waters, and the free Navigation of the Lakes appertain to us, yet, in Case of a rupture with Great Britain we should in all probability, find little benefits from the Communications with our upper Posts, by the Lakes Erie and Ontario; as it is to be presumed, that the Naval superiority which they now have on those Waters, will be maintained. It follows as a Consequence then, that we should open new or improve the present half explored Communications with Detroit and other Posts on the Lakes, by the Waters of the Susquehannah Potowmack or James River, to the Ohio, from whence, with short Portages several Communications by Water may be opened with Lake Erie. To do which, posts should be established at the most convenient places on the Ohio. This would open several doors for the supply of the Garrisons on the Lakes; and is absolutely necessary for such others as may be tho't advisable to establish upon the Mississippi. The Ohio affording the easiest, as well as the safest Route to the Illinois settlements, and the whole Country below on the Mississippi, quite to our Southern boundary.

To protect the Peltry and Fur Trade, to keep a watch upon our Neighbours, and to prevent their encroaching upon our Territory undiscovered, are all the purposes that can be answered by an extension of our Posts, at this time, beyond Detroit, to the Northward or Westward: but, a strong Post on the Scioto, at the carrying place between it and the River Sandusky, which empties into Lake Erie, . . . is indispensably necessary for the security of the present Settlers, and such as probably, will *immediately* settle within those Limits. And by giving security to the Country and covering its Inhabitants, will enable them to furnish supplies to the Garrisons Westward and Northward of these settlements, upon moderate and easy Terms.

The 2,631 Men beforementioned, I would have considered to

all Intents and purposes as Continental Troops; looking up to Congress for their Orders, their pay, and supplies of every kind. . . .

. . . It may also be observed, that in case of War and a necessity of assembling their Regiments in the Field, nothing more will be necessary, than to recruit 18 Men to each Compy. and give the Regiment its flank Company. Or if we should have occasion to add strength to the Garrisons, or increase the number of our Posts, we may augment 900 Men including Serjeants, without requiring more than the Officers of 4 Companies, or exceeding our present Establishment. In short, it will give us a Number of Officers well skilled in the Theory and Art of War, who will be ready on any occasion, to mix and diffuse their knowledge of Discipline to other Corps, without that lapse of Time, which, without such Provision, would be necessary to bring intire new Corps acquainted with the principles of it.

Besides the 4 Regiments of Infantry, one of Artillery will be indispensably necessary. The Invalid Corps should also be retained. Motives of humanity, Policy and justice will all combine to prevent their being disbanded. . . .

. . . The Regiment of Artillery, with the Artificers,[2] will furnish all the Posts in which Artillery is placed, in proportionate numbers to the Strength and importance of them. The residue, with the Corps of Invalids, will furnish Guards for the Magazines, and Garrison West Point. The importance of this last mentioned Post, is so great, as justly to have been considered, the key of America; It has been so pre-eminently advantageous to the defence of the United States, and is still so necessary in that view, as well as for the preservation of the Union, that the loss of it might be productive of the most ruinous Consequences. A Naval superiority at Sea and on Lake Champlain, connected by a Chain of Posts on the Hudson River, would effect an entire separation of the States on each side, and render it difficult, if not impracticable for them to co-operate.

[2] Technicians who would later be regarded as engineer or ordnance personnel [Ed.].

Altho' the total of the Troops herein enumerated does not amount to a large number, yet when we consider their detached situation, and the extent of Country they are spread over: the variety of objects that are to be attended to, and the close inspection that will be necessary to prevent abuses or to correct them before they become habitual; not less than two General Officers in my opinion will be competent to the Duties to be required of them. They will take their Instructions from the Secretary at War, or Person acting at the Head of the Military Department, who will also assign them their respective and distinct Districts. Each should twice a Year visit the Posts of his particular District, and notice the Condition they are in, Inspect the Troops, their discipline and Police, Examine into their Wants, and see that strict justice is rendered them and to the Public, they should also direct the Colonels, at what intermediate Times they shall perform the like duties at the Posts occupied by the Detachments of their respective Regiments. The visiting General ought frequently, if not always, to be accompanied by a Skillful Engineer, who should point out such alterations and improvements as he may think necessary from time to time, for the defence of any of the Posts; which, if approved by the General, should be ordered to be carried into execution. . . .

. . . The three Years Men now in service will furnish the proposed Establishment, and from these, it is presumed, the Corps must in the first Instance be composed. But as the pay of an American Soldier is much greater than any other we are acquainted with; and as there can be little doubt of our being able to obtain them in time of Peace, upon as good Terms as other Nations, I would suggest the propriety of inlisting those who may come after the present three years Men, upon Terms of similarity with those of the British, or any other the most liberal Nations. . . .

. . . Soldiers should not be inlisted for *less* than three Years, to commence from the date of their attestations; and the more difference there is in the commencement of their terms of Service, the better; this Circumstance will be the means of avoiding the danger and inconvenience of entrusting any important Posts to raw Recruits unacquainted with service.

Rum should compose no part of a Soldier's Ration; but Vinegar in large quantities should be issued. Flour or Bread, and a stipulated quantity of the different kinds of fresh or Salted Meat, with Salt, when the former is Issued, is all that should be contracted for.

Vegetables they can, and ought to be compelled to raise. If spruce, or any other kind of small Beer, could be provided, it ought to be given gratis, but not made part of the Compact with them. It might be provided also, that they should receive one or two days fish in a Week, when to be had; this would be a saving to the public, (the Lakes and most of the Waters of the Ohio and Mississippi abounding with Fish) and would be no disservice to the Soldier. . . .

. . . As a peace establishment may be considered as a change in, if not the Commencement of our Military system, it will be the proper time, to introduce new and beneficial regulations, and to expunge all customs, which from experience have been found unproductive of general good. Among the latter I would ask, if promotion by Seniority is not one? That it is a good general rule admits of no doubt, but that it should be an invariable one, is in my opinion wrong. It cools, if it does not destroy, the incentives to Military Pride and Heroic Actions. On the one hand, the sluggard, who keeps within the verge of his duty, has nothing to fear. On the other hand, the enterprising Spirit has nothing to expect. Whereas, if promotion was the *sure* reward of Merit, *all* would contend for Rank and the service would be benefited by their Struggles for Promotion. In establishing a mode by which this is to be done, and from which nothing is to be expected, or apprehended, either from favour or prejudice, lies the difficulty. Perhaps, reserving to Congress the right inherent in Sovereignties, of making all Promotions. A Board of superior Officers, appointed to receive and examine the claims to promotions out of common course, of any Officer, whether founded on particular merit, or extra service, and to report their opinion thereon to Congress;

might prove a likely means of doing justice. It would certainly give a Spur to Emulation, without endangering the rights, or just pretentions of the Officers. . . .

. . . I come next in the order I have prescribed myself, to treat of the Arrangements necessary for placing the Militia of the Continent [North America, i.e., the United States] on a respectable footing for the defence of the Empire [United States] and in speaking of this great Bulwark [the militia] of our Liberties and independence, I shall claim the indulgence of suggesting whatever general observations may occur from experience and reflection with the greater freedom, from a conviction of the importance of the subject; being persuaded, that the immediate safety and future tranquility of this extensive Continent depend in a great measure upon the peace Establishment now in contemplation; and being convinced at the same time, that the only probable means of preventing insult or hostility for any length of time and from being exempted from the consequent calamities of War, is to put the National Militia in such a condition as that they may appear truly respectable in the Eyes of our Friends and formidable to those who would otherwise become our enemies. . . .

. . . It may be laid down as a primary position, and the basis of our system, that every Citizen who enjoys the protection of a free Government, owes not only a proportion of his property, but even of his personal services to the defence of it, and consequently that the Citizens of America (with a few legal and official exceptions) from 18 to 50 Years of Age should be borne on the Militia Rolls, provided with uniform Arms, and so far accustomed to the use of them, that the Total strength of the Country might be called forth at a Short Notice on any very interesting Emergency, for these purposes they ought to be duly organized into Commands of the same formation; (it is not of *very* great importance, whether the Regiments are large or small, provided a sameness prevails in the strength and composition of them and I do not know that a better establishment, than that under which the Continental Troops now are, can be adopted. They ought to be regularly Mustered and trained, and to have their Arms and Accoutrements inspected at certain appointed times, not less than once or twice in the course of every [year] but as it is obvious, amongst such a Multitude of People (who may indeed be useful for temporary service) there must be a great number, who from domestic Circumstances, bodily defects, natural awkwardness or disinclination, can never acquire the habits of Soldiers; but on the contrary will injure the appearance of any body of Troops to which they are attached, and as there are a sufficient proportion of able bodied young Men, between the Age of 18 and 25, who, from a natural fondness for Military parade (which passion is almost ever prevalent at that period of life) might easily be enlisted or drafted to form a Corps in every State, capable of resisting any sudden impression which might be attempted by a foreign Enemy, while the remainder of the National forces would have time to Assemble and make preparations for the Field. I would wish therefore, that the former, being considered as a *denier* [*dernier*] *resort*, reserved for some great occasion, a judicious system might be adopted for forming and placing the latter on the best possible Establishment. And that while the Men of this description shall be viewed as the Van and flower of the American Forces, ever ready for Action and zealous to be employed whenever it may become necessary in the service of their Country; they should meet with such exemptions, privileges or distinctions, as might tend to keep alive a true Military pride, a nice sense of honour, and a patriotic regard for the public. Such sentiments, indeed, ought to be instilled into our Youth, with their earliest years, to be cherished and inculcated as frequently and forcibly as possible.

It is not for me to decide positively, whether it will be ultimately most interesting to the happiness and safety of the United States, to form this Class of Soldiers into a kind of Continental Militia, selecting every 10th 15th or 20th. Man from the Rolls of each State for the purpose; Organizing, Officering and Commissioning those Corps upon the same principle as is now practiced in the Continental Army. Whether it will be best to comprehend in this body, all the Men fit for service between some given Age and no others, for example between 18 and 25 or some similar description, or whether it will be preferable in every Regiment of the proposed Establishment to have one additional Company inlisted or drafted from the best Men for 3, 5, or 7 years and distinguished by the name of the additional or light Infantry Company, always to be kept complete. These Companies might then be drawn together occasionally and formed into particular Battalions or Regiments under Field Officers appointed for that Service. One or other of these plans I think will be found indispensably necessary, if we are in earnest to have an efficient force ready for Action at a moments Warning. And I cannot conceal my private sentiment, that the formation of additional, or light Companies will be most consistent with the genius of our Countrymen and perhaps in their opinion most consonant to the spirit of our Constitution. . . .

. . . It is likewise much to be wished, that it might be made agreeable to Officers who have served in the Army, to accept Commands in the Militia; that they might be appointed to them so far as can be done without creating uneasiness and jealousy, and that the principle Characters in the Community would give a countenance to Military improvements, by being present at public reviews and Exhibitions, and by bringing into estimation amongst their fellow Citizens, those who appear fond of cultivating Military knowledge and who excel in the Exercise of Arms. By giving such a tone to our Establishment; by making it universally reputable to bear Arms and disgraceful to decline having a share in the performance of Military duties; in fine, by keeping up in Peace "a well regulated, and disciplined Militia," we shall take the fairest and best method to preserve, for a long time to come, the happiness, dignity and Independence of our Country. . . .

. . . According to my recollection, five grand Magazines are proposed by the Secretary at War, one of which to be fixed at West Point. Now, as West Point is considered not only by our selves, but by all who have the least knowledge of the Country, as a post of the greatest importance, as it may in time of Peace, from its situation on the Water be somewhat obnoxious to surprise or

Coup de Main and as it would doubtless be a first object with any Nation which might commence a War against the United States, to seize that Post and occupy or destroy the Stores, it appears to me, that we ought particularly to guard against such an event, so far as may be practicable, and to remove some part of the Allurements to enterprise, by establishing the grand Arsenals in the Interior part of the Country, leaving only to West Point an adequate supply for its defence in almost any extremity.

I take the liberty also to submit to the consideration of the Committee, whether, instead of five great Arsenals, it would not be less expensive and equally convenient and advantageous to fix three general Deposits, one for the Southern, one for the Middle and one for the Eastern States, including New York, in each of which there might be deposited, Arms, Ammunition, Field Artillery, and Camp Equipage for thirty thousand Men, Also one hundred heavy Cannon and Mortars, and all the Apparatus of a Seige, with a sufficiency of Ammunition.

Under the fourth General Division of the subject, it was proposed to consider the Establishment of Military Academies and Manufacturies, as the means of preserving that knowledge and being possessed of those Warlike Stores, which are essential to the support of the Sovereignty and Independence of the United States. . . .

. . .That an Institution calculated to keep alive and diffuse the knowledge of the Military Art would be highly expedient, and that some kinds of Military Manufactories and Elaboratories [laboratories] may and ought to be established, will not admit a doubt; but how far we are able at this time to go into great and expensive Arrangements and whether the greater part of the Military Apparatus and Stores which will be wanted can be imported or Manufactured, in the cheapest and best manner: I leave those to whom the observations are to be submitted, to determine, as being more competent, to the decision than I can pretend to be. I must however mention some things, which I think cannot be dispensed with under the present or any other circumstances; Until a more perfect system of Education can be adopted, I would propose that Provision should be made at some

Post or Posts where the principle Engineers and Artillerists shall be stationed, for instructing a certain number of young Gentlemen in the Theory of the Art of War, particularly in all those branches of service which belong to the Artillery and Engineering Departments. Which, from the affinity they bear to each other, and the advantages which I think would result from the measure, I would have blended together; And as this species of knowledge will render them much more accomplished and capable of performing the duties of Officers, even in the Infantry or any other Corps whatsoever, I conceive that appointments to vacancies in the Established Regiments, ought to be made from the candidates who shall have completed their course of Military Studies and Exercises. As it does in an essential manner qualify them for the duties of Garrisons, which will be the principal, if not only service in which our Troops can be employed in time of Peace and besides the Regiments of Infantry by this means will become in time a nursery from whence a number of Officers for Artillery and Engineering may be drawn on any great or sudden occasion.

Of so great importance is it to preserve the knowledge which has been acquired thro' the various Stages of a long and arduous service, that I cannot conclude without repeating the necessity of the proposed Institution, unless we intend to let the Science become extinct, and to depend entirely upon the Foreigners for their friendly aid, if ever we should again be involved in Hostility. For it must be understood, that a Corps of able Engineers and expert Artillerists cannot be raised in a day, nor made such by any exertions, in the same time, which it would take to form an excellent body of Infantry from a well regulated Militia.

And as to Manufactories and Elaboratories it is my opinion that if we should not be able to go largely into the buisness at present, we should nevertheless have a reference to such establishments hereafter, and in the mean time that we ought to have such works carried on, wherever our principal Arsenals may be fixed, as will not only be sufficient to repair and keep in good order the Arms, Artillery, Stores &c of the Post, but shall also extend to Founderies and some other essential matters.

Thus have I given my sentiments without reserve on the four

different heads into which the subject seemed naturally to divide itself, as amply as my numerous avocations and various duties would permit. Happy shall I be, if any thing I have suggested may be found of use in forming an Establishment which will maintain the lasting Peace, Happiness and Independence of the United States.

4. The Military Clauses of the Constitution

THE CONSTITUTION OF 1787 WAS A MILITARY NO LESS THAN A PO-litical charter for the infant republic. Building on the experience of the Revolutionary War and, very largely, on the Articles of Confederation under which that struggle had been fought, the Philadelphia convention established the principles by which succeeding generations would seek to solve the basic problems of war and defense. The Constitution's clauses embody the guidelines of American military thought —civilian supremacy; a commander-in-chief with full executive responsibility, but checked by Congressional control over organization and appropriations; a small, national, professional army backed by state militia; and a people guaranteed in its right to bear arms. These principles governed, almost unchanged, for well over a century, and they are still controlling in popular and national attitudes, even though the events of the past fifty years have profoundly altered their application in practice.

We, the people of the United States, in order to form a more perfect union, establish justice, insure domestic tranquility, provide for the common defense, promote the general welfare, and secure the blessings of liberty to ourselves and our posterity, do ordain and establish this Constitution for the United States of America.

From *Documents Illustrative of the Formation of the Union of the American States* (Washington, D.C.: Government Printing Office, 1927), pp. 989–1001.

Article I

. . . SEC. 8. The Congress shall have power

To lay and collect taxes, duties, imposts and excises, to pay the debts and provide for the common defense and general welfare of the United States; but all duties, imposts, and excises shall be uniform throughout the United States;

To borrow money on the credit of the United States;

To regulate commerce with foreign nations, and among the several states, and with the Indian tribes;

To establish a uniform rule of naturalization, and uniform laws on the subject of bankruptcies throughout the United States;

To coin money, regulate the value thereof, and of foreign coin, and fix the standard of weights and measures;

To provide for the punishment of counterfeiting the securities and current coin of the United States;

To establish post offices and post roads;

To promote the progress of science and useful arts, by securing for limited times to authors and inventors the exclusive right to their respective writings and discoveries;

To constitute tribunals inferior to the Supreme Court;

To define and punish piracies and felonies committed on the high seas, and offenses against the law of nations;

To declare war, grant letters of marque and reprisal and make rules concerning captures on land and water;

To raise and support armies, but no appropriation of money to that use shall be for a longer term than two years;

To provide and maintain a navy;

To make rules for the government and regulation of the land and naval forces;

To provide for calling forth the militia to execute the laws of the Union, suppress insurrections and repel invasions;

To provide for organizing, arming, and disciplining the militia, and for governing such part of them as may be employed in the service of the United States, reserving to the states, respectively, the appointment of the officers, and the authority of training the militia according to the discipline prescribed by Congress; . . .

. . . To make all laws which shall be necessary and proper for carrying into execution the foregoing powers, and all other powers vested by this Constitution in the government of the United States, or in any department or officer thereof. . . .

. . . SEC. 10. No state shall enter into any treaty, alliance, or confederation; grant letters of marque and reprisal; coin money; emit bills of credit; make anything but gold and silver coin a tender in payment of debts; pass any bill of attainder, ex post facto law, or law impairing the obligation of contracts, or grant any title of nobility.

No state shall, without the consent of the Congress, lay any imposts or duties on imports or exports, except what may be absolutely necessary for executing its inspection laws: and the net produce of all duties and imposts, laid by any state on imports or exports shall be for the use of the treasury of the United States; and all such laws shall be subject to the revision and control of the Congress.

No state shall, without the consent of Congress, lay any duty of tonnage, keep troops, or ships of war in time of peace, enter into any agreement or compact with another state, or with a foreign power, or engage in war, unless actually invaded, or in such imminent danger as will not admit of delay.

Article II

SECTION 1. The executive power shall be vested in a President of the United States of America. He shall hold his office during the term of four years . . .

. . . SEC. 2. The President shall be commander-in-chief of the army and navy of the United States, and of the militia of the several states, when called into the actual service of the United States; he may require the opinion, in writing, of the principal officer in each of the executive departments, upon any subject relating to the duties of their respective offices, and he shall have power to grant reprieves and pardons for offenses against the United States, except in cases of impeachment.

He shall have power, by and with the advice and consent of the Senate, to make treaties, provided two-thirds of the Senators present concur; and he shall nominate, and by and with the advice and consent of the Senate, shall appoint ambassadors, other public ministers and consuls, judges of the Supreme Court, and all other officers of the United States, whose appointments are not herein otherwise provided for, and which shall be established by law; but the Congress may by law vest the appointment of such inferior officers, as they think proper, in the President alone, in the courts of law, or in the heads of departments.

The President shall have power to fill up all vacancies that may happen during the recess of the Senate, by granting commissions which shall expire at the end of their next session. . . .

Article III

SECTION 1. The judicial power of the United States shall be vested in one Supreme Court, and in such inferior courts as the Congress may from time to time ordain and establish. . . .

. . . SEC. 3. Treason against the United States shall consist only in levying war against them, or in adhering to their enemies, giving them aid and comfort. No person shall be convicted of treason unless on the testimony of two witnesses to the same overt act, or on confession in open court.

The Congress shall have power to declare the punishment of treason, but no attainder of treason shall work corruption of blood, or forfeiture except during the life of the person attainted.

Article IV

. . . SEC. 4. The United States shall guarantee to every state in this Union a republican form of government, and shall protect each of them against invasion; and on application of the legislature, or of the executive (when the legislature cannot be convened), against domestic violence. . . .

Constitutional Amendments

Article II

A well-regulated militia being necessary to the security of a free state, the right of the people to keep and bear arms sh. ll not be infringed.

Article III

No soldier shall, in time of peace, be quartered in any house, without the consent of the owner, nor in time of war, but in a manner to be prescribed by law.

Article V

No person shall be held to answer for a capital or otherwise infamous crime, unless on a presentment or indictment of a grand jury, except in cases arising in the land or naval forces, or in the militia, when in actual service in time of war or public danger; nor shall any person be subject for the same offense to be twice put in jeopardy of life or limb; nor shall be compelled in any criminal case to be a witness against himself, nor be deprived of life, liberty, or property, without due process of law; nor shall private property be taken for public use, without just compensation.

5. The Federalist: Jay, Hamilton, and Madison Discuss Defense Policy

IN THEIR GREAT ARGUMENT FOR RATIFICATION OF THE CONSTITUTION, John Jay, Alexander Hamilton, and James Madison, repeatedly returned to the basic problems of defense, of the war powers, of military organization, and of the relationship of military policy to both domestic and international politics. In these famous and thoughtful papers, one finds many of the ideas that were to recur again and again in American military thought; they are essential to an understanding of the later history.

3

Jay

UNION AS A REQUISITE FOR NATIONAL SAFETY

. . . Among the many objects to which a wise and free people find it necessary to direct their attention, that of providing for their *safety* seems to be the first. The *safety* of the people doubtless has relation to a great variety of circumstances and considerations, and consequently affords great latitude to those who wish to define it precisely and comprehensively.

At present I mean only to consider it as it respects security for the preservation of peace and tranquillity, as well as against dangers from *foreign arms and influence,* as from dangers of the *like kind* arising from domestic causes. Let us therefore proceed to examine whether the people are not right in their opinion that a cordial Union, under an efficient national government, affords them the best security that can be devised against *hostilities* from abroad. . . .

4

Jay

RELATIONS WITH FOREIGN POWERS

My last paper assigned several reasons why the safety of the people would be best secured by union against the danger it may be exposed to by *just* causes of war given to other nations; and those reasons show that such causes would only be more rarely given, but would also be more easily accommodated, by a national government than either by the State governments or the proposed little confederacies.

But the safety of the people of America against dangers from *foreign* force depends not only on their forbearing to give *just* causes of war to other nations, but also on their placing and continuing themselves in such a situation as not to *invite* hostility or insult; for it need not be observed that there are *pretended* as well as just causes of war.

It is too true, however disgraceful it may be to human nature, that nations in general will make war whenever they have a prospect of getting any thing by it; nay, absolute monarchs will often make war when their nations are to get nothing by it, but for purposes and objects merely personal, such as thirst for military glory, revenge for personal affronts, ambition, or private compacts to aggrandize or support their particular families or partisans. These and a variety of other motives, which affect only the mind of the sovereign, often lead him to engage in wars not sanctified by justice or the voice and interests of his people. But, independent of these inducements to war, which are more prevalent in absolute monarchies, but which well deserve our attention, there are others which affect nations as often as kings; and some of them will on examination be found to grow out of our relative situation and circumstances.

With France and with Britain we are rivals in the fisheries, and can supply their markets cheaper than they can themselves, notwithstanding any efforts to prevent it by bounties on their own or duties on foreign fish.

With them and with most other European nations we are rivals in navigation and the carrying trade; and we shall deceive ourselves if we suppose that any of them will rejoice to see it flourish; for, as our carrying trade cannot increase without in some degree diminishing theirs, it is more their interest, and will be more their policy, to restrain than to promote it.

In the trade to China and India, we interfere with more than one nation, inasmuch as it enables us to partake in advantages which they had in a manner monopolized, and as we thereby supply ourselves with commodities which we used to purchase from them.

The extension of our own commerce in our own vessels cannot

give pleasure to any nations who possess territories on or near this continent, because the cheapness and excellence of our productions, added to the circumstance of vicinity, and the enterprise and address of our merchants and navigators, will give us a greater share in the advantages which those territories afford, than consists with the wishes or policy of their respective sovereigns.

Spain thinks it convenient to shut the Mississippi against us on the one side, and Britain excludes us from the Saint Lawrence on the other; nor will either of them permit the other waters which are between them and us to become the means of mutual intercourse and traffic.

From these and such like considerations, which might, if consistent with prudence, be more amplified and detailed, it is easy to see that jealousies and uneasinesses may gradually slide into the minds and cabinets of other nations, and that we are not to expect that they should regard our advancement in union, in power and consequence by land and by sea, with an eye of indifference and composure.

The people of America are aware that inducements to war may arise out of these circumstances, as well as from others not so obvious at present, and that whenever such inducements may find fit time and opportunity for operation, pretences to color and justify them will not be wanting. Wisely, therefore, do they consider union and a good national government as necessary to put and keep them in *such a situation* as, instead of *inviting war,* will tend to repress and discourage it. That situation consists in the best possible state of defence, and necessarily depends on the government, the arms, and the resources of the country.

As the safety of the whole is the interest of the whole, and cannot be provided for without government, either one or more or many, let us inquire whether one good government is not, relative to the object in question, more competent than any other given number whatever.

One government can collect and avail itself of the talents and experience of the ablest men, in whatever part of the Union they may be found. It can move on uniform principles of policy. It can harmonize, assimilate, and protect the several parts and members, and extend the benefit of its foresight and precautions to each. In the formation of treaties, it will regard the interest of the whole, and the particular interests of the parts as connected with that of the whole. It can apply the resources and power of the whole to the defence of any particular part, and that more easily and expeditiously than State governments or separate confederacies can possibly do, for want of concert and unity of system. It can place the militia under one plan of discipline, and, by putting their officers in a proper line of subordination to the Chief Magistrate, will, as it were, consolidate them into one corps, and thereby render them more efficient than if divided into thirteen or into three or four distinct independent companies. . . .

. . . Leave America divided into thirteen or, if you please, into three or four independent governments—what armies could they raise and pay—what fleets could they ever hope to have? If one was attacked, would the others fly to its succor, and spend their blood and money in its defence? Would there be no danger of their being flattered into neutrality by its specious promises, or seduced by a too great fondness for peace to decline hazarding their tranquillity and present safety for the sake of neighbors, of whom perhaps they have been jealous, and whose importance they are content to see diminished. . . .

. . . But whatever may be our situation, whether firmly united under one national government, or split into a number of confederacies, certain it is, that foreign nations will know and view it exactly as it is; and they will act towards us accordingly. If they see that our national government is efficient and well administered, our trade prudently regulated, our militia properly organized and disciplined, our resources and finances discreetly managed, our credit re-established, our people free, contented, and united, they will be much more disposed to cultivate our friendship than provoke our resentment. If, on the other hand, they find us either destitute of an effectual government (each State doing right or wrong, as to its rulers may seem convenient), or split into three or four independent and probably discordant republics or confederacies, one inclining to Britain, another to France, and a third to Spain, and perhaps played off against each other by the three, what a poor, pitiful figure will America make in their eyes! How liable would she become not only to their contempt, but to their outrage; and how soon would dear-bought experience proclaim that when a people or family so divide, it never fails to be against themselves.

6

Hamilton

DISUNION AND DISSENSION AMONG THE STATES

. . . A man must be far gone in Utopian speculations who can seriously doubt that, if these States should either be wholly disunited, or only united in partial confederacies, the subdivisions into which they might be thrown would have frequent and violent contests with each other. To presume a want of motives for such contests as an argument against their existence, would be to forget that men are ambitious, vindictive, and rapacious. To look for a continuation of harmony between a number of independent, unconnected sovereignties in the same neighborhood, would be to disregard the uniform course of human events, and to set at defiance the accumulated experience of ages.

The causes of hostility among nations are innumerable. There are some which have a general and almost constant operation upon the collective bodies of society. Of this description are the love of power or the desire of pre-eminence and dominion—the jealousy of power, or the desire of equality and safety. There are others which have a more circumscribed though an equally operative influence within their spheres. Such are the rivalships and competitions of commerce between commercial nations. And there are others, not less numerous than either of the former, which take their origin entirely in private passions; in the attachments, enmities, interests, hopes, and fears of leading individuals in the communities of which they are members. Men of this class, whether the favorites of a king or of a people, have in too many instances abused the confidence they possessed; and assuming the pretext of some public motive, have not scrupled to sacrifice the national tranquillity to personal advantage or personal gratification. . . .

. . . But notwithstanding the concurring testimony of experience, in this particular, there are still to be found visionary or designing men, who stand ready to advocate the paradox of perpetual peace between the States, though dismembered and alienated from each other. The genius of republics (say they) is pacific; the spirit of commerce has a tendency to soften the manners of men, and to extinguish those inflammable humors which have so often kindled into wars. Commercial republics, like ours, will never be disposed to waste themselves in ruinous contentions with each other. They will be governed by mutual interest, and will cultivate a spirit of mutual amity and concord.

Is it not (we may ask these projectors in politics) the true interest of all nations to cultivate the same benevolent and philosophic spirit? If this be their true interest, have they in fact pursued it? Has it not, on the contrary, invariably been found that momentary passions, and immediate interests, have a more active and imperious control over human conduct than general or remote considerations of policy, utility, or justice? Have republics in practice been less addicted to war than monarchies? Are not the former administered by *men* as well as the latter? Are there not aversions, predilections, rivalships, and desires of unjust acquisitions, that affect nations as well as kings? Are not popular assemblies frequently subject to the impulses of rage, resentment, jealousy, avarice, and of other irregular and violent propensities? Is it not well known that their determinations are often governed by a few individuals in whom they place confidence, and are, of course, liable to be tinctured by the passions and views of those individuals? Has commerce hitherto done any thing more than change the objects of war? Is not the love of wealth as domineering and enterprising a passion as that of power or glory? Have there not been as many wars founded upon commercial motives since that has become the prevailing system of nations, as were before occasioned by the cupidity of territory or dominion? Has not the spirit of commerce, in many instances, administered new incentives to the appetite, both for the one and for the other? Let experience, the least fallible guide of human opinions, be appealed to for an answer to these inquiries. . . .

. . . What reason can we have to confide in those reveries which would seduce us into an expectation of peace and cordiality between the members of the present confederacy, in the state of separation? Have we not already seen enough of the fallacy and extravagance of those idle theories which have amused us with promises of an exemption from the imperfections, weaknesses, and evils incident to society in every shape? Is it not time to awake from the deceitful dream of a golden age, and to adopt as a practical maxim for the direction of our political conduct that we, as well as the other inhabitants of the globe, are yet remote from the happy empire of perfect wisdom and perfect virtue?

Let the point of extreme depression to which our national dignity and credit have sunk, let the inconveniences felt everywhere from a lax and ill administration of government, let the revolt of a part of the State of North Carolina, the late menacing disturbances in Pennsylvania, and the actual insurrections and rebellions in Massachusetts, declare——! . . .

8

Hamilton

CONSEQUENCES OF WARS BETWEEN STATES

. . . There is a wide difference, also, between military establishments in a country seldom exposed by its situation to internal invasions, and in one which is often subject to them, and always apprehensive of them. The rulers of the former can have no good pretext, if they are even so inclined, to keep on foot armies so numerous as must of necessity be maintained in the latter. These armies being, in the first case, rarely, if at all, called into activity for interior defence, the people are in no danger of being broken to military subordination. The laws are not accustomed to relaxations, in favor of military exigencies; the civil state remains in full vigor, neither corrupted, nor confounded with the principles or propensities of the other state. The smallness of the army renders the natural strength of the community an over-match for it; and the citizens, not habituated to look up to the military power for protection, or to submit to its oppressions, neither love nor fear the soldiery; they view them with a spirit of jealous acquiescence in a necessary evil, and stand ready to resist a power which they suppose may be exerted to the prejudice of their rights. The army under such circumstances may usefully aid the magistrate to suppress a small faction, or an occasional mob, or insurrection; but it will be unable to enforce encroachments against the united efforts of the great body of the people.

In a country in the predicament last described, the contrary of all this happens. The perpetual menacings of danger oblige the government to be always prepared to repel it; its armies must be numerous enough for instant defence. The continual necessity for their services enhances the importance of the soldier, and proportionably degrades the condition of the citizen. The military state becomes elevated above the civil. The inhabitants of territories, often the theatre of war, are unavoidably subjected to frequent infringements on their rights, which serve to weaken their sense of those rights; and by degrees the people are brought to consider the soldiery not only as their protectors but as their superiors. The transition from this disposition to that of considering them masters, is neither remote nor difficult; but it is very difficult to prevail upon a people under such impressions to make a bold or effectual resistance to usurpations supported by the military power.

The kingdom of Great Britain falls within the first description. An insular situation, and a powerful marine, guarding it in a great measure against the possibility of foreign invasion, supersede the necessity of a numerous army within the kingdom. A sufficient force to make head against a sudden descent, till the militia could have time to rally and embody, is all that has been deemed requisite. No motive of national policy has demanded, nor would public opinion have tolerated, a larger number of troops upon its domestic establishment. There has been, for a long time past, little room for the operation of the other causes, which have been enumerated as the consequences of internal war. This peculiar felicity of situation has, in a great degree, contributed to preserve the liberty which that country to this day enjoys, in spite of the prevalent venality and corruption. If, on the contrary, Britain had been situated on the continent, and had been compelled as she would have been, by that situation, to make her military establishments at home coextensive with those of the other great powers of Europe, she, like them, would in all probability be, at this day, a victim to the absolute power of a single man. 'T is possible, though not easy, that the people of that island may be enslaved from other causes; but it cannot be by the prowess of an army so inconsiderable as that which has been usually kept up within the kingdom.

If we are wise enough to preserve the Union we may for ages enjoy an advantage similar to that of an insulated situation. Europe is at a great distance from us. Her colonies in our vicinity will be likely to continue too much disproportioned in strength to be able to give us any dangerous annoyance. Extensive military establishments cannot, in this position, be necessary to our security. But if we should be disunited, and the integral parts should either remain separated, or, which is most probable, should be thrown together into two or three confederacies, we should be, in a short course of time, in the predicament of the continental powers of Europe. . . .

11

Hamilton

THE VALUE OF UNION TO COMMERCE AND
THE ADVANTAGES OF A NAVY

. . . A further resource for influencing the conduct of European nations towards us, in this respect, would arise from the establishment of a federal navy. There can be no doubt that the continuance of the Union under an efficient government, would put it in our power, at a period not very distant, to create a navy which, if it could not vie with those of the great maritime powers, would at least be of respectable weight if thrown into the scale of either of two contending parties. This would be more peculiarly the case in relation to operations in the West Indies. A few ships of the line, sent opportunely to the reinforcement of either side, would often be sufficient to decide the fate of a campaign, on the event of which interests of the greatest magnitude were suspended. Our position is, in this respect, a most commanding one. And if to this consideration we add that of the usefulness of supplies from this country, in the prosecution of military operations in the West Indies, it will readily be perceived that a situation so favorable would enable us to bargain with great advantage for commercial privileges. A price would be set not only upon our friendship, but upon our neutrality. By a steady adherence to the Union, we may hope, erelong, to become the arbiter of Europe in America, and to be able to incline the balance of European competitions in this part of the world as our interest may dictate.

But in the reverse of this eligible situation, we shall discover that the rivalships of the parts would make them checks upon each other, and would frustrate all the tempting advantages which nature has kindly placed within our reach. In a state so insignificant our commerce would be a prey to the wanton intermeddlings of all nations at war with each other; who, having nothing to fear from us, would with little scruple or remorse supply their wants by depredations on our property as often as it fell in their way. The rights of neutrality will only be respected when they are defended by an adequate power. A nation, despicable by its weakness, forfeits even the privilege of being neutral.

Under a vigorous national government, the natural strength and resources of the country, directed to a common interest, would baffle all the combinations of European jealousy to restrain our growth. This situation would even take away the motive to such combinations, by inducing an impracticability of success. An active commerce, an extensive navigation, and a flourishing marine would then be the offspring of moral and physical necessity. We might defy the little arts of the little politicians to control or vary the irresistible and unchangeable course of nature.

But in a state of disunion, these combinations might exist and might operate with success. It would be in the power of the maritime nations, availing themselves of our universal impotence, to prescribe the conditions of our political existence; and as they have a common interest in being our carriers, and still more in preventing our becoming theirs, they would in all probability combine to embarrass our navigation in such a manner as would in effect destroy it, and confine us to a PASSIVE COMMERCE. We should then be compelled to content ourselves with the first price of our commodities, and to see the profits of our trade snatched from us to enrich our enemies and persecutors. That unequalled spirit of enterprise, which signalizes the genius of the American merchants and navigators, and which is in itself an inexhaustible mine of national wealth, would be stifled and lost, and poverty and disgrace would overspread a country which, with wisdom, might make herself the admiration and envy of the world.

There are rights of great moment to the trade of America which are rights of the Union—I allude to the fisheries, to the navigation of the Western lakes, and to that of the Mississippi. The dissolution of the Confederacy would give room for delicate questions concerning the future existence of these rights; which the interest of more powerful partners would hardly fail to solve to our disadvantage. The disposition of Spain with regard to the Mississippi needs no comment. France and Britain are concerned with us in the fisheries, and view them as of the utmost moment to their navigation. They, of course, would hardly remain long indifferent to that decided mastery, of which experience has shown us to be possessed in this valuable branch of traffic, and by which we are able to undersell those nations in their own markets. What more natural than that they should be disposed to exclude from the lists such dangerous competitors?

This branch of trade ought not to be considered as a partial benefit. All the navigating States may, in different degrees, advantageously participate in it, and under circumstances of a greater extension of mercantile capacity, would not be unlikely to do it. As a nursery of seamen, it now is, or, when time shall have more nearly assimilated the principles of navigation in the several States, will become, a universal resource. To the establishment of a navy, it must be indispensable.

To this great national object, a NAVY, union will contribute in various ways. Every institution will grow and flourish in proportion to the quantity and extent of the means concentred towards its formation and support. A navy of the United States, as it would embrace the resources of all, is an object far less remote than a navy of any single State or partial confederacy, which would only embrace the resources of a single part. It happens, indeed, that different portions of confederated America possess each some peculiar advantage for this essential establishment. The more southern States furnish in greater abundance certain kinds of naval stores—tar, pitch, and turpentine. Their wood for the construction of ships is also of a more solid and lasting texture. The difference in the duration of the ships of which the navy might be composed, if chiefly constructed of Southern wood, would be of signal importance, either in the view of naval strength or of national economy. Some of the Southern and of the Middle States yield a greater plenty of iron, and of better quality. Seamen must chiefly be drawn from the Northern hive. The necessity of naval protection to external or maritime commerce does not require a particular elucidation, no more than the conduciveness of that species of commerce to the prosperity of a navy. . . .

23
Hamilton

THE NECESSITY OF AN ENERGETIC AND
ACTIVE NATIONAL GOVERNMENT

. . . The principal purposes to be answered by union are these— the common defence of the members; the preservation of the public peace, as well against internal convulsions as external attacks; the regulation of commerce with other nations and between the States; the superintendence of our intercourse, political and commercial, with foreign countries.

The authorities essential to the common defence are these: to raise armies; to build and equip fleets; to prescribe rules for the government of both; to direct their operations; to provide for their support. These powers ought to exist without limitation, *because it is impossible to foresee or define the extent and variety of national exigencies, or the correspondent extent and variety of the means which may be necessary to satisfy them.* The circumstances that endanger the safety of nations are infinite, and for this reason no constitutional shackles can wisely be imposed on the power to which the care of it is committed. This power ought to be co-extensive with all the possible combinations of such circumstances; and ought to be under the direction of the same councils which are appointed to preside over the common defence.

This is one of those truths which, to a correct and unprejudiced mind, carries its own evidence along with it; and may be obscured, but cannot be made plainer by argument or reasoning. It rests upon axioms as simple as they are universal; the *means* ought to be proportioned to the *end;* the persons, from whose agency the attainment of any *end* is expected, ought to possess the *means* by which it is to be attained.

Whether there ought to be a federal government intrusted with the care of the common defence, is a question in the first instance, open for discussion; but the moment it is decided in the affirmative, it will follow, that that government ought to be clothed with all the powers requisite to complete execution of its trust. And unless it can be shown that the circumstances which may affect the public safety are reducible within certain determinate limits; unless the contrary of this position can be fairly and rationally disputed, it must be admitted, as a necessary consequence, that there can be no limitation of that authority which is to provide for the defence and protection of community, in any matter essential to its efficacy—that is, in any matter essential to the *formation, direction,* or *support* of the NATIONAL FORCES.

Defective as the present Confederation has been proved to be, this principle appears to have been fully recognized by the framers of it; though they have not made proper or adequate provision for its exercise. Congress have an unlimited discretion to make requisitions of men and money; to govern the army and navy; to direct their operations. As their requisitions are made constitutionally binding upon the States, who are in fact under the most solemn obligations to furnish the supplies required of them, the intention evidently was, that the United States should command whatever resources were by them judged requisite to the "common defence and general welfare." It was presumed that a sense of their true interests, and a regard to the dictates of good faith, would be found sufficient pledges for the punctual performance of the duty of the members to the federal head.

The experiment has, however, demonstrated that this expectation was ill-founded and illusory; and the observations, made under the last head, will, I imagine, have sufficed to convince the impartial and discerning, that there is an absolute necessity for an entire change in the first principles of the system; that if we are in earnest about giving the Union energy and duration, we must abandon the vain project of legislating upon the States in their collective capacities; we must extend the laws of the federal government to the individual citizens of America; we must discard the fallacious scheme of quotas and requisitions, as equally impracticable and unjust. The result from all this is that the Union ought to be invested with full power to levy troops; to build and equip fleets; and to raise the revenues which will be required for the formation and support of an army and navy, in the customary and ordinary modes practised in other governments. . . .

41
Madison

POWERS DELEGATED TO THE GENERAL GOVERNMENT

. . . Is the aggregate power of the general government greater than ought to have been vested in it? This is the *first* question. . . . In all cases where power is to be conferred, the point first to be decided is, whether such a power be necessary to the public good; as the next will be, in case of an affirmative decision, to guard as effectually as possible against a perversion of the power to the public detriment.

That we may form a correct judgment on this subject, it will be proper to review the several powers conferred on the government of the Union; and that this may be the more conveniently done they may be reduced into different classes as they relate to the following different objects: 1. Security against foreign danger; 2. Regulation of the intercourse with foreign nations; 3. Maintenance of harmony and proper intercourse among the States; 4. Certain miscellaneous objects of general utility; 5. Restraint of the States from certain injurious acts; 6. Provisions for giving due efficacy to all these powers.

The powers falling within the *first* class are those of declaring war and granting letters of marque; of providing armies and fleets; of regulating and calling forth the militia; of levying and borrowing money.

Security against foreign danger is one of the primitive objects of civil society. It is an avowed and essential object of the American Union. The powers requisite for attaining it must be effectually confided to the federal councils.

Is the power of declaring war necessary? No man will answer this question in the negative. It would be superfluous, therefore, to enter into a proof of the affirmative. The existing Confederation establishes this power in the most ample form.

Is the power of raising armies and equipping fleets necessary? This is involved in the foregoing power. It is involved in the power of self-defence.

But was it necessary to give an INDEFINITE POWER of raising TROOPS, as well as providing fleets; and of maintaining both in PEACE, as well as in war?

The answer to these questions has been too far anticipated in another place to admit an extensive discussion of them in this place. The answer indeed seems to be so obvious and conclusive as scarcely to justify such a discussion in any place. With what color of propriety could the force necessary for defence be limited by those who cannot limit the force of offence? If a federal Constitution could chain the ambition or set bounds to the exertions of all other nations, then indeed might it prudently chain the discretion of its own government, and set bounds to the exertions for its own safety.

How could a readiness for war in time of peace be safely prohibited, unless we could prohibit, in like manner, the preparations and establishments of every hostile nation? The means of security can only be regulated by the means and the danger of attack. They will, in fact, be ever determined by these rules, and by no others. It is in vain to oppose constitutional barriers to the impulse of self-preservation. It is worse than in vain; because it plants in the Constitution itself necessary usurpations of power, every precedent of which is a germ of unnecessary and multiplied repetitions. If one nation maintains constantly a disciplined army, ready for the service of ambition or revenge, it obliges the most pacific nations who may be within the reach of its enterprises to take corresponding precautions. The fifteenth century was the unhappy epoch of military establishments in the time of peace. They were introduced by Charles VII. of France. All Europe has followed, or been forced into, the example. Had the example not been followed by other nations, all Europe must long ago have worn the chains of a universal monarch. Were every nation except France now to disband its peace establishments, the same event might follow. The veteran legions of Rome were an overmatch for the undisciplined valor of all other nations, and rendered her the mistress of the world.

Not the less true is it, that the liberties of Rome proved the final victim to her military triumphs; and that the liberties of Europe, as far as they ever existed, have, with few exceptions, been the price of her military establishments. A standing force, therefore, is a dangerous, at the same time that it may be a necessary, provision. On the smallest scale it has its inconveniences. On an extensive scale its consequences may be fatal. On any scale it is an object of laudable circumspection and precaution. A wise nation will combine all these considerations; and, whilst it does not rashly preclude itself from any resource which may become essential to its safety, will exert all its prudence in diminishing both the necessity and the danger of resorting to one which may be inauspicious to its liberties.

The clearest marks of this prudence are stamped on the proposed Constitution. The Union itself, which it cements and secures, destroys every pretext for a military establishment which could be dangerous. America united, with a handful of troops, or without a single soldier, exhibits a more forbidding posture to foreign ambition than America disunited, with a hundred thousand veterans ready for combat. It was remarked, on a former occasion, that the want of this pretext had saved the liberties of one nation in Europe. Being rendered by her insular situation and her maritime resources impregnable to the armies of her neighbors, the rulers of Great Britain have never been able, by real or artificial dangers, to cheat the public into an extensive peace establishment. The distance of the United States from the powerful nations of the world gives them the same happy security. A dangerous establishment can never be necessary or plausible, so long as they continue a united people. But let it never, for a moment, be forgotten that they are indebted for this advantage to the Union alone. The moment of its dissolution will be the date of a new order of things. The fears of the weaker, or the ambition of the stronger States, or Confederacies, will set the same example in the New, as Charles VII. did in the Old World. The example will be followed here from the same motives which produced universal imitation there. Instead of deriving from our situation the precious advantage which Great Britain has derived from hers, the face of America will be but a copy of that of the continent of Europe. It will present liberty everywhere crushed between standing armies and perpetual taxes. The fortunes of disunited America will be even more disastrous than those of Europe. The sources of evil in the latter are confined to her own limits. No superior powers of another quarter of the globe intrigue among her rival nations, inflame their mutual animosities, and render them the instruments of foreign ambition, jealousy, and revenge. In America the miseries springing from her internal jealousies, contentions, and wars, would form a part only of her lot. A plentiful addition of evils would have their source in that relation in which Europe stands to this quarter of the earth, and which no other quarter of the earth bears to Europe.

This picture of the consequences of disunion cannot be too highly colored, or too often exhibited. Every man who loves peace, every man who loves his country, every man who loves liberty, ought to have it ever before his eyes, that he may cherish in his heart a due attachment to the Union of America, and be able to set a due value on the means of preserving it. . . .

. . . A bad cause seldom fails to betray itself. Of this truth, the management of the opposition to the federal government is an unvaried exemplification. But among all the blunders which have been committed, none is more striking than the attempt to enlist on that side the prudent jealousy entertained by the people, of standing armies. The attempt has awakened fully the public attention to that important subject; and has led to investigations which must terminate in a thorough and universal conviction, not only that the Constitution has provided the most effectual guards against danger from that quarter, but that nothing short of a Constitution fully adequate to the national defence and the preservation of the Union, can save America from as many standing armies as it may be split into States or Confederacies, and from such a progressive augmentation, of these establishments in each, as will render them as burdensome to the properties and ominous to the liberties of the people, as any establishment that can become necessary, under a united and efficient government, must be tolerable to the former and safe to the latter.

The palpable necessity of the power to provide and maintain a navy has protected that part of the Constitution against a spirit of censure, which has spared few other parts. It must, indeed, be numbered among the greatest blessings of America, that as her Union will be the only source of her maritime strength, so this will be a principal source of her security against danger from abroad. In this respect our situation bears another likeness to the insular advantage of Great Britain. The batteries most capable of repelling foreign enterprises on our safety, are happily such as can never be turned by a perfidious government against our liberties. . . .

46
Madison

STATE AND FEDERAL POWERS COMPARED

. . . The only refuge left for those who prophesy the downfall of the State governments is the visionary supposition that the federal government may previously accumulate a military force for the projects of ambition. The reasonings contained in these papers must have been employed to little purpose indeed, if it could be necessary now to disprove the reality of this danger. That the people and the States should, for a sufficient period of time, elect an uninterrupted succession of men ready to betray both; that the traitors should, throughout this period, uniformly and systematically pursue some fixed plan for the extension of the military establishment; that the governments and the people of the States should silently and patiently behold the gathering storm, and continue to supply the materials, until it should be prepared to burst on their own heads, must appear to every one more like the incoherent dreams of a delirious jealousy, or the misjudged exaggerations of a counterfeit zeal, than like the sober apprehensions of genuine patriotism. Extravagant as the supposition is, let it however be made. Let a regular army, fully equal to the resources of the country, be formed; and let it be entirely at the devotion of the federal government: still it would not be going too far to say, that the State governments, with the people on their side, would be able to repel the danger. The highest number to which, according to the best computation, a standing army can be carried in any country, does not exceed one hundredth part of the whole number of souls; or one twenty-fifth part of the number able to bear arms. This proportion would not yield, in the United States, an army of more than twenty-five or thirty thousand men. To these would be opposed a militia amounting to near half a million of citizens with arms in their hands, officered by men chosen from among themselves, fighting for their common liberties, and united and conducted by governments possessing their affections and confidence. It may well be doubted, whether a militia thus circumstanced could ever be conquered by such a proportion of regular troops. Those who are best acquainted with the late successful resistance of this country against the British arms, will be most inclined to deny the possibility of it. Besides the advantage of being armed, which the Americans possess over the people of almost every other nation, the existence of subordinate governments, to which the people are attached, and by which the militia officers are appointed, forms a barrier against the enterprises of ambition, more insurmountable than any which a simple government of any form can admit of. Notwithstanding the military establishments in the several kingdoms of Europe, which are carried as far as the public resources will bear, the governments are afraid to trust the people with arms. And it is not certain, that with this aid alone they would not be able to shake off their yokes. But were the people to possess the additional advantages of local governments chosen by themselves, who could collect the national will and direct the national force, and of officers appointed out of the militia, by these governments, and attached both to them and to the militia, it may be affirmed with the greatest assurance, that the throne of every tyranny in Europe would be speedily overturned in spite of the legions which surround it. Let us not insult the free and gallant citizens of America with the suspicion, that they would be less able to defend the rights of which they would be in actual possession, than the debased subjects of arbitrary power would be to rescue theirs from the hands of their oppressors. Let us rather no longer insult them with the supposition that they can ever reduce themselves to the necessity of making the experiment, by a blind and tame submission to the long train of insidious measures which must precede and produce it. . . .

6. Thomas Paine on the Monarchical "War System"

TOM PAINE, THE FAMOUS REVOLUTIONARY PAMPHLETEER, IS NOT usually regarded as one of our military thinkers. He did, however, have ideas about war and the "war system" that, although unorthodox, advanced several themes, including that of general disarmament, that were to be of lasting significance. Paine's knowledge of war was not purely academic. A native of Norfolk, England, he early went to sea as a privateersman and later briefly served in the Continental Army. In 1791 he published *Rights of Man, Being an Answer to Mr. Burke's Attack on the French Revolution*. The discussion of the "war system" was fragmentary and incidental to the main arguments; Paine himself, later imprisoned by the very revolutionaries he sought to defend, was to be disillusioned in his belief in the pacific character of free nations. Even when he wrote, very few could have agreed with him.

. . . Monarchical sovereignty, the enemy of mankind, and the source of misery, is abolished; and sovereignty itself is restored to its natural and original place—the Nation. Were this the case throughout Europe, the cause of wars would be taken away.

It is attributed to Henry the Fourth of France, a man of an enlarged and a benevolent heart, that he proposed, about the year 1610, a plan for abolishing war in Europe. The plan consisted in constituting an European Congress, or as the French Authors style it, a Pacific Republic; by appointing delegates, from the several Nations, who were to act as a Court of Arbitration, in any disputes that might arise between Nation and Nation.

Had such a plan been adopted at the time it was proposed, the taxes of England and France, as two of the parties, would have been at least ten millions sterling annually to each Nation less than they were at the commencement of the French Revolution.

To conceive a cause why such a plan has not been adopted, and that instead of a Congress for the purpose of preventing war, it has been called only to terminate a war, after a fruitless ex-

From Thomas Paine, *Rights of Man* (London: R. Carlisle, 1819), Part I, pp. 110–112; Part II, pp. 17, 24–25, 114–116.

pence of several years, it will be necessary to consider the interest of Governments as a distinct interest to that of Nations.

Whatever is the cause of taxes to a Nation, becomes also the means of revenue to a Government. Every war terminates with an addition of taxes, and, consequently, with an addition of revenue; and in any event of war, in the manner they are now commenced and concluded, the powers and interests of Governments are increased. War, therefore, from its productiveness, as it easily furnishes the pretence of necessity for taxes, and appointments to places, and offices, becomes a principal part of the system of old Governments; and to establish any mode to abolish war, however advantageous it might be to Nations, would be to take from such Government the most lucrative of its branches. The frivolous matters upon which war is made, shew the disposition and avidity of Governments to uphold the system of war, and betray the motives upon which they act.

Why are not Republics plunged into war, but because the nature of their Government does not admit of an interest distinct from that of the Nation? Even Holland, though an ill-constructed Republic, and with a commerce extending over the world, existed nearly a century without war; and the instant the form of Government was changed in France, the republican principles of peace and domestic prosperity, and economy, arose with the new Government; and the same consequences would follow the same causes in other Nations.

As war is the system of Government on the old construction, the animosity which Nations reciprocally entertain, is nothing more than what the policy of their Governments excite, to keep up the spirit of the system. Each Government accuses the other of perfidy, intrigue, and ambition, as a means of heating the imagination of their respective Nations, and incensing them to hostilities. Man is not the enemy of Man, but through the medium of a false system of Government. Instead, therefore, of exclaiming against the ambition of Kings, the exclamation should be directed against the principles of such Governments; and, instead of seeking to reform the individual, the wisdom of a Nation should apply itself to reform the system. . . .

. . . The intrigue of Courts, by which the system of war is kept up, may provoke a confederation of Nations to abolish it; and an European Congress, to patronise the progress of free Government, and promote the civilization of Nations with each other, is an event nearer in probability, than once were the Revolutions and Alliance of France and America.

. . . As revolutions have begun, (and as the probability is always greater against a thing beginning than of proceeding after it has begun), it is natural to expect that other revolutions will follow. The amazing and still increasing expences with which old Governments are conducted, the numerous wars they engage in, or provoke, the embarrassments they throw in the way of universal civilization and commerce, and the oppression and usurpation they practise at home, have wearied out the patience, and exhausted the property of the world. In such a situation, and with the examples already existing, revolutions are to be looked for. They are become subjects of universal conversation, and may be considered as the *Order of the Day*.

If systems of Government can be introduced, less expensive, and more productive of general happiness, than those which have existed, all attempts to oppose their progress will, in the end, be fruitless. Reason, like time, will make its own way, and prejudice will fall in a combat with interest. If universal peace, civilization, and commerce, are ever to be the happy lot of man, it cannot be accomplished but by a revolution in the system of Governments. All the monarchical Governments are military. War is their trade; plunder and revenue their objects. While such Governments continue, peace has not the absolute security of a day. What is the history of all monarchical Governments, but a disgustful picture of human wretchedness, and the accidental respite of a few years' repose? Wearied with war, and tired with human butchery, they sat down to rest, and called it peace. This certainly is not the condition that Heaven intended for Man; and if *this be monarchy,* well might monarchy be reckoned among the sins of the Jews. . . .

It is impossible that such Governments as have hitherto existed in the world could have commenced by any other means than a total violation of every principle, sacred and moral. The obscurity in which the origin of all the present old Governments is buried, implies the iniquity and disgrace with which they began. The origin of the present Government of America and France will ever be remembered, because it is honourable to record it; but with respect to the rest, even flattery has consigned them to the tomb of time, without an inscription. It could have been no difficult thing in the early and solitary ages of the world, while the chief employment of men was that of attending flocks and herds, for a banditti of ruffians to overrun a country and lay it under contributions. Their power being thus established, the chief of the band contrived to lose the name of robber in that of monarch; and hence the origin of monarchy and kings.

The origin of the Government of England, so far as relates to what is called its line of monarchy being one of the latest, is, perhaps, the best recorded. The hatred which the Norman invasion and tyranny begat, must have been deeply rooted in the nation, to have outlived the contrivance to obliterate it. Though not a courtier will talk of the curfew-bell, not a village in England has forgotten it.

Those bands of robbers having parcelled out the world, and divided it into dominions, began, as is naturally the case, to quarrel with each other. What at first was obtained by violence, was considered by others as lawful to be taken, and a second plunderer succeeded the first. They alternately invaded the dominions which each had assigned to himself, and the brutality with which they treated each other explains the original character of monarchy. It was ruffian torturing ruffian. The conqueror considered the conquered, not as his prisoner, but his property. He led him in triumph rattling in chains, and doomed him at pleasure, to slavery or death. As time obliterated the history of their beginning, their successors assumed new appearances to cut off the entail of their disgrace, but their principles and objects remained the same. What, at first, was plunder, assumed the softer name of revenue; and the power originally usurped they affected to inherit.

From such beginning of Governments, what could be expected but a continual system of war and extortion? It has established itself into a trade. The vice is not peculiar to one more than to another, but is the common principle of all. There does not exist within such Governments sufficient stamina whereon to engraft reformation; and the shortest, easiest, and most effectual remedy, is to begin anew on the ground of the oration.

What scenes of horror, what perfection of iniquity, present themselves in contemplating the character, and reviewing the history of such Governments! If we would delineate human nature with a baseness of heart, and hypocrisy of countenance, that reflection would shudder at, and humanity disown, it is Kings, Courts, and Cabinets, that must sit for the portrait. Man, naturally as he is, with all his faults about him, is not up to the character.

Can we possibly suppose, that if Governments had originated in a right principle, and had not an interest in pursuing a wrong one, that the world could have been in the wretched and quarrelsome condition we have seen it? What inducement has the farmer, while following the plough, to lay aside his peaceful pursuit, and go to war with the farmer of another country? Or what inducement has the manufacturer? What is dominion to them, or to any class of men in a nation? Does it add an acre to any man's estate, or raise its value? Are not conquest and defeat each of the same price, and taxes the never-failing consequence? Though this reasoning may be good to a nation, it is not to a Government. War is the Pharo[1]-table of Governments, and nations the dupes of the games.

If there is any thing to wonder at in this miserable scene of Governments more than might be expected, it is the progress

[1] Faro, the card game [Ed.].

which the peaceful arts of agriculture, manufacture and commerce have made beneath such a long accumulating load of discouragement and oppression. It serves to shew, that instinct in animals does not act with stronger impulse than the principles of society and civilization operate in man. Under all discouragements, he pursues his object, and yields to nothing but impossibilities. . . .

. . . In the preceding part of this work I have spoken of an alliance between England, France, and America, for the purposes that were to be afterwards mentioned. Though I have no direct authority on the part of America, I have good reason to conclude, that she is disposed to enter into a consideration of such a measure, provided, that the Governments with which she might ally, acted as national Governments, and not as Courts enveloped in intrigue and mystery. That France as a nation, and a national Government, would prefer an alliance with England, is a matter of certainty. Nations, like individuals, who have long been enemies, without knowing each other, or knowing why, become the better friends when they discover the errors and impositions under which they had acted.

Admitting, therefore, the probability of such a connection, I will state some matters by which such an alliance, together with that of Holland, might render service, not only to the parties immediately concerned, but to all Europe.

It is, I think, certain, that if the fleets of England, France, and Holland were confederated, they could propose, with effect, a limitation to, and a general dismantling of, all the navies in Europe, to a certain proportion to be agreed upon.

First, That no new ship of war shall be built by any power in Europe, themselves included.

Secondly, That all the navies now in existence shall be put back, suppose to one-tenth of their present force. This will save France and England at least two millions sterling annually to each, and their relative force be in the same proportion as it is now. If men will permit themselves to think, as rational beings ought to think, nothing can appear more ridiculous and absurd, exclusive of all moral reflections, than to be at the expence of building navies, filling them with men, and then hauling them into the ocean, to try which can sink each other fastest. Peace, which costs nothing, is attended with infinitely more advantage, than any victory with all its expence. But this, though it best answers the purpose of nations, does not that of Court Governments, whose habited policy is pretence for taxation, places, and offices.

It is, I think, also certain, that the above confederated powers, together with that of the United States of America, can propose with effect, to Spain, the Independence of South America, and the opening those countries of immense extent and wealth to the general commerce of the world, as North America now is.

With how much more glory, and advantage to itself, does a nation act, when it exerts its powers to rescue the world from bondage, and to create itself friends, than when it employs those powers to encrease ruin, desolation, and misery. The horrid scene that is now acting by the English Government in the East Indies, is fit only to be told of Goths and Vandals, who, destitute of principle, robbed and tortured the world they were incapable of enjoying.

The opening of South America would produce an immense field of commerce, and a ready money market for manufactures, which the eastern world does not. The East is already a country full of manufactures, the importation of which is not only an injury to the manufactures of England, but a drain upon its specie. The balance against England by this trade is regularly upwards of half a million annually sent out in the East India ships in silver; and this is the reason, together with German intrigue, and German subsidies, there is so little silver in England.

But any war is harvest to such Governments, however ruinous it may be to a nation. It serves to keep up deceitful expectations, which prevent a people looking into the defects and abuses of Government. It is the *lo, here!* and the *lo, there!* that amuses and cheats the multitude. . . .

. . . When all the Governments of Europe shall be established on the Representative system, nations will become acquainted, and the animosities and prejudices fomented by the intrigue and artifice of courts, will cease. The oppressed soldier will become a freeman; and the tortured sailor, no longer dragged along the streets like a felon, will pursue his mercantile voyage in safety. It would be better that nations should continue the pay of their soldiers during their lives, and give them their discharge, and restore them to freedom and their friends, and cease recruiting, than retain such multitudes at the same expence, in a condition useless to society and themselves. As soldiers have hitherto been treated in most countries, they might be said to be without a friend. Shunned by the citizen on an apprehension of being enemies to liberty, and too often insulted by those who commanded them, their condition was a double oppression. But where genuine principles of liberty pervade a people, every thing is restored to order; and the soldier civilly treated, returns the civility. . . .

7. Congress Provides for the Militia

THE NEW CONSTITUTION WAS DECLARED IN FORCE AS OF MARCH 4, 1789. One of the first and most obvious duties it imposed upon the Congress was to "provide for calling forth the militia to execute the laws of the Union, suppress insurrections and repel invasions." In fulfilling this duty, the Congress had much good advice from George Washington, and Alexander Hamilton, among others, which it largely disregarded. The President's powers to call up the state militias were strictly confined to the repulse of invasion or the suppression of domestic disorder. In all of our wars thereafter, down to the adoption of peacetime conscription in 1941, it was never possible to use the bulk of our reserve manpower until it had been transmuted into "volunteers" with a federal rather than a state obligation. The Militia Act of 1792 was itself unrealistic. Attempting to create a great army, which should arm itself with the muskets and rifle equipment carefully prescribed, it in fact produced only a paper system that was never of much military value. On the eve of the War of 1812, the enrolled militia had a strength of over seven hundred thousand men, hardly any of it usable—it was poorly armed, poorly disciplined, and could not be ordered to service beyond the state's boundaries. Yet the act was to remain on the books for over a century, and was to dominate all reserve policy down to 1917, if not to 1940.

Chap. XXVIII.—*An Act to provide for calling forth the Militia to execute the laws of the Union, suppress insurrections and repel invasions.*

Section 1. *Be it enacted by the Senate and House of Representatives of the United States of America in Congress assembled,* That whenever the United States shall be invaded, or be in imminent danger of invasion from any foreign nation or Indian tribe, it shall be lawful for the President of the United States, to call forth such number of the militia of the state or states most convenient to the place of danger or scene of action, as he may judge necessary to repel such invasion, and to issue his orders for that purpose, to such officer or officers of the militia as he shall think proper; and in case of an insurrection in any state, against the government thereof, it shall be lawful for the President of the United States, on application of the legislature of such state, or of the executive (when the legislature cannot be convened) to call forth such number of the militia of any other state or states, as may be applied for, or as he may judge sufficient to suppress such insurrection.

Sec. 2. *And be it further enacted,* That whenever the laws of the United States shall be opposed, or the execution thereof obstructed, in any state, by combinations too powerful to be suppressed by the ordinary course of judicial proceedings, or by the powers vested in the marshals by this act, the same being notified to the President of the United States, by an associate justice or the district judge, it shall be lawful for the President of the United States to call forth the militia of such state to suppress such combinations, and to cause the laws to be duly executed. And if the militia of a state, where such combinations may hap-

From *United States Statutes at Large,* 2d Congress, Session 1 (1792), I, pp. 264–265, 271–274.

pen, shall refuse, or be insufficient to suppress the same, it shall be lawful for the President, if the legislature of the United States be not in session, to call forth and employ such numbers of the militia of any other state or states most convenient thereto, as may be necessary, and the use of militia, so to be called forth, may be continued, if necessary, until the expiration of thirty days after the commencement of the ensuing session.

Sec. 3. *Provided always, and be it further enacted,* That whenever it may be necessary, in the judgment of the President, to use the military force hereby directed to be called forth, the President shall forthwith, and previous thereto, by proclamation, command such insurgents to disperse, and retire peaceably to their respective abodes, within a limited time.

Sec. 4. *And be it further enacted,* That the militia employed in the service of the United States, shall receive the same pay and allowances, as the troops of the United States, who may be in service at the same time, or who were last in service, and shall be subject to the same rules and articles of war: And that no officer, non-commissioned officer or private of the militia shall be compelled to serve more than three months in any one year, nor more than in due rotation with every other able-bodied man of the same rank in the battalion to which he belongs. . . . Approved, May 2, 1792.

CHAP. XXXIII.—*An Act more effectually to provide for the National Defence by establishing an Uniform Militia throughout the United States.*

SECTION 1. *Be it enacted by the Senate and House of Representatives of the United States of America in Congress assembled,* That each and every free able-bodied white male citizen of the respective states, resident therein, who is or shall be of the age of eighteen years, and under the age of forty-five years (except as is herein after excepted) shall severally and respectively be enrolled in the militia by the captain or commanding officer of the company, within whose bounds such citizen shall reside, and that within twelve months after the passing of this act. And it shall at all times hereafter be the duty of every such captain or commanding officer of a company to enrol every such citizen, as aforesaid, and also those who shall, from time to time, arrive at the age of eighteen years, or being of the age of eighteen years and under the age of forty-five years (except as before excepted) shall come to reside within his bounds; and shall without delay notify such citizen of the said enrolment, by a proper non-commissioned officer of the company, by whom such notice may be proved. That every citizen so enrolled and notified, shall, within six months thereafter, provide himself with a good musket or firelock, a sufficient bayonet and belt, two spare flints, and a knapsack, a pouch with a box therein to contain not less than twenty-four cartridges, suited to the bore of his musket or firelock, each cartridge to contain a proper quantity of powder and ball: or with a good rifle, knapsack, shot-pouch and powder-horn, twenty balls suited to the bore of his rifle, and a quarter of a pound of powder; and shall appear, so armed, accoutred and provided, when called out to exercise, or into service, except, that when called out on company days to exercise only, he may appear without a knapsack. That the commissioned officers shall severally be armed with a sword or hanger and espontoon,[1] and that from and after five years from the passing of this act, all muskets for arming the militia as herein required, shall be of bores sufficient for balls of the eighteenth part of a pound. And every citizen so enrolled, and providing himself with the arms, ammunition and accoutrements required as aforesaid, shall hold the same exempted from all suits, distresses, executions or sales, for debt or for the payment of taxes.

SEC. 2. *And be it further enacted,* That the Vice President of the United States; the officers judicial and executive of the government of the United States; the members of both Houses of Congress, and their respective officers; all custom-house officers with their clerks; all post-officers, and stage drivers, who are employed in the care and conveyance of the mail of the post-office of the

[1] Spontoon, or half-pike [Ed.].

United States; all ferrymen employed at any ferry on the post road; all inspectors of exports; all pilots; all mariners actually employed in the sea service of any citizen or merchant within the United States; and all persons who now are or may hereafter be exempted by the laws of the respective states, shall be, and are hereby exempted from militia duty, notwithstanding their being above the age of eighteen, and under the age of forty-five years.

Sec. 3. *And be it further enacted,* That within one year after the passing of this act, the militia of the respective states shall be arranged into divisions, brigades, regiments, battalions and companies, as the legislature of each state shall direct; and each division, brigade and regiment, shall be numbered at the formation thereof; and a record made of such numbers in the adjutant-general's office in the state; and when in the field, or in service in the state, each division, brigade and regiment shall respectively take rank according to their numbers, reckoning the first or lowest number highest in rank. That if the same be convenient, each brigade shall consist of four regiments; each regiment of two battalions; each battalion of five companies; each company of sixty-four privates. That the said militia shall be officered by the respective states, as follows: To each division, one major-general and two aids-de-camp, with the rank of major; to each brigade, one brigadier-general, with one brigade inspector, to serve also as brigade-major, with the rank of a major; to each regiment, one lieutenant-colonel commandant; and to each battalion one major; to each company one captain, one lieutenant, one ensign, four sergeants, four corporals, one drummer and one fifer or bugler. That there shall be a regimental staff, to consist of one adjutant and one quartermaster, to rank as lieutenants; one paymaster; one surgeon, and one surgeon's mate; one sergeant-major; one drum-major, and one fife-major.

Sec. 4. *And be it further enacted,* That out of the militiia enrolled, as is herein directed, there shall be formed for each battalion at least one company of grenadiers, light infantry or riflemen; and that to each division there shall be at least one company of artillery, and one troop of horse: there shall be to each company of artillery, one captain, two lieutenants, four sergeants, four corporals, six gunners, six bombadiers, one drummer, and one fifer. The officers to be armed with a sword or hanger, a fusee,[2] bayonet and belt, with a cartridge-box to contain twelve cartridges; and each private or matross[3] shall furnish himself with all the equipments of a private in the infantry, until proper ordnance and field artillery is provided. There shall be to each troop of horse, one captain, two lieutenants, one cornet,[4] four sergeants, four corporals, one saddler, one farrier, and one trumpeter. The commissioned officers to furnish themselves with good horses of at least fourteen hands and an half high, and to be armed with a sword and pair of pistols, the holsters of which to be covered with bearskin caps. Each dragoon to furnish himself with a serviceable horse, at least fourteen hands and an half high, a good saddle, bridle, mailpillion[5] and valise, holsters, and a breast-plate and crupper, a pair of boots and spurs, a pair of pistols, a sabre, and a cartouch-box, to contain twelve cartridges for pistols. That each company of artillery and troop of horse shall be formed of volunteers from the brigade, at the discretion of the commander-in-chief of the state, not exceeding one company of each to a regiment, nor more in number than one eleventh part of the infantry, and shall be uniformly clothed in regimentals, to be furnished at their own expense; the colour and fashion to be determined by the brigadier commanding the brigade to which they belong.

SEC. 5. *And be it further enacted,* That each battalion and regiment shall be provided with the state and regimental colours by the field officers, and each company with a drum and fife, or bugle-horn, by the commissioned officers of the company, in such manner as the legislature of the respective states shall direct.

SEC. 6. *And be it further enacted,* That there shall be an adjutant-general appointed in each state, whose duty it shall be to

[2] A flintlock gun [Ed.].
[3] Private of artillery [Ed.].
[4] A Junior lieutenant of cavalry [Ed.].
[5] Saddlebag [Ed.].

distribute all orders from the commander-in-chief of the state to the several corps; to attend all public reviews when the commander-in-chief of the state shall review the militia, or any part thereof; to obey all orders from him relative to carrying into execution and perfecting the system of military discipline established by this act; to furnish blank forms of different returns that may be required, and to explain the principles on which they should be made; to receive from the several officers of the different corps throughout the state, returns of the militia under their command, reporting the actual situation of their arms, accoutrements, and ammunition, their delinquencies, and every other thing which relates to the general advancement of good order and discipline: all which the several officers of the divisions, brigades, regiments, and battalions, are hereby required to make in the usual manner, so that the said adjutant-general may be duly furnished therewith: from all which returns he shall make proper abstracts, and lay the same annually before the commander-in-chief of the state.

SEC. 7. *And be it further enacted,* That the rules of discipline, approved and established by Congress in their resolution of the twenty-ninth of March, one thousand seven hundred and seventy-nine, shall be the rules of discipline to be observed by the militia throughout the United States, except such deviations from the said rules as may be rendered necessary by the requisitions of this act, or by some other unavoidable circumstances. It shall be the duty of the commanding officer at every muster, whether by battalion, regiment, or single company, to cause the militia to be exercised and trained agreeably to the said rules of discipline.

SEC. 8. *And be it further enacted,* That all commissioned officers shall take rank according to the date of their commissions; and when two of the same grade bear an equal date, then their rank to be determined by lot, to be drawn by them before the commanding officer of the brigade, regiment, battalion, company, or detachment.

SEC. 9. *And be it further enacted,* That if any person, whether officer or soldier, belonging to the militia of any state, and called out into the service of the United States, be wounded or disabled while in actual service, he shall be taken care of and provided for at the public expense.

SEC. 10. *And be it further enacted,* That it shall be the duty of the brigade-inspector to attend the regimental and battalion meetings of the militia composing their several brigades, during the time of their being under arms, to inspect their arms, ammunition, and accoutrements; superintend their exercise and manœuvres, and introduce the system of military discipline before described throughout the brigade, agreeable to law, and such orders as they shall from time to time receive from the commander-in-chief of the state; to make returns to the adjutant-general of the state, at least once in every year, of the militia of the brigade to which he belongs, reporting therein the actual situation of the arms, accoutrements, and ammunition of the several corps, and every other thing which, in his judgment, may relate to their government and the general advancement of good order and military discipline; and the adjutant-general shall make a return of all the militia of the state to the commander-in-chief of the said state, and a duplicate of the same to the President of the United States.

And whereas sundry corps of artillery, cavalry, and infantry now exist in several of the said states, which by the laws, customs, or usages thereof have not been incorporated with, or subject to the general regulations of the militia:

SEC. 11. *Be it further enacted,* That such corps retain their accustomed privileges, subject, nevertheless, to all other duties required by this act, in like manner with the other militia.

APPROVED, May 8, 1792.

8. George Washington's Farewell Advice on War and Military Policy

As GEORGE WASHINGTON'S SECOND TERM WAS DRAWING TO ITS CLOSE in 1796, the world was assuming a far more threatening aspect than it had revealed eight years before. France had been swept by a social revolution that had turned, by 1793, into a new general war in

Europe. To Washington it seemed that if only we could avoid "permanent alliances," we could, if properly armed, remain free to "choose peace or war" as our own interests and as justice might demand. More than a century later, the Farewell Address was still the basic document for the problems of neutrality, which after 1914 once more assailed us. Its supplement in Washington's annual message of December 1796, with the plea for an effective Navy and the establishment of a military academy, was likewise to find its echoes in the future.

The Farewell Address, September 19, 1796

. . . Europe has a set of primary interests, which to us have none, or a very remote relation. Hence she must be engaged in frequent controversies, the causes of which are essentially foreign to our concerns. Hence therefore it must be unwise in us to implicate ourselves, by artificial ties, in the ordinary vicissitudes of her politics, or the ordinary combinations and collisions of her friendships, or enmities:

Our detached and distant situation invites and enables us to pursue a different course. If we remain one People, under an efficient government, the period is not far off, when we may defy material injury from external annoyance; when we may take such an attitude as will cause the neutrality we may at any time resolve upon to be scrupulously respected; when belligerent nations, under the impossibility of making acquisitions upon us, will not lightly hazard the giving us provocation; when we may choose peace or war, as our interest guided by our justice shall Counsel.

Why forego the advantages of so peculiar a situation? Why quit our own to stand upon foreign ground? Why, by interweaving our destiny with that of any part of Europe, entangle our peace and prosperity in the toils of European Ambition, Rivalship, Interest, Humour or Caprice?

'Tis our true policy to steer clear of permanent Alliances, with any portion of the foreign world. So far, I mean, as we are now

From *The Writings of Washington,* 35, pp. 234–236, 314–317.

at liberty to do it, for let me not be understood as capable of patronising infidility to existing engagements (I hold the maxim no less applicable to public than to private affairs, that honesty is always the best policy). I repeat it therefore, let those engagements be observed in their genuine sense. But in my opinion, it is unnecessary and would be unwise to extend them.

Taking care always to keep ourselves, by suitable establishments, on a respectably defensive posture, we may safely trust to temporary alliances for extraordinary emergencies.

Harmony, liberal intercourse with all Nations, are recommended by policy, humanity and interest. But even our Commercial policy should hold an equal and impartial hand: neither seeking nor granting exclusive favours or preferences; consulting the natural course of things; diffusing and deversifying by gentle means the streams of Commerce, but forcing nothing; establishing with Powers so disposed; in order to give to trade a stable course, to define the rights of our Merchants, and to enable the Government to support them; conventional rules of intercourse, the best that present circumstances and mutual opinion will permit, but temporary, and liable to be from time to time abandoned or varied, as experience and circumstances shall dictate; constantly keeping in view, that 'tis folly in one Nation to look for disinterested favors from another; that it must pay with a portion of its Independence for whatever it may accept under that character; that by such acceptance, it may place itself in the condition of having given equivalents for nominal favours and yet of being reproached with ingratitude for not giving more. There can be no greater error than to expect, or calculate upon real favours from Nation to Nation. 'Tis an illusion which experience must cure, which a just pride ought to discard.

In offering to you, my Countrymen these counsels of an old and affectionate friend, I dare not hope they will make the strong and lasting impression, I could wish; that they will controul the usual current of the passions, or prevent our Nation from running the course which has hitherto marked the Destiny of Nations: But if I may even flatter myself, that they may be productive of some partial benefit, some occasional good; that they may now and then recur to moderate the fury of party spirit, to warn against the mischiefs of foreign Intriegue, to guard against the Impostures of pretended patriotism; this hope will be a full recompence for the solicitude for your welfare, by which they have been dictated. . . .

Annual Message to Congress, December 1796

. . . To an active external Commerce, the protection of a Naval force is indispensable. This is manifest with regard to Wars in which a State itself is a party. But besides this, it is in our own experience, that the most sincere Neutrality is not a sufficient guard against the depredations of Nations at War. To secure respect to a Neutral Flag, requires a Naval force, organized, and ready to vindicate it, from insult or aggression. This may even prevent the necessity of going to War, by discouraging belligerent Powers from committing such violations of the rights of the Neutral party, as may first or last, leave no other option. From the best information I have been able to obtain, it would seem as if our trade to the mediterranean, without a protecting force, will always be insecure; and our Citizens exposed to the calamities from which numbers of them have but just been relieved.

These considerations invite the United States, to look to the means, and to set about the gradual creation of a Navy. The increasing progress of their Navigation, promises them, at no distant period, the requisite supply of Seamen; and their means, in other respects, favour the undertaking. It is an encouragement, likewise, that their particular situation, will give weight and influence to a moderate Naval force in their hands. Will it not then be adviseable, to begin without delay, to provide, and lay up the materials for the building and equipping of Ships of War; and to proceed in the Work by degrees, in proportion as our resources shall render it practicable without inconvenience; so that a future War of Europe, may not find our Commerce in the same unprotected state, in which it was found by the present.

Congress have repeatedly, and not without success, directed their attention to the encouragement of Manufactures. The object is of too much consequence, not to insure a continuance of their efforts, in every way which shall appear eligible. As a general rule, Manufactures on public account, are inexpedient. But where the state of things in a Country, leaves little hope that certain branches of Manufacture will, for a great length of time obtain; when these are of a nature essential to the furnishing and equipping of the public force in time of War, are not establishments for procuring them on public account, *to the extent of the ordinary demand for the public service,* recommended by strong considerations of National policy, as an exception to the general rule? Ought our Country to remain in such cases, dependant on foreign supply, precarious, because liable to be interrupted? If the necessary Articles should, in this mode cost more in time of peace, will not the security and independence thence arising, form an ample compensation? Establishments of this sort, commensurate only with the calls of the public service in time of peace, will, in time of War, easily be extended in proportion to the exigencies of the Government; and may even perhaps be made to yield a surplus for the supply of our Citizens at large; so as to mitigate the privations from the interruption of their trade. If adopted, the plan ought to exclude all those branches which are already, or likely soon to be, established in the Country; in order that there may be no danger of interference with pursuits of individual industry.

It will not be doubted, that with reference either to individual, or National Welfare, Agriculture is of primary importance. In proportion as Nations advance in population, and other circumstances of maturity, this truth becomes more apparent; and renders the cultivation of the Soil more and more, an object of public patronage. Institutions for promoting it, grow up, supported by the public purse: and to what object can it be dedicated with greater propriety? Among the means which have been employed to this end, none have been attended with greater success than the establishment of Boards, composed of proper characters, charged with collecting and diffusing information, and enabled by premiums, and small pecuniary aids, to encourage and assist a spirit of discovery and improvement. This species of establishment contributes doubly to the increase of improvement; by stimulating to enterprise and experiment, and by drawing to a common centre, the results everywhere of individual skill and observation; and spreading them thence over the whole Nation. Experience accordingly has shewn, that they are very cheap Instruments, of immense National benefits.

I have heretofore proposed to the consideration of Congress, the expendiency of establishing a National University; and also a Military Academy. The desirableness of both these Institutions, has so constantly increased with every new view I have taken of the subject, that I cannot omit the opportunity of once for all, recalling your attention to them.

The Assembly to which I address myself, is too enlightened not to be fully sensible how much a flourishing state of the Arts and Sciences, contributes to National prosperity and reputation. True it is, that our Country, much to its honor, contains many Seminaries of learning highly respectable and useful; but the funds upon which they rest, are too narrow, to command the ablest Professors, in the different departments of liberal knowledge, for the Institution contemplated, though they would be excellent auxiliaries.

Amongst the motives to such an Institution, the assimilation of the principles, opinions and manners of our Country men, but the common education of a portion of our Youth from every quarter, well deserves attention. The more homogeneous our Citizens can be made in these particulars, the greater will be our prospect of permanent Union; and a primary object of such a National Institution should be, the education of our Youth in the science of *Government*. In a Republic, what species of knowledge can be equally important? and what duty, more pressing on its Legislature, than to patronize a plan for communicating it to those, who are to be the future guardians of the liberties of the Country?

The Institution of a Military Academy, is also recommended by cogent reasons. However pacific the general policy of a Nation may be, it ought never to be without an adequate stock of Military knowledge for emergencies. The first would impair the energy of its character, and both would hazard its safety, or expose it to greater evils when War could not be avoided. Besides that War, might often, not depend upon its own choice. In proportion, as the observance of pacific maxims, might exempt a Nation from the necessity of practising the rules of the Military Art, ought to be its care in preserving, and transmitting by proper establishments, the knowledge of that Art. Whatever argument may be drawn from particular examples, superficially viewed, a thorough examination of the subject will evince, that the Art of War, is at once comprehensive and complicated; that it demands much previous study; and that the possession of it, in its most improved and perfect state, is always of great moment to the security of a Nation. This, therefore, ought to be a serious care of every Government: and for this purpose, an Academy, where a regular course of Instruction is given, is an obvious expedient, which different Nations have successfully employed. . . .

9. Benjamin Stoddert Calls for Massive Naval Expansion

AT THE TURN OF THE NINETEENTH CENTURY THE POLITICAL, DIPLOmatic, and military problems raised by the general wars in Europe accumulated rapidly. One of the first problems was that, having declared our independence of the British military system, our maritime commerce was no longer under the protection of the Royal Navy. In 1794 Congress authorized the construction of six heavy frigates ostensibly as a defense against the depredations of the Algerine corsairs in the Mediterranean. During the Revolution we had maintained small privateer and cruising forces (with which John Paul Jones had won his fame), but it was the "frigate bill" of 1794 which laid the first real foundations of American naval power.

By 1798, between the exactions of the warring great powers and the dissensions of domestic politics, there was a real threat of war. It was proposed to raise a ten thousand-man army under General Washington; at the same time, the Navy was removed from the jurisdiction of Henry Knox, the Secretary of War, and placed under an independent department with Benjamin Stoddert, a merchant and entrepreneur of Georgetown, Maryland, as the first Secretary of the Navy.

Stoddert threw himself with great energy into the task of building up the Navy as a powerful instrument of protective sea power. In his report of December 1798 he proposed a major and continuing program for building seventy-four-gun line-of-battleships—which had never before been attempted in the United States—with frigates and lesser vessels in proportion. But the war threat developed only into the Quasi-War with the French Directory; the large army was not raised, and Stoddert's battleships were not built. His reasoning is, however, still a landmark in the development of American military thinking.

[PHILADELPHIA]
Navy Department Dec [29] *1798*

JOSIAH PARKER Esqr
Chairman of the Committee of the
House of Representatives.

SIR I have given to the enquiries, you have done me the honor, as Chairman of a Committee of the House of Representatives, to make of me; all the Consideration my desire to comply promptly with the wishes of the Committee, would permit me—and now proceed with great diffidence, to submit the result. The protection of our Coast, the security of our extensive Country from invasion in some of its weaker parts, the safety of our important Commerce; and our future peace when the Maritime Nations of Europe, war with each other, all seem to demand, that our Naval force should be augmented;—so much augmented indeed, as to make the most powerfull nations desire our friendship,—the most unprincipled respect our nutrality.

The peacefull charrector of America will afford to the world

From *Naval Documents Related to the Quasi-War Between the United States and France*, II, (Washington, D.C.: Government Printing Office, 1935), pp. 129–131.

sufficient security, that we shall not be easily provoked to carry the war into the Country of an Enemy; and it well becomes the Wisdom of America to provide a cheap defence to keep from our own.

Twelve Ships of Seventy four Guns, as many Frigates, and twenty or thirty smaller Vessels, would probably be found, our Geographical situation, & our means of annoying the Trade of the Maritime powers, considered, a force sufficient to insure our future peace with the Nations of Europe. It would not perhaps be hazarding too much to say; that had we possessed this force a few years ago, we should not have lost by depredations on our Trade, four times the sum necessary to have created, & maintained it during the whole time the War has existed in Europe. If we do not profit by experience, and put ourselves in a situation to resent insults, and punish aggressions, nothing is more likely, than that in less than half a dozen years, another occasion may be presented, for a repetition of the same mortifying observation.

In another and a still more interesting view of this subject; mutual safety was a leading motive, & must ever remain, a strong cement of our Union. Whether this security can be afforded unless we are able to Command our own Coast,—and whether the union of all the States can be long preserved without it, are questions which merit the most serious, & attentive consideration of American Legislators. I forbear to dwell on this fruitfull, perhaps delicate topic, However, to attend to our more pressing concerns; We cannot feel intirely secure that we are not to be exposed to great calamities from the ambition, or animosity of France, untill a considerable addition be made to our Naval force. If twelve Ship of Seventy four Guns are added to our Navey; an Invasion of any part of our Country would be rendered so difficult, that it would scarcely be attempted.—For it is not possible to conceive, that France would promise herself any advantage by an Invasion of this country, equal to the enormous expence, & still more enormous risk, if we should be so prepared to resist her; She would be obliged to employ more than double the Number of Ships of equal force, to convoy her armies, provisions, and Stores, and to keep the communication open between her armies, & her own Country.—France can calculate, and will calculate the loss and probable gain of her enterprize.—When she find's that she cannot deceive us, that she cannot arm our Citizens to carry on this work of subjugation, Insolent, and unfounded expectation! that we are determined, on manly resistance, and that we take vigorous measures, to put ourselves into a proper posture of defence.— Even France with all her Pride, and all her Heroism, will consult her Interest and avoid war with America, and like other Nations, she will discover that it will not only be just, but politic to indulge us in our favorite wish of preserving peace with all the world. Thus then, in whatever views the subject is considered; whether our object be to prevent Invasion, to protect our Commerce, to obtain a speedy, and a proper peace, to maintain peace hereafter, or by affording security to every part of our Country, to guard against the long train of Ills, which must result from disunion; the wisest, cheapest, and most peacable means of obtaining the end we aim at, will be prompt, & vigorous measures for the Creation of a Navy sufficient for defence, but not for Conquest.—

The United States are doubtless able to bear any expence necessary for their present safety, and future tranquillity; no country increases so fast in population, and resources,—and no country can incur a Debt, with such an absolute certainty of discharging it, without laying more burthens on the people; our revenue arising from the Imports, and other sources, must increase in proportion to the increase of population; and the increase of the latter is certain, no Country ever had less to fear, from the consequences of incurring any debt necessary for defence and safety.—

On the Subject of procuring Ships of 74 Guns, we probably have it in our option, to buy them or to build them; The former will be the most expeditious mode of procuring them, but the latter, if the pressure of our affairs will admit, will be the most honorable & the most advantageous for our Country.—If we buy them from a foreign Nation, it is not to be expected that we shall be able to obtain those of the best quality; & the sum given for them will not be kept at home, and distributed amongst our own Citizens; but will operate against us like an unfavourable balance of trade; my own Idea is that we certainly ought to build the Vessels, in preference to purchasing them, that immediate Measures should be taken, to secure all the Necessary timber; but that the President should be authorized to obtain, as the exigency of our affairs may require, 12 Ships of 74 Guns by purchase or otherwise. If it should be found necessary to procure them sooner than they can be built; the Timber may be preserved by Docking, untill those purchased decay, or for a Century, if it should not be wanted sooner.—

The Estimates herewith will shew the expence of building, and equipping 12 Ships of 74 Guns, and 6 Brigs or Schooners, to mount not exceding 18 Guns. The latter would be highly usefull in scouring the West Indies, and we have not a sufficient proportion of this Size.—

Three of the largest of the 24 Gun Ships, might be converted into Frigates of 32 Guns; The whole annual expence—of Maintaining the Navy; would then be 5,383,540–6/100 Dollars [$5,383,540.60], the Annual expence of the existing navy is 2,434,261.10/100 Dollars.—The difference would be the annual expence of the proposed addition 2,949,278–96/100.—

In time of peace a small proportion of this sum would be sufficient to keep the Ships, in a State of preservation.—Every material article for the building, and equipment of Ships of War, Copper excepted, and probably copper also, may be procured, the growth or manufacture, of our own Country.—It is true that we have heretofore used cordage, made of hemp of foreign growth, and imported Canvas,—and these articles constitute, if ware and tear be included, one third part of the expence of building, equiping, and refitting our Vessels of War. But Manufactories of Canvas have been theretofore established in the Eastern States; and with proper public encouragement, may be received, and made to supply, at least the public demand;—and it is most certain that any quantity of hemp, can be raised, on the Ohio, & Mississippia, the Susquehana, the Potomak, James River, and other parts of the

United States; if the growers of it are assured of a ready Market, and at a price, less than that given for imported hemp; though if the prices of Cordage, and Canvas, the intire growth, & Manufacture of the Country, should be found at first a little dearer than the imported; the good policy of paying the difference, to our own Citizens, to render ourselves independent of Foreign Countries, for articles so essential to our defence cannot for a moment be doubted.—. . .

PART TWO

Isolated Security:
1817–1861

10. John C. Calhoun Outlines a Large Defense Policy

JOHN C. CALHOUN, AS REPRESENTATIVE FROM SOUTH CAROLINA, HAD
been one of the leading Congressional "war hawks" in 1812. To attempt to follow military thought through the ineptitudes and disasters of the conflict that they precipitated is unnecessary. But by 1816
peace had been restored, in Europe as in America; and it was necessary once more to face the questions of permanent military establishment and military policy. In his speech on the revenue bill in January
1816, Calhoun discussed both in the broadest terms. He proclaimed
his "certainty" that "bloody" wars with England would recur and
boldly outlined the measures of preparedness he believed necessary.
Congress and the country, it may be added, failed to follow him.

Mr. Calhoun commenced his remarks by observing, that there
were in the affairs of nations, not less than that of individuals,
moments, on the proper use of which depended their fame,
prosperity and duration. Such he conceived to be the present situation of this nation. Recently emerged from a war, we find ourselves in posession of a physical and moral power of great magnitude; and, impressed by the misfortunes which have resulted from
want of forecast heretofore, we are disposed to apply our means
to the purposes most valuable to the country. He hoped, that in

From: Robert L. Merriwether (ed.), *The Papers of John C. Calhoun*, I
(Columbia: University of South Carolina Press, 1959) pp. 316–327. Reprinted by permission of the publisher.

this interesting situation, we should be guided by the dictates of truth and wisdom only, that we should prefer the lasting happiness of our country to its present ease, its security to its pleasure, fair honor and reputation, to inglorious and inactive repose.

We are now called on to determine what amount of revenue is necessary for this country in time of peace; this involves the additional question, what are the means which the true interests of this country demand? The principal expence of our government grows out of measures necessary for its defence; and in order to decide what those measures ought to be, it will be proper to enquire what ought to be our policy towards other nations, and what will probably be theirs towards us? . . .

Beginning with the policy of this country, it ought, he said, to correspond with the character of its political institutions. What then is their character? They rest on justice and reason. Those being the foundations of our government, its policy ought to comport with them. It is the duty of all nations, especially of one whose institutions recognize no principle of force, but appeal to virtue for their strength, to act with justice and moderation; with moderation approaching to forbearance. In all possible conflicts with foreign powers, our government should be able to make it manifest to the world, that it has justice on its side. We should always forbear, if possible, until all should be satisfied, that when we take up arms, it is not for the purpose of conquest, but maintaining our essential rights. Our government, however, is also founded on equality; it permits no man to exercise violence; it permits none to trample on the rights of his fellow citizen with impunity. These maxims we should also carry into our intercourse with foreign nations, and as we render justice to all, so we should be prepared to exact it from all. Our policy should not only be moderate and just, but as high minded as it is moderate and just. This, said Mr. C. appears to me the true line of conduct. In the policy of nations, said he, there are two extremes: one extreme in which justice and moderation may sink into feebleness—another in which that lofty spirit, which ought to animate all nations, particularly free ones, may mount up to military violence. These extremes ought to be equally avoided: but of the two, he considered the first far the most dangerous, far the most fatal. . . .

. . . Having dismissed this part of the subject, Mr. C. proceeded to consider another part of it, in his opinion equally important, viz.: What will be the probable policy of other nations? With the world at large, said he, we are now at peace. I know of no nation with which we shall probably come into collision, unless it be with Great Britain and Spain. With both of these nations we have considerable points of collision: I hope this country will maintain, in regard to both of them, the strictest justice: but with both these nations there is a possibility, sooner or later, of our being engaged in war. As to Spain, I will say nothing, because she is the inferior of the two, and those measures which apply to the superior power, will include also the inferior. I shall consider our relations then with England only.

Peace now exists between the two countries. As to its duration, I will give no opinion, except that I believe the peace will last the longer for the war which has just ended. Evidences have been furnished during the war of the capacity and character of this nation, which will make her indisposed to try her strength with us on slight grounds. But, what is the probable course of events respecting the future relations between the two countries? England is the most formidable power in the world. She has the most numerous army and navy at her command. We, on the contrary, are the most growing nation on earth; most rapidly improving in those very particulars in which she excels. This question then presents itself: will the greater power permit the less to attain its destined greatness by natural growth, or will she take measures to disturb it? Those who know the history of nations, will not believe that a rival will look unmoved on this prosperity. It has been said, that nations have heads, but no hearts. Every statesman, every one who loves his country, who wishes to maintain the dignity of that country, to see it attain the summit of greatness and prosperity, regards the progress of other nations with a jealous eye. The English statesmen have always so acted. I find no fault with them on that account, but rather to point it out as a principle which ought also to govern our conduct in regard to them. Will Great Britain permit us to go on in an uninterrupted march to the height of national greatness and prosperity? I fear not. But, admitting the councils on that side of the water to be governed by a degree of magnanimity and justice, the world has never experienced from them, and I am warranted in saying never will, may not some unforeseen collision involve you in hostilities with Great Britain? Gentlemen on the other side have said, that there are points of difference with that nation, (existing prior to the war) which are yet unsettled. I grant it. If such, then, be the fact, does it not shew that points of collision remain—that whenever the same condition of the world that existed before the war shall recur, the same collisions will probably take place? If Great Britain sees the opportunity of enforcing the same doctrines we have already contested, will she not seize it?

Admitting this country to maintain that policy which it ought; that its councils be governed by the most perfect justice and moderation, we yet see, said Mr. Calhoun, that by a difference of views on essential points, the peace between the two nations is liable to be jeopardized. I am sure, that future wars with England are not only possible, but, I will say more, that they are highly probable—nay, that they will certainly take place. Future wars, I fear, with the honorable Speaker, future wars, long and bloody, will exist between this country and Great Britain: I lament it—but I will not close my eyes on future events; I will not betray the high trust reposed in me; I will speak what I believe to be true. You will have to encounter British jealousy and hostility in every shape, not immediately manifested by open force or violence, perhaps, but by indirect attempts to check your growth and prosperity. As far as they can, they will disgrace every thing connected with you; her reviewers, paragraphists and travellers will assail you and your institutions, and no means will be left untried to bring you to contemn yourselves, and be contemned by others. I thank my God, they have not now the means of effecting it which they once had. No; the late war has given you a mode of feeling and thinking which forbids the acknowledgment of national inferiority, that first of political evils. Had we not encountered Great Britain, we should not have had the brilliant points to rest on which we now have. We, too, have now *our* heroes and illustrious actions. If Britain has her Wellington, we have our Jacksons, Browns and Scotts. If she has her naval heroes, we have them not less renowned, for they have snatched the laurel from her brows. It is impossible that we can now be degraded by comparisons; I trust we are equally above corruption and intrigue; it only remains then to try the contest by force of arms.

Let us now, said Mr. C. consider the measures of preparation which sound policy dictates. First, then, as to extent, without reference to the kind: They ought to be graduated by a reference to the character and capacity of both countries. England excels in means all countries that now exist, or ever did exist; and has besides great moral resources—intelligent and renowned for masculine virtues. On our part our measures ought to correspond with that lofty policy which becomes freemen determined to defend our rights. Thus circumstanced on both sides, we ought to omit no preparation fairly in our means. Next, as to the species of preparation, which opens subjects of great extent and importance. The navy most certainly, in any point of view, occupies the first place. It is the most safe, most effectual, and the cheapest mode of defence. For, let the fact be remembered, our navy costs less per man, including all the amount of extraordinary expenditures on the Lakes, than our army. This is an important fact, which ought to be fixed in the memory of the House; for, if that force be the most efficient and safe, which is at the same time the cheapest, on that should be our principal reliance. We have heard much of the danger of standing armies to our liberties—the objection cannot be made to the navy. Generals, it must be acknowledged, have often advanced at the head of armies to imperial rank and power; but in what instance had an admiral usurped on the liberties of his country? Put our strength in the navy for foreign defence, and we shall certainly escape the whole catalogue of possible ills, painted by gentlemen on the other side. A naval power attacks that country, from whose hostility alone we have any thing to dread, where she is most assailable, and defends this country where it is weakest. Where is Great Britain most vulnerable? In what point is she most accessible to attack? In her commerce—in her navigation. There she is not only exposed, but the blow is fatal. There is her strength; there is the secret of her power. Here, then, if ever it become necessary, you ought to strike.

But where are *you* most exposed? On the Atlantic line; a line so long and so weak, that you are peculiarly liable to be assailed in it. How is it to be defended? By a navy, and by a navy alone can it be efficiently defended. Let us look back to the time when the enemy was in possession of the whole line of the sea coast, moored in your rivers, and ready to assault you at every point. The facts are too recent to require to be painted—I will only generally state that your commerce was cut up; your specie circulation destroyed; your internal communications interrupted, your best and cheapest high way being entirely in possession of the enemy; your ports foreign, the one to the other; your treasury exhausted, in merely defensive preparations and militia requisitions, not knowing where you would be assailed, you had at the same moment, to stand prepared at every point. A recurrence of this state of things, so oppressive to the country, in the event of another war, could be prevented only by the establishment and maintenance of a sufficient naval force. Mr. C. said he had thought proper to press this point thus strongly, because, though it was generally assented to that the navy ought to be increased, he found that assent too cold, and the approbation bestowed on it too negative in its character. It ought, it is said, to be gradually increased. If the navy is to be increased at all, let its augmentation be limited only by your ability to build, officer and man. If it is the kind of force most safe, and at the same time most efficient to guard against foreign invasion, or repel foreign aggression, you ought to put your whole force on the sea side. It is estimated that we have in our country eighty thousand sailors. This would enable us to man a considerable fleet, which, if well directed, would give us the habitual command on our own coast, an object, in every point of view, so desirable. Not that we ought, hastily, without due preparation, under present circumstances, build a large number of vessels; but we ought to commence preparation, establish docks, collect timber and naval stores, and, as soon as the materials are prepared, we ought to commence building, to the extent which I have mentioned. If any thing can preserve the country in its most imminent dangers from abroad, it is this species of armament. If we desire to be free from future wars, as I hope we may, this is the only way to effect it. We shall have peace then, and what is of still higher moment, with perfect security.

In regard to our present military establishment, Mr. C. said, it was small enough. That point the honorable Speaker had fully demonstrated: it was not sufficiently large at present to occupy all our fortresses. Gentlemen had spoken in favor of the militia, and against the army. In regard to the militia, said Mr. C. I would go as far as any gentleman, and considerably further than those would who are so violently opposed to our small army. I would not only arm the militia, but I would extend their term of service, and make them efficient. To talk about the efficiency of militia called into service for six months only, is to impose on the people; it is to ruin them with false hopes. I know the danger of large standing armies, said Mr. C. I know the militia are the true force; that no nation can be safe at home and abroad, which has not an efficient militia; but the time of service ought to be enlarged, to enable them to acquire a knowledge of the duties of the camp, to let the habits of civil life be broken. For though militia, freshly drawn from their homes, may in a moment of enthusiasm, do great service, as at New Orleans, in general they are not calculated for service in the field, until time is allowed for them to acquire habits of discipline and subordination. Your defence ought to depend on the land, on a regular draft from the body of the people. It is thus in time of war the business of recruiting will be dispensed with; a mode of defending the country every way uncongenial with our republican institutions; uncertain, slow in its operation and expensive, it draws from society its worse materials, introducing into our army, of necessity, all the severities, which are exercised in that of the most despotic government. Thus compounded, our army in a great degree, lose that enthusiasm which citizen-soldiers, conscious of liberty, and fighting in defence of their country, have ever been animated.

All free nations of antiquity entrusted the defence of the country, not to the dregs of society, but to the body of citizens; hence that heroism which modern times may admire but cannot equal. I know that I utter truths unpleasant to those who wish to enjoy liberty without making the efforts necessary to secure it. Her favor is never won by the cowardly, the vicious or indolent. It has been said by some physicians that life is a forced state; the same may be said of freedom. It requires efforts; it presupposes mental and moral qualities of a high order to be generally diffused in the society where it exists. It mainly stands on the faithful discharge of two great duties which every citizen of proper age owes the republic; a wise and virtuous exercise of the right of suffrage; and a prompt and brave defence of the country in the hour of danger. The first symptom of decay has ever appeared in the backward and negligent discharge of the latter duty. Those who are acquainted with the historians and orators of antiquity know the truth of this assertion. The least decay of patriotism, the least verging towards pleasure, and luxury will there immediately discover itself. Large standing and mercenary armies then become necessary; and those who are not willing to render the military service essential to the defence of their rights, soon find, as they ought to do, a master. It is the order of nature and cannot be reversed. This would at once put an adequate force in your hands, and render you secure. I cannot agree with those who think that we are free from danger, and need not to prepare for it, because we have no nation in our immediate neighborhood to dread. Recollect that the nation with whom we have recently terminated a severe conflict, lives on the bosom of the deep; that although three thousand miles of ocean intervene between us, she can attack you with as much facility as if she had but 200 or 250 miles over land to march. She is as near you as if she occupied Canada instead of the islands of Great Britain. You have the power of assailing as well as being assailed; her provinces border on our territory, the dread of losing which if you are prepared to attack them will contribute to that peace which every honest man is anxious to maintain as long as possible with that country.

Mr. C. then proceeded to a point of less but yet of great importance—he meant, the establishment of roads and opening canals in various parts of the country. Your country, said he, has certain points of feebleness and certain points of strength about it. Your feebleness should be removed, your strength improved. Your population is widely dispersed. Though this is greatly advantageous in one respect, that of preventing the country from being permanently conquered, it imposes a great difficulty in defending your territory from invasion, because of the difficulty of transportation from one point to another of your widely extended frontier. We ought to contribute as much as possible to the formation of good military roads, not only on the score of general political economy, but to enable us on emergencies to collect the whole mass of our military means on the point menaced. . . .

Mr. C. proceeded to another topic—the encouragement proper to be afforded to the industry of the country. In regard to the question, how far manufactures ought to be fostered, Mr. C. said it was the duty of this country, as a means of defence, to encourage the domestic industry of the country, more especially that part of it which provides the necessary materials for clothing and defence. Let us look at the nature of the war most likely to occur. England is in the possession of the ocean; no man, however sanguine, can believe that we can deprive her soon of her predominance there. That control deprives us of the means of maintaining our army and navy cheaply clad. The question relating to manufactures must not depend on the abstract principle, that industry left to pursue its own course, will find in its own interest all the encouragement that is necessary. I lay the claims of the manufacturers entirely out of view, said Mr. C.—but on general principles, without regard to their interest, a certain encouragement should be extended at least to our woollen and cotton manufactures.

There was another point of preparation which, Mr. C. said, ought not to be overlooked—the defence of our coast, by means other than the navy, on which we ought to rely mainly but not entirely. The coast is our weak part, which ought to be rendered strong, if it be in our power to make it so. There are two points on our coast particularly weak, the mouths of the Mississippi and the Chesapeake Bay, which ought to be cautiously attended to, not however neglecting others. The administration which leaves these two points in another war without fortification, ought to receive the execration of the country. . . .

11. James Monroe and Post-Napoleonic Military Policy

IN HIS INAUGURAL ADDRESS OF MARCH 4, 1817, PRESIDENT MONROE offered a military policy more general in its terms and considerably more modest than that which John C. Calhoun had envisaged the year before. In fact, Monroe was to continue naval building and begin an extensive program of seacoast fortification. But neither he nor his successors, could reform the militia system, despite its lamentable showing in the War of 1812; Congress and the country were soon to lose interest in military expenditure in a time of profound peace. Monroe's inaugural is typical of a long line of similar Presidential statements, announcing generalized military policy to which the nation paid little or no attention.

. . . Dangers from abroad are not less deserving of attention. Experiencing the fortune of other nations, the United States may be again involved in war, and it may in that event be the object of the adverse party to overset our Government, to break our Union, and demolish us as a nation. Our distance from Europe and the just, moderate, and pacific policy of our Government may form some security against these dangers, but they ought to be antici-

From James D. Richardson (ed.), *Compilation of the Messages and Papers of the Presidents,* II (New York: Bureau of National Literature), pp. 576–577.

pated and guarded against. Many of our citizens are engaged in commerce and navigation, and all of them are in a certain degree dependent on their prosperous state. Many are engaged in the fisheries. These interests are exposed to invasion in the wars between other powers, and we should disregard the faithful admonition of experience if we did not expect it. We must support our rights or lose our character, and with it, perhaps, our liberties. A people who fail to do it can scarcely be said to hold a place among independent nations. National honor is national property of the highest value. The sentiment in the mind of every citizen is national strength. It ought therefore to be cherished.

To secure us against these dangers our coast and inland frontiers should be fortified, our Army and Navy, regulated upon just principles as to the force of each, be kept in perfect order, and our militia be placed on the best practicable footing. To put our extensive coast in such a state of defense as to secure our cities and interior from invasion will be attended with expense, but the work when finished will be permanent, and it is fair to presume that a single campaign of invasion by a naval force superior to our own, aided by a few thousand land troops, would expose us to greater expense, without taking into the estimate the loss of property and distress of our citizens, than would be sufficient for this great work. Our land and naval forces should be moderate, but adequate to the necessary purposes—the former to garrison and preserve our fortifications and to meet the first invasions of a foreign foe, and, while constituting the elements of a greater force, to preserve the science as well as all the necessary implements of war in a state to be brought into activity in the event of war; the latter, retained within the limits proper in a state of peace, might aid in maintaining the neutrality of the United States with dignity in the wars of other powers and in saving the property of their citizens from spoliation. In time of war, with the enlargement of which the great naval resources of the country render it susceptible, and which should be duly fostered in time of peace, it would contribute essentially, both as an auxiliary of defense and as a powerful engine of annoyance, to diminish the calamities of war and to bring the war to a speedy and honorable termination.

But it ought always to be held prominently in view that the safety of these States and of everything dear to a free people must depend in an eminent degree on the militia. Invasions may be made too formidable to be resisted by any land and naval force which it would comport either with the principles of our Government or the circumstances of the United States to maintain. In such cases recourse must be had to the great body of the people, and in a manner to produce the best effect. It is of the highest importance, therefore, that they be so organized and trained as to be prepared for any emergency. The arrangement should be such as to put at the command of the Government the ardent patriotism and youthful vigor of the country. If formed on equal and just principles, it can not be oppressive. It is the crisis which makes the pressure, and not the laws which provide a remedy for it. This arrangement should be formed, too, in time of peace, to be the better prepared for war. With such an organization of such a people the United States have nothing to dread from foreign invasion. At its approach an overwhelming force of gallant men might always be put in motion. . . .

12. John C. Calhoun Proposes the "Expansible Army"

HOWEVER TEMPERATE HIS OWN VIEWS ON MILITARY POLICY, PRESIDENT Monroe made Calhoun his Secretary of War in October 1817, and the Army was maintained for some time at a strength of about ten thousand men. In the spring of 1820, however, an increasingly economy-minded Congress peremptorily ordered the Secretary to submit a plan for reducing the force to no more than six thousand. Calhoun reasoned that if the force was to be reduced to this minimal level, it should at least be done in a way permitting of its rapid reexpansion in the event of emergency. His report of December 1820 represents perhaps the first serious effort by American military thinkers on the problem of how to maintain a necessarily small peacetime Army and yet enable it promptly to respond to the exigencies of war. At the time, Congress reduced the Army without accepting the essential features of the Calhoun plan. But the problems of a mobilizable reserve, of adequate reserve training, and of mobilization planning have remained with us from that day. The "organization of the army ought to have reference," as Calhoun observed in 1820, "to the objects for which it is maintained." Almost a century later Elihu Root was putting the same idea into similar words when he said that the object of having an Army was "to provide for war" (see Document 27). And even after the Civil War, Calhoun's report was still being quoted as the final word on adequate military policy.

Reduction of the Army.

COMMUNICATED TO THE HOUSE OF REPRESENTATIVES,
DECEMBER 12, 1820.

SIR: WAR DEPARTMENT, *December* 12, 1820.

In obedience to a resolution of the House of Representatives of the 11th of May last, "directing that the Secretary of War report to this House, at the commencement of the next session, a plan for the reduction of the army to six thousand, non-commissioned officers, musicians, and privates, and preserving such parts of the corps of engineers, as, in his opinion, without regard to that number, it may be for the public interest to retain; and, also, what saving of the public revenue will be produced by such an arrangement of the army as he may propose in conformity with this resolution," I have the honor to make the following report:

I deem it proper, before a plan is presented in detail for reducing the army, as proposed in the resolution, to state briefly the general principles on which it is conceived our military peace establishment ought to be organized. It will be readily admitted, that the organization of the army ought to have reference to the objects for which it is maintained, and ought to be such as may be

From *American State Papers, Military Affairs,* 16th Congress, Session 2 (1820), II, pp. 188–193.

best calculated to effect such objects; as it must be obvious, on the slightest reflection, that on considerations connected therewith ought to depend, not only its members, but also the principles on which it ought to be formed.

The necessity of a standing army in peace is not believed to be involved in the subject under consideration, as the resolution presupposes the propriety of maintaining one; and in fact its necessity is so apparent, that, even those least friendly to the army have never attempted to abolish it, or even to reduce it, since the late war, much below the number proposed in the resolution. The objects for which a standing army in peace ought to be maintained may be comprised under two classes; those which, though they have reference to a state of war, yet are more immediately connected with its duties in peace; and those which relate immediately and solely to war. Under the first class may be enumerated, as the leading objects, the garrisoning of the forts along our Atlantic frontier in order to preserve tnem, and to cause the sovereignty of the United States to be respected in their immediate neighborhood, and the occupying of certain commanding posts in our inland frontier to keep in check our savage neighbors, and to protect our newly formed and feeble settlements in that quarter. These are, doubtless, important objects; but are by no means so essential as those which relate immediately and solely to a state of war; and, though not to be neglected wholly, ought not to have any decided influence in the organization of our peace establishment. Without, therefore, making any further remark on this point of the inquiry, I will proceed to consider the other class, on which, as it comprises the great and leading inducement to maintain in this country a regular army in peace, the prominent features of its organization ought to depend.

However remote our situation from the great powers of the world, and however pacific our policy, we are, notwithstanding, liable to be involved in war; and, to resist, with success, its calamities and dangers, a standing army in peace, in the present improved state of the military science, is an indispensable preparation. The opposite opinion cannot be adopted, without putting to hazard the independence and safety of the country. I am aware that the militia is considered, and in many respects justly, as the great national force; but, to render them effective, every experienced officer must acknowledge, that they require the aid of regular troops. Supported by a suitable corps of trained artillerists, and by a small well-disciplined body of infantry, they may be safely relied on to garrison our forts, and to act in the field as light troops. In these services, their zeal, courage, and habit of using fire-arms, would be of great importance, and would have their full effect. To rely on them beyond this, to suppose our militia capable of meeting in the open field the regular troops of Europe, would be to resist the most obvious truth, and the whole of our experience as a nation. War is an art, to attain perfection in which, much time and experience, particularly for the officers, are necessary. It is true, that men of great military genius occasionally appear, who, though without experience, may, when an army is already organized and disciplined, lead it to victory; yet I know of no instance, under circumstances nearly equal, in which the greatest talents have been able, with irregular and undisciplined troops, to meet with success those that were regularly trained. Genius without much experience may command, but it cannot go much further. It cannot at once organize and discipline an army, and give it that military tone and habit which only, in the midst of imminent danger, can enable it to perform the most complex evolutions with precision and promptitude. Those qualities which essentially distinguish an army from an equal assemblage of untrained individuals, can only be acquired by the instruction of experienced officers. If they, particularly the company and regimental officers, are inexperienced, the army must remain undisciplined, in which case, the genius, and even experience of the commander, will be of little avail. The great and leading objects, then, of a military establishment in peace, ought to be to create and perpetuate military skill and experience; so that, at all times, the country may have at its command a body of officers, sufficiently numerous, and well instructed in every branch of duty, both of the line and staff; and the organization of the army ought to be such as to enable the Government, at the commencement of hostilities, to obtain a regular force, adequate to the emergencies of the country, properly organized and prepared for actual service. It is thus only that we can be in the condition to meet the first shocks of hostilities with unyielding firmness; and to press on an enemy, while our resources are yet unexhausted. But if, on the other hand, disregarding the sound dictates of reason and experience, we should in peace neglect our military establishment, we must, with a powerful and skilful enemy, be exposed to the most distressing calamities. Not all the zeal, courage, and patriotism of our militia, unsupported by regularly trained and disciplined troops, can avert them. Without such troops, the two or three first campaigns would be worse than lost. The honor of our arms would be tarnished, and the resources of the country uselessly lavished; for, in proportion to the want of efficiency, and a proper organization, must, in actual service, be our military expenditures. When taught by sad experience, we would be compelled to make redoubled efforts, with exhausted means, to regain those very advantages which were lost for the want of experience and skill. In addition to the immense expenditure which would then be necessary, exceeding manifold what would have been sufficient to put our peace establishment on a respectable footing, a crisis would be thus brought on of the most dangerous character. If our liberty should ever be endangered by the military power gaining the ascendency, it will be from the necessity of making those mighty and irregular efforts to retrieve our affairs, after a series of disasters, caused by the want of adequate military knowledge; just as, in our physical system, a state of the most dangerous excitement and paroxysm follows that of the greatest debility and prostration. To avoid these dangerous consequences, and to prepare the country to meet a state of war, particularly at its commencement, with honor and safety, much must depend on the organization of our military peace establishment, and I have, accordingly, in a plan about to be proposed for the reduction of the army, directed my attention mainly to that point, believing it to be of the greatest importance.

To give such an organization the leading principles in its formation ought to be, that, at the commencement of hostilities, there should be nothing either to new model or to create. The only difference, consequently, between the peace and the war formation of the army ought to be in the increased magnitude of the latter; and the only change in passing from the former to the latter, should consist in giving to it the augmentation which will then be necessary.

It is thus, and thus only, the dangerous transition from peace to war may be made without confusion or disorder; and the weakness and danger, which otherwise would be inevitable, be avoided. Two consequences result from this principle. First, the organization of the staff in a peace establishment ought to be such, that every branch of it should be completely formed, with such extension as the number of troops and posts occupied may render necessary; and, secondly, that the organization of the line ought, as far as practicable, to be such that, in passing from the peace to the war formation, the force may be sufficiently augmented; without adding new regiments or battalions; thus raising the war on the basis of the peace establishment, instead of creating a new army to be added to the old, as at the commencement of the late war. The next principle to be observed is, that the organization ought to be such as to induce, in time of peace, citizens of adequate talents and respectability of character to enter and remain in the military service of the country, so that the Government may have officers at its command, who, to the requisite experience, would add the public confidence. The correctness of this principle can scarcely be doubted; for, surely, if it is worth having an army at all, it is worth having it well commanded.

These are the general principles upon which I propose to form the organization of the army, as proposed to be reduced under the resolution. . . . The present organization of the staff, with its branches, is retained, with slight alterations. . . .

. . . It is also proposed to retain the two majors and four brigadier generals. Although it is not probable that there will be concentrated, in time of peace, at any one point, the force equal to the command of a single major or even a brigadier general, yet it is conceived that it is important to the service that they should be retained. As two regiments, with a proper proportion of artillery and light troops, constitute, in our service, one brigade, and two brigades a division, the command of a major general, the number of regiments and battalions, under the proposed organization, thus gives a command equal to that of two majors and four brigadier generals. But a more weighty, and, in my opinion, decisive reason why they should be retained, may be found in the principle already stated, that the organization of the peace establishment ought to be such as to induce persons of talent and respectability to enter and continue in the military service. To give to the officers of the army the necessary skill and acquirements, the military academy is an invaluable part of our establishment; but that alone will be inadequate. For this purpose respectability of rank and compensation must be given to the officers of the army, in due proportion to the other pursuits of life. Every prudent individual, in selecting his course of life, must be governed, making some allowance for the natural disposition, essentially by the reward which attends the various pursuits open to him. Under our free institutions, every one is left free to make his selection; and most of the pursuits of life, followed with industry and skill, lead to opulence and respectability. The profession of arms, in the well established state of things which exist among us, has no reward but what is attached to it by law; and if that should be inferior to other professions, it would be idle to suppose individuals, possessed of the necessary talents and character, would be induced to enter it. A mere sense of duty ought not, and cannot be safely relied on. It supposes that individuals would be actuated by a stronger sense of duty towards the Government than the latter towards them. . . .

. . . No position connected with the organization of the peace establishment is susceptible of being more rigidly proved, than that the proportion of its officers to the rank and file ought to be greater than in a war establishment. It results immediately from a position, the truth of which cannot be fairly doubted, and which I have attempted to illustrate in the preliminary remarks, that the leading object of a regular army in time of peace ought to be, to enable the country to meet with honor and safety, particularly at the commencement of war, the dangers incident to that state; to effect this object as far as practicable, the peace organization ought, as has been shown, to be such, that in passing to a state of war, there should be nothing either to new model or to create; and that the difference between that and the war organization, ought to be simply in the greater magnitude of the latter. The application of this principle has governed in that portion of the formation of the proposed military establishment now under consideration. The companies, both of the artillery and infantry, are proposed to be reduced to their minimum peace formation, the former to consist of sixty-four privates and non-commissioned officers, and the latter of thirty-seven, which will give to the aggregate of both corps thus formed, six thousand three hundred and sixteen non-commissioned officers, musicians, and privates. Without adding an additional officer, or a single company, they may be augmented, should a just precaution, growing out of our foreign relations, render it necessary, to eleven thousand five hundred and fifty-eight; and, pending hostilities, by adding two hundred and eighty-eight officers, the two corps, on the maximum of the war formation, may be raised to the respectable force of four thousand five hundred and forty-five of the artillery, and fourteen thousand four hundred and ninety of the infantry, making, in the aggregate, nineteen thousand and thirty-five officers, non-commissioned officers, and privates. . . . The war organization, thus raised on the basis of the peace establishment, will bring into effective operation the whole of the experience and skill of the latter, which, with attention, would, in a short period, be communicated to the new recruits, and the officers recently appointed, so as to constitute a well disciplined force. . . .

. . . Economy is certainly a very high political virtue, intimately connected with the power and the public virtue of the community. In military operations, which, under the best management, are so expensive, it is of the utmost importance; but, by no propriety of language can that arrangement be called economical, which, in order that our military establishment in peace should be rather less expensive, would, regardless of the purposes for which it ought to be maintained, render it unfit to meet the dangers incident to a state of war.

With a single observation, which was omitted in its proper place, I will conclude my remarks. The plan proposed for the reduction of the army gives six thousand three hundred and sixteen non-commissioned officers, musicians, and privates, instead of six thousand, the number fixed in the resolution. It was found difficult to form an organization on proper principles, which would give that precise number, and as the difference was not deemed very material, I have ventured to deviate to that extent, from the terms of the resolution. . . .

Organization of the Army as proposed under the resolution of the House of Representatives of May 11, 1820.

Staff.

The chief reduction which is practicable in the staff is that of the purchasing department. It is reduced to one commissary general stationed at Washington, one assistant and two storekeepers at New York and Philadelphia, where all stores purchased for the army will be concentrated, and from whence they will be distributed to the quartermasters of every corps. By abolishing the distinction between the battalion and regimental paymasters, several corps may occasionally, when assembled on one point, be paid by the same officer. The difficulty of finding suitable persons willing to accept of the appointment of surgeons' mates has likewise been the reason for suppressing that rank, and allowing in their steads a certain number of assistant surgeons with the rank and appointment of post surgeons, and abolishing all distinctions of rank and pay between surgeons employed in a post, battalion, or regiment. In small posts the assistant commissaries of subsistence may be charged with the functions of quartermasters.

Artillery

By uniting the three corps of the ordinance, light artillery, and artillery in one, appointing one general staff at the head of it, and

Artillery.

1 Colonel commandant.
1 Colonel of ordnance.
1 Lieutenant colonel of ordnance.
2 Majors of ordnance.
5 Lieutenant colonels of battalions.
5 Majors,   do
7 Captains of ordnance.
5   do   of light artillery.
40   do   of artillery.
10 Lieutenants of light artillery.
80   do   of artillery.
10 Second lieutenants of light
      artillery.
80 Second lieutenants of artillery.

247 Officers.

15 Sergeants of light artillery.
120   do   of artillery.
30 Corporals of light artillery.
240   do   of artillery.
5   do   of the train.
5 Armorers.
5 Smiths, (light artillery.)
5 Trumpets, (light artillery.)
40 Drummers.
90 Gunners, (light artillery.)
720   do   artillery.
180 Matrosses, (light artillery.)

1,440 Matrosses, artillery.
10 Workmen.
45 Soldiers of the train,
      (light artillery.)

2,950 Total.

Infantry.

9 Colonels.
9 Lieutenant colonels.
9 Majors.
90 Captains.
90 First lieutenants.
90 Second lieutenants.

297 Officers.

360 Sergeants.
360 Corporals.
9 Armorers.
9 Drum majors.
90 Drummers.
2,520 Privates.
18 Workmen.

3,366 Total.

75 Artificers, workmen
      of ordnance.
6,391 Rank and file.

NOTE.—To each regiment and battalion a subaltern will be assigned as adjutant, and one as quartermaster, and in all cases where officers of the line are assigned to the staff, their pay in the line is merged in that of the staff, which is in fact but an additional allowance for the extra expense attending such situations.

making its officers pass in rotation through the three services, the organization of the army will be rendered more simple, and the instruction of the officers much more complete. The present regiment of light artillery being organized to manoeuvre sixty guns, is stronger than our occasions require; being on foot, and performing garrison duty, it cannot practise its peculiar manoeuvres, nor qualify itself for the service which it will be called upon to perform in the field. It is therefore proposed to convert it into an additional regiment of foot artillery, which will only be changing its denomination, and to add a company of light artillery to each of the five regiments of artillery. This arm will thus be distributed on the frontier, and by allowing twenty-eight saddle and thirty-two train horses to each company, with ten soldiers of the train to serve them, it will be enabled to manoeuvre two pieces at a time, with their caissons.

Two lieutenants and two second lieutenants in each company are more than the service indispensably require. A certain number of officers of this rank can, therefore, always be spared from regimental service, and appointed as assistants in the ordnance department. But it is necessary to maintain some supernumerary captains for this purpose; for, if their number did not pass that of the companies of artillery, it would be impossible to spare a captain of artillery from his company. Lest misapprehension should arise on this subject, it is proper to state that officers of artillery detailed on the ordnance service are exclusively under the control of the ordnance department. The service of the arsenals is to be provided for out of the artillery; and the cannoneers will thus perfect themselves in the composition of fireworks, &c. A single company of ordnance artificers will be retained in peace.

As three or four experienced pointers are sufficient for each piece, it is proposed to form them into a peculiar class, as in Europe. All augmentations or reductions of the artillery will then fall on the matrosses, who can be trained in a few weeks. The proposed organization allows three sergeants, commanding two guns, to each company, (of whom the senior may perform the duties of orderly and quartermaster sergeant,) six corporals, commanding each one gun, three gunners, and six matrosses (the least number that can manoeuvre it) to each gun. By raising the force of each company to 100 men, in time of war, the whole corps will be able to manoeuvre 90 guns in the field, viz: 30 by the light artillery, and 60 by ten companies of foot; and 900, or even 1,800 guns in forts and batteries, by allowing six cannoniers, or even three, with the aid of the militia, to serve alternately two guns.

Infantry.

The proposed organization in the reduction of each regiment to the minimum force, will leave it adapted to the purposes of military service and instruction, by preserving in each corps all its necessary component parts. To execute the modern manoeuvres of the field, each battalion must divide itself into two half battalions, four divisions, eight platoons, sixteen sections, and thirty-two squads, exclusive of its flank companies. Experience has pointed out that, in time of war, its front should not pass 200 files, exclusive of flank companies, lest it become weak and wavering. But it cannot, in peace, be reduced below 128 files, or 64 to a half battalion, 32 to a division, 16 to a platoon, 8 to a section, 4 to a squad, as the various fractions would become too diminutive for any service, if reduced below that number.

The propriety of reducing each regiment to its minimum force, rather than reducing the number of regiments, and making them somewhat stronger, has been chiefly deduced from the following principle, the desire of avoiding to create new regiments, with raw inexperienced officers at their head, in the time of war. Each regiment of the army can be formed into two battalions, equally intermixed with old soldiers at the approach of war, and that by a very simple operation, provided that, some time previously, care may have been taken to augment the number of their officers, and fill up their ranks to a higher complement. Nine regiments, which, on the proposed organization, form only 3,663 men in time of peace, may then be raised to near 16,000 in time of war, without creating new corps—by doubling the number of battalions, and raising their front to 250 files, including the flank companies, and forming them in three ranks. It is therefore evident that the reduction of each regiment of infantry, when formed on this small scale, whilst it makes a very trifling economy for the present, deprives us of the power of forming a large and effective force in time of war.

The mode of doubling the battalion is simply to form a battalion of each half battalion, a division of each platoon, a platoon of each section, &c., and fill up their ranks to the proper number, with a care to place the recruits in the second ranks.

NOTE.—As this estimate is predicated on the smallest numbers that can perform the requisite manoeuvres in the school of company and battalion, and as experience proves that no organization can be kept full, an increase of one-sixth to the rank and file would render the corps at all times efficient and perfect, and would greatly improve the proposed organization.

13. A Program for the Fortification of the Seacoasts

SINCE THE BEGINNING OF MONROE'S PRESIDENCY, A BOARD OF MILITARY engineers, of which Joseph G. Totten, brevet lieutenant colonel of Engineers, is the best remembered—he is commemorated by Fort Totten, at the western entrance to Long Island Sound—had been reporting on the proper design of a system of coastal fortification. The report of February 1821, which Calhoun transmitted to the Speaker of the House, not only outlined an extensive program of construction but supplied a complete rationale for fortification as it appeared in the military thinking of the time. It is as instructive for the general tenor of military thought as it is on engineering problems of fort-building.

SIR: CITY OF WASHINGTON, *February* 7, 1821.

The following summary of the operations of the Board of Engineers, called for by your order, is respectfully submitted.

The commission charged with reconnoitring the frontiers of the United States has completed the three most important sections of

From *American State Papers, Military Affairs, II*, pp. 305–310.

the maritime boundaries, viz: The coast of the gulf of Mexico, the coast between Cape Hatteras and Cape Cod, and the coast between Cape Cod and the river St. Croix. The coast between Cape Hatteras and Cape Fear has likewise been surveyed; and the only section which remains to be examined, to complete the reconnoissance of the coast, is South Carolina and Georgia.

The reports presented in 1818, 1819, 1820, and 1821, to the honorable Secretaries of the War and Navy Departments, were accompanied by every necessary plan, table, &c. and embrace every naval and military consideration, both as to the attack and as to the defence of the frontier, as to fixing the sites for the great naval depots, and as to protecting, by the general system of defence, the general system of internal navigation. We must refer to the details of these reports to show the importance of establishing a complete system for the protection of the frontiers, and the necessity of building this system upon principles harmonizing with the modern system of warfare. It will be seen that most of the existing forts only defend single points, and satisfy only a few essential conditions; and that they have not been planned with a view to the defence of the frontiers, considered as one great and combined system, whose several parts should be connected, and should mutually support each other. The navy yards (excepting that of Charlestown, near Boston) have all been improperly placed; the conveniences for the erection of the necessary establishments having alone been taken into consideration, while all the other requisites for points so important, such as security against attack by sea or land, facility for receiving all kinds of building materials in time of war as well as in time of peace, vicinity to a place of rendezvous, have been overlooked.

A defensive system for the frontiers of the United States is therefore yet to be created; its bases are: first, a navy; second, fortifications; third, interior communication by land and water; and fourth, a regular army and well organized militia: these means must all be combined, so as to form a complete system.

The navy must, in the first place, be provided with proper establishments for construction and repair, harbors of rendezvous, stations, and ports of refuge. It is only by taking into view the general character, as well as the details of the whole frontier, that we can fix on the most advantageous points for receiving these naval depots, harbors of rendezvous, stations, and ports of refuge. . . .

. . . After determining the general and connected system of naval depots, harbors of rendezvous, stations, and ports of refuge, the commission in the next place traced the scheme of fortifications necessary to protect this system, and at the same time to guard the whole frontier against invasion. The forts projected by the commission for this purpose satisfy one or more of the following conditions:

1. To close important harbors to an enemy, and secure them to the navy of the country.

2. To deprive an enemy of strong positions, where, protected by his naval superiority, he might fix permanent quarters in our territory, maintain himself during the war, and keep the whole frontier in perpetual alarm.

3. To cover our great cities against attack.

4. To prevent as much as possible the great avenues of interior navigation from being blockaded by a naval force, at their entrance into the ocean.

5. To cover the coastwise and interior navigation, and give to our navy the means necessary for protecting this navigation.

6. To cover the great naval establishments. . . .

. . . From the general exposition which we have given, it will be seen that all the fortifications projected by the board are not of the same pressing necessity, nor of like importance; that some are required immediately, and that the commencement of others may be delayed. In classing them, we shall observe that the works of the most urgent necessity are those which are destined to prevent an enemy, in time of war, from forming a permanent establishment, or even a momentary one, on the soil of the Union; those which defend our great naval arsenals; and those which protect our chief commercial cities.

In the second grade we will place those which defend stations for our navy, and commercial cities of secondary importance, which, either from natural or artificial defences, existing works, &c., are not entirely without protection, and can wait until the chief and more important points are secured, at least against a first attack.

Finally, in the third class, we will range the works which will complete the defensive system in all its parts, but whose construction may, without imminent danger, be deferred until the frontier has received all the successive degrees of strength which the gradual erection of the forts of the first and second class will give to it.

The table A, joined to this report, has been drawn up on this principle, and shows:

1st. That the works to be erected during the first period will cost $8,010,054; will require 2,540 men, at most, to garrison them in time of peace, and 20,305 in case of siege.

2d. That the works of the second class will cost $4,711,031; will require 1,030 men, at most, to garrison them in peace, and 8,615 in case of siege.

3d. That the expense of the works belonging to the third class will amount to $5,073,970; their garrisons, in time of peace, to 1,120 men, and, in case of a siege, to 9,042 men.

4th. That the total expense of completely fortifying the maritime frontier will amount to $17,795,055; the troops necessary to guard these fortifications, in peace, to 4,690 men, at most, and 37,962 men in time of war; supposing them, which is beyond all probability, all besieged at once.

The time required to construct these works must depend entirely upon the annual appropriations which the nation may grant to this branch of the public service. All that can be said upon this subject is, that, in an undertaking of such vital importance to the safety, prosperity, and greatness of the Union, there should not be an instant's relaxation of effort and perseverance. A work of such magnitude must, with every possible effort, be the work of years; but each year, with *limited* means, will produce its fruit, and the final result is to endure for ages. However long it may be before sensible effects are produced, the result will be certain; and should no danger threaten the republic in our own days, future generations may owe the preservation of their country to the precaution of their forefathers. France was at least fifty years in completing her maritime and interior defences; but France, on more than one occasion since the reign of Louis XIV., has been saved by the fortifications erected by his power, and by the genius of Vauban. However slow the progress of this system may be, from the necessity of a sparing application of the public funds to this purpose, it is essential to disburse something in this way each year, so as to give to the frontier an annual increase of strength. We must therefore insist upon the advantage of dividing the construction of the works into several periods, according to their more or less immediate urgency, and of beginning them successively in that order. By these means, satisfactory results as to the augmentation of the strength of the frontier will be obtained as early as possible; whilst, if we were to begin them all at once, we should be a great while without defence upon any one point.

We shall now enter into the question of the expense of erecting these forts, and garrisoning them for war, and compare it with the expense of defending the coast in its present state. To render this question as clear as possible, we shall only examine it with respect to New Orleans, Norfolk, Baltimore, Philadelphia, New York, and Narraganset bay.

Supposing that an enemy had concentrated about twenty thousand men at Halifax or Bermuda; the United States must, on hearing of this force, at once prepare to receive them at all the points mentioned above. As it will be impossible to foresee on which of these points the first blow will be struck, it will be necessary to have troops encamped at each of them; and to meet an attack with a force at least numerically equal to that of the assailant, the force kept constantly under arms in these camps must be at least equal to one-half of the hostile expedition, whilst as many more must be kept in readiness, and within call. The points are so immediately accessible in some cases, and so remote from succor in others, that, after the point of attack is known by the appearance of the enemy before it, there will remain no time for reinforcements to arrive. By manœuvring in front of any of these places, he will induce us to concentrate our forces there, when, suddenly profiting of a favorable breeze, he will sail to another, which he may reach in a few hours and seize, if a force is not stationed there likewise at least equal to his own. Neither, in such a case, can reinforcements be directed against him in time; for all the forces under march will have received a direction upon the point he has just quitted. Our whole coast will thus, by a single expedition, be kept in alarm from Louisiana to Maine; and such is the extent and exposure of the maritime frontier, that an enemy may ruin us by a war of mere threatenings. If our cities are not garrisoned, they will become his prey at once; if they are, the treasury will be gradually emptied, the credit of the Government exhausted, the wearied and starving militia will desert to their homes, and nothing can avert the direful consummation of tribute, pillage, and conflagration.

The table B, joined to this report, shows that, to be in readiness on every vulnerable point, it will be necessary to maintain 67,000 men encamped and under arms at the six places above mentioned, and 53,000 ready to march, and within call. This number is really below that which would be required; for these points being exposed, according to our hypothesis, to an attack from 20,000 regular and disciplined troops, 20,000 militia would not be able to repel them, unless aided by entrenchments, requiring a time to perfect them which would not be allowed us, and involving expenses which we have not comprised in our estimates. Besides, to have 20,000 men, and especially new levies, under arms, it will be necessary, considering the epidemics which always attack such troops, to carry the formation of this corps to at least 25,000 men. The State of Louisiana, being more remote from all succor, requires a larger force under arms than the other points; we have fixed this force at 17,000, considering that the State might furnish 3,000 within call. . . .

From these bases, the 67,000 men of the militia necessary to guard the above mentioned points, in the present situation of the maritime frontier, will cost, in a campaign of six months, $16,750,000.

In strict justice, we should add to this expense, which is, we believe, greatly undervalued, amongst many other things, the loss of time, and the interruption of the labor of the citizens who have left their business to assume arms for their defence. This is a real loss to the nation, and a heavy tax on individuals. And while reflecting on the dreadful mortality which rages in the camps of men unaccustomed to the fatigues and privations of a military life, we cannot help remarking how much greater the loss of a citizen is than of a soldier.

The latter is generally an isolated being; he has prepared the sacrifice of his life by entering the army; it is the peculiar and constant duty of his profession. The former is a man of business, the father of a family, and his loss involves with it a large circle of domestic sorrow and suffering.

The total expense of constructing the works at New Orleans, Norfolk, Baltimore, Philadelphia, New York, and Narraganset bay, will amount to $11,147,695. . . . Their garrisons might consist of the same number of regular troops in time of war as in time of peace; and the remainder might be furnished by the militia held in readiness to throw themselves into the forts on the first appearance of an enemy. By these means, 2,720 regulars, and 21,000 militia, either in the forts or in small corps upon advantageous positions, making 23,720 men, would suffice after the erection of these works, and 36,280 might be kept in readiness to march when called upon. We should have only 23,720 to pay and support, instead of 67,000; and the expense would be $5,658,000, instead of $16,750,000. The difference $11,092,000 being about equal to the expense of the forts, it follows that the cost of their erection will be compensated by the saving they make in a single campaign of six months. It is proper to add that though the expense of these works be great, that expense is never to be renewed; while with troops, on the contrary, the expense is annually repeated, if not increased, until the end of the war. Besides, the disbursements for fortifications are made in time of peace, slowly, and to an extent exactly correspondent with the financial prosperity of the country. Armies, however, are most wanted, and must be paid in periods of great emergency, when the ordinary sources of revenue are dried up, and when the treasury can only be kept supplied by a resort to means the most disagreeable to, and the most burthensome upon, the people.

The defence of our maritime frontier by permanent fortifications, and even the expense of erecting these fortifications, will thus be a real and positive economy. The points of attack being reduced to a few, instead of awaiting an attack on every point, and holding ourselves every where in readiness to repel it, we shall force an enemy to direct his efforts against these few points, with which we shall be well acquainted beforehand, and which we shall have disposed to withstand all his attempts. There is no doubt but that such circumstances will render an enemy more backward in risking his expeditions, and that we shall not only therefore be better able to resist attack, but that we shall also be less frequently menaced with invasion.

Some prominent military writers have opposed the principle of fortifying an extensive land frontier; but no military or political writer has ever disputed the necessity of fortifying a maritime frontier. The practice of every nation, ancient and modern, has been the same in this respect. On a land frontier, a good, experienced, and numerous infantry may dispense with permanent fortifications, although they would prove excellent auxiliaries and supports when properly disposed and organized; but though disciplined troops can, rigorously speaking, without their aid, cover and protect a frontier, undisciplined troops never can. On a maritime frontier the case is totally different. Troops cannot supply the place of the strong batteries which are disposed along the important places. The uncertainty of the point on which an enemy may direct his attack, the suddenness with which he may reach it, and the powerful masses which he can concentrate at a distance out of our reach and knowledge, or suddenly, and at the very moment of attack, are reasons for erecting defences on every

exposed point, which may repel his attack, or retard it until reinforcements can arrive, or the means of resistance be properly
organized. By land we are acquainted with the motions of an
enemy, with the movements and directions of his columns; we
know the roads by which he must pass. But the ocean is a vast
plain without obstacles; there his movements are performed out
of our sight and knowledge, and we can receive no intelligence of
his approach until he has already arrived within the range of the
eye. In a word, the vulnerable points of a seacoast frontier are
left to their fate, if they are not covered by permanent fortifications; and their only chance of safety must then depend upon the
issue of a battle, always uncertain, even when regular and well-
disciplined troops, inured to danger, have been assembled beforehand, and have made all possible preparation for the combat. . . .

. . . Lastly, the defensive system of our seacoast by permanent
fortifications being completed, and the Union being protected
against all danger of invasion from that quarter, she can direct all
her resources towards her navy. Her national quarrels will then
all be decided upon the ocean, and no longer upon her own
territory; her wars will all be maritime; a species of warfare in
unison with the institutions of the country, less costly in men and
money, and which, by keeping off all aggressions from her own
territory, will preserve untouched her industry, her agriculture,
her financial resources, and all the other means of supporting a
just and honorable war.

As for the garrisons which these forts will require in time of
war, a small portion of them, equal in number to the garrisons
necessary in time of peace, may be composed of regular troops;
the surplus, of militia practised to the manœuvres of artillery; for
the greatest part of the troops required for the defence and service of these great coast batteries should be composed of artillery.

To this end every state might organize a certain number of battalions of militia artillery, proportioned to the exigencies and
armament of the forts upon its coast, or within the sphere of
activity of its military force. These battalions should be within
call of the forts as long as no invading expedition is announced;

but as soon as some operation of an enemy should menace the frontier, they should throw themselves into the forts, and remain there as long as the precise point of attack should remain uncertain. This system of defence for the coast was established in France, where it succeeded very well. It appears to us to harmonize as well with the institutions and spirit of the country, as with the principles of economy which should direct and govern all the expenses of the Government. . . .

. . . If to our general system of permanent fortifications and naval establishments we connect a system of interior communications by land and water, adapted both to the defence and to the commercial interests of the country; if to these we add a well-constituted regular army, and perfect the organization of our militia, the Union will not only completely secure its territory, but preserve its national institutions from those violent shocks and revolutions which, in every age and in every nation, have been too often incident to a state of war. . . .

All which is most respectfully submitted.

Bernard, *Brigadier General.*

J. D. Elliott, *Captain U. S. Navy.*

Joseph G. Totten,
Major of Engineers, Brevet Lieut. Col.

14. John Quincy Adams: The Declining Interest in Military Affairs

THE WAY IN WHICH THE MILITARY PROBLEM APPEARED IN THE PEACE-ful times of James Monroe's successor is well illustrated by Adams' second annual message. The peacetime duties of the Army, even its "moral character," had become more significant than its readiness for war. The condition of the militia is still acknowledged to be "defective." Adams indicates something of the fate that had overtaken the large fort-building and naval-construction programs adopted after the War of 1812, and the very minor role that military considerations had assumed in American affairs.

From the reports herewith communicated of the Secretaries of War and of the Navy, with the subsidiary documents annexed to them, will be discovered the present condition and administration of our military establishment on the land and on the sea. The organization of the Army having undergone no change since its reduction to the present peace establishment in 1821, it remains only to observe that it is yet found adequate to all the purposes for which a permanent armed force in time of peace can be needed or useful. It may be proper to add that, from a difference of opinion between the late President of the United States and the Senate with regard to the construction of the act of Congress of 2d March, 1821, to reduce and fix the military peace establishment of the United States, it remains hitherto so far without execution that no colonel has been appointed to command one of the regiments of artillery. A supplementary or explanatory act of the Legislature appears to be the only expedient practicable for removing the difficulty of this appointment.

In a period of profound peace the conduct of the mere military establishment forms but a very inconsiderable portion of the duties devolving upon the administration of the Department of War. It will be seen by the returns from the subordinate departments of the Army that every branch of the service is marked with order, regularity, and discipline; that from the commanding general through all the gradations of superintendence the officers feel themselves to have been citizens before they were soldiers, and that the glory of a republican army must consist in the spirit of freedom, by which it is animated, and of patriotism, by which it is impelled. It may be confidently stated that the moral character of the Army is in a state of continual improvement, and that all the arrangements for the disposal of its parts have a constant reference to that end.

But to the War Department are attributed other duties, having, indeed, relation to a future possible condition of war, but being purely defensive, and in their tendency contributing rather to the security and permanency of peace—the erection of the fortifications provided for by Congress, and adapted to secure our

From *Messages of the Presidents*, II, pp. 925–929.

shores from hostile invasion; the distribution of the fund of public gratitude and justice to the pensioners of the Revolutionary war; the maintenance of our relations of peace and of protection with the Indian tribes, and the internal improvements and surveys for the location of roads and canals, which during the last three sessions of Congress have engaged so much of their attention, and may engross so large a share of their future benefactions to our country.

By the act of the 30th of April, 1824, suggested and approved by my predecessor, the sum of $30,000 was appropriated for the purpose of causing to be made the necessary surveys, plans, and estimates of the routes of such roads and canals as the President of the United States might deem of national importance in a commercial or military point of view, or necessary for the transportation of the public mail. The surveys, plans, and estimates for each, when completed, will be laid before Congress.

In execution of this act a board of engineers was immediately instituted, and have been since most assiduously and constantly occupied in carrying it into effect. The first object to which their labors were directed, by order of the late President, was the examination of the country between the tide waters of the Potomac, the Ohio, and Lake Erie, to ascertain the practicability of a communication between them, to designate the most suitable route for the same, and to form plans and estimates in detail of the expense of execution.

On the 3d of February, 1825, they made their first report, which was immediately communicated to Congress, and in which they declared that having maturely considered the circumstances observed by them personally, and carefully studied the results of such of the preliminary surveys as were then completed, they were decidedly of opinion that the communication was practicable.

At the last session of Congress, before the board of engineers were enabled to make up their second report containing a general plan and preparatory estimate for the work, the Committee of the House of Representatives upon Roads and Canals closed the session with a report expressing the hope that the plan and estimate of the board of engineers might at this time be prepared, and that the subject be referred to the early and favorable consideration of Congress at their present session. That expected report of the board of engineers is prepared, and will forthwith be laid before you.

Under the resolution of Congress authorizing the Secretary of War to have prepared a complete system of cavalry tactics, and a system of exercise and instruction of field artillery, for the use of the militia of the United States, to be reported to Congress at the present session, a board of distinguished officers of the Army and of the militia has been convened, whose report will be submitted to you with that of the Secretary of War. The occasion was thought favorable for consulting the same board, aided by the results of a correspondence with the governors of the several States and Territories and other citizens of intelligence and experience, upon the acknowledged defective condition of our militia system, and of the improvements of which it is susceptible. The report of the board upon this subject is also submitted for your consideration.

In the estimates of appropriations for the ensuing year upward of $5,000,000 will be submitted for the expenditures to be paid from the Department of War. Less than two-fifths of this will be applicable to the maintenance and support of the Army. A million and a half, in the form of pensions, goes as a scarcely adequate tribute to the services and sacrifices of a former age, and a more than equal sum invested in fortifications, or for the preparations of internal improvement, provides for the quiet, the comfort, and happier existence of the ages to come. The appropriations to indemnify those unfortunate remnants of another race unable alike to share in the enjoyments and to exist in the presence of civilization, though swelling in recent years to a magnitude burdensome to the Treasury, are generally not without their equivalents in profitable value, or serve to discharge the Union from engagements more burdensome than debt.

In like manner the estimate of appropriations for the Navy Department will present an aggregate sum of upward of $3,000,000.

About one-half of these, however, covers the current expenditures of the Navy in actual service, and one-half constitutes a fund of national property, the pledge of our future glory and defense. It was scarcely one short year after the close of the late war, and when the burden of its expenses and charges was weighing heaviest upon the country, that Congress, by the act of 29th April, 1816, appropriated $1,000,000 annually for eight years to the *gradual increase of the Navy*. At a subsequent period this annual appropriation was reduced to half a million for six years, of which the present year is the last. A yet more recent appropriation the last two years, for building ten sloops of war, has nearly restored the original appropriation of 1816 of a million for every year. The result is before us all. We have twelve line-of-battle ships, twenty frigates, and sloops of war in proportion, which, with a few months of preparation, may present a line of floating fortifications along the whole range of our coast ready to meet any invader who might attempt to set foot upon our shores. Combining with a system of fortifications upon the shores themselves, commenced about the same time under the auspices of my immediate predecessor, and hitherto systematically pursued, it has placed in our possession the most effective sinews of war and has left us at once an example and a lesson from which our own duties may be inferred. The gradual increase of the Navy was the principle of which the act of 29th April, 1816, was the first development. It was the introduction of a system to act upon the character and history of our country for an indefinite series of ages. It was a declaration of that Congress to their constituents and to posterity that it was the destiny and the duty of these confederated States to become in regular process of time and by no petty advances a great naval power. That which they proposed to accomplish in eight years is rather to be considered as the measure of their means than the limitation of their design. They looked forward for a term of years sufficient for the accomplishment of a definite portion of their purpose, and they left to their successors to fill up the canvas of which they had traced the large and prophetic outline. The ships of the line and frigates which they had in contemplation will be shortly completed. The time which they had allotted for the accomplishment of the work has more than elapsed. It remains for your consideration how their successors may contribute their portion of toil and of treasure for the benefit of the succeeding age in the gradual increase of our Navy. There is perhaps no part of the exercise of the constitutional powers of the Federal Government which has given more general satisfaction to the people of the Union than this. The system has not been thus vigorously introduced and hitherto sustained to be now departed from or abandoned. In continuing to provide for the gradual increase of the Navy it may not be necessary or expedient to add for the present any more to the number of our ships; but should you deem it advisable to continue the yearly appropriation of half a million to the same objects, it may be profitably expended in providing a supply of timber to be seasoned and other materials for future use in the construction of docks or in laying the foundations of a school for naval education, as to the wisdom of Congress either of those measures may appear to claim the preference.

Of the small portions of this Navy engaged in actual service during the peace, squadrons have continued to be maintained in the Pacific Ocean, in the West India seas, and in the Mediterranean, to which has been added a small armament to cruise on the eastern coast of South America. In all they have afforded protection to our commerce, have contributed to make our country advantageously known to foreign nations, have honorably employed multitudes of our seamen in the service of their country, and have inured numbers of youths of the rising generation to lives of manly hardihood and of nautical experience and skill. The piracies with which the West India seas were for several years infested have been totally suppressed, but in the Mediterranean they have increased in a manner afflictive to other nations, and but for the continued presence of our squadron would probably have been distressing to our own. The war which has unfortunately broken out between the Republic of Buenos Ayres and the Brazilian Government has given rise to very great irregularities among the naval officers of the latter, by whom principles in relation to blockades and to neutral navigation have been brought forward to which we can not subscribe and which our own commanders have found it necessary to resist. From the friendly disposition toward the United States constantly manifested by the Emperor of Brazil, and the very useful and friendly commercial intercourse between the United States and his dominions, we have reason to believe that the just reparation demanded for the injuries sustained by several of our citizens from some of his officers will not be withheld. Abstracts from the recent dispatches of the commanders of our several squadrons are communicated with the report of the Secretary of the Navy to Congress. . . .

15. Policy Under Andrew Jackson, the Second Military President

GENERAL ANDREW JACKSON WAS OUR SECOND MILITARY PRESIDENT. While hardly a professional officer in the modern sense, he had made his career largely in war. And when he was elected in 1828, he was the nation's outstanding soldier. The military policy that he announced in his first inaugural was conventional, however, and with its doubtless politic reliance on the militia seems to dispute much of Jackson's own practical experience. Nor was there much urgency so far as military matters were concerned in his subsequent messages. His Farewell Address in March 1837 spoke in stronger terms for building up the Navy. Yet it was still theoretic and pale by comparison with the farewell advice that Washington offered amid the pressing practical issues of the Napoleonic era.

The First Inaugural Address, March 3, 1829

. . . Considering standing armies as dangerous to free governments in time of peace, I shall not seek to enlarge our present

From *Messages of the Presidents*, III, pp. 1000–1001, 1089; IV, pp. 1525–1526.

establishment, nor disregard that salutary lesson of political experience which teaches that the military should be held subordinate to the civil power. The gradual increase of our Navy, whose
flag has displayed in distant climes our skill in navigation and
our fame in arms; the preservation of our forts, arsenals, and
dockyards, and the introduction of progressive improvements in
the discipline and science of both branches of our military service are so plainly prescribed by prudence that I should be excused
for omitting their mention sooner than for enlarging on their importance. But the bulwark of our defense is the national militia,
which in the present state of our intelligence and population must
render us invincible. As long as our Government is administered
for the good of the people, and is regulated by their will; as long
as it secures to us the rights of person and of property, liberty of
conscience and of the press, it will be worth defending; and so
long as it is worth defending a patriotic militia will cover it with
an impenetrable ægis. Partial injuries and occasional mortifica-
tions we may be subjected to, but a million of armed freemen,
possessed of the means of war, can never be conquered by a
foreign foe. To any just system, therefore, calculated to strengthen
this natural safeguard of the country I shall cheerfully lend all the
aid in my power. . . .

The Second Annual Message, December 6, 1830

. . . Your attention is again invited to the subjects connected
with that portion of the public interests intrusted to the War Department. Some of them were referred to in my former message,
and they are presented in detail in the report of the Secretary of
War herewith submitted. I refer you also to the report of that
officer for a knowledge of the state of the Army, fortifications,
arsenals, and Indian affairs, all of which it will be perceived have
been guarded with zealous attention and care. It is worthy of
your consideration whether the armaments necessary for the
fortifications on our maritime frontier which are now or shortly
will be completed should not be in readiness sooner than the

customary appropriations will enable the Department to provide them. This precaution seems to be due to the general system of fortification which has been sanctioned by Congress, and is recommended by that maxim of wisdom which tells us in peace to prepare for war.

I refer you to the report of the Secretary of the Navy for a highly satisfactory account of the manner in which the concerns of that Department have been conducted during the present year. Our position in relation to the most powerful nations of the earth, and the present condition of Europe, admonish us to cherish this arm of our national defense with peculiar care. Separated by wide seas from all those Governments whose power we might have reason to dread, we have nothing to apprehend from attempts at conquest. It is chiefly attacks upon our commerce and harassing inroads upon our coast against which we have to guard. A naval force adequate to the protection of our commerce, always afloat, with an accumulation of the means to give it a rapid extension in case of need, furnishes the power by which all such aggressions may be prevented or repelled. The attention of the Government has therefore been recently directed more to preserving the public vessels already built and providing materials to be placed in depot for future use than to increasing their number. With the aid of Congress, in a few years the Government will be prepared in case of emergency to put afloat a powerful navy of new ships almost as soon as old ones could be repaired.

The modifications in this part of the service suggested in my last annual message, which are noticed more in detail in the report of the Secretary of the Navy, are again recommended to your serious attention. . . .

The Farewell Address, March 4, 1837

. . . While I am thus endeavoring to press upon your attention the principles which I deem of vital importance in the domestic concerns of the country, I ought not to pass over without notice the important considerations which should govern your policy toward foreign powers. It is unquestionably our true interest to cultivate the most friendly understanding with every nation and to avoid by every honorable means the calamities of war, and we shall best attain this object by frankness and sincerity in our foreign intercourse, by the prompt and faithful execution of treaties, and by justice and impartiality in our conduct to all. But no nation, however desirous of peace, can hope to escape occasional collisions with other powers, and the soundest dictates of policy require that we should place ourselves in a condition to assert our rights if a resort to force should ever become necessary. Our local situation, our long line of seacoast, indented by numerous bays, with deep rivers opening into the interior, as well as our extended and still increasing commerce, point to the Navy as our natural means of defense. It will in the end be found to be the cheapest and most effectual, and now is the time, in a season of peace and with an overflowing revenue, that we can year after year add to its strength without increasing the burdens of the people. It is your true policy, for your Navy will not only protect your rich and flourishing commerce in distant seas, but will enable you to reach and annoy the enemy and will give to defense its greatest efficiency by meeting danger at a distance from home. It is impossible by any line of fortifications to guard every point from attack against a hostile force advancing from the ocean and selecting its object, but they are indispensable to protect cities from bombardment, dockyards and naval arsenals from destruction, to give shelter to merchant vessels in time of war and to single ships or weaker squadrons when pressed by superior force. Fortifications of this description can not be too soon completed and armed and placed in a condition of the most perfect preparation. The abundant means we now possess can not be applied in any manner more useful to the country, and when this is done and our naval force sufficiently strengthened and our militia armed we need not fear that any nation will wantonly insult us or needlessly provoke hostilities. We shall more certainly preserve peace when it is well understood that we are prepared for war.

In presenting to you, my fellow-citizens, these parting counsels, I have brought before you the leading principles upon which I endeavored to administer the Government in the high office with which you twice honored me. Knowing that the path of freedom is continually beset by enemies who often assume the disguise of friends, I have devoted the last hours of my public life to warn you of the dangers. The progress of the United States under our free and happy institutions has surpassed the most sanguine hopes of the founders of the Republic. Our growth has been rapid beyond all former example in numbers, in wealth, in knowledge, and all the useful arts which contribute to the comforts and convenience of man, and from the earliest ages of history to the present day there never have been thirteen millions of people associated in one political body who enjoyed so much freedom and happiness as the people of these United States. You have no longer any cause to fear danger from abroad; your strength and power are well known throughout the civilized world, as well as the high and gallant bearing of your sons. . . .

16. John Rodgers: Naval Policy at the End of the Age of Sail

JOHN RODGERS WAS THE FOUNDER OF THE FAMOUS NAVAL FAMILY whose members have served with distinction in all our wars, from those with the Barbary corsairs onward. In 1836, nearing the end of his life, he was serving as president of the Board of Navy Commissioners, when the Secretary of the Navy, Mahlon Dickerson, called upon him to submit a broad naval program adequate to provide for the "security and welfare of the Union." The times were still untroubled by any threats of war, but this was the period when steam was just beginning to replace sail power—an awkward age of technological transition, the implications of which could not be clearly foreseen. Rodgers' solution was to recommend a massive fleet of sailing men-of-war, boldly scaled to the maximum number that could be manned in war and backed by a smaller number of steamers for coastal work. His reasoning and estimates are set forth in this report, which again was accepted only in small part by Congress.

NAVY COMMISSIONERS' OFFICE, *March* 2, 1836.

SIR: The board of navy commissioners have the honor to acknowledge the receipt of your letter of the 26th ultimo, requesting a report on the probable amount that would be necessary to supply the United States with the ordnance, arms, and munitions of war (so far as may be wanted for the purposes of the navy) which a proper regard to self-defence would require to be always on hand; and on the probable amount that would be necessary to place the naval defences of the United States (including the increase of the navy, navy yards, dock yards, and steam or floating batteries) upon the footing of strength and respectability which is due to the security and welfare of the Union. . . .

. . . The second object of inquiry, as to "the probable amount that would be necessary to place the naval defences of the United States (including the increase of the navy, navy yards, dock yards, and steam or floating batteries) upon the footing of strength and respectability which is due to the security and welfare of the Union," embraces a wide range, requires an examination of several subjects of great importance, and the expression of opinions upon which differences of opinion may and probably will exist. Before any estimate can be formed of the probable *amount* that would be necessary for the purposes proposed, an examination must be had, and an opinion formed of the *nature* and *extent* of the naval force which is "necessary to place the naval defences of the United States upon the footing of strength and respectability which is due to the security and welfare of the Union," and the time within which it ought to be or might be advantageously prepared.

Taking into view the geographical position of the United States with reference to other nations with whom we are most likely to be brought into future collision; the great extent of our maritime frontier, and the extreme importance of securing the communications of the whole valley of the Mississippi through the Gulf of Mexico, and the intercourse between all parts of the coast; the

From *American State Papers, Military Affairs*, VI, pp. 400–403.

efficient protection of our widely-extended and extremely valuable commerce under all circumstances; and the great naval and fiscal resources of the country, the board consider the proper limit for the *extent* of the naval force to be that which can be properly manned when the country may be involved in a maritime war.

In estimating this extent, it is assumed that about ninety thousand seamen are employed in the foreign and coasting trade and fisheries. As the navigation has been generally increasing, there is little reason to apprehend any immediate diminution during peace. In any war which would require the employment of all our naval force, it is believed that such interruptions would occur to our commerce as would enable the navy to obtain without difficulty at least thirty thousand seamen and ordinary seamen; and if it should continue long, it is probable that a larger number might be engaged. The number of 30,000, with the landsmen who may be safely combined with them, will therefore be assumed as the number for which vessels ought to be prepared for the commencement of a state of hostilities.

With respect to the *nature* of the force which it would be most advantageous to prepare, there will undoubtedly be differences of opinion. The materials for the larger vessels, as ships-of-the-line and frigates, would be obtained with great difficulty, under circumstances which should interfere with our coasting trade, whilst sloops-of-war and smaller vessels could be built with greater comparative facility under such circumstances.

The preparation of a considerable number of steam vessels, ready to defend our great estuaries, to aid the operations of our other naval force, and in the concentration of movements of the military force, as circumstances might require, is believed to demand serious and early attention.

Having due regard to these and other considerations, the board propose that the force to be prepared, ready for use when circumstances may require it, shall consist of 15 ships-of-the-line, 25 frigates, 25 sloops-of-war, 25 steamers, and 25 smaller vessels; and that the frames and other timber, the copper, ordnance, tanks, and chain cables, shall also be prepared for 10 ships-of-the-line and 10 frigates.

The force proposed to be prepared, ready for use, will employ and can be manned by the 30,000 seamen and others which have been considered available in a state of war. The materials for the ten ships-of-the-line and ten frigates will constitute a necessary reserve for increasing the number of those vessels, should they be required, or for supplying losses from decay or casualties.

To estimate the amount necessary to prepare this force, it is proposed to ascertain the whole probable cost, including ordnance, by the average cost of similar vessels already built, (steam vessels excepted,) and of materials already procured, and then to deduct the value of the present force, and all other present available means. . . .

. . . The next subject for consideration is the nature and extent of force proper to be kept employed in a time of peace for the protection of our commercial interests, and to prepare the officers and others for the efficient management of the force proposed for a state of war.

Our commerce is spread over every ocean; our tonnage is second only to that of Great Britain; and the value of articles embarked is believed by many to be fully equal to those transported by the ships of that nation. In the safety and prosperity of this commerce all the other interests of the United States are deeply interested. It is liable to be disturbed and injured in various modes, unless the power of the country, exerted through its naval force, is ready to protect it. It is therefore proposed that small squadrons should be employed upon different stations, subject at all times, however, to such modifications as circumstances may require.

Of these squadrons, one might be employed in the *Mediterranean,* and attend to our interests on the west coasts of Spain and Portugal, and southward to the western coast of Morocco and Madeira.

One in the *Indian ocean:* to visit, successively, the most important commercial points east of the Cape of Good Hope; to

China; then to cross the Pacific; visit the northern whaling stations and islands; cruise some time upon the west coast of America; and return by way of Cape Horn, the coast of Brazil and the windward West India islands.

One in the *Pacific ocean:* to attend to our interests upon the west coast of America; keeping one or more vessels at or near the Sandwich and other islands which are frequented by our whale ships and other vessels; and, in succession, cross the Pacific, visiting the islands and southern whaling stations of China and other commercial places; and return, by the way of the Cape of Good Hope, to the United States.

A squadron upon the *coast of Brazil,* or east coast of South America, might be charged with attention to our interests on the whole of that coast, and upon the north coast, so far as to include the Oronoco. If a ship-of-the-line should be employed on this station, it might be occasionally sent round to the Pacific.

A squadron in the *West Indies and Gulf of Mexico* will be necessary for, and may be charged with attention to, the protection of our commerce amongst the West India islands and along the coast of South America, from the Oronoco round to the Gulf of Mexico.

A small *coast squadron* upon our Atlantic coast might be very advantageously employed in making our officers familiarly and thoroughly acquainted with all our ports and harbors, which would be very useful in a state of war. The vessels would also be ready for any unexpected service, either to transport information or orders, to reinforce other squadrons, or to visit our eastern fisheries. Besides this cruising force, it is recommended that a ship-of-the-line be kept in a state of readiness for service, *men excepted* at Boston, New York, and Norfolk, and used as receiving ships for the recruits as they are collected. This would give the means of furnishing a considerable increase of force, with a very small addition to the current expense. . . .

Considering this force with reference to its power of giving experience to the officers and qualifying them for the management of the force proposed for war, it appears that, for the force proposed to be *actually employed at sea* in peace and in war, the peace force will require and employ about two-thirds the number of commanders of squadrons, about one-third the captains, and forty one-hundredths of the commanders and lieutenants and masters which the proposed war, force would demand, and midshipmen sufficient to supply the additional number of these last classes which a change to a state of war would require.

Supposing the foregoing force to be that which is to be kept in commission, the next question is, what force will be necessary to keep *afloat* to provide the necessary reliefs? The board believe that this force should be the *least* which will answer the object proposed, as every vessel when launched is exposed to a decay which is much more rapid than when left under the cover of a tight ship-house.

We have already six ships-of-the-line afloat, which will be fully equal to our present wants when they are repaired. A reserve of three frigates may be required, but only to be launched when the necessity for it shall arise; for the sloops-of-war and smaller vessels it will probably be sufficient to merely keep up the cruising force as proposed, except some extraordinary demand should arise. The force of steam vessels proposed, when distributed at Boston, New York, Norfolk, and Pensacola, would probably meet all the demands of a state of peace, and furnish useful schools for officers, to prepare them for the proper management of others when they are required. The force to be kept afloat, then, will be assumed at six ships-of-the-line, eleven frigates, fifteen sloops-of-war, four steamers, and ten smaller vessels. The annual amount necessary to keep this force in a state of repair, and to supply the wear and tear of stores of cruising vessels, is estimated at $950,000. . . .

Before concluding this report, the board would respectfully offer some remarks upon the form of the appropriations, and suggest some attention to existing acts of Congress.

By the separate acts for the gradual increase of the navy, for the gradual improvement of the navy, for building and rebuilding different vessels, altogether seven in number, each appropriation is rendered separate and distinct, although the general object is the same, and requires the use of the same kinds of materials. It is necessary, in conformity to the law of the 3d of March, 1809, that the vouchers, receipts, expenditures and accounts of each should be kept separately; and, in strictness, no article purchased for one can be applied to the use of another, however desirable or economical such use may be.

It is suggested, therefore, for consideration, whether it might not be very advantageous for Congress to determine, by some general act or resolution, the number and classes of vessels which the President might be authorized to have built, or for which materials might be procured; and then appropriate specially the amounts which might be devoted to those objects, and for keeping the force afloat in repair, under the general head of "For building and repairing vessels, and for purchase of materials and stores."

The adoption of some such plan, and removing the special restrictions which now exist, and requiring, as at present, detailed estimates for the current repairs, and reports of proceedings in building vessels, and for purchase of materials, would, it is believed, greatly simplify and diminish the number of accounts at the Treasury Department and in all the navy yards, without infringing in any degree the principle of special appropriations; would furnish to Congress all the information they now receive, and would enable us at all times to use those materials which are best prepared and most appropriate for the different objects for which they might be wanted. . . .

JOHN RODGERS.

Hon. M. Dickerson, *Secretary of the Navy.*

17. Henry Wager Halleck: The Scholar in Uniform

Halleck was raised in Oneida County, New York. Graduating from the United States Military Academy in 1839, he was an exemplar of the new type of West Point–trained professional soldier, then filling the junior ranks of the officer corps—a type that was to supply most of the high command on both sides in the Civil War. Thoughtful and scholarly, he was probably the best educated, in an academic sense, among them; he won the sobriquet of "Old Brains" from his less studious colleagues. He was to serve Lincoln as commanding general and chief of staff—titles then denoting a good deal less than at present—in the Civil War. The bent of his mind is indicated by the fact that on retirement he devoted himself to the study of international law and jurisprudence.

As a young lieutenant of engineers, Halleck was sent abroad to study the European military systems and military literature. On his return, he prepared a course of lectures, *Elements of Military Art and Science*, intended primarily for militia officers, which was published in 1846, just as the Mexican War was beginning. The discussion was largely theoretical and formal, dealing in an abstract way with the military technology of the time; but because it was to remain the leading American text on the subject down to the Civil War era, it cannot be ignored in any documentation of military thinking. The extracts given below (including one of his numerous learned footnotes) have been selected to indicate the tenor of Halleck's mind and approach, rather than the substance of his course of instruction.

. . . All modern ethical writers regard *unjust* war as not only immoral, but as one of the greatest of crimes—murder on a large scale. Such are all wars of mere ambition, engaged in for the purpose of extending regal power or national sovereignty; wars of plunder, carried on from mercenary motives; wars of propagandism, undertaken for the unrighteous end of compelling men to adopt certain religious or political opinions, whether from the alleged motives of "introducing a more orthodox religion," or of "extending the area of freedom." Such wars are held in just abhorrence by all moral and religious people: and this is believed to be the settled conviction of the great mass of our own citizens.

But in addition to that respectable denomination of Christians who deny our right to use arms under any circumstances, there are many religious enthusiasts in other communions who, from causes already noticed, have adopted the same theory, and hold *all* wars, even those in self-defence, as unlawful and immoral. This opinion has been, within the last few years, pressed on the public with great zeal and eloquence, and many able pens have

From H. Wager Halleck, *Elements of Military Art and Science* (New York: D. Appleton & Company, 1846), pp. 8–9, 34–37, 139–144.

been enlisted in its cause. One of the most popular, and by some regarded one of the most able writers on moral science, has adopted this view as the only one consonant with the principles of Christian morality.

It has been deemed proper, in commencing a course of lectures on war, to make a few introductory remarks respecting this question of its justifiableness. We know of no better way of doing this than to give on the one side the objections to war as laid down in Dr. Wayland's[1] Moral Philosophy, and on the other side the arguments by which other ethical writers have justified a resort to war. We do not select Dr. Wayland's work for the purpose of criticizing so distinguished an author; but because he is almost the only writer on ethics who advocates these views, and because the main arguments against war are here given in brief space, and in more moderate and temperate language than that used by most of his followers. I shall give his arguments in his own language.

"I. All wars are contrary to the revealed will of God."

It is said in reply, that if the Christian religion condemns all wars, no matter how just the cause, or how necessary for self-defence, we must expect to find in the Bible some direct prohibition of war, or at least a prohibition fairly implied in other direct commandments. But the Bible nowhere prohibits war: in the Old Testament we find war and even conquest positively commanded, and although war was raging in the world in the time of Christ and his apostles, still they said not a word of its unlawfulness and immorality. Moreover, the fathers of the church amply acknowledge the right of war, and directly assert, that when war is justly declared, the Christian may engage in it either by stratagem or open force. If it be of that highly wicked and immoral character which some have recently attributed to it, most assuredly it would be condemned in the Bible in terms the most positive and unequivocal.

But it has been said that the use of the sword is either directly or typically forbidden to the Christian, by such passages as "Thou

[1] Francis Wayland, President of Brown University (1827–1845) and Professor of Moral Philosophy there [Ed.].

shalt not kill," (Deut. v. 17,) "I say unto you, that ye resist evil:
but whosoever shall smite thee on thy right cheek, turn to him
the other also," (Matt. v. 39,) &c. If these passages are to be
taken as literal commands, as fanatics and religious enthusiasts
would have us believe, not only is war unlawful, but also all our
penal statutes, the magistracy, and all the institutions of the state
for the defence of individual rights, the protection of the inno-
cent, and the punishment of the guilty. But if taken in conjunction with the whole Bible, we must infer that they are hyperboli-
cal expressions. . . .

. . . It has been said by some that the duties of patriotism are
less binding upon us than upon our ancestors; that, whatever may
have been the practice in years that are past, the present generation can in no manner bear arms in their country's cause, such a
course being not only *dishonorable,* but in the eye of the Christian, *wicked,* and even *infamous!* It is believed, however, that
such are not the general opinions and sentiments of the religious
people of this country. Our forefathers lighted the fires of Religion and Patriotism at the same altar; it is believed that their
descendants have not allowed either to be extinguished, but that
both still burn, and will continue to burn, with a purer and
brighter flame. Our forefathers were not the less mindful of their
duty to their God, because they also faithfully served their country. If we are called upon to excel them in works of charity, of
benevolence, and of Christian virtue, let it not be said of us that
we have forgotten the virtue of patriotism . . . [2]

[2] For further discussion of this subject the reader is referred to Lieber's
Political Ethics, Part II., book vii. chap. 3; Paley's Moral and Political
Philosophy; Legare's Report of June 13, 1838, in the House of Representa-
tives; Mackintosh's History of the Revolution of 1688, chap. x.; Bynkershock;
Vatel; Puffendorf; Clausewitz; and most other writers on international law
and the laws of war.

Dr. Wayland's view of the question is advocated with much zeal by Dy-
mond in his Inquiry into the Accordancy of War with the Principles of
Christianity; Jay's Peace and War; Judd's Sermon on Peace and War; Pea-
body's Address, &c.; Coue's Tract on What is the Use of the Navy? Sumner's
True Grandeur of Nations.

Strategy.

WAR has been defined, "A contest between nations and states carried on by force." But this definition is by some considered defective, inasmuch as it would exclude all civil wars.

When war is commenced by attacking a nation in peace, it is called *offensive,* and when undertaken to repel invasion, or the attacks of an enemy, it is called *defensive.* A war may be essentially defensive even where we begin it, if intended to prevent an attack or invasion which is under preparation. Besides this general division of war, military writers have made numerous others, such as—

Wars of intervention, in which one state interferes in favor of another. This intervention may either have respect to the *internal* or to the *external* affairs of a nation. . . . Most liberal publicists consider intervention in the internal affairs of nations as indefensible; but the principle is supported by the advocates of the old monarchies of Europe.

Wars of insurrection to gain or to regain liberty; as was the case with the Americans in 1776, and the modern Greeks in 1821.

Wars of independence from foreign dictation and control, as the wars of Poland against Russia, of the Netherlands against Spain, of France against the several coalitions of the allied powers, of the Spanish Peninsula against France, and of China and India against England. . . .

Wars of opinion, like those which the Vendeans have sustained in support of the Bourbons, and those France has sustained against the allies, as also those of propagandism, waged against the smaller European states by the republican hordes of the French Revolution. To this class also belong—

Religious wars, like those of Islamism, of the crusades, and of the Reformation.

Wars of conquest, like those of the Romans in Gaul, of the English in India, of the French in Egypt and Africa, and of the Russians in Circassia.

National wars, in which the great body of the people of a state engage, like those of the Swiss against Austria and the Duke of Burgundy, of the Catalans in 1712, of the Americans against England, of the Dutch against Phillip II., and of the Poles and Circassians against Russia.

Civil wars, where one portion of the state fights against the other, as the war of the Roses in England, of the league in France, of the Guelphs and Ghibelines in Italy, and of the factions in Mexico and South America.

It is not the present intention to enter into any discussion of these different kinds of war, but rather to consider the general subject, and to discuss such general principles and rules as may be applicable to all wars.

War in its most extensive sense may be regarded both as a *science* and an *art.* It is a science so far as it investigates general principles and institutes an analysis of military operations; and an art when considered with reference to the practical rules for conducting campaigns, sieges, battles, &c. So is engineering a science so far as it investigates the general principles of fortification, and also artillery, in analyzing the principles of gunnery; but both are arts when considered with reference to the practical rules for the construction, attack, and defence of forts, or for the use of cannon.

This distinction has not always been observed by writers on this subject, and some have asserted that strategy is the *science,* and tactics the *art* of war. This is evidently mistaking the general distinction between science, which investigates principles, and art, which forms practical rules.

In popular language, however, it is usual to speak of *the military art* when we refer to the general subject of war, and of *the military sciences* when we wish to call attention more particularly to the scientific principles upon which the art is founded. We shall here consider the military art in this general sense, as including the entire subject of war.

As thus defined, the military art may be divided into four distinct branches, viz.: 1st. *Strategy;* 2d. Fortification, or *Engineering;* 3d. *Logistics;* 4th. *Tactics.* Several general treatises on this art add another branch, called *The Polity of War,* or the relations of war with the affairs of state. . . .

Military Polity.

. . . From these data we see that the great European powers at the present day maintain, in time of peace, military establishments equal to about one-hundredth part of their entire population.

The geographical position of a country also greatly influences the degree and character of its military preparation. It may be bordered on one or more sides by mountains and other obstacles calculated to diminish the probability of invasion; or the whole frontier may be wide open to an attack: the interior may be of such a nature as to furnish security to its own army, and yet be fatal to the enemy should he occupy it; or it may furnish him advantages far superior to his own country. It may be an island in the sea, and consequently exposed only to maritime descents— events of rare occurrence in modern times.

Again, a nation may be placed between others who are interested in its security, their mutual jealousy preventing the molestation of the weaker neighbor. On the other hand, its political institutions may be such as to compel the others to unite in attacking it in order to secure themselves. The republics of Switzerland could remain unmolested in the midst of powerful monarchies; but revolutionary France brought upon herself the armies of all Europe. . . .

. . . For any nation to postpone the making of military preparations till such time as they are actually required in defence, is to waste the public money, and endanger the public safety. The closing of an avenue of approach, the security of a single road or river, or even the strategic movement of a small body of troops, often effects, in the beginning, what afterwards cannot be accomplished by large fortifications, and the most formidable armies. Had a small army in 1812, with a well-fortified dépôt on Lake Champlain, penetrated into Canada, and cut off all reinforcements and supplies by way of Quebec, that country would inevitably have fallen into our possession. In the winter of 1806-7, Napoleon crossed the Vistula, and advanced even to the walls of Königsberg, with the Austrians in his rear, and the whole power of Russia before him. If Austria had pushed forward one hundred thousand men from Bohemia, on the Oder, she would, in all probability, says the best of military judges, Jomini, have struck a fatal blow to the operations of Napoleon, and his army must have been exceedingly fortunate even to regain the Rhine. But Austria preferred remaining neutral till she could increase her army to four hundred thousand men. She then took the offensive, and was beaten; whereas, with one hundred thousand men brought into action at the favorable moment, she might, most probably, have decided the fate of Europe.

"Defensive war," says Napoleon, "does not preclude attack, any more than offensive war is exclusive of defence," for frequently the best way to counteract the enemy's operations, and prevent his conquests, is, at the very outset of the war, to invade and cripple him. But this can never be attempted with raw troops, ill supplied with the munitions of war, and unsupported by fortifications. Such invasions must necessarily fail. Experience in the wars of the French revolution has demonstrated this; and even our own short history is not without its proof. In 1812, the conquest of Canada was determined on some time before the declaration of war; an undisciplined army, without preparation or apparent plan, was actually put in motion, eighteen days previous to this declaration, for the Canadian peninsula. With a disciplined army of the same numbers, with an efficient and skilful leader, directed against the vital point of the British possessions at a time when the whole military force of the provinces did not exceed three thousand men, how different had been the result!

While, therefore, the permanent defences of a nation must be subordinate to its resources, position, and character, they can in no case be dispensed with. No matter how extensive or important the temporary means that may be developed as necessity requires, there must be some force kept in a constant state of efficiency, in order to impart life and stability to the system. The one can never properly replace the other; for while the former constitutes the basis, the latter must form the main body of the military edifice, which, by its strength and durability, will offer shelter and protection to the nation; or, if the architecture and materials be defective, crush and destroy it in its fall.

The permanent means of military defence employed by modern nations, are—

1st. An army; 2d. A navy; 3d. Fortifications.

The first two of these could hardly be called permanent, if we were to regard their *personnel;* but looking upon them as institutions or organizations, they present all the characteristics of durability. They are sometimes subjected to very great and radical changes; by the hot-house nursing of designing ambition or rash legislation, they may become overgrown and dangerous, or the storms of popular delusion may overthrow and apparently sweep them away. But they will immediately spring up again in some form or other, so deeply are they rooted in the organization of political institutions.

Its army and navy should always be kept within the limits of a nation's wants; but pity for the country which reduces them in number or support so as to degrade their character or endanger their organization. "A government," says one of the best historians of the age, "which neglects its army, under whatever pretext, is a government culpable in the eyes of posterity, for it is preparing humiliations for its flag and its country, instead of laying the foundation for its glory."

One of our own distinguished cabinet ministers remarks, that the history of our relations with the Indian tribes from the beginning to the present hour, is one continued proof of the necessity of maintaining an efficient military force in time of peace, and that the treatment we received for a long series of years from European powers, was a most humiliating illustration of the folly of attempting to dispense with these means of defence.

"Twice," says he, "we were compelled to maintain, by open war, our quarrel with the principal aggressors. After many years of forbearance and negotiation, our claims in other cases were at length amicably settled; but in one of the most noted of these cases, it was not without much delay and imminent hazard of war that the execution of the treaty was finally enforced. No one acquainted with these portions of our history, can hesitate to ascribe much of the wantonness and duration of the wrongs we endured, to a knowledge on the part of our assailants of the scantiness and inefficiency of our military and naval force.

"If," said Mr. Calhoun, "disregarding the sound dictates of reason and experience, we, in peace, neglect our military establishment, we must, with a powerful and skilful enemy, be exposed to the most distressing calamities."

These remarks were made in opposition to the reduction of our military establishment, in 1821, below the standard of thirteen thousand. Nevertheless, the force was reduced to about six or seven thousand; and we were soon made to feel the consequences. It is stated, in a report of high authority, that if there had been two regiments available near St. Louis, in 1832, the war with Black Hawk would have been easily avoided; and that it cannot be doubted that the scenes of devastation and savage warfare which overspread the Floridas for nearly seven years would also have been avoided, and some thirty millions have been saved the country, if two regiments had been available at the beginning of that conflict.[3]

We must, in this country, if we heed either the dictates of reason or experience, maintain in time of peace a skeleton military and naval force, capable of being greatly expanded, in the event of danger, by the addition of new troops. . . .

[3] We may now add to these remarks, that if our government had occupied the country between the Nueces and the Rio Grande with a well-organized army of twelve thousand men, war with Mexico might have been avoided; but to push forward upon Matamoras a small force of only two thousand, in the very face of a large Mexican army was holding out to them the strongest inducements to attack us. The temporary economy of a few thousands in reducing our military establishment to a mere handful of men, again results in a necessary expenditure of many millions of dollars and a large sacrifice of human life.

18. James C. Dobbin: The Naval Revival Under Franklin Pierce

BY 1853 THE REVOLUTIONARY IMPLICATIONS OF STEAM POWER WERE becoming clear. The invention of the screw propeller, supplanting the short-radius and vulnerable paddle wheels of John Rodgers' day, had made steam "unquestionably the great agent to be used on the ocean, as well for purposes of war as of commerce." Again, there was no threat of foreign war, but the Pierce administration, for numerous and contradictory reasons, mainly of domestic politics, was to use this fact to launch a new program of naval revival. The Secretary of the Navy, James C. Dobbin, proposed in his annual report for 1853 the construction of six propeller sloops-of-war. Dobbin went back to all the old and abstract arguments for naval strength in general; the nation was still a long way from the later Mahanite concepts of sea power, and Dobbin argued only for a Navy "at least large enough to command our own seas and coast." This time, however, the program, as well as others that followed, was accepted by Congress, in part because the Southerners believed the ships might facilitate the acquisition of new slave states in the Caribbean. In fact they were to provide the Union Navy in 1861 with an effective core for the great fleet that was to blockade and crush the Confederacy.

The result of my investigation of this subject is a decided conviction that the maintenance of our proper and elevated rank among the great powers of the world; the just protection of our wide-spread and growing commerce; the defence of our thousands of miles of coast along the Atlantic and Pacific oceans, the lakes, and the Gulf of Mexico; the recent marked improvements in the art of naval architecture adopted by other nations—all unite in demonstrating the policy, the necessity, of an increase of the navy. It is true, indeed, our policy is peace. No lust of dominion, no spirit of aggression, marks out *our* course. Our national mission is, by the moral force of example, to illustrate the blessings of liberty and peace, civilization and religion. But the reasonable inquiry is, can peace be best maintained by the exhibition of

From *Annual Report of the Secretary of the Navy, 1853*, 33d Congress, Session 1, House Executive Documents, pp. 307–310.

comparative weakness, or by a display of strength and a preparation which, while it invites not a conflict, at least defies assault? What are the objects of a navy—what the considerations to guide us to a correct conclusion as to the size and character of the naval force of a republic situated, geographically and politically, as the United States? Do not wisdom and prudence admonish the careful statesman in his calculations for the future, while he takes thought of the commerce, the rights, the coast to be protected by this right arm of defence, at the same time not to be unmindful of the comparative force, efficiency, and character of the navies of the great powers with whom, with all our cherished love of peace, we may have to contend? Is it the suggestion of a sound discretion to rely exclusively upon the sudden preparation of a patriotic people when the perilous emergency starts up before them, and shut our eyes with quiet composure to our real condition? Or is it wiser to make that preparation which a considerate glance at the true state of facts shall persuade us is essential to our security?

I believe that it is only necessary to present the case as it truly exists to the attention of those who have the power to produce the desired results.

The American navy consists of about seventy vessels, embracing all from the ships-of-the-line to the smallest brig, schooner, and store-ship. Of these many ships-of-the-line, frigates, steamers, and sloops-of-war are not only unfit for service, but, I am advised by the Bureau of Construction, Equipment, and Repair, are not worth repairing. There are not now in the Navy forty vessels which could be brought into service in ninety days, if needed. There is no steamer in the Pacific or African squadron, but one of two guns in the Brazil squadron, and we have no steamer of more than ten guns. The law only authorizes the enlistment of 7,500 men, which, with an allowance of a proper complement for each vessel, would not man a fleet of fifty vessels, with a fair proportion of large ships. On referring to authentic papers, it will be found that, in *point of size* at least, our navy is much less than one-fifth of that of several of the greatest powers of Europe; and, whatever may be its relative superiority and efficiency, is not larger than that of certain other powers of Europe which are not of the first rank in the scale of nations.

And however much we may desire to cultivate terms of amity, these are the powers with whom we are most likely to contend in future conflicts, and the great deep is the theatre on which future contests may be decided. I am not unmindful of the mighty development of strength and force which the patriotism, the energy, the nautical skill, and mercantile marine, of a great nation would soon rally to our assistance. Other nations, in addition to their large navies, have *their* immense mercantile marine, and *their* mail steamships also. But, again, what have we to defend and protect? We have an Atlantic coast of much more than two thousand miles, stretching from the Rio Grande to the St. Croix, studded with magnificent cities and thriving towns. We now have a Pacific coast extending for many hundred miles, from the confines of Mexico to the far northwest; an inviting country, rapidly populating, totally unfortified, separated by mountains and deserts from the military power of the government. A new empire has, as by magic, sprung into existence. San Francisco promises, at no distant day, to become another New York, and our prosperous trade in the Pacific, amid the wonders of commerce, to bear the same relation to China and Japan which that of the Atlantic coast bears to the continent of Europe and Great Britain. We have over four millions of tonnage; American vessels, freighted with the rich fruits of American industry, penetrating every sea; and thousands of our countrymen, whom busy enterprise has borne to distant lands, or whom misfortune has wrecked on some inhospitable shore, all look to their country's flag to protect them. Is our present navy sufficient for all these great purposes of defence and protection? I am very far from intimating an opinion that we should steadily maintain a naval force as large as that of some of the powers mentioned. They have large colonial settlements on islands and continents remote from their seat of government. Their jealousies, their proximity to each other, their peculiar form of government, all combine to require for their purposes a far larger naval force than we need. But while they are annually enlarging theirs, shall we allow the disparity annually to become greater? The following warning admonition on this point by Washington, in his eighth annual message, enforces this view: "To an active external commerce, the protection of a naval force is indispensable. This is manifest with regard to wars in which a State itself is a party. But, besides this, it is in our own experience that the most sincere neutrality is not a sufficient guard against the depredations of nations at war. *To secure respect to a neutral flag requires a naval force, organized and ready to vindicate it from insult and aggression.* This may prevent even the necessity of going to war, by discouraging belligerent powers from committing such violations of the rights of the neutral party as may first or last leave no other option. These considerations invite the United States to look to means, and to set about the gradual increase of a navy. Will it not, then, be advisable to begin without delay to provide and lay up the materials for the building and equipping of ships-of-war, and to proceed in the work by degrees, in proportion as our resources shall render it practicable without inconvenience, so that a future war of Europe may not find our commerce in the same unfortunate state in which it was found by the present?" I take it to be a fair proposition that our navy should, *at least, be large enough to command our own seas and coast.* Otherwise, it would seem to be not only a useless appendage, but fall an easy prey to the enemy and add to his strength. And, in view of this point, it may be well to remember the positions overlooking our home commerce, the Bermudas and West Indies, well fortified and held by other nations. It may be said that we have strong fortifications, and that they can be relied upon for defence. But our fortifications, with their conceded importance, without a navy, have well been compared to a shield without a sword. Perhaps it may be alleged that our navy was comparatively small in the war of 1812, when our gallant officers achieved brilliant victories, won for themselves imperishable renown, and broke the charm of the enemy's naval invincibility. Those were, indeed, great achievements, and we still have proud spirits in the navy whom opportunity would call forth, and who would again accomplish all that valor and patriotism could accomplish. But without enlarging upon the circumstances which helped to occasion success then, or dwelling upon the disasters that then befel our commerce, when we call to mind the formidable, growing, and, in numbers at least, the overwhelming strength of the navies of the many great nations with whom we claim equal rank, may it not be well to consider that it may even be possible to tax too severely the valor and skill of our small navy, however gallant? As, however, we have enjoyed a season of profound peace, with the exception of the war with a nation without a navy, it is, perhaps, not to be regretted that we have deferred enlarging ours thus long, as we can now advantageously avail ourselves of the vast improvements suggested by the tests of experience and the inventive genius of the architects of our own and other countries.

Steam is unquestionably the great agent to be used on the ocean, as well for purposes of war as of commerce. The improved system of screw-propellers, instead of side-wheels, is one of the grand desiderata to render the use of steam effective in naval warfare—the one being exposed to the shot of the enemy, the other submerged and comparatively secure. When the bayonet was added to the musket, the invention was applauded, for placing in the hands of the soldier, at one time, two engines of *destruction;* and the introduction of the screw-propeller has been similarly appreciated, as combining, without confusion, two elements of *progress*—the sail and the steam-engine. Side-wheel steamers are much impaired in their capacity for sailing, and consume too much coal for distant cruises. Those now on hand can be made to answer well for short cruises and as despatch vessels. The screw-propeller, being upon a principle not so much interfering with the sailing capacity, with the improved models of the present day, can be so constructed as to sail as well as the best clipper-ships, and reserve the use of steam for emergencies when greatest speed is required, or when, in a calm, a desirable position can be the more promptly and surely taken. The great necessary expense incident to the expedition to Japan could have been materially, indeed one-half curtailed, had it been in the power of the department to have supplied the squadron with screw-propellers instead of the side-wheel steamers, now costing so much from the consumption of coal.

I recommend, therefore, that the department be authorized to have constructed at least six first-class steam-frigate propellers. The opinion is entertained that that number may be built in our several yards in addition to the work now going on, and the repairs usually needed on the return of vessels from long cruises. It is estimated that they will cost between four and five millions of dollars, and can be built in about twenty months. With the exception of some deficiency in the supply of white oak and yellow pine, which can be without much difficulty procured, we have on hand at the various yards ample material to accomplish what is recommended. It will be perceived, on referring to the estimates of the Bureau of Construction, &c., that an estimate is made of the entire cost—of the cost without purchasing any material, and of the probable amount which would be expended during the fiscal year without regard to great despatch. This was done in order that the subject might be understood properly, and that such action might be taken as appeared wisest. As it is deemed desirable to make this addition to our naval forces as early as practicable, in consideration of the number of vessels which will soon be unfit for service and not worth repairing, and as it is important to retain on hand for emergency a reasonable supply of building material, I venture to suggest the policy of making the appropriation at an early day, to enable the department to build them with despatch, and purchase a supply of material so as not to diminish the amount on hand. . . .

PART THREE

Isolated Security: 1862–1898

19. William Tecumseh Sherman: Forerunner of the "New" Warfare

THE CIVIL WAR WAS THE FIRST TOTAL OR NEAR-TOTAL WAR IN AMERIcan experience. As such, it was to influence the American people profoundly in nearly every aspect of their lives. It had, however, little effect upon their attitudes toward military policy or even, in the early postwar years, on professional military thought. We were to continue until 1898 with substantially the same military system and the same structure of military ideas with which we had faced the crisis of 1861. William T. Sherman (whose offhand remark "War is hell" later became world famous) was one of the few even among the generals who seemed to grasp the implications of the new and dreadful lineaments of war, as they were now appearing out of the womb of the industrial revolution. And Sherman himself did not reduce his insights to theoretical or philosophical statement. Preeminently a man of action, one has to seek his contribution to military thought in what he did rather than in what he wrote. His correspondence, mainly with Grant, in the autumn of 1864 in which the famous march through Georgia was planned and launched, has been selected as indicating not only his grasp of the "strategic" and total warfare of the future, but also the flair and style that he brought to conventional military thinking.

CITY POINT, VA., *September 10, 1864—10 a.m.*
Major-General SHERMAN:
As soon as your men are sufficiently rested and preparations can be made, it is desirable that another campaign should be

From *Official Records of the War of the Rebellion,* Series I, Volume XXXIX, Part 2, p. 335–Part 3, p. 661.

commenced. We want to keep the enemy constantly pressed to the end of the war. If we give him no peace while the war lasts, the end cannot be distant. Now that we have all of Mobile Bay that is valuable, I do not know but it will be the best move to transfer Canby's troops to act upon Savannah whilst you move on Augusta. I should like to hear from you, however, on this matter.

U. S. Grant,
Lieutenant-General.

HDQRS. MILITARY DIVISION OF THE MISSISSIPPI,
Atlanta, Ga., September 20, 1864.

Lieut. Gen. U. S. GRANT,
Commanding Armies of the United States, City Point, Va.:

GENERAL: I have the honor to acknowledge at the hands of Lieutenant-Colonel Porter, of your staff, your letter of September 12, and accept with thanks the honorable and kindly mention of the services of this army in the great cause in which we are all engaged. I send by Colonel Porter all official reports which are completed, and will, in a few days, submit a list of names which I deem worthy of promotion. I think we owe it to the President to save him the invidious task of election among a vast number of worthy aspirants, and have ordered my army commanders to prepare their lists with great care and to express their preferences based upon claims of actual capacity and services rendered. These I will consolidate and submit in such a form that if mistakes are committed they will at least be sanctioned by the best contemporaneous evidence of merit, for I know that vacancies do not exist equal in number to that of the officers that really deserve promotion. As to the future, I am pleased to know your army is being steadily reenforced by a good class of men, and I hope it will go on until you have a force that is numerically double that of your antagonist, so that with one part you can watch him and with the other you can push out boldly from your left flank, occupy the South Shore [Side] Railroad, compel him to attack you in position, or accept battle on your own terms. We ought to ask our country for the largest possible armies that can be raised, as so important a thing as the "self-existence of a great nation" should not be left to the fickle chances of war. Now that Mobile is shut out to the commerce of our enemy it calls for no further effort on our part, unless the capture of the city can be followed up by the occupation of the whole Alabama River and the railroad across to Columbus, Ga., when that place would at once become a magnificent auxiliary to my farther progress into Georgia, but until General Canby is much reenforced, and until he can more thoroughly subdue the scattered armies west of the Mississippi, I suppose that much cannot be attempted as against the Alabama River and Columbus, Ga.

The utter destruction of Wilmington, N. C., is of importance only in connection with the necessity of cutting off all foreign trade to our enemy, and if Farragut can get across the bar, and the move can be made quick, I suppose it will succeed. From my knowledge of the mouth of Cape Fear, I anticipate more difficulty in getting the heavy ships across the bar than in reaching the town of Wilmington, but of course the soundings of the channel are well known at Washington as well as the draft of his ironclads, so that it must be demonstrated as feasible or else it would not be attempted. If successful, I suppose that Fort Caswell will be occupied and the fleet at once sent to the Savannah River. Then the reduction of the city is the only question. If once in our possession, and the river open to us, I would not hesitate to cross the State of Georgia with 60,000 men, hauling some stores and depending on the country for the balance. Where a million of people live my army won't starve; but, as you know, in a country like Georgia, with few roads and innumerable streams, an inferior force could so delay an army and harass it that it would not be a formidable object, but if the enemy knew that we had our boats on the Savannah I could rapidly move to Milledgeville, where there is abundance of corn and meat, and would so threaten Macon and Augusta that he would give up Macon for Augusta;

then I would move to interpose between Augusta and Savannah, and force him to give me Augusta, with the only powder mills and factories remaining in the South, or let us have the Savannah River. Either horn of the dilemma would be worth a battle. I would prefer his holding Augusta as the probabilities are; for then, with the Savannah River in our possession, the taking of Augusta would be a mere matter of time. This campaign could be made in winter. But the more I study the game the more am I convinced that it would be wrong for me to penetrate much farther into Georgia without an objective beyond. It would not be productive of much good. I can start east and make a circuit south and back, doing vast damage to the State, but resulting in no permanent good; but by mere threatening to do so I hold a rod over the Georgians who are not overloyal to the South. I will therefore give my opinion that your army and Canby's should be re-enforced to the maximum; that after you get Wilmington, you strike for Savannah and the river; that General Canby be instructed to hold the Mississippi River and send a force to get Columbus, Ga., either by the way of the Alabama or the Appalachicola, and that I keep Hood employed, and put my army in fine order for a march on Augusta, Columbia, and Charleston, to be ready as soon as Wilmington is sealed as to commerce, and the city of Savannah is in our possession. I think it will be found that the movements of Price and Shelby west of the Mississippi are mere diversions. They cannot hope to enter Missouri save as raiders, and the truth is Rosecrans should be ashamed to take my troops for such a purpose. If you will secure Wilmington and the city of Savannah from your center, and let Canby have the Mississippi River and west of it, I will send a force to the Alabama and Appalachicola, provided you give me 100,000 of the drafted men to fill up my old regiments, and if you will fix a day to be in Savannah, I will insure our possession of Macon and a point on the river below Augusta.

The possession of the Savannah River is more than fatal to the possibility of a Southern independence; they may stand the fall of Richmond, but not of all Georgia. I will have a long talk with

Colonel Porter and tell him everything that may occur to me of interest to you. In the mean time know that I admire your dogged perseverance and pluck more than ever. If you can whip Lee and I can march to the Atlantic I think Uncle Abe will give us a twenty days' leave of absence to see the young folks.

Ever, yours,

W. T. Sherman,
Major-General.

Washington, *September 28, 1864.*
Major-General Sherman, *Atlanta, Ga.:*

General: Your communications of the 20th in regard to the removal of families from Atlanta and the exchange of prisoners, and also the official report of your campaign, are just received. I have not had time as yet to examine your report. The course which you have pursued in removing rebel families from Atlanta and in the exchange of prisoners is fully approved by the War Department. Not only are you justified by the laws and usages of war in removing these people, but I think it was your duty to your own army to do so. Moreover, I am fully of opinion that the nature of your position, the character of the war, the conduct of the enemy, and especially of non-combatants and women of the territory which we have heretofore conquered and occupied, will justify you in gathering up all the forage and provisions which your army may require both for a siege of Atlanta and for your supply in your march farther into the enemy's country. Let the disloyal families of the country thus stripped go to their husbands, fathers, and natural protectors in the rebel ranks. We have tried three years of conciliation and kindness without any reciprocation. On the contrary, those thus treated have acted as spies and guerrillas in our rear and within our lines. The safety of our armies and a proper regard for the lives of our soldiers require that we apply to our inexorable foes the severe rules of war. We certainly are not required to treat the so-called non-combatants and rebels better than they themselves treat each other. Even here in Virginia, within fifty miles of Washington, they strip their own families of provisions, leaving them as our army advances to be fed by us or to starve within our lines. We have fed this class of people long enough. Let them go with their husbands and fathers in the rebel ranks, and if they won't go we must send them to their friends and natural protectors. I would destroy every mill and factory within my reach which I did not want for my own use. This the rebels have done, not only in Maryland and Pennsylvania, but also in Virginia and other rebel States, when compelled to fall back before our armies. In many sections of the country they have not left a mill to grind grain for their own suffering families, lest we might use them to supply our armies. We must do the same. I have endeavored to impress these views upon our commanders for the last two years. You are almost the only one who has properly applied them. I do not approve of General Hunter's course in burning private houses, or uselessly destroying private property—that is barbarous; but I approve of taking or destroying whatever may serve as supplies to us or to the enemy's armies.

Very respectfully, your obedient servant,

H. W. Halleck,
Major-General and Chief of Staff.

ATLANTA, *October 1, 1864—1 p. m.*
(Received 7 p. m.)

Lieutenant-General GRANT, *City Point:*

Hood is evidently on the west side of Chattahoochee below Sweet Water. If he tries to get on my road this side of the Etowah I shall attack him, but if he goes over to the Selma and Talladega road why would it not do for me to leave Tennessee to the force which Thomas has and the reserves soon to come to Nashville, and for me to destroy Atlanta, and then march across Georgia to Savannah or Charleston, breaking roads and doing irreparable damage? We cannot remain on the defensive.

W. T. Sherman,
Major-General.

HDQRS. MILITARY DIVISION OF THE MISSISSIPPI,
In the Field, Allatoona, Ga., October 9, 1864—7.30 p. m.
(Received 11 a. m. 10th.)

Lieutenant-General GRANT,
City Point, Va.:

It will be a physical impossibility to protect the roads, now that Hood, Forrest, and Wheeler, and the whole batch of devils, are turned loose without home or habitation. I think Hood's movements indicate a diversion to the end of the Selma and Talladega Railroad at Blue Mountain, about sixty miles southwest of Rome, from which he will threaten Kingston, Bridgeport, and Decatur, Ala. I proposed we break up the railroad from Chattanooga, and strike out with wagons for Milledgeville, Millen, and Savannah. Until we can repopulate Georgia, it is useless to occupy it, but the utter destruction of its roads, houses, and people will cripple their military resources. By attempting to hold the roads we will lose 1,000 men monthly, and will gain no result. I can make the march, and make Georgia howl. We have over 8,000 cattle and 3,000,000 of bread, but no corn; but we can forage in the interior of the State.

W. T. Sherman,
Major-General, Commanding.

CITY POINT, VA., *October 11, 1864—11 a. m.*
Major-General SHERMAN, *Atlanta, Ga.:*

Your dispatch received. Does it not look as if Hood was going to attempt the invasion of Middle Tennessee, using the Mobile and Ohio and Memphis and Charleston roads to supply his base on the Tennessee River, about Florence or Decatur? If he does this he ought to be met and prevented from getting north of the Tennessee River. If you were to cut loose, I do not believe you would meet Hood's army, but would be bushwhacked by all the old men, little boys, and such railroad guards as are still left at home. Hood would probably strike for Nashville, thinking by going north he could inflict greater damage upon us than we could upon the rebels by going south. If there is any way of getting at Hood's army, I would prefer that, but I must trust to your own judgment. I find I shall not be able to send a force from here to act with you on Savannah. Your movements, therefore, will be independent of mine, at least until the fall of Richmond takes place. I am afraid Thomas, with such lines of road as he has to protect, could not prevent Hood going north. With Wilson turned loose with all your cavalry, you will find the rebels put much more on the defensive than heretofore.

U. S. Grant,
Lieutenant-General.

KINGSTON, GA., *October 11, 1864—10 a. m.*
Lieutenant-General GRANT, *City Point, Va.:*

Hood moved his army from Palmetto Station across by Dallas and Cedartown, and is now on the Coosa River, south of Rome. He threw one corps on my road at Acworth, and I was forced to follow. I hold Atlanta with the Twentieth Corps, and have strong detachments along my line. These reduce my active force to a comparatively small army. We cannot remain now on the defensive. With 25,000 men, and the bold cavalry he has, he can constantly break my road. I would infinitely prefer to make a wreck of the road and of the country from Chattanooga to Atlanta, including the latter city, send back all my wounded and worthless, and, with my effective army, move through Georgia, smashing things to the sea. Hood may turn into Tennessee and Kentucky, but I believe he will be forced to follow me. Instead of being on the defensive, I would be on the offensive; instead of guessing at what he means to do, he would have to guess at my plans. The difference in war is full 25 per cent. I can make Savannah, Charleston, or the mouth of the Chattahoochee. Answer quick, as I know we will not have the telegraph long.

W. T. Sherman,
Major-General

CITY POINT, VA., *October 11, 1864—11.30 p. m.*
(Received 7.55 a. m. 12th.)

Maj. Gen. W. T. SHERMAN, *Kingston, Ga.:*

Your dispatch of to-day received. If you are satisfied the trip to the sea-coast can be made, holding the line of the Tennessee firmly, you may make it, destroying all the railroad south of Dalton or Chattanooga, as you think best.

U. S. Grant,
Lieutenant-General.

HDQRS. MILITARY DIVISION OF THE MISSISSIPPI,
In the Field, Kingston, October 11, 1864.

General HALLECK,
Washington:

DEAR GENERAL: Yours of September 28 is just received and is exceedingly to my liking because it is the judgment of history. I don't care about the silly titles of Southern or Northern editors, but I do want to do right, and at Memphis and Vicksburg I experienced in my own sphere of action the unwisdom of expending millions of money and thousands of lives and then turn to and rent or entertain claims of indemnity for property fairly won. I think the gage of battle was made to us and if we win we are entitled to the conquests. And how soon was I forced to realize my crude judgment. Hood at once moved against my communications, and by contracting my lines I left a corps impregnable in Atlanta, with ninety days' food, and sallied out prepared to fight him wherever he chose. No army can keep an enemy off my long line, but its vital points are secure. Allatoona prevented the occupation of my line and covered 8,000 cattle, which are necessary to me. I am here at a point where if Hood passes up toward Chattanooga I can cross at Rome and be on his rear. I have Rome strongly held also, but I am loath to remain on the defensive, and want to break up this line back to Chattanooga, leave Thomas to defend Tennessee, and collect my forces and go to the seashore, taking Macon, Milledgeville, and Savannah en route. I can do it. Still I am acting to defend Atlanta and its defenses, a harder task than to take them. I have just got a mail and letters from everybody, McClellan[1] included, the first I ever remember to have received; also several inclosing a slip from a newspaper saying that I pledge 99 votes of every 100 of this army for McClellan. It is like newspaper assertions, a pure fabrication. I am not the citizen of any State; my State allegiance is divided between Ohio, California, Missouri, and Louisiana, and by the laws of no one State could I vote. Not being a voter I abstain from all expressions; indeed, I cannot conceive how my opinion is pertinent to the occasion. I deny ever having said or thought of such a thing as here indicated. I hate to express a political opinion, because it is tested, not by reason or general principles, but by some dirty party platform. Again let me say that I value your opinion of matters of importance above those of any other, because I know you to be frank, honest, and learned in the great principles of history. Both Grant and I are deficient in these and are mere actors in a grand drama, the end of which we do not see. . . . Show this to the President, except this conclusion: Damn the mischievous newspapers.

Your friend,

W. T. Sherman.

CITY POINT, VA., *October 17, 1864—3.30 p. m.*
Major-General SHERMAN, *Tilton, Ga.:*

The moment I know you have started south stores will be shipped to Hilton Head, where there are transports ready to take them to meet you at Savannah. In case you go south I would not propose holding anything south of Chattanooga, certainly not south of Dalton. Destroy in such case all of military value in Atlanta.

U. S. Grant,
Lieutenant-General.

---

[1] George B. McClellan had been removed from command of the Union forces in 1862 by Lincoln. He was nominated as Democratic candidate for President in 1864 but was soundly defeated [Ed.].

SPECIAL FIELD ORDERS, ⎱ HDQRS. MIL. DIV. OF THE MISS.,
                                   In the Field, Ship's Gap, Ga.,
No. 93.   ⎰   *October 17, 1864.*

I. Army commanders will at once park their trains at points convenient to roads leading south. Each army will make up a train of the most indifferent wagons and worthless mules and horses, and prepare to send them to Chattanooga, together with the sick and wounded, prisoners of war, surplus servants, tents, chairs, cots, and the furniture that now fill our wagons and disgrace the army––in other words, each army will strip its trains to the best teams, loaded only with the essentials for a long march, depending on the country for forage and vegetables. Each army commander will report at what time of to-day or to-night he will be ready to send back such a train, and hold it at a point convenient to move toward Ringgold, but not dispatch it until further orders.

II. Major-General Howard will continue to reconnoiter well forward; also down along the ridge about as far south as La Fayette. General Stanley will examine roads toward Dirt Town, and General Cox will do the same, but the armies will not move until further orders based on more complete intelligence of the plans and designs of the enemy.

By order of Maj. Gen. W. T. Sherman:

L. M. Dayton,
Aide-de-Camp.

HDQRS. MILITARY DIVISION OF THE MISSISSIPPI,
In the Field, Gaylesville, Ala., October 22, 1864—8 a. m.
General GRANT,
City Point, Va.:

I feel perfectly master of the situation here. I still hold Atlanta and the road, with all bridges and vital points well guarded, and I have in hand an army before which Hood has retreated precipitately down the valley of the Coosa. It is hard to divine his future plans, but by abandoning Georgia, and taking position with his rear to Selma, he threatens the road from Chattanooga to Atlanta, and may move to Tennessee by Decatur. He cannot cross the Tennessee except at Muscle Shoals, for all other points are patrolled by our gun-boats. I am now perfecting arrangements to put into Tennessee a force able to hold the line of the Tennessee whilst I break up the railroad in front of Dalton, including the city of Atlanta, and push into Georgia, and break up all its railroads and depots, capture its horses and negroes, make desolation everywhere, destroy the factories at Macon, Milledgeville, and Augusta, and bring up with 60,000 men on the seashore about Savannah or Charleston. I think this far better than defending a long line of railroad. I will leave General George H. Thomas to command all my division behind me, and take with me only the best fighting material. Of course I will subsist on the bountiful corn-fields and potato patches, as I am now doing luxuriously. I have now all your dispatches, and there will be time to give me any further instructions. Canby should be most active as against Selma from the direction of Mobile, and I will order similar movements from the Mississippi River and Decatur, provided Beauregard follows me, as he will be forced to do by public clamor.

W. T. Sherman,
Major-General, Commanding.

CITY POINT, VA., *November 1, 1864—6 p. m.*
Major-General SHERMAN,
Atlanta, Ga.:
Do you not think it advisable now that Hood has gone so far north to entirely settle him before starting on your proposed campaign? With Hood's army destroyed you can go where you please with impunity. I believed, and still believe, that if you had started south whilst Hood was in the neighborhood of you he would have been forced to go after you. Now that he is so far away, he might look upon the chase as useless and go in one direction whilst you are pushing in the other. If you can see the

chance for destroying Hood's army, attend to that first and make your other move secondary.

U. S. Grant,
Lieutenant-General.

HDQRS. MILITARY DIVISION OF THE MISSISSIPPI,
In the Field, Kingston, Ga., November 2, 1864.
Lieut. Gen. U. S. GRANT,
City Point, Va.:

If I turn back the whole effect of my campaign will be lost. By my movements I have thrown Beauregard well to the west, and Thomas will have ample time and sufficient troops to hold him until re-enforcements reach him from Missouri and recruits. We have now ample supplies at Chattanooga and Atlanta to stand a month's interruption to our communications, and I don't believe the Confederate army can reach our lines, save by cavalry raid, and Wilson will have cavalry enough to checkmate that. I am clearly of opinion that the best results will follow me in my contemplated movement through Georgia.

W. T. Sherman,
Major-General, Commanding.

CITY POINT, VA., *November 2, 1864—11.30 a. m.*
Major-General SHERMAN,
Rome, Ga.:

Your dispatch of 9 a. m. yesterday is just received. I dispatched you the same date, advising that Hood's army, now that it had worked so far north, be looked upon more as the objective. With the force, however, you have left with Thomas, he must be able to take care of Hood and destroy him. I do not really see that you can withdraw from where you are to follow Hood, without giving up all we have gained in territory. I say, then, go as you propose.

U. S. Grant,
Lieutenant-General.

Hdqrs. Military Division of the Mississippi,
In the Field, Kingston, Ga., November 2, 1864.
Lieutenant-General Grant,
City Point, Va.:
Dispatch of 11.30 a. m. received. I will go on and complete my arrangements and in a few days notify you of the day of my departure. General Thomas reports to-day that his cavalry reconnoitered within three miles of Florence yesterday, and found Beauregard intrenching. I have ordered him to hold Nashville, Chattanooga, and Decatur, all well supplied for a siege. All the rest of his army to assemble about Pulaski and to fight Beauregard cautiously and carefully. At the same time for A. J. Smith and all re-enforcements to get up to enable him to assume a bold offensive, and to enable Wilson to get a good mount of cavalry. I think Jeff. Davis will change his tune when he finds me advancing into the heart of Georgia instead of retreating, and I think it will have an immediate effect on your operations at Richmond.

W. T. Sherman,
Major-General, Commanding.

Hdqrs. Military Division of the Mississippi,
In the Field, Kingston, Ga., November 6, 1864.
Lieut. Gen. U. S. Grant,
Commander-in-Chief, City Point, Va.:
Dear General: I have heretofore telegraphed and written you pretty fully, but I still have some thoughts in my busy brain that should be confided to you as a key to future developments. The taking of Atlanta broke upon Jeff. Davis so suddenly as to disturb the equilibrium of his usually well-balanced temper, so that at Augusta, Macon, Montgomery, and Columbia, S. C., he let out some of his thoughts which otherwise he would have kept to himself. As he is not only the President of the Southern Confederacy but also its Commander-in-Chief, we are bound to attach more importance to his words than we would to those of a mere civil chief magistrate. The whole burden of his song con-

sisted in the statement that Sherman's communications must be broken and his army destroyed. Now, it is a well-settled principle that if we can prevent his succeeding in his threat we defeat him and derive all the moral advantages of a victory. Thus far Hood and Beauregard conjointly have utterly failed to interrupt my supplies or communications with my base. My railroad and telegraph are now in good order from Atlanta back to the Ohio River. His losses at Allatoona, Resaca, Ship's Gap, and Decatur exceed in number (his losses in men) ours at the block-houses at Big Shanty, Allatoona Creek, and Dalton; and the rapidity of his flight from Dalton to Gadsden takes from him all the merit or advantage claimed for his skillful and rapid lodgment made on my railroad. The only question in my mind is whether I ought not to have dogged him far into Mississippi, trusting to some happy accident to bring him to bay and to battle. But I then thought that by so doing I would play into his hands by being drawn or decoyed too far away from our original line of advance. Besides, I had left at Atlanta a corps and railroad guards back to Chattanooga, which might have fallen an easy prey to his superior cavalry. I felt compelled to do what is usually a mistake in war, divide my forces, send a part back into Tennessee, retaining the balance here. As I have heretofore informed you, I sent Stanley back directly from Gaylesville and Schofield from Rome, both of whom have reached their destinations, and thus far Hood, who had brought up at Florence, is farther from my communications than when he started, and I have in Tennessee a force numerically greater than his, well commanded and well organized, so that I feel no uneasiness on the score of Hood reaching my main communications. My last accounts from General Thomas are to 9.30 last night, when Hood's army was about Florence in great distress about provisions, as he well must be. But that devil Forrest was down about Johnsonville and was making havoc among the gun-boats and transports. But Schofield's troops were arriving at Johnsonville and a fleet of gun-boats reported coming up from below, able to repair that trouble. But you know that that line of supplies was only opened for summer use when the Cumberland is not to be depended upon. We now have abundant supplies at Atlanta, Chattanooga, and Nashville, with the Louisville and Nashville Railroad and the Cumberland River unmolested, so that I regard Davis' threat to get his army on my rear, or on my communications, as a miserable failure. Now as to the second branch of my proposition, I admit that the first object should be the destruction of that army, and if Beauregard moves his infantry and artillery up into that pocket about Jackson and Paris, I will feel strongly tempted to move Thomas directly against him and myself move rapidly by Decatur and Purdy to cut off his retreat. But this would involve the abandonment of Atlanta and a retrograde movement, which would be very doubtful of expediency or success; for, as a matter of course, Beauregard, who watches me with his cavalry and his friendly citizens, would have timely notice and would slip out and escape to regain what we have earned at so much cost. I am more than satisfied that Beauregard has not the men to attack fortifications or meet me in battle, and it would be a great achievement for him to make me abandon Atlanta by mere threats and maneuvers. These are the reasons which have determined my former movements. I have employed the last ten days in running to the rear the sick and wounded and worthless, and all the vast amount of stores accumulated by our army in the advance, aiming to organize this branch of my army into four well-commanded corps, encumbered by only one gun to 1,000 men, and provisions and ammunition which can be loaded up in our mule teams, so that we can pick up and start on the shortest notice. I reckon that by the 10th instant this end will be reached, and by that date I also will have the troops all paid, the Presidential election over and out of our way, and I hope the early storms of November, now prevailing, will also give us the chance of a long period of fine healthy weather for campaigning. Then the question presents itself, What shall be done? On the supposition always that Thomas can hold the line of the Tennessee, and very shortly be able to assume the offensive as against Beauregard, I propose to act in such a manner against the material resources of the South as utterly to negative

Davis' boasted threat and promises of protection. If we can march a well-appointed army right through his territory, it is a demonstration to the world, foreign and domestic, that we have a power which Davis cannot resist. This may not be war, but rather statesmanship, nevertheless it is overwhelming to my mind that there are thousands of people abroad and in the South who will reason thus: If the North can march an army right through the South, it is proof positive that the North can prevail in this contest, leaving only open the question of its willingness to use that power.

Now, Mr. Lincoln's election, which is assured, coupled with the conclusion thus reached, makes a complete, logical whole. Even without a battle, the result operating upon the minds of sensible men would produce fruits more than compensating for the expense, trouble, and risk. Admitting this reasoning to be good, that such a movement per se be right, still there may be reasons why one route would be better than another. There are three from Atlanta, southeast, south, and southwest, all open, with no serious enemy to oppose at present. The first would carry me across the only east and west railroad remaining in the Confederacy, which would be destroyed and thereby sever the communications between the armies of Lee and Beauregard. Incidentally, I might destroy the enemy's depots at Macon and Augusta and reach the seashore at Charleston or Savannah, from either of which points I could re-enforce our armies in Virginia. The second and easiest route would be due south, following substantially the valley of the Flint River, which is very fertile and well supplied, and fetching up on the navigable waters of the Appalachicola, destroying en route the same railroad, taking up the prisoners of war still at Andersonville, and destroying about 400,000 bales of cotton near Albany and Fort Gaines. This, however, would leave the army in a bad position for future movements. The third, down the Chattahoochee to Opelika and Montgomery, thence to Pensacola or Tensas Bayou, in communication with Fort Morgan. This latter route would enable me at once to co-operate with General Canby in the reduction of Mobile and occupation of the line of the Alabama. In my judgment the first would have a material effect upon your campaign in Virginia, the second would be the safest of execution, but the third would more properly fall within the sphere of my own command and have a direct bearing upon my own enemy, Beauregard. If, therefore, I should start before I hear further from you or before further developments turn my course, you may take it for granted that I have moved via Griffin to Barnesville; that I break up the road between Columbus and Macon good, and then, if I feint on Columbus, will move, via Macon and Millen, to Savannah, or if I feint on Macon you may take it for granted I have shot off toward Opelika, Montgomery, and Mobile Bay or Pensacola. I will not attempt to send couriers back, but trust to the Richmond papers to keep you well advised. I will give you notice by telegraph of the exact time of my departure. General Steedman is here to clear the railroad back to Chattanooga, and I will see that the road is broken completely between the Etowah and the Chattahoochee, including their bridges, and that Atlanta itself is utterly destroyed.

I am, with respect,

W. T. Sherman,
Major-General.

20. Ulysses S. Grant Looks to a Peaceful Future

IN 1868 THE NATION, AS IT HAD DONE BEFORE AND WAS TO DO AGAIN, elected its leading soldier to the Presidency. As on the other occasions, the result was not the militarization of American policy. When Grant came to the problems of foreign affairs in his second inaugural, March 4, 1873, he took a remarkably calm view of all military issues (it was a time when both the Army and the Navy were sinking toward their nadir in efficiency and in popular respect), relying instead, upon a vision of the time when the world would "become one nation" and "armies and navies will be no longer required."

Fellow-Citizens: Under Providence I have been called a second time to act as Executive over this great nation. It has been

From *Messages of the Presidents*, IX, pp. 4175–4176.

my endeavor in the past to maintain all the laws, and, so far as lay in my power, to act for the best interests of the whole people. My best efforts will be given in the same direction in the future, aided, I trust, by my four years' experience in the office.

When my first term of the office of Chief Executive began, the country had not recovered from the effects of a great internal revolution, and three of the former States of the Union had not been restored to their Federal relations.

It seemed to me wise that no new questions should be raised so long as that condition of affairs existed. Therefore the past four years, so far as I could control events, have been consumed in the effort to restore harmony, public credit, commerce, and all the arts of peace and progress. It is my firm conviction that the civilized world is tending toward republicanism, or government by the people through their chosen representatives, and that our own great Republic is destined to be the guiding star to all others.

Under our Republic we support an army less than that of any European power of any standing and a navy less than that of either of at least five of them. There could be no extension of territory on the continent which would call for an increase of this force, but rather might such extension enable us to diminish it.

The theory of government changes with general progress. Now that the telegraph is made available for communicating thought, together with rapid transit by steam, all parts of a continent are made contiguous for all purposes of government, and communication between the extreme limits of the country made easier than it was throughout the old thirteen States at the beginning of our national existence.

The effects of the late civil strife have been to free the slave and make him a citizen. Yet he is not possessed of the civil rights which citizenship should carry with it. This is wrong, and should be corrected. To this correction I stand committed, so far as Executive influence can avail. . . .

. . . The States lately at war with the General Government are now happily rehabilitated, and no Executive control is exercised in any one of them that would not be exercised in any other State under like circumstances. . . .

. . . In future, while I hold my present office, the subject of acquisition of territory must have the support of the people before I will recommend any proposition looking to such acquisition. I say here, however, that I do not share in the apprehension held by many as to the danger of governments becoming weakened and destroyed by reason of their extension of territory. Commerce, education, and rapid transit of thought and matter by telegraph and steam have changed all this. Rather do I believe that our Great Maker is preparing the world, in His own good time, to become one nation, speaking one language, and when armies and navies will be no longer required.

My efforts in the future will be directed to the restoration of good feeling between the different sections of our common country; to the restoration of our currency to a fixed value as compared with the world's standard of values—gold—and, if possible, to a par with it; to the construction of cheap routes of transit throughout the land, to the end that the products of all may find a market and leave a living remuneration to the producer; to the maintenance of friendly relations with all our neighbors and with distant nations; to the reestablishment of our commerce and share in the carrying trade upon the ocean; to the encouragement of such manufacturing industries as can be economically pursued in this country, to the end that the exports of home products and industries may pay for our imports—the only sure method of returning to and permanently maintaining a specie basis; to the elevation of labor; and, by a humane course, to bring the aborigines of the country under the benign influences of education and civilization. It is either this or war of extermination. Wars of extermination, engaged in by people pursuing commerce and all industrial pursuits, are expensive even against the weakest people, and are demoralizing and wicked. Our superiority of strength and advantages of civilization should make us lenient toward the Indian. The wrong inflicted upon him should be taken into account and the balance placed to his credit. The moral view of the question should be considered and the question asked, Can not the Indian be made a useful and productive member of society by proper teaching and treatment? If the effort is made in good faith, we will stand better before the civilized nations of the earth and in our own consciences for having made it. . . .

21. Generals Discuss Army Reorganization in the 1870's

IN THE LATE 1870's CONGRESS, AGAIN BENT MAINLY ON ECONOMY, set up a joint Senate-House committee to study Army reorganization. Headed by General Ambrose E. Burnside, who had commanded the Union forces at Fredericksburg at the end of 1862 and was now a Senator from Rhode Island, it sought the views of many of the surviving military leaders, including Sherman, James A. Garfield, Winfield Scott Hancock, and George B. McClellan. The committee's own report, made in 1879, is of no special interest, but some examples of the generals' responses are given, to indicate how the problems of military organization and defense appeared to the Civil War commanders ten years after the end of the great holocaust.

William T. Sherman

. . . The experience of a few years . . . seems to have demonstrated that the modern regiment was better adapted to administration than the legion composed of all arms; and we find that by an act of Congress of March 6, 1802, the Army was reorganized into a regiment of artillery, two regiments of infantry, a corps of engineers, and a general staff, aggregating 3,356. Many changes followed in quick succession, embracing the period of the war with Great Britain of 1812–'14; and in 1817 we find the Army to have consisted of a general staff, corps of engineers, Ordnance Department, a regiment of light artillery, a corps of artillery, eight regiments of infantry, and one of rifles, aggregating 8,221 men.

From House and Senate Joint Committee Report, Senate Report, 555, 45th Congress, Session 3, II, pp. 104–107, 121–125, 426–428, 454–457.

Then, as now, the country was staggering under the effect of a large debt, incurred in the then recent war, which called for a reduction of the expenses of the general government. Under a resolution of the House of Representatives, of April 17, 1818, the Hon. John C. Calhoun, then Secretary of War, submitted a special report on the subject of army organization and administration; and subsequently, on January 12, 1820, another on the same general subject, which reports seem to me so exhaustive, and so applicable to the present occasion, that nothing more need be written, further than to apply his principles and reasoning to the new state of facts.[1]

. . . Since the date of that report the country has had the experience of three great wars and innumerable conflicts with the Indians, yet the principles enunciated are the same to-day as in 1820. The various changes of organization and of the strength of parts are better illustrated by the documents and tables herewith than by any written statement I might attempt, but it is seen clearly that the present organization and strength of the Army result logically from antecedent events; and that measured by any standard—of the population of the country, its wealth, the extent of territory, the number of posts to be maintained, the routes of travel to be guarded, the public lands from which trespassers are to be excluded, or indeed by any fair inference of necessity—it can be demonstrated that the existing military establishment, including all officers and enlisted men, aggregating 27,489, is less in proportion than was the Legion of the United States, fixed by General Washington in 1792.

Therefore it would seem to be the part of wisdom to let well enough alone, and to allow the existing Army to increase or diminish by natural causes, according to the necessities of the country.

But on the supposition that the present commission prefer to accomplish a thorough reorganization, I have prepared the accompanying table, exhibiting an organization easily reached from

[1] Sherman quotes extensively from Calhoun, here. See Document 10 [Ed.].

the present standard, and which would better fulfill the second of Mr. Calhoun's principles, of being enlarged to a war standard with the least possible "confusion or disorder" and "at the least possible expense."

It will be observed that I assume the new force, or peace establishment, to consist of five regiments of artillery, ten of cavalry, and twenty of infantry, each to have the same identical organization, leaving to the artillery and cavalry the same number of companies as now, and diminishing the number of infantry regiments by five, but adding two companies to each regiment, thus only disbanding ten of the existing companies. I take from the artillery and cavalry fifteen majors, and give twenty to the infantry, an increase of five; and give to each company of cavalry and infantry two first lieutenants, the same that the artillery now have. This will increase the number of first lieutenants in the Army by three hundred and sixty; a most valuable increase, because they are the active "duty-officers," and they constitute the school from which the country will, in times of war and danger, habitually draw the chief officers for hard service.

Examining the table further, we find that each regiment of every arm of service is composed of twelve companies, susceptible of being grouped into three battalions of four companies each, to command and administer which are—

One colonel, one lieutenant-colonel, two majors (one field-officer to command each battalion), one adjutant, and one quartermaster and commissary, making six officers; and

One sergeant-major, one quartermaster-sergeant, one commissary-sergeant, and one principal musician, making four noncommissioned staff.

Each company will have one captain, two first lieutenants, and one second lieutenant, making four officers; one orderly-sergeant, three sergeants, three corporals, two artificers, two musicians, and fifty privates, making four officers and sixty-one enlisted men.

Each regiment would then contain, for a *peace establishment*, fifty-four officers and seven hundred and thirty-six enlisted men, aggregating seven hundred and ninety; or the

5 regiments of artillery=	60 companies =	270 officers, and	3,680 men.
10 " cavalry	120 "	540 "	7,360 "
20 " infantry	240 "	1,080 "	14,720 "
		1,890	25,760

aggregating, officers and men, 27,650.

To increase to the *war standard,* simply add to each company one sergeant, one corporal, and fifty privates, which would result as follows:

5 regiments of artillery=	60 companies =	270 officers and	6,800 men.
10 " cavalry	120 "	540 "	13,600 "
20 " infantry	240 "	1,080 "	27,200 "
		1,890	47,600

To further increase for war purposes, add four new companies to each battalion, and we have—

5 regiments of artillery =	120 companies =	510 officers and	13,700 men.
10 " cavalry	240 "	1,020 "	27,400 "
20 " infantry	480 "	2,040 "	54,800 "
		3,570	95,900

The Germans now use companies as large as two hundred and fifty men, so that a battalion of eight companies numbers two thousand men. Assuming that as the *maximum,* we will have—

5 regiments =	15 battalions of artillery =	30,000
10 "	30 " cavalry	60,000
20 "	60 " infantry	120,000
	Making an army of	210,000

on a *minimum,* or peace basis, of 27,650. Thus an effective and well-organized army of over 200,000 can be created promptly, "without the least confusion or disorder," fulfilling all the conditions of Mr. Calhoun's second great principle, which he regarded as of more national importance than the first. . . .

James A. Garfield

. . . Whatever may be the merits of the controversy between the staff and line of the Army (and it is an old one, not only here but in other countries), the importance of a trained staff can hardly be overstated. Adapting to our own times the figure employed by a military author who wrote early in the century, it may be said that the functions of the staff are the Army's life-breath in the Departments of Orders; its character in the Department of Inspection; its food in the Subsistence; its limbs and raiment in the Quartermaster's; its health in the Medical; its defense in the Engineer's; its weapons in the Ordnance; its rights and discipline in the Judge-Advocate's, and its reward in the Pay Department.

An effective Army staff is, of necessity, a work of years. It cannot be created in an emergency, and sent at once to the field, ready for efficient work. Without thoroughly well-organized staff and supply departments, made efficient by long previous training, an army is "foredoomed to dogs and vultures." No expenditure at the moment, however lavish, can supply these wants or avert this doom. An eminent military critic of England has said:

"The parsimony of the House of Commons, during the later years of the Duke of Wellington's command, practically abolished any supply department for our troops at home, and kept up a staff wholly inadequate to the wants of a field army. Consequently, the instant the real strain of a campaign in the field came upon our force, it may be said to have perished. Our army which was enrolled in 1854 was a collection of magnificent isolated battalions, the finest this country ever produced; but they were bound together by a rope of sand. Irresistible in the battlefield, they melted away like snow before the first touch of the hardships and inclemencies of winter; and their loss was the direct, necessary, and inevitable consequence of the ignorant economy of the Parliament of Britain. This was the great lesson which the Crimean war taught this country."

Any military legislation, therefore, which destroys the staff puts out the eyes of the Army, impairs its intelligence, and fatally cripples its strength.

The staff of our Army rendered efficient and distinguished service during the late war, and is still an honorable, intelligent, and effective body of public servants. But its functions have been distorted by the usurpations of the Secretaries of War.

The generals of the Army, the commanders of military divisions, districts, and posts complain, with reason, that they are deprived of that authority over officers of the staff which proper subordination and the efficiency of the service demand. And this arises, in large measure, from the extent to which the numerous details of authority and service have been centralized in the War Department and in the several staff departments. Of course, the fact cannot be lost sight of that many staff officers are charged with the disbursement of large sums of money, and are under heavy bonds to account for the same in accordance with law and the rules of the War and Treasury Departments. But these obligations ought to be entirely compatible with the subordination of staff officers to military commanders, who are presumed to understand and respect the statutes and regulations which make disbursing officers accountable, in all matters of administration, to the Secretary of War. . . .

. . . It is a significant fact that, while numberless petitions and remonstrances upon almost all subjects of legislation have been constantly pouring into Congress, yet during the last eight years, not one petition has been addressed to either the Senate or the House praying for the decrease of our military establishment or for the reduction of the pay of its officers or enlisted men. Our people remember with gratitude the great captains who, in the late war, led their soldiers to victory to save the republic from overthrow. They thoroughly learned the lesson that, in times of extreme peril, the preservation of liberty and peace depends upon the disciplined valor of the nation, and that the science and art of war can be acquired only by the thorough and patient study and practice of its elements. This work they expect of the Army; and the annual amount which they cheerfully pay for its support is the cost of national insurance against foes from without and anarchy within. They expect Congress and the Executive to make the Army worthy of a great nation; and this can be done only by the hearty co-operation of Congress with those eminent and patriotic soldiers who have devoted their lives to the study and practice of military science.

Our Army should be large enough to accomplish the two leading objects for which the military establishment was created; the first and chief of these is to keep alive the knowledge and practice of military science, so that at any time, in case of foreign or domestic war, the nation may know how to defend itself against the most skillful enemy. The necessity of an army for this purpose was never more strongly stated than in the report made in 1820 by Secretary Calhoun, one of our very ablest Secretaries of War. The fundamental doctrine of his report was, that our Army should at all times be so complete in its organization that, "at the commencement of hostilities, there should be nothing either to new-model or to create;" that, in passing from peace to war, nothing should be needed but to increase the force of enlisted men.

In addition to securing this primary object, the Army should be large enough to preserve inviolate our national boundaries, and protect our widely-extended frontier settlements against Indian hostilities; to keep the peace and protect the public property in all places subject to the jurisdiction of the United States; and to aid the several States in case of invasion or insurrection too powerful to be controlled by their local authorities. . . .

. . . It is the unanimous testimony of our foremost officers—men whom the nation long ago learned to trust and honor—that the present organization is barely sufficient to accomplish the objects of its creation and to perform the other important duties which have been imposed upon it by law.

The people have not asked for its reduction. They demand an honest and economical administration of the government; but they cherish and cheerfully support the Army which affords them a perpetual guarantee of national safety and domestic peace.

No doubt changes can be made by which the Army will be greatly improved. For example, a reorganization of the infantry on the basis proposed by General Sherman in his letter already quoted, diminishing the number of infantry regiments by five, adding two companies to each remaining regiment, adopting the three-battalion formation, and increasing the maximum strength of each company, would realize the conditions prescribed by Secretary Calhoun, and enable Congress to pass from the peace to the war basis by expanding the force from 25,000 to 200,000 without adding new regiments.

This plan would have the additional advantage of keeping constantly in the field two strong battalions of each regiment, while the third was performing post duty, supplying details, and enlisting and drilling recruits for the whole regiment.

Another reform would also be effected. Enlistments would be made, and the recruits would be commanded, from the first, by officers of the regiment in which they were to serve. This suggestion is adopted in the bill now pending in the House of Representatives; but it is coupled with a reduction of the infantry force which would seriously impair the efficiency of the Army. Besides reducing the line of the Army below the limit of safety, the bill fatally cripples the staff. . . .

. . . It is evident that during the last three years there has been manifested in Congress a growing spirit of unfriendliness, if not of positive hostility, toward the Army. Near the close of the last Congress, after failing in its attempt to cut down our military force 33 per cent, the House of Representatives insisted upon adding to the Army appropriation bill a provision which plainly violated the constitutional rights of the President as Commander-in-Chief; and, rather than abandon its revolutionary attempt, allowed the appropriation to fail, subjected the country to the expense and inconvenience of an extra session of Congress, and left the Army to serve for many months without pay. . . .

Winfield Scott Hancock

. . . What the strength, composition, and organization of the Army should be depend on the purpose for which it is maintained.

A *large* standing army is against the settled policy of the nation. We rely upon creating armies from our population when the necessity for them has actually arisen or is impending. But "in peace prepare for war" is an accepted and respected maxim amongst us. Under the operations of these somewhat contradictory principles we have been led to the compromise of a small standing army which is expected to keep pace with the progress of the profession, construct adequate and suitable national defenses, hold some of our most important military positions, preventing their sudden seizure by an enemy, his occupation of our harbors and destruction of our great commercial cities; be prepared at all times to supply the national forces with the most improved weapons, implements, and munitions of war, and to guard these and other public property until distributed for service; be ready at a moment's notice to organize, equip, and supply, with efficiency and economy, armies of any magnitude which the occasion may call for; and, lastly, to serve as a nucleus for the raw levies raised as needed.

These I understand to be the main purposes for which our Regular Army is maintained. As *a physical force*, our little standing Army can never be of appreciable importance after a great contest has set in. Its value consists in its serving as a model and a standard for the militia, and in the knowledge and system, the spirit of discipline, and the military information which its members store up in peace and disseminate among the "national forces" when the struggle comes.

What, then, should be the strength, composition, and organization of the Army, that it may best accomplish the objects of its existence?

Looking from the stand-point assumed, the first question which presents itself is the question of cost. What, during peace, are the people able and willing to pay in the way of insurance by military proficiency and preparation against heavy loss in case of war? If *nothing*, then the Army as a permanent institution ought to be dispensed with. A discussion of the questions arising from our Indian frontier is omitted in this connection. The Indian furnishes only incidental duty for part of the Army. The service is of secondary importance, and is comparatively temporary in its

nature. It must for a few years longer occupy the attention of
our cavalry and infantry, and some parts of the staff, and, from
time to time, influence the strength and organization of these
arms, but it is entitled to no weight in considering the question
just proposed.

If the people are willing in peace, as they have always shown
themselves to be, to guarantee their own protection in case of war,
by intrusting to an army the accomplishment of the objects here-
inbefore enumerated, then the main question is closed, and the
resulting ones of the strength, &c., of the force to be kept up are
opened.

Infantry and Cavalry.

As a general proposition, it may be said that every arm of the
service, in order that it may be a model for the national forces,
ought to be large enough to give full development at whatever
cost of time and money, to its own specialty. This for infantry
and cavalry would require but a small force, smaller than we now
have in service. The duties of these arms, especially the former,
are not only readily acquired by our people, but they are of
such a nature that a large part of the "national forces" are always
voluntarily or under State auspices practicing them. Hence the
expenses imposed on the General Government for fostering them
in behalf of the *theory* of war should be comparatively small. But
it happens that these arms are called upon for a vast amount of
difficult and dangerous special service on the Indian frontier, and
so long as this service is necessary they must be kept strong
enough to perform it efficiently. I have no doubt that under the
demands of this service our cavalry and infantry have been prevented from reaching that state of discipline and instruction
which they would otherwise have attained. Companies and posts
have been small and isolated. The time of the men, when not
engaged in actual hostilities, has, in the main, been necessarily
devoted to providing for their own pressing wants, leaving but
little to bestow upon the practice of their formal military duties.
Furthermore, the point to which the *instruction* of a command, as

well as its *esprit*, can be carried depends largely upon the extent of the organization. In our cavalry and infantry it has, in late years, not generally been practicable to carry instruction effectually beyond the school of the individual soldier, and rarely beyond the school of the company. The evils of this condition of things appear to have been recognized, and a partial and temporary remedy was applied by the act of August 5, 1876, authorizing an increase of the enlisted strength of cavalry companies to one hundred. For the sake of general instruction and proficiency as well as for their greater usefulness on frontier service, this increase authorized for companies of cavalry should be made permanent and extended to all companies of infantry. This would probably make the infantry arm larger than required even in the present state of the frontier. I would, therefore, offset the increase proposed in the strength of infantry companies by reducing the number of them, having say eight in a regiment instead of ten, as now.

The question of any further reduction of these arms than that just suggested should, I think, be deferred a few years longer, until our Indian frontiers are in a more settled condition. If no other disturbances have arisen I have no doubt that these arms could with safety be still further reduced, if then deemed advisable.

The Artillery.

We have five regiments of artillery, each containing twelve batteries or companies; that is, sixty companies of artillery, five of them being armed and equipped as light artillery, the other fifty-five being armed as infantry, but in addition receiving such instructions in the use of heavy guns as circumstances permit. In the organization of an army for active service sixty batteries of artillery would certainly be an extravagant supply of that arm for twenty-five regiments of infantry; but it must be borne in mind that the different branches of our military peace establishment are not constituted to form due proportions of an active army.

The relative strength of the different parts of our standing

Army cannot be governed either by the principles of organization for large armies in the field, established by our own experience, or by the principles developed by the more matured experience of foreign nations. On the contrary, in relation to their strength the different branches of our peace establishment are quite independent of each other, each being intended, not for a proportional integral of our twenty-five thousand men, but to supply a recognized want of our nation.

Artillery, if not the most, is one of the most important abstruse and progressive branches of military science. Much time, practice, favorable opportunity, and hard study are absolutely necessary to master and keep pace with it. *Very* expensive under the most skillful, in untrained hands it becomes *enormously* so. This is true of the heavy as well as of the light artillery. Every shot, for example, from the 15-inch guns of one of our forts costs, for powder and projectile alone, $63.78, to say nothing of the original cost of the gun, the carriage, implements, &c. The Government only, and not States or individuals, as in the case of cavalry or infantry, can take care of this branch of the military profession. If not protected and fostered by the General Government it is lost.

Proceeding, as we do, upon the possibility of war, it would certainly be unwise, if not foolish, to build defenses, cast cannon, devise projectiles, and then neglect in peace to teach those things in relation to the use of them which it will be *too late* to learn after war begins. Without multiplying arguments, I may state my conclusion that our true policy is to maintain a comparatively large force of artillery and keep it well instructed in its specialty. That arm is not now too large, perhaps in rank and file not large enough. If the number of enlisted men cannot be increased—and probably it ought not to be at this time, then certainly the men should be concentrated into fewer companies, so that each company shall contain a hundred. Instruction in artillery is seriously retarded under the present system. (By the latest orders eighteen of the artillery companies in this division are limited to thirty enlisted men, the other fifteen companies being authorized to have fifty-four.)

A company of thirty or even fifty-four enlisted men in one of our permanent forts—where they must be to find the guns, &c., for their instruction—is, practically speaking, a guard and police force, and not a *garrison*. There are so few men that nearly all their time is consumed in guarding and carrying out the measures necessary to preserve the public property. If the present system of occupying a great number of forts is to continue, larger companies would partially remove the difficulty just mentioned. In addition to this a considerable increase of ammunition for practice should be authorized. But I am inclined to think that the welfare of the service would be promoted by keeping the greater part of the artillery always concentrated for instruction at two or three of the largest forts. . . .

. . . A considerable saving of expense would result from the reductions and consolidations proposed in the cavalry, artillery and infantry. The concentration of enlisted men, so as to have fewer and larger companies, would be a departure from the old theory that our Army in peace, especially the line, should be a *skeleton* to be filled out for war. This theory, false in principle, has always failed in practice. It involves just that lack of power so much complained of during peace—companies too small for instruction, drill, and other duty—and when war comes, in lieu of filling out the skeleton, we take entire new organizations from the volunteers or militia. Our standing Army should be a small, complete, compact, vigorous, healthy body, always in a thorough state of discipline and instruction, serving as a model and a standard for the national forces, and not preserved as a skeleton into which it is expected to infuse vitality, activity and knowledge at the moment an emergency arises. . . .

George B. McClellan

. . . The question of the organization of the armed force of a nation is one of the highest importance, for upon its wise solution will necessarily depend important considerations of economy, and perhaps the honor and safety of the country. It is a question which rises far above all considerations of party or personal interest, and to its solution should be brought the highest qualities of the statesman, aided by the best available military knowledge and experience. The statesmen must control, but if wise and equal to the responsibility they will obtain their data from *not too many* soldiers of wisdom and experience, and, after determining the general principles, will leave most of the details to the professional men. In determining the proper organization of our Army, it would appear indispensable first to establish the conditions of the problem in some such way as this.

Modern weapons and the modern system of warfare insure great advantage to well-trained and thoroughly organized troops, in contradistinction to new levies, especially in an offensive campaign; so that great economy in time, money, and life will result from the employment of the first-mentioned class of troops. While modern warfare and weapons demand a very high order of intelligence, and offer greater advantage than ever to intelligent soldiers, such as the Americans are, they make it more than ever necessary that that intelligence should be guided and controlled by instruction and discipline to produce the most useful and inexpensive results. Certain special arms of service, such as the engineer troops, artillery, and cavalry, from the nature of their duties and the weapons they employ, require longer and more careful instruction than the infantry, and should therefore in time of peace be kept nearer to the war standard than the infantry. Recruits become efficient soldiers much more rapidly and infinitely more economically by placing them in old regiments already provided with good officers and non-commissioned officers and a just proportion of well-instructed private soldiers than by forming them into new regiments. The system of very small companies on the peace footing is injurious to discipline, instruction, and economy. When a prompt and large increase of the Army must be made to meet an emergency, it is of the first importance that a sufficient number of staff officers, *i. e.,* adjutants-general, inspectors-general, engineers, quartermasters, commissaries, surgeons, and aids-de-camp, should be at once available, already instructed and experienced in their duties. Nothing was more clearly proved by the late war than this.

The permanent strength of the Regular Army should be sufficient to enable it to perform with promptness, vigor, economy, and certainty all its ordinary duties; and its organization should be so elastic as to permit a rapid, economical, and efficient increase of its numbers. If an army is maintained at all, true economy requires that it should be thoroughly efficient in all respects and adequate to the work devolving upon it. Large posts, that is, posts with large garrisons, if well selected, promote discipline and economy, and enable the troops to perform much more efficient and economical service than if scattered among a number of small posts.

The experience of our own and other countries proves that it is false economy to reduce the peace establishment of the Army unduly, for the reason that the employment of large masses of new troops upon the breaking out of war involves an immense expenditure, out of all proportion with the savings resulting from reducing the peace establishment too much. For similar reasons it is wise and necessary to furnish in peace due supplies of all war materials not liable to deterioration.

When the peace establishment is judiciously organized any portion of its cost which refers to future wants and not to current needs of the day, may be regarded in the light of an insurance against the heavy losses to which every nation is liable when it foolishly regulates all timely and moderate preparations for war; and this refers not only to the mere money question, but to those more important points of loss and time, sacrifice of life and disaster which so often characterize the beginning of wars by unprepared nations. . . .

. . . In the event of any important war, we must, no doubt, rely upon the volunteers to form the greater part of our armies, supported by as large bodies as practicable of instructed regular troops, so that a just conclusion would appear to be that, in time of peace, the Regular Army should be of sufficient force to enable it to perform all of its duties against the Indians and on the

Rio Grande frontier with promptness and effect, and to take reasonable care of the other frontiers; and that it should be so organized as to permit a large and rapid expansion when necessary. . . .

. . . In regard to the infantry, the experience of European nations has of late years led them to the adoption of what are called "strong companies," so that the generally-received infantry organization on the war establishment is now 250 non-commissioned officers and men to a company, four companies to a battalion, and three battalions to a regiment. In brief terms, the reasons for this are that a company of 250 men is found to be a much more effective unit in battle than the old-fashioned small company of 100 men or less: that it can be thoroughly controlled and handled by a competent captain, assisted by four lieutenants, and that a larger company would be too much for one captain. Experience has also shown that a battalion of 1,000 men is about the limit of the useful command of a field-officer, and that the operations of four strong companies can be more effectually controlled and kept in harmony than those of the old-fashioned ten weak companies, as it is far easier to have unity in the action of four captains than in that of ten. The same principle gives three battalions to the colonel for his regiment.

Again, it is the most economical arrangement, as requiring fewer officers, and it admits of the greatest possible expansion in time of war, for on the peace footing the number of privates is usually reduced to about 100.

But to render this organization effective the battalions should be permanently organized during peace with a proper staff, and the company officers and non-commissioned officers must be thoroughly efficient.

Under our present system the regiments are often so completely broken up that the colonels lose their proper control. With battalions composed of four companies it would be proper and possible to establish the rule that no permanent post should be held by less than a battalion, leaving any smaller posts that might be necessary to be held by temporary detachments from the nearest battalion posts.

Another question which merits careful consideration, and comes to a great extent within the domain of the statesman, is whether the arms, equipments, ammunition, &c., for the Army should be made in the arsenals or obtained by purchase from private firms, under a system of rigid inspection. There enters here not only the question of costs, including interest on capital invested, &c., but also the consideration of encouraging private companies in time of peace, so that in emergencies the government may have larger facilities at their disposal. . . .

22. Emory Upton: Critical Analyst of Military Policy

IN THE BURNSIDE PAPERS THERE ARE SEVERAL REFERENCES TO THE work of "General Upton," a younger officer whose influence on American military thought was ultimately to prove at least comparable to that of the far more famous Alfred Thayer Mahan. Like Henry Wager Halleck, Emory Upton came from upstate New York. He was graduated from West Point, with the May class of 1861, directly into the Civil War, where he made a brilliant record; twice wounded, he was a brevet major general at the age of twenty-four. After the war, he remained in the Army, returning to West Point, where he developed an improved tactical system and served, after 1870, as commandant of cadets and instructor in tactics. In 1875 he was sent westward around the world to study the Asian military systems (mainly those maintained by the European colonial powers) as well as the European armies themselves. After publishing *The Armies of Asia and Europe* in 1878, he devoted himself to completing *The Military Policy of the United States,* the first serious critical study of the subject. The Introduction, datelined "Fort Monroe, Virginia, 1880," contains the essentials of the argument that the body of the book sustains by detailed historical analysis. Upton, the victim of an "incurable disease," killed himself the following year; and the book was not formally published until 1904, when Elihu Root exhumed it from the War De-

From Emory Upton, *The Military Policy of the United States* (Washington, D.C.: Government Printing Office, 1904), pp. vii–xv.

partment files to support his program of Army reform. But its influence among professional soldiers was strong from the beginning.

Shortly after the disastrous battle of Camden, Washington wrote to the President of Congress "what we need is a good army, not a large one." Unfortunately for the country, the object sought by this assertion, so thoroughly in harmony with our cherished institutions, has only been partially attained in time of peace.

In view of the growth of our neighbors, the vast extent of our territory, and the rapid increase of our floating population, the time must speedily arrive when all intelligent and law-abiding people will accept, and adhere to, the opinion of John Adams that "the National defense is one of the cardinal duties of a statesman."

Our military policy, or, as many would affirm, our want of it, has now been tested during more than a century. It has been tried in foreign, domestic, and Indian wars, and while military men, from painful experience, are united as to its defects and dangers, our final success in each conflict has so blinded the popular mind, as to induce the belief that as a nation we are invincible.

With the greater mass of people, who have neither the time nor the inclination to study the requirements of military science, no error is more common than to mistake military resources for military strength, and particularly is this the case with ourselves.

History records our triumph in the Revolution, in the War of 1812, in the Florida War, in the Mexican War, and in the Great Rebellion, and as nearly all of these wars were largely begun by militia and volunteers, the conviction has been produced that with us a regular army is not a necessity.

In relating the events of these wars, the historian has generally limited himself to describing the battles that have been fought, without seeking to investigate the delays and disasters by which they have been prolonged, till, in nearly every instance, the national resources have been exhausted.

The object of this work is to treat historically and statistically, our military policy up to the present time, and to show the enormous and unnecessary sacrifice of life and treasure, which has attended all our armed struggles.

Whether we may be willing to admit it or not, in the conduct of war, we have rejected the practice of European nations and with little variation, have thus far pursued the policy of China.

All of our wars have been prolonged for want of judicious and economical preparation, and often when the people have impatiently awaited the tidings of victory, those of humiliating defeat have plunged the nation into mourning.

The cause of all this is obvious to the soldier and should be no less obvious to the statesman. It lies partly in the unfounded jealousy of not a large, but even a small standing army; in the persistent use of raw troops; in the want of an expansive organization, adequate for every prospective emergency; in short and voluntary enlistments, carrying with them large bounties; and in a variety of other defects which need not here be stated. In treating this subject, I am aware that I tread on delicate ground and that every volunteer and militiaman who has patriotically responded to the call of his country, in the hour of danger, may possibly regard himself as unjustly attacked.

To such I can only reply, that where they have enlisted for the period of three months, and, as at Bladensburg and on many other fields, have been hurled against veteran troops, they should not hold me responsible for the facts of history, which I have sought impartially to present. To such volunteers as enlisted for the period of the Mexican War, and particularly for two and three years during the War of the Rebellion, with whom it is my pride to have served and to whom I owe all of my advancement in the service, I but express the opinion of all military men, in testifying that their excellence was due, not to the fact that they were volunteers, but to the more important fact that their long term of service enabled them to become, in the highest sense, regulars in drill, discipline, and courage.

With a keen appreciation of their own ignorance and helplessness when they entered the service, the veterans of Gettysburg laughed at the militia who assisted in driving Lee across the Potomac, satirically asking the full regiments fresh from home, "Where they buried their dead?" The same men who felt hostile to the regular troops because of their superior discipline, found as they approached the same standard that no gulf lay between them, and with the recollections of Bull Run fresh in their memories they in turn ever after made sport of the raw troops which came temporarily to their aid.

Every battlefield of the war after 1861 gave proof to the world of the valor of the disciplined American soldier; but in achieving this reputation the nation was nearly overwhelmed with debt from which we are still suffering, while nearly every family in the land was plunged in mourning.

Already we are forgetting these costly sacrifices, and unless we now frame and bequeath to the succeeding generation a military system suggested by our past experience and commended by the example of other enlightened nations, our rulers and legislators in the next war will fall into the same errors and involve the country in the same sacrifices as in the past.

It has been truly remarked by one of our philosophers that "We follow success and not skill."

Should my labors in a field thus far unoccupied, and which I do not pretend to exhaust, be instrumental in aiding our future statesmen to achieve national success through skill, to the saving of life and treasure, it will be my satisfaction to have discharged a duty which every patriotic soldier and citizen owes to his country.

Up to this time in our history our military policy has been largely shaped by the Anglo-Saxon prejudice against "standing armies as a dangerous menace to liberty." Assuming that with this as one of his premises the reader has come to the erroneous conclusion that the officers of the army are wholly given over to selfishness and ambition it ought not to be difficult to convince him that no one of their number can suggest any change or modification of our system without being false to his guild.

No one can study the subject without acknowledging that our military policy is weak and that it invites and inevitably produces long wars, and that in the race for military laurels the professional soldier usually distances all competitors.

A century is a short period in the life of a nation, but its history may convey many valuable lessons as the result of the system which we cherish as our own invention; thus, the War of the Revolution lasted seven years, the War of 1812 three years, the Florida War seven years, the Mexican War two years, and the Rebellion four years, not to mention the almost incessant Indian wars of this period. In other words, since the publication of the Declaration of Independence to this time these figures show that for every three years of peace we have had one year of actual war.

The same prejudice has led our people to another false conclusion. If standing armies are dangerous to liberty, then it ought to follow that officers of the army should be inimical to republican institutions. But here again, if the lessons of history be read and accepted, it will be admitted that of all forms of government the republican, or democratic, is most favorable to the soldier. There is not a well-read officer in our service who does not know that monarchy sets a limit to military ambition, while in republics military fame is frequently rewarded with the highest civic honors.

The history of Rome, Greece, and Carthage affords abundant support for this statement, while, on the other hand, that of England shows that of all her great heroes Cromwell alone, in the days of the Commonwealth, stepped from the head of the army to the head of the state. After the restoration, Marlborough and Wellington received titles and estates, but those were bestowed by the Crown instead of the people.

In France, Turenne and Condé added the luster of their achievements to the glory of the King, but the wars of the Revolution filled Europe with the fame of republican generals, Napoleon at their head. When through popular favor he became First Consul and finally rose to supreme power he gave rank and titles to his generals, but the fame of his marshals was merged in the glory of the Emperor. He knew how to exalt and how to abase; he could tolerate no rival; a line in the Moniteur[1] could at any time make or destroy the reputation of a marshal.

In our day Bismarck planned the political unity of Germany, while Von Moltke alone made it possible by destroying in two campaigns the military power of Austria and France.

Had Germany been a republic both would have risen to the chief magistracy of the state, but under a monarchy they had to content themselves with fame, titles, and estates, and the patronizing favor of a kind-hearted Emperor.

The French, on the contrary, after establishing a republic, elevated to the presidency the marshal who surrendered the Imperial army at Sedan.[2]

Our own people, no less than the Romans, are fond of rewarding our military heroes. The Revolution made Washington President for two terms; the war of 1812 elevated Jackson and Harrison to the same office, the first for two terms, the latter for one; the Mexican war raised Taylor and Pierce to the Presidency, each for one term; the rebellion has already made Grant President for two terms, Hayes for one term, while the present Chief Magistrate, Garfield, owes his high office as much to his fame as a soldier as to his reputation as a statesman.

Long wars do not reward the highest commanders only. After the Revolution Knox, Dearborn, and Armstrong rose to the office of Secretary of War; Hamilton was Secretary of the Treasury; while Monroe, first Secretary of State, was finally elected President for two terms. During the Rebellion nearly 150 regular officers rose to the grade of brigadier and major general who, but for the four years' struggle, would have been unknown outside of the military profession.

[1] A French newspaper, the official organ of government information under Napoleon [Ed.].

[2] In the Franco-Prussian War. Comte Marie Edmé Patrice Maurice Mac-Mahon, Marshal of France, was second President of the Third Republic [Ed.].

Since the war, distinguished officers of volunteers have filled nearly every office in the gift of the people. They have been · elected chief magistrates of their States, and to-day on both floors of Congress they are conspicuous alike for their numbers and influence.

The rewards following long wars apply chiefly to the combatant branch of the Army, but if we assume that all officers are devoid of patriotism there is another large class, namely, the staff, who should denounce any change in our system.

The officers of the supply department know that money is power and that the disbursement of it commands influence and friends. During the four years before the rebellion the total disbursements of the Quartermaster's Department was less than thirty-five millions of dollars. During the four years of war, they exceeded a thousand millions. Up to 1861 the Quartermaster-General could give no orders to persons outside of his own officers; during the war he issued general orders to more than a hundred thousand employees, and became admiral of a fleet of more than a thousand vessels.

The Surgeon-General, before 1861, could not control a single sick or convalescent soldier. During the war he was put in command of all the general hospitals and had subject to his orders more than a hundred thousand men. In other departments there was a similar increase of authority not enjoyed alone by their respective officers, who, except for the war, would never have been known as agents of the Government.

Free from danger and from lust of power, if the noncombatant officers love war more than peace, it is manifest that they, too, should join the ambitious soldier and the demagogue in the cry, "Standing armies are dangerous to liberty." But who are our officers that they should be charged with mere selfishness and ambition? If we take those educated by the Government from their youth, are they not selected by the representatives of the people and from every class of society?

Are not their fathers, mothers, and their own sons in civil life, and in common with them, are they not citizens of the same country enjoying the blessings of the same Government? Nurtured by this Government, taught to love and defend its flag, are they alone a large family connection most likely to prove false to the institutions which have placed us first among nations? Is death on the field of battle no evidence of love for one's country? Have the officers of our Army to-day no sense of duty? In time of universal peace are those who continually expose their lives in Indian wars to open up to civilization the rich lands of the far West, actuated by no other motive than love of promotion? These questions to the reader are all pertinent in enabling him to penetrate the motive of the author. Whether or not he will concede to the Army a patriotism as bright and enduring as that which prevails in civil life, he no doubt will admit that as the man who uses a weapon is the best judge of its fitness, so a professional soldier should be the best judge of what constitutes a good military system.

In every civilized country success in war depends upon the organization and application of its military resources. The resources themselves consist of men, material, and money. Their organization is wholly within the province of the statesman. Under our Constitution Congress has the power to raise and support armies, and, subject to the supervision of the President, only professional soldiers should command them.

In time of war the civilian as much as the soldier is responsible for defeat and disaster. Battles are not lost alone on the field; they may be lost beneath the Dome of the Capitol, they may be lost in the Cabinet, or they may be lost in the private office of the Secretary of War. Wherever they may be lost, it is the people who suffer and the soldiers who die, with the knowledge and the conviction that our military policy is a crime against life, a crime against property, and a crime against liberty. The author has availed himself of his privileges as a citizen to expose to our people a system which, if not abandoned, may sooner or later prove fatal. The time when some one should do this has arrived.

Up to the Mexican War there was little that was glorious in our military history.

In the Revolution, the Continentals or Regulars often displayed a valor deserving of victory, but which was snatched away by the misconduct of undisciplined troops.

In the War of 1812 the discipline and victories of the Navy alone saved the country from dishonor. On the land the historian of the Army was glad to slur over needless disasters, to dwell on the heroism in the open field displayed by the Regulars at Chippewa and Lundys Lane. The Mexican war was a succession of victories. The Volunteers as well as the Regulars were disciplined troops.

The Rebellion began with the defeat at Bull Run, but a multitude of subsequent battles again proved that the valor of disciplined American troops, be they Regulars or Volunteers, can not be excelled by the best armies of Europe.

No longer compelled to doubt the prowess of our armies, the time has come to ask what was the cause of defeats like those of Long Island, Camden, Queenstown, Bladensburg, and Bull Run. The people who, under the war powers of the Constitution, surrender their liberties and give up their lives and their property have a right to know why our wars are unnecessarily prolonged. They have a right to know whether disasters have been brought about through the neglect and ignorance of Congress, which is intrusted with the power to raise and support armies, or through military incompetency. Leaving their representatives free to pay their own salaries, the people have a right to know whether they have devoted their time to studying the art of government. John Adams wrote the maxim that "The national defense is the cardinal duty of a statesman."

War, it need scarcely be said, affects the life, liberty, and property of the individual citizen, and beyond that the life of the nation. On its issue necessarily depends the fate of governments and the happiness of millions of human beings, present and future.

From the known method of selecting generals in most of our wars, no one assumes that the title implies knowledge of the art of war. Conscious that our legislators make a merit of neglecting the national defense, shall they, too, like our generals, enjoy unearned titles, or the highest of all titles, that of statesman?

Foreign governments, surrounded by powerful neighbors, act on the theory that military commanders can be educated, no less than captains and lieutenants. The same theory is true of statesmen. A general does not so much regard the causes of war; his duty is to be familiar with military history and to know the details and principles upon which successful war is conducted.

The statesman, on the contrary, should study peace and the causes which tend to preserve or destroy it. History will teach him that peace ends in war and war again ends in peace. If the causes which terminate peace and produce war can not be removed, and if the legislator does not recognize and know how to create a powerful army, he ceases to be a statesman.

In the course of his labors, the author has met with many discouragements. As a rule it has only been necessary to mention to his brother officers the words "military policy" to provoke the reply that "We have no military policy;" that everything is left to luck or to chance. While apparently true, this conclusion is nevertheless a mistake.

Laws whose operation have been the same in all our wars constitute a system, wise or unwise, safe or unsafe, according to their fruit. Contemplating the same results in the rebellion as in the Revolution and the War of 1812, it can not be denied that the impression has sunk deep into the Army that no change will ever be made for the better. There is ample reason for such a conviction. Ultimate success in all our wars has steeped the people in the delusion that our policy is correct and that any departure from it would be no less difficult than dangerous.

Again, our remoteness from powerful nations has led to another delusion—that we shall forever be free from foreign invasion. Within the present year (1880) a Senator of the United States, standing on the parapet of Fort Monroe and witnessing the firing of worthless smoothbore artillery, assured the author that we would not have another war in a century. No statesman would have made such a prediction. He would have recalled the Revolution, the War of 1812, and the Mexican War. He would have pointed to the British possession on the north, to Mexico on the west, and Spain on the south; he would not have forgotten the affair of the *Virginius* and the frequent complications on the Rio Grande as proof that at any moment we may be plunged into another foreign war. He would, furthermore, have condemned the useless ordnance before him, and would have declared that wisdom and economy demand that we should be ready for any war whenever and wherever it may occur.

He would not have stopped there; accepting the truth that the nation is governed best which is governed least, and that ours is a government of the people, he would nevertheless have told the Senator that the military policy of a republic should look more to the dangers of civil commotion than to the possibility of foreign invasion. He need not have referred to the forty years of anarchy and civil war which terminated in the establishment of the Roman Empire; he could have appealed to our own history and informed the Senator that in less than a century our peace had been disturbed by Shays's Rebellion, the Whisky Rebellion, the Great Rebellion, and more recently still the Railroad Riots of 1877. He could have informed the Senator that if our policy in foreign wars has been feeble and childish, at least half the expenditure and bloodshed has been borne by our enemies, while in civil commotion the loss of every dollar and the sacrifice of every life fall upon the citizens of the Republic.

He could have continued his lecture and told the Senator that as a nation we can afford to imitate the daily example of our citizens. The pioneer who seeks a home in the forest first builds a cabin, then a log house, and next a frame house. He does not accuse himself of extravagance. The cabin answered his purposes when he was poor and without family, but when his children multiplied he tore it down and put such material as was worth saving into the log house. This, too, satisfied his wants, but when he began to have neighbors, when roads were opened and friends and strangers began to visit him, he saw that he lacked room and, having become prosperous, he abandoned the log home and for comfort and appearance built a house and barn which excited the admiration of every passer-by.

Looking at the example of every pioneer, as well as the prosperous man of business, the statesman could have informed the Senator that the military policy of an agricultural nation of 3,000,000 people just emerging from the forest, was no policy for a nation extending from ocean to ocean and now numbering more than fifty millions. But bad as is our system it would be unpatriotic to attack it if at the same time no remedy could be suggested. In order that this work may not be misjudged we will first indicate to the reader the chief causes of weakness of our present system, and next will outline the system which ought to replace it.

The causes of the weakness are as follows:

First. The employment of militia and undisciplined troops commanded by generals and officers utterly ignorant of the military art.

Second. Short enlistments from three months to three years, instead of for or during the war.

Third. Reliance upon voluntary enlistments, instead of voluntary enlistments coupled with conscription.

Fourth. The intrusion of the States in military affairs and the consequent waging of all our wars on the theory that we are a confederacy instead of a nation.

Fifth. Confusing volunteers with militia and surrendering to the States the right to commission officers of volunteers the same as officers of militia.

Sixth. The bounty—a national consequence of voluntary enlistments.

Seventh. The failure to appreciate military education, and to distribute trained officers as battalion, regimental, and higher commanders in our volunteer armies.

Eighth. The want of territorial recruitment and regimental depots.

Ninth. The want of post-graduate schools to educate our officers in strategy and the higher principles of the art of war.

Tenth. The assumption of command by the Secretary of War.

The main features of the proposed system are as follows:

First. In time of peace and war the military forces of the country to consist of—

The Regular Army.

The National Volunteers, and

The Militia.

The Regular Army in time of peace to be organized on the expansive principle and in proportion to the population, not to exceed one thousand in one million.

The National Volunteers to be officered and supported by the Government, to be organized on the expansive principle and to consist in time of peace of one battalion of two hundred men to each Congressional district.

The Militia to be supported exclusively by the States and as a last resort to be used only as intended by the Constitution, namely, to execute the laws, suppress insurrections, and repel invasions.

The author is well aware that in suggesting this system he will be accused of favoring centralization and strong government. This is a charge which he would neither covet nor deny. No soldier in battle ever witnessed the flight of an undisciplined army without wishing for a strong government, but a government no stronger than was designed by the fathers of the Republic.

Founded in the affections of the people, the Constitution in time of danger gives Congress absolute power to raise and support armies and to lay its hands upon every man and every dollar within the territory of the nation.

Recognizing, moreover, that the individual life is to be sacrificed to the life of a state, the same Constitution permits the suspension of the writ of habeas corpus, giving to Congress and to the President power not only over life and property, but over the liberty of every citizen of the Republic. It is a popular delusion that armies make wars; the fact is wars inevitably make armies. No matter what the form of government, war, at the discretion of the rulers, means absolute despotism, the danger from which increases as the war is prolonged. Armies in time of peace have seldom if ever overthrown their governments, but in time of anarchy and war the people have often sought to dictate, and purchase peace at the expense of their liberty. If we would escape this danger we should make war with a strong arm. No foreign invader should ever be allowed a foothold on our soil. Recognizing, too, that under popular institutions the majority of the people create the government and that the majority will never revolt, it should be our policy to suppress every riot and stamp out every insurrection before it swells to rebellion. This means a strong government, but shall we find greater safety in one that is weaker?

Military resources are one thing and military strength another. For military resistance, the strength of a government is the power it can wield on the field of battle. In the War of 1812 the strength of the Government at the battle of Bladensburg was measured by 6,000 militia; at Bull Run it was measured by 35,000 of the same kind of troops. In one case the capital fell into the hands of the enemy, while in the other our existence as a nation possibly depended upon the irresolution and supineness of a band of insurgents. At Gettysburg the wave of rebellion was resisted by 80,000 veteran troops; had we trusted to the same number of militia the capital would have been captured and the Government hopelessly destroyed. Unable to suppress in two years an insurrection which culminated in a great rebellion, the representatives of the people were forced to adopt conscription and to concentrate in the hands of the President all the war powers granted by the Constitution, whereupon weakness gave place to strength, but at the expense of a needless sacrifice of life and property.

If in time of rebellion our own Government grew more despotic as it grew stronger, it is not to be inferred that there is any necessary connection between despotism and military strength.

Twenty thousand regular troops at Bull Run would have routed the insurgents, settled the question of military resistance, and relieved us from the pain and suspense of four years of war.

China, the most despotic of Governments, has no military strength; numbering 400,000,000 people, she has been twice conquered by a few despised Tartars, and only a few years ago 20,000 English and French dictated peace at the walls of the capital. In Persia the Shah can lop off the heads of his subjects or wall them up alive at his pleasure, and yet it has been said that a single foreign battalion could overthrow his throne, while a brigade would starve in his dominions.

In seeking to avoid the dangers of weakness and despotism the author would not have it imagined that his work will produce immediate effect, or that his system will be adopted in five, ten, or even twenty years. Such a revolution in our military policy must be preceded by a change in popular sentiment.

Foreign governments for more than a hundred years have recognized us as a nation, but, strange to say, a fact patent to all the world, is as yet recognized by scarcely a majority of our people.

Our forefathers hated Great Britain because she repeatedly subverted the government of the colonies. A large portion of their descendants, confusing states rights with state sovereignty, look upon the General Government as equally hostile to the States. When this feeling is abandoned; when it is understood that the life of the State is bound up in the life of the nation; when it is appreciated that republicanism, State and national, guaranteed by the Constitution, is the natural bulwark against the two forms of despotism—absolute monarchy on the one side and absolute democracy on the other—then, and not till then, will the views of the author be accepted. Should his work be received unkindly he will at least have the satisfaction that he has sought to be true to the Republic, and that in view of its increasing grandeur he has endeavored to present a military system which, recognizing the opposition to large standing armies, will still be compatible with the safety, honor, and the liberty of our people.

E. U.

FORT MONROE, VIRGINIA, 1880.

23. Chester A. Arthur: Military Revival in the 1880's

IN THE EARLY 1880's A MODEST BUT DEFINITE MILITARY REVIVAL began. The obsolete state of the Navy, the Army's seacoast forts, the National Guard, and the heavy-armaments industry began to awake attention. In his annual message of December 4, 1883, President Arthur described these beginnings and urged that they be carried forward. He did so, however, in very mild, if not tepid, language. The final paragraphs of this section of his message indicate how little these stirrings reflected any change in the traditional passive and defensive military policies, or in the traditional suspicious and penurious attitudes toward military appropriations.

. . . From the report of the Secretary of War it will be seen that in only a single instance has there been any disturbance of the quiet condition of our Indian tribes. A raid from Mexico into Arizona was made in March last by a small party of Indians, which was pursued by General Crook into the mountain regions from which it had come. It is confidently hoped that serious outbreaks will not again occur and that the Indian tribes which have for so many years disturbed the West will hereafter remain in peaceable submission.

I again call your attention to the present condition of our extended seacoast, upon which are so many large cities whose wealth and importance to the country would in time of war invite attack from modern armored ships, against which our existing defensive works could give no adequate protection. Those works were built before the introduction of modern heavy rifled guns into maritime warfare, and if they are not put in an efficient condition we may easily be subjected to humiliation by a hostile power greatly inferior to ourselves. As germane to this subject, I call your attention to the importance of perfecting our submarine-torpedo defenses. The board[1] authorized by the last Congress to report upon the method which should be adopted for the manufacture of heavy ordnance adapted to modern warfare has visited the principal iron and steel works in this country and in Europe. It is hoped that its report will soon be made, and that Congress will thereupon be disposed to provide suitable facilities

From *Messages of the Presidents*, X, pp. 4767–4769.

[1] The Gun-Foundry Board [Ed.].

and plant for the manufacture of such guns as are now impera-
tively needed.

On several occasions during the past year officers of the Army
have at the request of the State authorities visited their militia encampments for inspection of the troops. From the reports of these
officers I am induced to believe that the encouragement of the
State militia organizations by the National Government would be
followed by very gratifying results, and would afford it in sudden
emergencies the aid of a large body of volunteers educated in
the performance of military duties.

The Secretary of the Navy reports that under the authority of
the acts of August 5, 1882, and March 3, 1883, the work of
strengthening our Navy by the construction of modern vessels has
been auspiciously begun. Three cruisers are in process of construction—the *Chicago*, of 4,500 tons displacement, and the
Boston and *Atlanta*, each of 2,500 tons. They are to be built of
steel, with the tensile strength and ductility prescribed by law,
and in the combination of speed, endurance, and armament are
expected to compare favorably with the best unarmored war vessels of other nations. A fourth vessel, the *Dolphin*, is to be constructed of similar material, and is intended to serve as a fleet
dispatch boat.

The double-turreted monitors *Puritan, Amphitrite,* and *Terror*
have been launched on the Delaware River and a contract has
been made for the supply of their machinery. A similar monitor,
the *Monadnock*, has been launched in California.

The Naval Advisory Board and the Secretary recommend the
completion of the monitors, the construction of four gunboats,
and also of three additional steel vessels like the *Chicago, Boston,*
and *Dolphin.*

As an important measure of national defense, the Secretary
urges also the immediate creation of an interior coast line of wa-
terways across the peninsula of Florida, along the coast from
Florida to Hampton Roads, between the Chesapeake Bay and
the Delaware River, and through Cape Cod.

I feel bound to impress upon the attention of Congress the

necessity of continued progress in the reconstruction of the Navy. The condition of the public Treasury, as I have already intimated, makes the present an auspicious time for putting this branch of the service in a state of efficiency.

It is no part of our policy to create and maintain a Navy able to cope with that of the other great powers of the world.

We have no wish for foreign conquest, and the peace which we have long enjoyed is in no seeming danger of interruption.

But that our naval strength should be made adequate for the defense of our harbors, the protection of our commercial interests, and the maintenance of our national honor is a proposition from which no patriotic citizen can withhold his assent. . . .

24. The Endicott Board: Modernizing the Coast Defenses

THE CLEVELAND ADMINISTRATION NOT ONLY PRESSED FORWARD WITH the Naval modernization begun under President Arthur, but also started upon the rehabilitation of the coast defenses. With the new Secretary of War, William C. Endicott, as its head, a board largely composed of officers (it included both Brigadier General Stephen V. Benét, grandfather of the later famous poet, and Commander W. T. Sampson, the subsequent victor at the battle of Santiago) was set up to study the problem. The report is notable for the sweeping character of the program it recommended, calling not only for hundreds of batteries of heavy and light ordnance, but also for searchlight, mine, and torpedo-boat defenses. It is notable also for its exposition of the military technology of the time and for its strategic reasoning. The latter is still almost wholly theoretical. It still sees war as primarily a problem in cost accounting and is consequently still preoccupied with the possible "plunder" of the coast cities. It was so detached from political and historical actuality that it could even recommend a massive re-fortification of the demilitarized Canadian border.

The Canadian border was not refortified, and the board's program, soon to undergo the inevitable wear and tear of advancing technology, was never more than partially fulfilled. It initiated, nevertheless, an extensive effort toward modernizing the coast defenses. The rebuilding of the Navy in the 1880's and 1890's is a familiar story; not many are today aware of the simultaneous rebuilding and rearming of the forts, which by the early years of the twentieth century had given the United States a reasonably adequate and modern coast-defense system.

Order of the President.

Executive Mansion, *Washington, May* 12, 1885.

Under a provision of an act of Congress entitled "An act making appropriations for fortifications and other works of defense, and for the armament thereof for the fiscal year ending June thirtieth, eighteen hundred and eighty-six, and for other purposes," approved March 3, 1885, a Board, to consist of the officers and civilians hereinafter named, is appointed to "examine and report at what ports fortifications or other defenses are most urgently required, the character and kind of defenses best adapted for each, with reference to armament," and "the utilization of torpedoes, mines, or other defensive appliances:"

Hon. William C. Endicott, Secretary of War, president of the Board.
Brigadier-General Stephen V. Benét, Chief of Ordnance.
Brigadier-General John Newton, Chief of Engineers.
Lieutenant-Colonel Henry L. Abbot, Corps of Engineers.
Captain Charles S. Smith, Ordnance Department.
Commander W. T. Sampson, U. S. Navy.
Commander Caspar F. Goodrich, U. S. Navy.
Mr. Joseph Morgan, jr., of Pennsylvania.
Mr. Erastus Corning, of New York.

Grover Cleveland.

The Board convened by order of the President has the honor to submit the following report:

From *Report of the Board on Fortifications or Other Defenses,* House Executive Documents, 49th Congress, Session 1, pp. 5–10, 13–15, 26–27.

The reports of the Chief of Engineers of the Army have annually laid before the country the condition of the national defenses, and attention is specially invited to those of 1880, 1881, 1882, and 1884.

Without enlarging upon this subject, it suffices to state that the coast fortifications, which in 1860 were not surpassed by those of any country for efficiency, either for offense or defense, and were entirely competent to resist vessels of war of that period, have, since the introduction of rifled guns of heavy power and of armor plating in the navies of the world, become unable to cope with modern iron or steel-clad ships of war; far less to prevent their passage into the ports destined for attack.

Prior to 1860 the largest gun in service was the 10-inch Rodman smooth-bore, the energy of whose projectile was 2,000 foot-tons. The forts of that period were more than competent to resist its projectile; it should form, therefore, no subject of reproach because at present they cannot withstand the shock of 20,000, 30,000, and 45,000 foot-tons of energy, without mentioning the new guns under construction expected to deliver 61,000 foot-tons of energy. . . .

. . . It is of no advantage to conceal the fact that the ports along our sea-coast—a length of about 4,000 miles, not including Alaska—invite naval attack; nor that our richest ports, from their greater depth of water and capacity to admit the largest and most formidable armored ships, are of all the most defenseless.

The property at stake exposed to easy capture and destruction would amount to billions of dollars, and the contributions which could be levied by a hostile fleet upon our sea-ports should be reckoned at hundreds of millions.

It is impossible to understand the supineness which has kept this nation quiet—allowing its floating and shore defenses to become obsolete and effete—without making an effort to keep progress with the age, while other nations, besides constructing powerful navies, have not considered themselves secure without large expenditures for fortifications, including armored forts.

Our nearest neighbor, though reasoning from the past, she

should have no occasion to dread a naval attack from us, has nevertheless constructed armored forts at Halifax and Bermuda, both as a refuge for her fleets and as outposts for offensive operations.

In the mean time we have acquired great riches and apparently dreamed that prosperity should inspire friendship and not envy in less favored peoples—forgetting that riches are a temptation, and that the plunder of one of our sea-ports might abundantly reimburse an enemy for the expenses of a war conducted against us. . . .

. . . The objects against which a naval attack would be directed are—

First, the important commercial ports, containing, in addition to the shipping, large magazines of the products of commerce, and which are, on account of public and private wealth, tempting marks to an enemy. Such cities are also railroad centers, and their capture by an enemy would derange not only the internal commerce by land, but also interfere with the transportation of troops and *matériel* of war; and this might occur at critical junctures during military operations. And if, in addition, these places should be the sites of navy-yards, naval stations, and of depots of military and naval stores, the loss and injury to the country would be greatly increased.

In the second place, vessels in the foreign trade must be protected—this at sea could be performed only by the Navy—but when these arrive upon the coast, they should find fortified harbors of refuge provided for their security.

The third object of attack and capture would be the vessels employed in the coasting trade. A glance at the map of the coast will clearly indicate the dangers to which this commerce is exposed. An enemy having superior naval power might intercept all communication coastwise between New York and the ports of New England, by cruising in Vineyard and Long Island Sounds. His cruisers watching Sandy Hook, the mouths of Delaware and Chesapeake Bays, the coasts of Georgia and the Carolinas, the Florida straits and the Gulf coasts, would subject this trade to such risk of capture, that during war it would be virtually suspended. . . .

. . . The Board, in stating "at what ports fortifications or other defenses are most urgently required," presents the following list:

1. New York.   5. Hampton Roads.   9. Baltimore.
2. San Francisco.   6. New Orleans.   10. Portland, Me.
3. Boston.   7. Philadelphia.   11. Rhode Island ports in
4. The Lake ports.   8. Washington.   Narragansett Bay.

In the sequel the objects to be gained by the defense of the principal ports, as well as of others named in this report, will be commented upon. The Board will now consider "the character and kind of defenses best adapted for each, with reference to armament" and "the utilization of torpedoes, mines, or other defensive appliances," taking up the subject in the order in which it is presented to it.

The defenses, as to character and kind with reference to armament, should be fixed and floating, one or both, according to locality, armed with powerful cannon needed to repel attack from the most formidable ships.

In the phrase "floating defenses" just used, the armored seagoing ship of the Navy is not referred to. We have none of that kind, and if hereafter built in sufficient number and power they would act offensively and not be confined to the defense of ports. The floating defenses mean floating batteries designed specially for operating in harbors or close to the land—armored more heavily and armed with heavier guns than any probable adversary. Of considerably less draught than the armored seagoing ship they could, by operating among the shoals, avoid ramming, and even torpedoes. To gain such advantages speed must be sacrificed, but it is quite evident that for the defense of harbors and bays the advantages of extra thickness of armor and of superior power of gun more than compensate for that loss. These batteries are costly, and their use should be restricted to cases of necessity; as, for instance, where the port is so near to deep water that a bombardment may not otherwise be prevented; also in localities where the nature of the foundations forbids the construction of fixed defenses, or where the width of the channel is too great to be well swept from shore batteries. . . .

. . .The shore batteries may be armored turrets revolving or fixed, armored casemates, and emplacements in barbette. . . .

. . . It is not generally considered possible to bar the progress of an armored fleet by the mere fire of the battery; some obstruction sufficient to arrest the ships within effective range of the guns is necessary. The kind of obstruction now relied upon is the torpedo in the form of a submarine mine, and except in special cases exploded by electric currents, which are so managed that the operator on shore can either ignite the mine under the ship's bottom or allow the ship to explode it by contact. . . .

. . . Special batteries of guns are instituted for the defense of the lines of mines against the attempt of unarmored or light armored boats to countermine or grapple for their attachments. . . .

. . .When practicable every mine-field should be commanded by electric search-lights, so that the enemy's attempts at night to tamper with the mines may be detected and rendered abortive.

Movable torpedoes operated from shore stations are still in the experimental stage; and no definite recommendation except for experimental trials could now be made. The successful operation of these torpedoes would add another element to the defense of the mines.

Torpedo boats would prove of great use in defeating attempts against the mines, made either with small or large vessels.

Heavy batteries and submarine mines are correlative terms of a good defense from the shore. Without powerful guns in the defense the armored ships of the enemy would proceed deliberately to the removal of the mines, either ignoring or silencing the fire of the works, and without the aid of the mines the enemy's vessels could not generally be prevented from running past the batteries. . . .

. . . Rapid-firing guns also would be of use against the torpedo boats and the unarmored portions of ships, and a certain number should be provided in the defense. Machine guns for flanking defenses and sweeping mine-fields, for repelling assaults upon the works, and for other purposes, will be necessary. . . .

. . . Among the most important means of conducting an active defense of the coast is the torpedo boat, which, although recently developed, has received the sanction of the nations of Europe, each one of which now possesses a large number of these vessels. Their use will be quite general, first, in disturbing blockades and preventing these from being made close, as no fleet would like to lie *over night* within striking distance of a station of these boats; second, in attacking an enemy's ship enveloped in fog or smoke; third, in relieving a vessel pursued by the enemy; fourth, in defending the mines by night and day against attempts at countermining, and in many other ways not necessary to recapitulate.

Impressed with the utility of this mode of defense, the Board has recommended the construction of 150 of these boats, and desires further to say that in its opinion this service requires a special corps of officers and men from the Navy trained to their use.

The self-moving torpedo, one example being the "Whitehead," would be the main reliance. The spar torpedo might be used from launches, but as in general this service would be of the nature of a forlorn hope, and liable to fail of success, its principal recommendation would be ease of improvising and the absence of other suitable means to the end.

Submarine boats have not passed the experimental stage, and the Board has at present no recommendation to make in their regard.

Aerial torpedoes with large charges of high explosives projected in curved or vertical fire, while they demand consideration, have not yet arrived at a stage of development demanding practical discussion.

LIST OF PORTS, WITH DESCRIPTION OF FORTIFICATIONS AND OTHER DEFENSES, WITH REFERENCE TO ARMAMENT, MINES, TORPEDOES, ETC.

(1) *New York.*—This important port must be fortified at both entrances in the most thorough manner. *Fortifications:* Turrets,

armored casemates, barbette batteries, mortar batteries. Submarine mines will form a part of the defense. Eighteen torpedo boats are recommended for service in this harbor.

Proposed armament.

Caliber.	Kind.	Number.	Remarks.
16-inch	110-ton guns	18	B. L. R. [Breech-Loading Rifle]
14-inch	80-ton guns	2	B. L. R.
12-inch	50-ton guns	40	B. L. R.
10-inch	27-ton guns	20	B. L. R.
8-inch	13-ton guns	15	B. L. R.
12-inch	Mortars	144	Rifled.

(2) *San Francisco.*—This is a most exposed point, and, owing to the width across the channel, difficult to be defended by guns from the shore. Floating batteries are consequently required to be added to the defense. *Fortifications:* Turrets, barbette batteries, mortar batteries. Submarine mines will form a part of the defense. Eighteen torpedo boats are recommended for service at this harbor. Three floating batteries are recommended for the defense in addition to the land batteries.

Proposed armament.

Caliber.	Kind.	Number.	Remarks.
16-inch	110-ton guns	10	B. L. R.
14-inch	80-ton guns	4	B. L. R.
12-inch	50-ton guns	20	B. L. R.
10-inch	27-ton guns	71	B. L. R.
8-inch	13-ton guns	5	B. L. R.
12-inch	Mortars	128	Rifled.

(3) *Boston.*—This port has a wide opening to seaward, with three approaches, and consequently requires extensive works of defense. *Fortifications:* Turrets, armored casemates, barbette batteries, mortar batteries. Submarine mines will form a part of the defense. Eighteen torpedo-boats are recommended for service here.

Proposed armament.

Caliber.	Kind.	Number.	Remarks.
16-inch	110-ton guns	8	B. L. R.
12-inch	50-ton guns	10	B. L. R.
10-inch	27-ton guns	15	B. L. R.
8-inch	13-ton guns	10	B. L. R.
12-inch	Mortars	132	Rifled.

(4) *The Lake ports.*—The situation being peculiar, an explanation becomes necessary. The treaty of 1817 between the United States and England limited each party to an insignficant naval force upon the Lakes. At that time the country on both sides was undeveloped; with the exception of Detroit there was nothing perhaps deserving the name of town upon the Upper Lakes. Everything has changed; large cities as centers of commerce now dot the coasts of the lake, and the wealth and property liable to capture and destruction are enormous in amount. In the mean while our neighbors over the line have surmounted the rapids of the Saint Lawrence and the Falls of Niagara by canals which, in their present condition, permit the passage of boats of 9 feet draught, and when the improvements shall have been finished will have a depth of 14 feet. The present draught will admit many gunboats now in the possession of Great Britain, and when the depth of water is increased, armored vessels from the other side of the Atlantic may float in the waters of Lake Erie. A state of war, therefore, with that power, would at this time, unless something be done to avert the consequences, involve the lake cities in frightful losses or even destruction. These cities, being upon the shore, could not by land forts be protected from bombardment. Fort Wayne, on the Detroit River, if supplied with suitable armament well placed, could, with the assistance of submarine mines and torpedoes, prohibit a passage into Lake Huron. The canal at the Sault Ste. Marie would also demand a fort to protect it from destruction.

Our commerce on the Upper Lakes is much more extensive

than that of Canada, and doubtless many of the steamers might at a pinch be converted into light-armed naval vessels. But to do this, with any prospect of anticipating the arrival of British gunboats after the declaration of war, the vessels should be inspected, beginning now, and the inspections continued, so that a perfect knowledge might be obtained of the number and description of all that might be fit for the service designed, and plans of their modification to receive the guns be made and kept, so that when the vessels are wanted there should be no unnecessary delay in preparing them for service. It is needless to state that the guns and other necessary material should also be provided, ready for use at a moment's warning.

Upon Lake Ontario the Canadian commerce is superior to ours. Some protection, however, would be needed here, which, imperfect as it is, might serve a good purpose. It is proposed to keep in one of the interior lakes of New York vessels armed with light guns and furnished with self-moving torpedoes, to be sent when needed, by canal, into Lake Ontario. Some might be sent to Buffalo for service in the Upper Lakes. A port of refuge against the superior naval force of England should be provided in the lower part of Lake Ontario.

The fort at Rouse's Point is sufficient, with the addition of a few 8-inch rifles, to secure Lake Champlain from an inroad.

It may be observed that one or more fortifications on the Saint Lawrence River would be required, which, in the event of hostilities, could at once protect our frontier and command the water approaches to the Lakes. They would be more reliable than an improvised fleet upon Lake Erie, though they could not wholly take its place.

Proposed armament.

Locality.	Caliber.	Kind.	Number.	Remarks.
Fort Wayne	10-inch	27-ton guns	3	B. L. R.
	8-inch	13-ton guns	3	B. L. R.
	6-inch	5-ton guns	4	B. L. R.
	10-inch	Mortars	8	Rifled.

Proposed fort on Saint				
Lawrence River	12-inch	50-ton guns	2	B. L. R.
	10-inch	27-ton guns	6	B. L. R.
	10-inch	Mortars	8	Rifled.
Fort Montgomery, Rouse's				
Point	8-inch	13-ton guns	4	B. L. R.
	10-inch	Mortars	8	Rifled.

[After considering the lesser ports in turn, making similar though smaller recommendations for each, the board turned to the industrial problem.]

... After a careful study of the extensive plant required for the production of steel-gun forgings and armor-plates of sizes, thicknesses, and qualities suitable for such manufacture, and after an inspection of our principal works and foundries, the conclusion is forced upon the Board that the necessary facilities for the production of such large masses of steel, and the machines for fashioning this metal into guns and armor, are not now to be found in this country. . . .

. . . It is clear that to effect the object of the act of Congress under which this Board was appointed, the manufacture and tempering of steel in enormous masses must be provided for by Congressional legislation.

The same can be said of the large and extensive workshops, and tools for machining the steel.

The Board, basing its estimates upon the report of the Gun-Foundry Board, considered that, to accomplish the work and accomplish it well, the plant necessary for making the tempered steel for the parts of guns up to the largest calibers will cost about $850,000, and that the plant for fabricating such guns will cost about $900,000,—this sum being exclusive of expenditures necessary to arm the Navy.

The vital question then arises, in what manner can such steel works and machine shops be best created?

It cannot be expected that even the richest and most flourishing of our steel works, with millions of capital to uphold it, will venture such an amount of money in plant, merely in the doubtful hope that the Government may give a contract sufficiently large to save it from loss.

Business men know that the action of one Congress does not control the action of subsequent Congresses, and that, unless the appropriation is made permanent, running through several years, pledging the United States to such an expenditure, there is no certainty as to the future, and the risk is far greater than the chances of profit.

After due consideration of the subject, this Board indorses the conclusions of the Gun-Foundry Board contained in the supplementary report of December 20, 1884, as follows, viz:

> The question whether the fabrication can be better and more economically performed in Government establishments, or by private contract, or by a combined system, has been carefully considered, and the Board has been unable to discover any reason to modify the unanimous opinion expressed in its report of February 16, 1884, that "it is more judicious to establish gun factories;" that there should be "two gun factories under the control of the Government; and that the Army and Navy should be provided with separate establishments."

The requirements of the two services in this respect are sufficiently distinct to justify two separate establishments, which, in the interests of the national defense, would be fully occupied for many years to come—probably long enough to exhaust their capacity for good work.

An appropriation, therefore, of $1,000,000 for a factory is recommended and should be made at once, as it would require about two years to erect and equip it. The money required for machining and completing the guns at the factory could be appropriated in the following year, when the forgings would be about ready for delivery [by the private manufacturers]. . . .

25. Alfred Thayer Mahan: Philosopher of Sea Power

IN 1886, THE YEAR OF THE ENDICOTT BOARD REPORT, CAPTAIN ALFRED Thayer Mahan arrived at the new War College at Newport, Rhode

Island, as professor of naval history and tactics. The son of "Old Dennis" Mahan, who at West Point had taught military engineering and tactics to most of the future leaders of the Civil War, Captain Mahan was himself of studious bent, and his carefully researched lectures soon began to attract attention. Opposed by the shellbacks among the professional seamen, Mahan and the War College were to find powerful allies among the new forces in politics and industry coming to the fore in the late 1880's. Theodore Roosevelt, for example, then a rising young politician already noted as the author of a naval history of the War of 1812, gave a jingoistic speech at the War College.

Mahan's lectures were influential even before the book based upon them, *The Influence of Sea Power Upon History, 1660–1783*, was published in 1890. His full sea-power theory developed rather slowly through many later books and papers; it can be only briefly represented here; but the style, method, and much of the argument appear in the first chapter of the first and most famous volume.

The first and most obvious light in which the sea presents itself from the political and social point of view is that of a great highway; or better, perhaps, of a wide common, over which men may pass in all directions, but on which some well-worn paths show that controlling reasons have led them to choose certain lines of travel rather than others. These lines of travel are called trade routes; and the reasons which have determined them are to be sought in the history of the world.

Notwithstanding all the familiar and unfamiliar dangers of the sea, both travel and traffic by water have always been easier and cheaper than by land. The commercial greatness of Holland was due not only to her shipping at sea, but also to the numerous tranquil water-ways which gave such cheap and easy access to her own interior and to that of Germany. This advantage of carriage by water over that by land was yet more marked in a period when roads were few and very bad, wars frequent and society unsettled, as was the case two hundred years ago. Sea traffic then went

From Captain A. T. Mahan, *The Influence of Sea Power upon History, 1660–1783* (Boston: Little, Brown and Company, 1890), pp. 25–89.

in peril of robbers, but was nevertheless safer and quicker than that by land. A Dutch writer of that time, estimating the chances of his country in a war with England, notices among other things that the water-ways of England failed to penetrate the country sufficiently; therefore, the roads being bad, goods from one part of the kingdom to the other must go by sea, and be exposed to capture by the way. As regards purely internal trade, this danger has generally disappeared at the present day. In most civilized countries, now, the destruction or disappearance of the coasting trade would only be an inconvenience, although water transit is still the cheaper. Nevertheless, as late as the wars of the French Republic and the First Empire, those who are familiar with the history of the period, and the light naval literature that has grown up around it, know how constant is the mention of convoys stealing from point to point along the French coast, although the sea swarmed with English cruisers and there were good inland roads.

Under modern conditions, however, home trade is but a part of the business of a country bordering on the sea. Foreign necessaries or luxuries must be brought to its ports, either in its own or in foreign ships, which will return, bearing in exchange the products of the country, whether they be the fruits of the earth or the works of men's hands; and it is the wish of every nation that this shipping business should be done by its own vessels. The ships that thus sail to and fro must have secure ports to which to return, and must, as far as possible, be followed by the protection of their country throughout the voyage.

This protection in time of war must be extended by armed shipping. The necessity of a navy, in the restricted sense of the word, springs, therefore, from the existence of a peaceful shipping, and disappears with it, except in the case of a nation which has aggressive tendencies, and keeps up a navy merely as a branch of the military establishment. As the United States has at present no aggressive purposes, and as its merchant service has disappeared, the dwindling of the armed fleet and general lack of interest in it are strictly logical consequences. When for any reason sea trade is again found to pay, a large enough shipping interest will reappear to compel the revival of the war fleet. It is possible that when a canal route through the Central-American Isthmus is seen to be a near certainty, the aggressive impulse may be strong enough to lead to the same result. This is doubtful, however, because a peaceful, gain-loving nation is not far-sighted, and far-sightedness is needed for adequate military preparation, especially in these days.

As a nation, with its unarmed and armed shipping, launches forth from its own shores, the need is soon felt of points upon which the ships can rely for peaceful trading, for refuge and supplies. In the present day friendly, though foreign, ports are to be found all over the world; and their shelter is enough while peace prevails. It was not always so, nor does peace always endure, though the United States have been favored by so long a continuance of it. In earlier times the merchant seaman, seeking for trade in new and unexplored regions, made his gains at risk of life and liberty from suspicious or hostile nations, and was under great delays in collecting a full and profitable freight. He therefore intuitively sought at the far end of his trade route one or more stations, to be given to him by force or favor, where he could fix himself or his agents in reasonable security, where his ships could lie in safety, and where the merchantable products of the land could be continually collecting, awaiting the arrival of the home fleet, which should carry them to the mother-country. As there was immense gain, as well as much risk, in these early voyages, such establishments naturally multiplied and grew until they became colonies; whose ultimate development and success depended upon the genius and policy of the nation from which they sprang, and form a very great part of the history, and particularly of the sea history, of the world. All colonies had not the simple and natural birth and growth above described. Many were more formal, and purely political, in their conception and founding, the act of the rulers of the people rather than of private individuals; but the trading-station with its after expansion, the work simply of the adventurer seeking gain, was in its reasons and essence the same as the elaborately organized and chartered colony. In both cases the mother-country had won a foothold in a foreign land, seeking a new outlet for what it had to sell, a new sphere for its shipping, more employment for its people, more comfort and wealth for itself.

The needs of commerce, however, were not all provided for when safety had been secured at the far end of the road. The voyages were long and dangerous, the seas often beset with enemies. In the most active days of colonizing there prevailed on the sea a lawlessness the very memory of which is now almost lost, and the days of settled peace between maritime nations were few and far between. Thus arose the demand for stations along the road, like the Cape of Good Hope, St. Helena, and Mauritius, not primarily for trade, but for defence and war; the demand for the possession of posts like Gibraltar, Malta, Louisburg, at the entrance of the Gulf of St. Lawrence,—posts whose value was chiefly strategic, though not necessarily wholly so. Colonies and colonial posts were sometimes commercial, sometimes military in their character; and it was exceptional that the same position was equally important in both points of view, as New York was.

In these three things—production, with the necessity of exchanging products, shipping, whereby the exchange is carried on, and colonies, which facilitate and enlarge the operations of shipping and tend to protect it by multiplying points of safety—is to be found the key to much of the history, as well as of the policy, of nations bordering upon the sea. The policy has varied both with the spirit of the age and with the character and clear-sightedness of the rulers; but the history of the seaboard nations has been less determined by the shrewdness and foresight of governments than by conditions of position, extent, configuration, number and character of their people,—by what are called, in a word, natural conditions. It must however be admitted, and will be seen, that the wise or unwise action of individual men has at certain periods had a great modifying influence upon the growth of sea power in the broad sense, which includes not only the military strength afloat, that rules the sea or any part of it by force of arms, but also the peaceful commerce and shipping from which alone a military fleet naturally and healthfully springs, and on which it securely rests.

The principal conditions affecting the sea power of nations may be enumerated as follows: I. Geographical Position. II. Physical Conformation, including, as connected therewith, natural productions and climate. III. Extent of Territory. IV. Number of Population. V. Character of the People. VI. Character of the Government, including therein the national institutions.

I. *Geographical Position.*—It may be pointed out, in the first place, that if a nation be so situated that it is neither forced to defend itself by land nor induced to seek extension of its territory by way of the land, it has, by the very unity of its aim directed upon the sea, an advantage as compared with a people one of whose boundaries is continental. This has been a great advantage to England over both France and Holland as a sea power. The strength of the latter was early exhausted by the necessity of keeping up a large army and carrying on expensive wars to preserve her independence; while the policy of France was constantly diverted, sometimes wisely and sometimes most foolishly, from the sea to projects of continental extension. These military efforts expended wealth; whereas a wiser and consistent use of her geographical position would have added to it.

The geographical position may be such as of itself to promote a concentration, or to necessitate a dispersion, of the naval forces. Here again the British Islands have an advantage over France. The position of the latter, touching the Mediterranean as well as the ocean, while it has its advantages, is on the whole a source of military weakness at sea. The eastern and western French fleets have only been able to unite after passing through the Straits of Gibraltar, in attempting which they have often risked and sometimes suffered loss. The position of the United States upon the two oceans would be either a source of great weakness or a cause of enormous expense, had it a large sea commerce on both coasts. . . .

. . . Two remarks, however, are here appropriate.

Circumstances have caused the Mediterranean Sea to play a greater part in the history of the world, both in a commercial and a military point of view, than any other sheet of water of the same size. Nation after nation has striven to control it, and the strife still goes on. Therefore a study of the conditions upon which preponderance in its waters has rested, and now rests, and of the relative military values of different points upon its coasts, will be more instructive than the same amount of effort expended in another field. Furthermore, it has at the present time a very marked analogy in many respects to the Caribbean Sea,—an analogy which will be still closer if a Panama canal-route ever be completed. A study of the strategic conditions of the Mediterranean, which have received ample illustration, will be an excellent prelude to a similar study of the Caribbean, which has comparatively little history.

The second remark bears upon the geographical position of the United States relatively to a Central-American canal. If one be made, and fulfil the hopes of its builders, the Caribbean will be changed from a terminus, and place of local traffic, or at best a broken and imperfect line of travel, as it now is, into one of the great highways of the world. Along this path a great commerce will travel, bringing the interests of the other great nations, the European nations, close along our shores, as they have never been before. With this it will not be so easy as heretofore to stand aloof from international complications. The position of the United States with reference to this route will resemble that of England to the Channel, and of the Mediterranean countries to the Suez route. As regards influence and control over it, depending upon geographical position, it is of course plain that the centre of the national power, the permanent base, is much nearer than that of other great nations. The positions now or hereafter occupied by them on island or mainland, however strong, will be but outposts of their power; while in all the raw materials of military strength no nation is superior to the United States. She is, however, weak in a confessed unpreparedness for war; and her geographical nearness to the point of contention loses some of its value by the character of the Gulf coast, which is deficient in ports combining security from an enemy with facility for repairing war-ships of the first class, without which ships no country can pretend to control any part of the sea. In case of a contest for supremacy in the Caribbean, it seems evident from the depth of the South Pass of the Mississippi, the nearness of New Orleans, and the advantages of the Mississippi Valley for water transit, that the main effort of the country must pour down that valley, and its permanent base of operations be found there. The defence of the entrance to the Mississippi, however, presents peculiar difficulties; while the only two rival ports, Key West and Pensacola, have too little depth of water, and are much less advantageously placed with reference to the resources of the country. To get the full benefit of superior geographical position, these defects must be overcome. Furthermore, as her distance from the Isthmus, though relatively less, is still considerable, the United States will have to obtain in the Caribbean stations fit for contingent, or secondary, bases of operations; which by their natural advantages, susceptibility of defence, and nearness to the central strategic issue, will enable her fleets to remain as near the scene as any opponent. With ingress and egress from the Mississippi sufficiently protected, with such outposts in her hands, and with the communications between them and the home base secured, in short, with proper military preparation, for which she has all necessary means, the preponderance of the United States on this field follows, from her geographical position and her power, with mathematical certainty.

II. *Physical Conformation.*—The peculiar features of the Gulf coast, just alluded to, come properly under the head of Physical Conformation of a country, which is placed second for discussion among the conditions which affect the development of sea power.

The seaboard of a country is one of its frontiers; and the easier the access offered by the frontier to the region beyond, in this case the sea, the greater will be the tendency of a people toward intercourse with the rest of the world by it. If a country be imagined having a long seaboard, but entirely without a harbor, such a country can have no sea trade of its own, no shipping, no navy. . . .

... Numerous and deep harbors are a source of strength and wealth, and doubly so if they are the outlets of navigable streams, which facilitate the concentration in them of a country's internal trade; but by their very accessibility they become a source of weakness in war, if not properly defended. The Dutch in 1667 found little difficulty in ascending the Thames and burning a large fraction of the English navy within sight of London; whereas a few years later the combined fleets of England and France, when attempting a landing in Holland, were foiled by the difficulties of the coast as much as by the valor of the Dutch fleet. In 1778 the harbor of New York, and with it undisputed control of the Hudson River, would have been lost to the English, who were caught at disadvantage, but for the hesitancy of the French admiral. With that control, New England would have been restored to close and safe communication with New York, New Jersey, and Pennsylvania; and this blow, following so closely on Burgoyne's disaster of the year before, would probably have led the English to make an earlier peace. The Mississippi is a mighty source of wealth and strength to the United States; but the feeble defences of its mouth and the number of its subsidiary streams penetrating the country made it a weakness and source of disaster to the Southern Confederacy. And lastly, in 1814, the occupation of the Chesapeake and the destruction of Washington gave a sharp lesson of the dangers incurred through the noblest water-ways, if their approaches be undefended; a lesson recent enough to be easily recalled, but which, from the present appearance of the coast defences, seems to be yet more easily forgotten. Nor should it be thought that conditions have changed; circumstances and details of offence and defence have been modified, in these days as before, but the great conditions remain the same....

... Except Alaska, the United States has no outlying possession, —no foot of ground inaccessible by land. Its contour is such as to present few points specially weak from their saliency, and all important parts of the frontiers can be readily attained,—cheaply by water, rapidly by rail. The weakest frontier, the Pacific, is far removed from the most dangerous of possible enemies. The internal resources are boundless as compared with present needs;

we can live off ourselves indefinitely in "our little corner," to use the expression of a French officer to the author. Yet should that little corner be invaded by a new commercial route through the Isthmus, the United States in her turn may have the rude awakening of those who have abandoned their share in the common birthright of all people, the sea.

III. *Extent of Territory.*—The last of the conditions affecting the development of a nation as a sea power, and touching the country itself as distinguished from the people who dwell there, is Extent of Territory. This may be dismissed with comparatively few words.

As regards the development of sea power, it is not the total number of square miles which a country contains, but the length of its coast-line and the character of its harbors that are to be considered. As to these it is to be said that, the geographical and physical conditions being the same, extent of sea-coast is a source of strength or weakness according as the population is large or small. A country is in this like a fortress; the garrison must be proportioned to the *enceinte*. A recent familiar instance is found in the American War of Secession. Had the South had a people as numerous as it was warlike, and a navy commensurate to its other resources as a sea power, the great extent of its sea-coast and its numerous inlets would have been elements of great strength. The people of the United States and the Government of that day justly prided themselves on the effectiveness of the blockade of the whole Southern coast. It was a great feat, a very great feat; but it would have been an impossible feat had the Southerners been more numerous, and a nation of seamen. What was there shown was not, as has been said, how such a blockade can be maintained, but that such a blockade is possible in the face of a population not only unused to the sea, but also scanty in numbers. . . .

IV. *Number of Population.*—. . . In point of population it is not only the grand total, but the number following the sea or at least readily available for employment on ship-board and for the creation of naval material, that must be counted. . . .

[Here, Mahan argues the importance of reserves both of trained seamen and of skilled shipwrights to meet initial reverses in war. "It may be admitted," he concludes, "that a great population following callings related to the sea, is now, as formerly, a great element of sea power; that the United States is deficient in that element; and that its foundations can be laid only in a large commerce under her own flag."]

V. *National Character.*—The effect of national character and aptitudes upon the development of sea power will next be considered. . . .

[The gist of this section is that "a tendency to trade, involving of necessity the production of something to trade with, is the national characteristic most important to the development of sea power"; to this, Mahan adds another characteristic, "the capacity for planting healthy colonies." In both respects he contrasts the Spanish, French, and Dutch characters unfavorably to that of the British. He thought the national character of Americans, with their "instinct for commerce, bold enterprise in the pursuit of gain, and a keen sense for the trails that lead to it," would provide an admirable basis for the development of American sea power.]

VI. *Character of the Government.*—In discussing the effects upon the development of a nation's sea power exerted by its government and institutions, it will be necessary to avoid a tendency to over-philosophizing, to confine attention to obvious and immediate causes and their plain results, without prying too far beneath the surface for remote and ultimate influences.

Nevertheless, it must be noted that particular forms of government with their accompanying institutions, and the character of rulers at one time or another, have exercised a very marked influence upon the development of sea power. The various traits of a country and its people which have so far been considered constitute the natural characteristics with which a nation, like a man, begins its career; the conduct of the government in turn corresponds to the exercise of the intelligent will-power, which, according as it is wise, energetic and persevering, or the reverse, causes success or failure in a man's life or a nation's history.

It would seem probable that a government in full accord with the natural bias of its people would most successfully advance its growth in every respect; and, in the matter of sea power, the most brilliant successes have followed where there has been intelligent direction by a government fully imbued with the spirit of the people and conscious of its true general bent. Such a government is most certainly secured when the will of the people, or of their best natural exponents, has some large share in making it; but such free governments have sometimes fallen short, while on the other hand despotic power, wielded with judgment and consistency, has created at times a great sea commerce and a brilliant navy with greater directness than can be reached by the slower processes of a free people. The difficulty in the latter case is to insure perseverance after the death of a particular despot.

England having undoubtedly reached the greatest height of sea power of any modern nation, the action of her government first claims attention. In general direction this action has been consistent, though often far from praiseworthy. It has aimed steadily at the control of the sea. . . .

. . . At the peace [of Utrecht, 1713], while Holland received compensation by land, England obtained, besides commercial privileges in France, Spain, and the Spanish West Indies, the important maritime concessions of Gibraltar and Port Mahon in the Mediterranean; of Newfoundland, Nova Scotia, and Hudson's Bay in North America. The naval power of France and Spain had disappeared; that of Holland thenceforth steadily declined. Posted thus in America, the West Indies, and the Mediterranean, the English government thenceforth moved firmly forward on the path which made of the English kingdom the British Empire. For the twenty-five years following the Peace of Utrecht, peace was the chief aim of the ministers who directed the policy of the two great seaboard nations, France and England; but amid all the fluctuations of continental politics in a most unsettled period, abounding in petty wars and shifty treaties, the eye of England was steadily fixed on the maintenance of her sea power. . . . While England's policy thus steadily aimed at widening and strengthening the bases of her sway upon the ocean, the other governments of Europe seemed blind to the dangers to be feared from her sea growth. The miseries resulting from the overweening power of Spain in days long gone by seemed to be forgotten; forgotten also the more recent lesson of the bloody and costly wars provoked by the ambition and exaggerated power of Louis XIV. Under the eyes of the statesmen of Europe there was steadily and visibly being built up a third overwhelming power, destined to be used as selfishly, as aggressively, though not as cruelly, and much more successfully than any that had preceded it. This was the power of the sea, whose workings, because more silent than the clash of arms, are less often noted, though lying clearly enough on the surface. It can scarcely be denied that England's uncontrolled dominion of the seas, during almost the whole period chosen for our subject, was by long odds the chief among the military factors that determined the final issue. . . . When war broke out with Spain in 1739, the navy of England was in numbers more than equal to the combined navies of Spain and France; and during the quarter of a century of nearly uninterrupted war that followed, this numerical disproportion increased. In these wars England, at first instinctively, afterward with conscious purpose under a government that recognized her opportunity and the possibilities of her great sea power, rapidly built up that mighty colonial empire whose foundations were already securely laid in the characteristics of her colonists and the strength of her fleets. In strictly European affairs her wealth, the outcome of her sea power, made her play a conspicuous part during the same period. The system of subsidies, which began half a century before in the wars of Marlborough and received its most extensive development half a century later in the Napoleonic wars, maintained the efforts of her allies, which would have been crippled, if not paralyzed, without them. Who can deny that the government which with one hand strengthened its fainting allies on the continent with the life-blood of money, and with the other drove its own enemies off the sea and out of their chief possessions, Canada, Martinique, Guadeloupe, Havana, Manila, gave to its country the foremost role in European politics; and who can fail to see that the power which dwelt in that government, with a land narrow in extent and poor in resources, sprang directly from the sea? . . .

. . . This steady keeping to a general line of policy was doubtless made specially easy for successive English governments by the clear indications of the country's conditions. Singleness of purpose was to some extent imposed. The firm maintenance of her sea power, the haughty determination to make it felt, the wise state of preparation in which its military element was kept, were yet more due to that feature of her political institutions which practically gave the government, during the period in question, into the hands of a class,—a landed aristocracy. Such a class, whatever its defects otherwise, readily takes up and carries on a sound political tradition, is naturally proud of its country's glory, and comparatively insensible to the sufferings of the community by which that glory is maintained. It readily lays on the pecuniary burden necessary for preparation and for endurance of war. Being as a body rich, it feels those burdens less. Not being commercial, the sources of its own wealth are not so immediately endangered, and it does not share that political timidity which characterizes those whose property is exposed and business threatened,— the proverbial timidity of capital. Yet in England this class was not insensible to anything that touched her trade for good or ill. Both houses of Parliament vied in careful watchfulness over its extension and protection, and to the frequency of their inquiries a naval historian attributes the increased efficiency of the executive power in its management of the navy. Such a class also naturally imbibes and keeps up a spirit of military honor, which is of the first importance in ages when military institutions have not yet provided the sufficient substitute in what is called *esprit-de-corps*. But although full of class feeling and class prejudice, which made themselves felt in the navy as well as elsewhere, their practical sense left open the way of promotion to its highest honors to the more humbly born; and every age saw admirals who had sprung from the lowest of the people. In this the temper of the English upper class differed markedly from that of the French. As late as 1789, at the outbreak of the Revolution, the French Navy List still bore the name of an official whose duty was to verify the proofs of noble birth on the part of those intending to enter the naval school.

Since 1815, and especially in our own day, the government of England has passed very much more into the hands of the people at large. Whether her sea power will suffer therefrom remains to be seen. Its broad basis still remains in a great trade, large mechanical industries, and an extensive colonial system. Whether a democratic government will have the foresight, the keen sensitiveness to national position and credit, the willingness to insure its prosperity by adequate outpouring of money in times of peace, all which are necessary for military preparation, is yet an open question. Popular governments are not generally favorable to military expenditure, however necessary, and there are signs that England tends to drop behind. . . .

[It is seen that the influence of government upon the sea career of its people can work in two distinct but closely related ways.]

First, in peace: The government by its policy can favor the natural growth of a people's industries and its tendencies to seek adventure and gain by way of the sea; or it can try to develop such industries and such sea-going bent, when they do not naturally exist; or, on the other hand, the government may by mistaken action check and fetter the progress which the people left to themselves would make. In any one of these ways the influence of the government will be felt, making or marring the sea power of the country in the matter of peaceful commerce; upon which alone, it cannot be too often insisted, a thoroughly strong navy can be based.

Secondly, for war: The influence of the government will be felt in its most legitimate manner in maintaining an armed navy, of a size commensurate with the growth of its shipping and the importance of the interests connected with it. More important even than the size of the navy is the question of its institutions, favoring a healthful spirit and activity, and providing for rapid development in time of war by an adequate reserve of men and of ships and by measures for drawing out that general reserve power which has before been pointed to, when considering the character and pursuits of the people. Undoubtedly under this second head of warlike preparation must come the maintenance of suitable naval stations, in those distant parts of the world to which the armed shipping must follow the peaceful vessels of commerce. The protection of such stations must depend either upon direct military force, as do Gibraltar and Malta, or upon a surrounding friendly population, such as the American colonists once were to England, and, it may be presumed, the Australian colonists now are. Such friendly surroundings and backing, joined to a reasonable military provision, are the best of defences, and when combined with decided preponderance at sea, make a scattered and extensive empire, like that of England, secure; for while it is true that an unexpected attack may cause disaster in some one quarter, the actual superiority of naval power prevents such disaster from being general or irremediable. History has sufficiently proved this. England's naval bases have been in all parts of the world; and her fleets have at once protected them, kept open the communications between them, and relied upon them for shelter.

Colonies attached to the mother-country afford, therefore, the surest means of supporting abroad the sea power of a country. In peace, the influence of the government should be felt in promoting by all means a warmth of attachment and a unity of interest which will make the welfare of one the welfare of all, and the quarrel of one the quarrel of all; and in war, or rather for war, by inducing such measures of organization and defence as shall be felt by all to be a fair distribution of a burden of which each reaps the benefit.

Such colonies the United States has not and is not likely to have. As regards purely military naval stations, the feeling of her people was probably accurately expressed by an historian of the English navy a hundred years ago, speaking then of Gibraltar and Port Mahon. "Military governments," said he, "agree so little with the industry of a trading people, and are in themselves so repugnant to the genius of the British people, that I do not wonder that men of good sense and of all parties have inclined to give up these, as Tangiers was given up." Having therefore no foreign establishments, either colonial or military, the ships of war of the United States, in war, will be like land birds, unable to fly far from their own shores. To provide resting-places for them, where they can coal and repair, would be one of the first duties of a government proposing to itself the development of the power of the nation at sea.

As the practical object of this inquiry is to draw from the lessons of history inferences applicable to one's own country and service, it is proper now to ask how far the conditions of the United States involve serious danger, and call for action on the part of the government, in order to build again her sea power. It will not be too much to say that the action of the government since the Civil War, and up to this day, has been effectively directed solely to what has been called the first link in the chain which makes sea power. Internal development, great production, with the accompanying aim and boast of self-sufficingness, such has been the object, such to some extent the result. In this the government has faithfully reflected the bent of the controlling elements of the country, though it is not always easy to feel that such controlling elements are truly representative, even in a free country. However that may be, there is no doubt that, besides having no colonies, the intermediate link of a peaceful shipping, and the interests involved in it, are now likewise lacking. In short, the United States has only one link of the three.

The circumstances of naval war have changed so much within the last hundred years, that it may be doubted whether such disastrous effects on the one hand, or such brilliant prosperity on the other, as were seen in the wars between England and France, could now recur. In her secure and haughty sway of the seas England imposed a yoke on neutrals which will never again be borne; and the principle that the flag covers the goods is forever secured. The commerce of a belligerent can therefore now be safely carried on in neutral ships, except when contraband of war or to blockaded ports; and as regards the latter, it is also certain that there will be no more paper blockades. Putting aside therefore the question of defending her seaports from capture or contribution, as to which there is practical unanimity in theory and entire indifference in practice, what need has the United States of sea power? Her commerce is even now carried on by others; why should her people desire that which, if possessed, must be defended at great cost? So far as this question is economical, it is outside the scope of this work; but conditions which may entail suffering and loss on the country by war are directly pertinent to it. Granting therefore that the foreign trade of the United States, going and coming, is on board ships which an enemy cannot touch except when bound to a blockaded port, what will constitute an efficient blockade? The present definition is, that it is such as to constitute a manifest danger to a vessel seeking to enter or leave the port. . . . To avoid such blockades there must be a military force afloat that will at all times so endanger a blockading fleet that it can by no means keep its place. Then neutral ships, except those laden with contraband of war, can come and go freely, and maintain the commercial relations of the country with the world outside.

It may be urged that, with the extensive sea-coast of the United States, a blockade of the whole line cannot be effectively kept up. No one will more readily concede this than officers who remember how the blockade of the Southern coast alone was maintained. But in the present condition of the navy, and, it may be added, with any additions not exceeding those so far proposed by the government, the attempt to blockade Boston, New York, the Delaware, the Chesapeake, and the Mississippi, in other words, the great centres of export and import, would not entail upon one of the large maritime nations efforts greater than have been made before. England has at the same time blockaded Brest, the Biscay coast, Toulon, and Cadiz, when there were powerful squadrons lying within the harbors. It is true that commerce in neutral ships can then enter other ports of the United States than those named; but what a dislocation of the carrying traffic of the country, what failure of supplies at times, what inadequate means of transport by rail or water, of dockage, of lighterage, of warehousing, will be involved in such an enforced change of the ports of entry! Will there be no money loss, no suffering, consequent upon this? And when with much pain and expense these evils have been partially remedied, the enemy may be led to stop the new inlets as he did the old. The people of the United States will certainly not starve, but they may suffer grievously. As for supplies which are contraband of war, is there not reason to fear that the United States is not now able to go alone if an emergency should arise?

The question is eminently one in which the influence of the government should make itself felt, to build up for the nation a navy which, if not capable of reaching distant countries, shall at least be able to keep clear the chief approaches to its own. The eyes of the country have for a quarter of a century been turned from the sea; the results of such a policy and of its opposite will be shown in the instance of France and of England. Without asserting a narrow parallelism between the case of the United States and either of these, it may safely be said that it is essential to the welfare of the whole country that the conditions of trade and commerce should remain, as far as possible, unaffected by an external war. In order to do this, the enemy must be kept not only out of our ports, but far away from our coasts.

Can this navy be had without restoring the merchant shipping? It is doubtful. History has proved that such a purely military sea power can be built up by a despot, as was done by Louis XIV.; but though so fair seeming, experience showed that his navy was like a growth which having no root soon withers away. But in a representative government any military expenditure must have a strongly represented interest behind it, convinced of its necessity. Such an interest in sea power does not exist, cannot exist here without action by the government. How such a merchant shipping should be built up, whether by subsidies or by free trade, by constant administration of tonics or by free movement in the open air, is not a military but an economical question. Even had the United States a great national shipping, it may be doubted whether a sufficient navy would follow; the distance which separates her from other great powers, in one way a protection, is also a snare. The motive, if any there be, which will give the United States a navy, is probably now quickening in the Central American Isthmus. Let us hope it will not come to the birth too late.

Here concludes the general discussion of the principal elements which affect, favorably or unfavorably, the growth of sea power in nations. . . . There will next be examined the general history of Europe and America, with particular reference to the effect exercised upon that history, and upon the welfare of the people, by sea power in its broad sense. From time to time, as occasion offers, the aim will be to recall and reinforce the general teaching, already elicited, by particular illustrations. The general tenor of the study will therefore be strategical, in that broad definition of naval strategy which has before been quoted and accepted: "Naval strategy has for its end to found, support, and increase, as well in peace as in war, the sea power of a country."

26. Benjamin F. Tracy: The Beginning of the Battleship Fleet

ALFRED THAYER MAHAN, AS HE HIMSELF SAID, HAD EMBARKED UPON his studies with only a "superficial" acquaintance with naval history, but with the idea that closer analysis of this subject "would at least serve to imbue his hearers with an exalted sense of the mission of their calling; and might also, by throwing light upon the political bearings of naval force, contribute to give the service and the country a more definite impression of the necessity to provide a fleet adequate to great undertakings, lest, if an occasion should arise for what he has ventured to call 'statesmanship directing arms,' we should be found unprepared, through having no sufficient arms to direct."[1] In the latter purpose he was brilliantly to succeed. The Cleveland administration had pushed

[1] Alfred Thayer Mahan, *The Influence of Sea Power Upon the French Revolution and Empire* (Boston: Little, Brown and Company, 1892), p. iv.

on with naval and fort building; but Benjamin Harrison and the Republicans, who succeeded to power in 1889, were even more favorable to naval expansion, for a complex of reasons having little or nothing to do with foreign policy or foreign threats. The new Secretary of the Navy, Benjamin F. Tracy, turned to Mahan for advice; and Tracy's first annual report, presenting a bold new rationale of naval building and calling for an initial authorization of no less than eight seagoing battleships, was probably written by Mahan. Presented in November 1889, the report was supplemented in the following January by an even more expansive long-range analysis from the Navy Policy Board, in which Mahanite doctrine of naval requirements and naval policy was prominent. The result was a major and impassioned debate over naval policy, in which Mahan's book, appearing in 1890, had a great effect. In the end, Congress voted only three battleships—the first it had ever voted—in place of the eight for which Tracy (and Mahan) had initially asked, but the vote was a turning point in military policy and set the nation, eight years before the Spanish American War, on the course, of global sea power and world politics.

Report
of
the Secretary of the Navy.

NAVY DEPARTMENT,
November 30, 1889.

To the President:

The effective force of the United States Navy, when all the ships now authorized are completed, excluding those which by the process of decay and the operation of law will by that date have been condemned, will comprise 11 armored vessels, of which only three are battle-ships, and 31 unarmored vessels, making a total of 42.

The following statement shows the number of war vessels on the effective list of the principal foreign powers, built, building, or

From *Annual Report of the Secretary of the Navy, 1889*, House Executive Documents, 51st Congress, Session 1, pp. 3–6, 10–14; *Report of Policy Board, 1890*, Senate Executive Documents, 51st Congress, Session 1, pp. 3–7.

projected, at the present time, and exclusive of sailing and practice ships:

Country.	Armored.	Unarmored.	Total.
England	76	291	367
France	57	203	260
Russia	49	119	168
Germany	40	65	105
Holland	24	70	94
Spain	12	78	90
Italy	19	67	86
Turkey	15	66	81
China	7	66	73
Sweden and Norway	20	44	64
Austria	12	44	56

The table shows that even when the present building program is completed, the United States can not take rank as a naval power.

The purpose for which the United States maintains a navy is not conquest, but defense. For reasons of economy and public policy, the force should be as small as is consistent with this object. But it appears from the above comparison, that with all the additions authorized by the legislation of the last seven years, the country, as far as its capacity for defense is concerned, will be absolutely at the mercy of states having less than one-tenth of its population, one-thirtieth of its wealth, and one hundredth of its area. While the element of defensive strength is thus clearly deficient, the vulnerable points open to an enemy's attack, and the interests liable at all times to injury, are numerous and important. A coast line of 13,000 miles upon which are situated more than twenty great centers of population, wealth, and commercial activity, wholly unprotected against modern weapons, affords an inviting object of attack, with a wide range of choice as to the points to be selected. Any one of the powers named could, without serious difficulty, even after the completion of our fleet as now authorized, secure in a single raid upon our coast, an amount of money sufficient to meet the expenses of a naval war; an amount, one-half of which, if judiciously expended over a series of years, would be sufficient to afford this country a guaranty of perpetual peace.

The defense of the United States absolutely requires the creation of a fighting force. So far the increase has been mainly in the direction of unarmored cruisers. These vessels, while useful in deterring commercial states from aggression and as an auxiliary to secure celerity and efficiency in larger operations, do not constitute a fighting force, even when it is intended exclusively for defense. To meet the attack of ironclads, ironclads are indispensable. To carry on even a defensive war with any hope of success we must have armored battle-ships. The capture or destruction of two or three dozen or two or three score of merchant vessels is not going to prevent a fleet of ironclads from shelling our cities or exacting as the price of exemption a contribution that would pay for their lost merchantmen ten times over. We must do more than this. We must have the force to raise blockades, which are almost as disastrous to commercial cities as bombardment. We must have a fleet of battle-ships that will beat off the enemy's fleet on its approach, for it is not to be tolerated that the United States, with its population, its revenue, and its trade, is to submit to attack upon the threshold of its harbors. Finally, we must be able to divert an enemy's force from our coast by threatening his own, for a war, though defensive in principle, may be conducted most effectively by being offensive in its operations.

If the country is to have a navy at all, it should have one that is sufficient for the complete and ample protection of its coast in time of war. If we are to stop short of this, we might better stop where we are, and abandon all claim to influence and control upon the sea. It is idle to spend our money in building small, slow-going steamers, that are unnecessary in peace and useless for war. It is little better than a repetition of the mistaken policy that prevailed in our early history, of building gunboats that were laid up or sold as soon as war broke out. The country needs a navy that will exempt it from war, but the only navy that will accomplish this is a navy that can wage war.

The policy of military aggrandizement is totally repugnant to American institutions, and is not likely ever to be entered upon. The present question has nothing to do with such a policy. It is a practical business question of insuring our property and our trade, in which the commercial cities of the coast, the ports on our lake frontier, and the centers of production in the interior are alike interested. The naval force before the war, when the population numbered thirty millions, included ninety vessels of all classes. Before the completion of the present program, which will give a total of less than half that number, the population will have more than doubled, and the wealth on our coast subject to injury or destruction will have increased tenfold. The annual increase of wealth in this country is estimated to equal that of England, France, and Germany, and before it can create an effective navy its population is certain to exceed that of any two of these powers combined. Such a nation can not be indifferent to events taking place in close proximity to its own coasts, threatening the freedom of its commerce and the security of its sea-port cities. The questions that have arisen and that will continue to arise in the Gulf of Mexico and the Pacific concern the prosperity and development of the United States too closely to be further ignored, and our interests in these localities are too important to be left longer unprotected.

The cost of building a navy casts no perceptible burden upon a country of our vast resources. It is the premium paid by the United States for the insurance of its acquired wealth and its growing industries. Compared with the interests that are secured, the rate is low. It is a cheap price to pay for safety. We collect in duties in six months at a single port a greater sum than we could spend in building a new navy in six years. For the past two years the Government has paid its creditors for the privilege of discounting its debt before it was due twice the sum we have spent in reconstruction. And the fact must be remembered that of the amount which we spend for the construction of a ship, only a small fraction, perhaps one-tenth, goes for absolutely raw material, while the remaining nine-tenths represents, in one form or another, the earnings of American labor.

It is sometimes asserted that there need be no haste about building ships, upon the supposition that our reserve strength is sufficient to improvise a force in time of war. This is a fatal mistake. Naval wars in the future will be short and sharp. It is morally certain that they will be fought out to the end with the force available at the beginning. The nation that is ready to strike the first blow will gain an advantage which its antagonist can never offset, and inflict an injury from which he can never recover.

Under the most favorable circumstances, with the largest experience and the best mechanical appliances, the construction of war-ships takes a long time. In the United States much has been learned in the last eight years, and facilities have been greatly enlarged, but much still remains to be done, and a longer time is required here than in the ship-yards of Europe. The design and construction of the innumerable and complex details of a modern war-ship can not be hurried. There is no branch of mechanical art in which haste leads more certainly to wastefulness and imperfection. The limited capacity of our establishments, public and private, is a further cause of delay. If Congress were ready to-day to authorize the construction of all the ships that we need it would be a mechanical impossibility for the country, with its present appliances, to furnish them within fifteen years; while the first six months of hostilities would not only see our exposed cities forced to submit to heavy contributions, but every ship-yard in the country, public or private, destroyed, and thus the last hope extinguished of creating a navy to meet the emergency of war.

The new cruisers are eight in number, the *Chicago, Boston, Atlanta,* and *Dolphin,* contracted for in 1883, and the *Baltimore, Charleston, Yorktown,* and *Petrel,* contracted for in 1886 and 1887.

In looking back at the work of naval reconstruction, begun seven years ago, the country has reason to be congratulated on the success of the undertaking. . . .

. . . To stop now in the work of reconstruction, is to abandon everything we have gained. We have proved that at a time when war-ship construction had seemed almost a lost art in this country, American mechanics could create it anew and place the United States where it was seventy years ago, when the vessels of its Navy were the best of their class afloat. We have fostered and developed a branch of industry in America which may, if kept up, attract to itself no inconsiderable share of the profits that now go to ship-builders abroad. We have secured for our Navy a certain number of excellent and useful vessels of the unprotected cruiser type, at a fair and reasonable cost. We have thus laid a solid foundation. But we must not for a moment deceive ourselves by supposing that we have an effective Navy. We have two distinct and widely separated ocean frontiers to protect, and there is only one way in which they can be protected, namely, by two separate fleets of armored battle-ships, with coast-defense ships suitably distributed to cover the most exposed localities. . . .

. . . The necessities of our vulnerable position therefore demand the immediate creation of two fleets of battle-ships, of which eight should be assigned to the Pacific and twelve to the Atlantic and Gulf. They must be the best of their class in four leading characteristics: armament, armor, structural strength, and speed. The last is nearly as essential to the battle-ship as it is to the cruiser. It may safely be assumed that, other things being equal, the battle-ship of the highest speed will as a rule be the victor in action, for she can choose her position and keep the enemy at a disadvantage. Not only must the speed of our battle-ships be high, but it must be uniformly high, for the speed of the fleet is regulated by that of the slowest vessel.

In addition to the battle-ships, the situation of the country requires at least twenty vessels for coast and harbor defense. These vessels, although restricted in their range of effectiveness, are necessary components of a naval force which has a sea-coast to defend. Their employment as floating fortresses requires that they should have a powerful battery and the heaviest of armor, combined with moderate draft. At the present time eight vessels of this type are under construction, five of which are reconstructed monitors.

The one problem now before the Government, in the matter of a naval policy, is to get these forty vessels built at the earliest possible moment. The steps necessary to their completion, namely, legislation, design, and construction, can not take less than five years in the case of each one. Unless the existing yards, public and private, are enlarged and restocked with plant, not more than eight could be built at one time, and the construction of the others would have to wait for the launching of the first. Using the utmost promptness, the ships most essential to efficient protection could not be supplied in less than twelve or fifteen years.

It is therefore recommended that the construction of eight armored vessels be authorized at the coming session, and that they be of the type of battle-ships rather than coast-defense ships; the former being more generally serviceable, and there being only three of them now in process of construction as against eight of the latter.

In reference to fast cruisers, all modern experience goes to show that they are essential adjuncts of an armored fleet, and the proportion of three cruisers to one battle-ship is believed to be sound and reasonable. This would make the future navy consist of 20 battle-ships, 20 coast-defense ships, and 60 cruisers, or 100 vessels in all, which is believed to be a moderate estimate of the proper strength of the fleet. Of the 60 cruisers required, 31 are now built or authorized. For an increase in the number of cruisers, considered simply as auxiliaries to the fighting force of battle-ships, we may wisely wait until the latter are in process of construction.

It must be remembered, however, that cruisers have another and equally important function in the attack and defense of commerce. Any stanch vessel with a good coal capacity and the highest rate of speed, armed with a few rapid-firing guns, though built and used principally for commercial purposes, may by certain adaptations in her construction be made readily available for this form of warfare. The fast transatlantic liners, nationalized in foreign countries, but supported and maintained by American trade and American passengers—many of them, even, owned by American citizens—are a powerful factor in the naval force of the Governments whose flag they bear and at whose disposal they must place themselves in time of war.

It is a matter for serious consideration whether steps may not be taken towards the creation of such a fleet of specially adapted steamers of American construction, owned by American merchants, carrying the American flag, and capable, under well-defined conditions, of temporary incorporation in the American Navy. The advantages of such an arrangement, which enlarges the merchant marine and makes it at the same time self-protecting, are overwhelmingly great. The difficulty is that American capital will not be drawn into the enterprise unless it can be sure of specific compensation for the concessions which it makes to the Government, first, in the adaptation of its vessels to the latter's needs, and secondly, in the surrender of a privilege to use them when the exigency arises. . . .

. . . Our deficiency should be supplied either by a line of fast merchant-men, constructed with special reference to use in time of war, which will enable the Government to avail itself of their services at critical moments, or we should build a fleet of at least five first-class cruisers of the very highest rate of speed, certainly not less than 22 knots. The displacement of these vessels should not be less than 4,000 tons. Even such a fleet will not supply the want of swift merchant-steamers for coaling and transport service. Colliers and transports must alike be fast, for they can not fight; and the collier can take no chances of capture, for she carries the life of the fleet.

. . . Apart from the want of battle-ships the most marked defect of the present fleet is in torpedo-boats. The number of these boats owned by fifteen foreign States is as follows:

Country	Torpedo-boats.	Country	Torpedo-boats.
England	207	China	26
France	191	Denmark	22
Russia	138	Japan	21
Italy	128	Sweden and Norway	19
Germany	98	Holland	16
Austria	60	Spain	15
Greece	51	Brazil	15
Turkey	29		

The United States has one such boat under construction. This branch of defense can not safely be neglected any longer. It is high time that steps should be taken to supply these essential constituents of a naval force. I therefore recommend that the construction of at least five torpedo-boats of the first and second classes, in suitable proportions, be authorized, as a beginning, at the coming session of Congress. . . .

Report of Policy Board.

NAVY DEPARTMENT,
Washington, January 20, 1890.

SIR: . . . It may be stated that a navy is essential (1) for waging war and (2) to prevent war; and the second purpose may be far more important than the first. The Board in making this statement does not overlook the many important duties which a navy has to perform in time of peace, but a navy which is adjusted to meet the requirements of the country in time of war will, undoubtedly, be ample to perform the duty required of it in time of peace; and it may be rigidly accepted that there is no real ultimate economy in the maintenance of vessels apparently adapted to the more economical performance of the latter duty, if ill adapted to the former. The magnitude of the naval force to be maintained by a government should be adjusted on the one hand to the chances of war, and the magnitude of the naval force which a war would bring against it; and, on the other hand, it should be commensurate with the wealth of the country and the interests at stake in case of war. If the chances of war are slight and the interests to be guarded are unimportant, certainly the naval force to be maintained need not be great:—if the chances of war are great, then the naval force which should be maintained ought to be limited by nothing but the limits of the nation's wealth;—for, in case of war, its life is at stake. Whatever may be the chances of war, if the interests to be guarded are great, then the naval force to be maintained should also be great.

In these cases, it is assumed that the protection required is best given by a naval force. For the United States it may confidently be asserted that the chances of war are much less than for most European nations, or at least that the chances of war with any nation comparable with this in wealth and power are much less than the chances of war among the nations of Europe. The isolated position of this country removes many incentives to war.

We fear no encroachments upon our territory, nor are we tempted at present to encroach upon that of others. Our territory does not obstruct the free passage to the sea of the commerce of any nation, nor is our own obstructed in any similar way. We have no colonies, nor any apparent desire to acquire them, nor will this desire probably arise until the population of this country has overflowed its vast limits or its great resources become strained to maintain it.

At present our foreign commerce is carried in foreign vessels, and our manufactures compete with those of other nations in but few markets, when we consider the manufacturing resources of this country.

All these reasons combine to make the United States self-contained to a greater degree than any other important nation, and, as a consequence, we are brought into conflict with the interests of other nations to the least possible extent. For this reason, the chances of war would seem to be at a minimum. But there are not wanting indications that this comparative isolation will soon cease to exist, and that it will gradually be replaced by a condition of affairs which will bring this nation into sharp commercial competition with others in every part of the world. Even now our commercial relations with our nearest neighbors are clamoring for modification both by sea and land, and in the adjustment of our trade with a neighbor we are certain to reach out and obstruct the interests of foreign nations.

The time can not be distant when we shall compete in earnest with others for the vast and increasing ocean-carrying trade; the time is near at hand when our own people will find it profitable to carry at least their own goods to foreign markets.

The construction of a canal to form an ocean route between the

Atlantic and Pacific will place this nation under great responsibility which may be a fruitful source of danger. . . .

. . . When we consider the wealth of our country, or our ability to maintain a navy, and the interests at stake in case of war, we are again forced to admit that our Navy is insignificant and totally disproportionate to the greatness of the country and to the task which would certainly fall to it in case of war.

If we omit entirely from consideration the property along our coast which is now exposed to destruction, and consider only the exports and imports which are exposed upon the high seas, we find that the value of such property is annually $1,500,000,000. This does not include our coastwise trade, which would double these figures; and this trade would also be exposed to destruction in case of a naval war. While more than 75 per cent. of this vast foreign traffic is carried in foreign ships, the exports represent a part of the nation's wealth and would be subject to capture. Nor does the loss of this property adequately represent the loss to the country which would result from its capture in whatever ships it might be carried. The enormous home industries and inland transportation directly dependent upon the continuance of these exports would be paralyzed.

It matters not whether this commerce is carried in foreign ships, if it were to cease it would produce wide-spread misery. It is not, then, alone sufficient that our sea-ports should be protected against bombardment,—they must not be blockaded—our commerce must be free to enter and leave at its accustomed ports. The Board feels that it can not emphasize this too strongly. If the port of New York alone were blockaded for even three months, it would produce greater confusion and loss than would be directly inflicted by a bombardment of the city, even in its present unprotected condition. . . .

. . . While the Atlantic and Pacific furnish a practically insurmountable barrier to an invading army, our extended coast line is a constant temptation to an enemy to assail us from the sea. When we consider the simplicity of the means required to resist an invasion and remember the greatness of our population from which armies are to be recruited, and the railway and other facilities for concentrating them upon any threatened points of our coast, we must be convinced that only a powerful army would venture to invade our territory. The vast means of ocean transportation demanded for any considerable army and the difficulties to be overcome in keeping up its supplies would, manifestly, render it impossible to invade our country. We have, then, only to fear a naval attack which may vary from the marauding attack of a few cruisers upon our shores or commerce, up to the organized and destructive attack of a well-appointed fleet of armor-clads. How shall we best protect ourselves against these? Shall we place our main dependence upon fortifications for our principal ports, and permit ourselves to be shut up within them, and suffer our vast commerce to be driven from the seas? or, shall we be prepared to maintain our rights at sea, to keep our ports open to our trade and, incidentally, protect the ports?

While feeling reasonably secure against any invasion of our territory by an enemy, we should redouble our efforts to protect ourselves against the one certain form of attack in case of war, and the only complete protection is to be found in an efficient and sufficient navy. Considering, then—

(1) That we are a nation possessed of great and increasing wealth:

(2) That much of this wealth must pass to and fro across the ocean or along our coast, where it is exposed to capture or destruction in case of war:

(3) That we are now totally unprepared—even against second-rate powers—to protect our commerce, to prevent the blockade of our ports, or to maintain our rights and honor away from home:

(4) That these objects can only be secured by a navy:

(5) That while we are now at peace with all nations this fortunate condition of affairs may not always continue:

it is evident that we should proceed with all possible dispatch to provide a navy of such a character and magnitude as will efficiently serve these purposes.

To do this is a naval problem which depends for its complete solution upon several conditions, which, in turn, are fixed or known with a moderate degree of exactness. . . .

. . . First, then, if other conditions were equal, we should maintain a navy at least equal in strength to the most powerful navy in the world, on the theory that we might have to fight such a nation. But the second condition, viz.—proximity of bases of supply, greatly modifies this estimate as far as the magnitude of the navy required for the protection of our interests in the western hemisphere is concerned, and these are our greatest interests; for in this part of the world we should be acting near our own base, while most European nations would be separated several thousands of miles from any base of supply, a fact which would serve to exclude some of the most powerful ships in the world from acting against us, provided our naval strength was sufficient to prevent our enemy from seizing some of the islands along our coast and establishing the necessary bases, or taking possession of Long Island Sound, Chesapeake Bay, or other suitable body of water where colliers could anchor in security. . . .

. . . We find, then, in this consideration, a limit fixed for our naval strength which, it is probable, we need not exceed and with less than which we can not rest secure.

To be able in case of war to completely destroy, at its outbreak, every base of supplies belonging to our enemy which should be in proximity to our country, and at the same time to protect the converging highways of our commerce, both foreign and coastwise, would represent the principal demand to be made upon our Navy for purposes of defense, and, hence, for any purpose. . . .

PART FOUR

The United States
as a World Power:
1899–1922

27. Elihu Root: The Reorganization of the Army

IN 1899 PRESIDENT MCKINLEY DRAFTED ELIHU ROOT, A NEW YORK corporation lawyer, as Secretary of War, thinking that the post would be chiefly concerned with the legal and administrative problems stemming from the War Department's control over the new overseas dependencies. Root quickly realized, however, that to be an effective colonial administrator he would have to have an effective Army and that his first task would be to reform the moss-grown and clearly "defective" military machine he had inherited. He attacked the problem in his first annual report, in 1899; and in a series of masterful reports thereafter he did much to modernize American military thinking. He secured a group of notable reforms—the establishment of the Army War College; a Chief of Staff and the general staff system; the replacement of the Militia Act of 1792 with the Dick Act of 1903, recognizing the National Guard as the "organized militia" and bringing it into a more effective relationship with the Regular Army; improved promotion and training systems; and an Army-Navy Joint Board, ancestor of the Joint Chiefs of Staff. He was unable to get everything he wanted, but he at least began the transformation of the Army from a more or less ritualistic military order into an instrument for waging war in the new world emerging after 1900.

Army Reorganization

Extract from the Report of the Secretary of War for 1899

Before July 1, 1901, when, under existing law, the present volunteer force must be disbanded and the present regular force restored to its peace basis of 26,610, we shall be compelled to face the practical necessity of providing for some increase of the regular army. It is manifest that however speedily the insurrection in the Philippines may be quelled, we shall be required to maintain for a long time in those islands a considerable force to furnish the protection which the inhabitants are entitled to receive from us, and to maintain order among the savage and semi-civilized tribes which still exist in nearly every island. There is no occasion to doubt that the expense of this portion of the military establishment can readily and properly be defrayed from the insular revenues.

It is not conceivable that a practical people should expend the great sums we are devoting to our seacoast fortifications, and the delicate and complicated machinery of modern ordnance with which we are equipping them, and not provide an adequate force of men to care for, preserve, and become familiar with the use of the guns and machinery. An increase in our artillery force will be absolutely necessary for this purpose. The present heavy-artillery force is about one-fifth of the requisite number.

I beg to suggest that the manifold services which have been rendered by officers of the army of the United States during the past year in almost every branch of civil government, and the effective zeal and devotion which they have exhibited in succoring the distressed, teaching the ignorant, establishing and maintaining civil law, fighting against pestilence, introducing sanitary reforms, and promoting and aiding peaceful industry should be regarded as proof, if any were needed, that American soldiers do not cease to be American citizens, and that no danger is to be apprehended from a reasonable enlargement of the army which affords such evidence of its character and spirit.

It is greatly to be desired that at the same time, while the lessons drawn from the experience of recent war are fresh in our

Reprinted by permission of the publishers, from Elihu Root, edited by Robert Bacon and James Brown Scott, *The Military and Colonial Policy of the United States,* (Cambridge, Mass.: Harvard University Press, 1916), pp. 350–363, 442–447, 420–433.

minds, some improvements should be made in the organization of the army.

For many years various criticisms upon our present organization have been made and discussed, and a number of measures for improvement have been recommended by my predecessors or embodied in bills introduced in Congress. Some marked improvements have been made, notably the three-battalion form of regimental organization, which, after being urged by several successive Secretaries of War and advocated by all the high military authorities in the country for a generation, was finally authorized by the act of April 26, 1898.

As to most of the proposed changes, however, there has not been a sufficient public interest in the subject or a sufficiently strong conviction of the importance of good organization to overcome the diversity of opinions and personal interests desirous of being left undisturbed.

The method of proposing and considering, one by one, specific remedies for specific defects does not seem to be an adequate treatment of the subject. It seems to me that the best course would be to settle upon the true principle which should govern the use to be made of the army and then inquire in what respect our present arrangement fails to conform to that principle, and make it conform.

Two propositions seem to me fundamental in the consideration of the subject:

First. That the real object of having an army is to provide for war.

Second. That the regular establishment in the United States will probably never be by itself the whole machine with which any war will be fought.

The first of these statements seems like a truism, and it will probably be received everywhere without conscious denial. Yet the precise contrary is really the theory upon which the entire treatment of our army proceeded for the thirty-three years between the Civil War and the war with Spain. Present utility was really the controlling consideration, and the possibility of war seemed at all times so vague and unreal that it had no formative power in shaping legislation regarding the army. The result was an elaborate system admirably adapted to secure pecuniary accountability and economy of expenditure in time of peace; a large number of small and separate commands, well officered and well disciplined, very efficient for police duty against Indians, and as separate commands unsurpassed anywhere in fighting qualities; and a class of officers most of whom were of a high order of individual excellence, who rendered valuable service in the construction of public works, as instructors in colleges, and in a great variety of professional duties at separate posts and with their commands, but who, with the exception of the general officers, were arranged in rank without any reference whatever to their respective abilities to command or to render effective service. The result did not include the effective organization and training of the army as a whole for the purposes of war. This was not because the army did not wish such organization and training, but because it was not permitted to organize and train for that object. The army has many able, educated, and competent officers who have thought much upon the subject and deeply regretted this condition, but who have been unable to secure a change.

I believe that without any revolutionary interference with the general scheme of organization or with individual rights, and without excessive expense, a great improvement can be made in the way of conforming the organization and training of the army to its true purpose. It is not reorganization which is needed, but the grant of opportunities for development along lines which are well understood and appreciated by the army itself.

The preparation of an army for war involves at least these four things:

First. Systematic study by responsible officers of plans for action under all contingencies of possible conflict, and with this, study of the larger problems of military science and the most complete information regarding it, study of the constant improvements in implements and methods of warfare, and of the adaptability of improvements and inventions for the purpose of carry-

ing out the plans devised, and study of the arrangement of territorial and tactical organizations, and the establishment of depots,
camps, fortifications, and lines of communication with reference
to these plans, so that all expenditures for each separate step of
development may contribute toward the practical realization of
a comprehensive and consistent scheme. This requirement is not
to be met by the separate study and reflection of single officers
not charged with the duty or able to give effect to their conclusions. The responsibility of declared duty, the comparison of
different views, the contribution of different minds, the correction and evolution by discussion, the long-continued, laborious,
and systematic application of a considerable number of minds
of a high order, and with a recognized status giving authority to
their conclusions, are needed to produce the desired result.

To illustrate: The War Department has recently received numerous applications from different parts of the country for the acquisition of tracts of land and the establishment of permanent
camping places for the encampment and training of soldiers in
large bodies, which the people of the country evidently realize
ought to be provided for. There are different ways in which these
applications may be treated. They may be rejected or favored
with reference to the advantages which they will afford to the
people of the towns in the neighborhood of the proposed camps
through the business which would result from the maintenance
of troops there, or they may be rejected or favored according to
the healthfulness of the locations and the conveniences which
they will afford and the ease of access from the points whence
troops would naturally be drawn. Neither of these methods is at
all satisfactory. If such camps are to be established, their locations
should be selected with reference to carefully devised and comprehensive plans, one feature of which consists in determining
the points at which troops can most usefully be mobilized for immediate use in case of war, so that by sending troops to them in
time of peace we should be doing the very same thing which we
have to do in time of urgent necessity, and so that every railroad that is built, every side track that is laid, and every building

that is erected will leave so much less to do when war threatens. Such plans cannot be improvised; they cannot be produced by any other process than that above indicated.

Second. The preparation of material of war, keeping pace with the progress of military science and adapted to the conditions to be anticipated when war shall arise.

Gratifying progress has been made recently in this respect, but with the restoration of peace we may apprehend that there will be to some extent a return to the same indifference which left us without smokeless powder or small-bore magazine rifles in the spring of 1898. Under such conditions it is necessary that questions as to the character and form of material should be settled by authority beyond reasonable question, and that the things which ought to be done should be indicated clearly and positively. In no other way is it possible that such things can be done. At present the opinions of the artillery or infantry using a weapon, of the ordnance officers making it, of the department commander, and of the major-general commanding the army, may all differ on such questions, and there is no way of settling them after an appropriation, except by the decision of the Secretary of War, who cannot possibly study the subject thoroughly, or before the appropriation, by a committee of Congress with whom the differing opinions naturally tend to destroy each other and to prevent any action whatever. Some body of competent men whose business it is to be familiar with the whole field of invention, to consider it, to discuss it, and to reach conclusions upon it, alone can furnish those authoritative determinations which are necessary to effective demands for adequate material.

Third. An adequate process of selection according to merit and effectiveness among the officers of the army, so that the men of superior ability and power may be known and placed in positions involving responsibility and authority.

Without some such process in time of peace the selection has to be made after war has commenced, at the expense always of treasure and of life, and sometimes of temporary failure and humiliation. Such a process of selection will necessarily at the same time afford an incentive to exertion and a reward for professional attainments and effective service, while stimulating the development of the capable officer and bringing to the front the men best able to bear responsibility and perform the difficult duties to be confronted in actual hostilities.

Fourth. The exercise and training of the officers and men of the army in the movements of large bodies of troops by brigade, division, and corps under conditions approaching as nearly as possible those to be anticipated in executing the plans devised for their action in war.

Officers who have never seen a corps, division, or brigade organized and on the march cannot be expected to perform perfectly the duties required of them when war comes. The collection of large bodies of men presents, not the same difficulties presented by a small body, multiplied or increased in degree, but entirely new difficulties which only experience can qualify men to meet. The sanitation, the care, the discipline, and many of the duties are new to the man who has dealt only with a company or a regiment. The highest efficiency under these conditions can be attained only by giving experience approximating as nearly as possible to that which will be encountered when the war machinery is required to do its proper work.

I think the following steps may be taken to advantage:

(1) An army war college should be established, which shall be composed of the heads of the staff departments, properly so called, and a number of the ablest and most competent officers of high rank in the army (including, of course, the major-general commanding), these officers to be detailed for service in the college for limited periods, so that while the college shall be continuous in records, character, and performance, it shall continually and gradually change in its personal elements. It should be the duty of this body of officers to direct the instruction and intellectual exercise of the army, to acquire the information, devise the plans, and study the subjects above indicated, and to advise the Commander-in-Chief upon all questions of plans, armament, transportation, mobilization, and military preparation and movement.

This college should have combined with it, reënforced and enlarged in its scope and effectiveness, the present division of military information of the Adjutant-General's Office, where its records and its conclusions should be preserved. It should not supersede, but should incorporate, continue, and bring under the same general management the present service schools, supplementing where it is necessary their courses, which now, so far as instruction is concerned, largely cover the ground. Its instruction would, at the outset and perhaps permanently, be given through these schools, but it should give unity, influence, authority, and effectiveness in military affairs to the work and the thought developed in them, aside from mere instruction, and a weight and utility to their records of the efficiency and merit of their pupils not hitherto accorded to them in proportion to the high character of the work they have done.

(2) Every officer of the army below the rank of a field officer, and not already a graduate of one of the service schools, should be detailed for some fixed period during his service to receive instruction at this college in the science of war, including the duties of the staff, and in all matters pertaining to the application of military science to national defense; provision should be made for the continuance of such instruction by correspondence after the expiration of the period of each officer's detail, and all officers should be invited and entitled to present, as a part of the regular course and for credit on their efficiency records, written papers and reports upon the results of their investigations, explorations, reflections, and professional and scientific work, and upon such special subjects as may be prescribed by the college.

(3) All staff appointments other than medical should hereafter be made from the line of the army for a fixed period of, say, four or five years, the holder to return to the line at the end of the period, and not to be eligible to reappointment until after at least one year's service in the line, and after the expiration of a reasonable period the selection of staff appointments should be made on the basis of proficiency and fitness, as shown in the war college (or heretofore in the service schools), including as elements for consideration both the work done during the period of detail, and

the post-graduate work. Excepting, however, that such appointments should also be permitted for gallant and meritorious conduct in the field, shown by recommendations of commanding officers for brevet promotion made during the progress of a war, and excepting that for the technical and scientific branches of Engineering, Ordnance, and Signal Service, examinations should be continued; all promotions in the staff itself should be upon the basis prescribed for original appointment, combined with efficiency of service in the staff.

(4) The present system of promotion by seniority should be modified as to all officers now or hereafter below field rank, by making a specific proportion of the promotions to each grade for seniority, and a specific proportion on the basis either of efficiency records in the war college, or heretofore in the service schools, including both elements of work done during actual attendance and subsequent thereto, or for gallantry in the field during war, or both, accompanied in each case by evidence of faithful performance of the ordinary duties of the line.

(5) All selections of candidates for staff appointments and for staff promotions and for line promotions, other than those made for seniority, should be made by boards of officers appointed for that purpose, upon an examination and estimate of the efficiency records exhibiting the grounds for appointment or promotion above stated. Nothing can be more important than that the officers of the army shall feel that their rise in rank depends upon what they do; that ability, intellectual activity, faithful performance of duty, and gallant conduct are more certain claims to preferment than social or political influence. A system of promotions which is divorced from the efficiency record is not merely unjust, but it destroys ambition and checks the effort of the army. The way to prevent the separation is by a systematic provision to enable every officer to show what there is in him, and to preserve a full record of what he does, by providing a competent and disinterested body to pass judgment on the record, and by a law making the judgment reached on this basis the imperative and sole ground of selection for promotion.

These provisions will go far toward accomplishing results which are provided for in the organization of every considerable army in the world, and which under our organization are not the business of anybody in particular, and for the most part cannot be accomplished by any one whomsoever; and if Congress will then make the appropriations necessary for periodical mobilization and maneuvers, the four requisites of preparation for war above stated can be substantially attained. The only element in these recommendations which does not result necessarily from a statement of the requirements is the limitation on the period of staff duty and the periodical return to the line. I think this will be beneficial to the staff, and will do away with the feeling quite prevalent in the line that the staff is a privileged class, divorced from its old associates, and a tendency toward unfriendly criticism which seems to me to be prejudicial to good discipline and effective service.

Another function which is now performed to a very slight degree, and which is of very great importance, should be performed by the proposed war college acting in coöperation with the existing naval war college, that is, the union of the army and the navy in the collection and utilization of information, studying and formulating plans for defense and attack, and the testing and selection of material of war. Communication, conference, and interchange of instructors between the two institutions could not fail to be of great value to both services, and to make easier and more certain that perfect coöperation which is so essential both in forming and executing the plans which involve the operations of both forces. . . .

. . . The second proposition which I stated as underlying the consideration of this subject—that the regular establishment is not the whole machine with which a war will ever be fought—has been too signally illustrated both in the Civil War and in the war with Spain and the Philippine war to require further demonstration. Our method is, and always will be, immediately upon the outbreak of a war, to create an army of which the regular army on its peace footing forms but a part, and usually but a small part, and the great body of which is composed of volunteers.

That the relations between the regulars and volunteers in this new force shall be such that they shall constitute a homogeneous body, using the same arms, familiar with the same drill, answering to the same ideas of discipline, inspired by the same spirit, and capable of equal and even performance, and that the preparation of the regular army in time of peace for the event of war shall to the greatest possible extent conduce to the benefit of the whole army, both regular and volunteer, and make it easy to put that body in a state of preparation, is an end toward which the best military thought of the country may well be addressed.

It should be a special subject of consideration by the war college, and upon it that body should invite the conference and coöperation of the military authorities of the several states. As one step toward attaining the end, courses of instruction in the college should be open to officers of the National Guard of the states, and the efficiency records of such officers in the college, and written papers and reports contributed by them after their terms of instruction have ended, should be made a part of the records of the War Department as the authorized and accepted basis of appointments to office in any volunteer force which may be raised.

The provisions of the act of March 2, 1899, under which the army now serving in the Philippines was created, partly out of the old regular force, partly by new recruits in the regular establishment, and partly by additional volunteer regiments, made a long step in advance toward attaining the homogeneity which I have endeavored to describe. The fact that the officers of the entire army receive their commissions from the same source, and look for their promotions and rewards to the same authority, while in every volunteer regiment regular officers have been joined with volunteer officers in forming, training, and commanding the regiment, produce this result to a degree not previously attained.

Following these lines and working through the methods which I have described, a permanent plan ought to be wrought out with the concurrence of the military authorities of the several states, and enacted by Congress, for the creation of a war army composed of both regulars and volunteers whenever such an army is required. The part to be taken by the regular army in the new organization and the part to be taken by the volunteers should be prescribed, and the parts should be so assigned that the new organization shall have the fullest possible benefit of the preparation of the regular army.

The form and the machinery for the organization of the new army and the part to be taken in the raising of the army by the military authorities and organizations of the several states should be indicated, so that whenever war threatens, and long before it is declared, the multitude of men who are to do the work of organization may know, without waiting for an act of Congress, what will be required of them when the hour strikes, and may be engaged in the quiet and deliberate preparation so necessary in advance of action to prevent confusion and mistake. . . .

Militia and Volunteers

Extract from the Report of the Secretary of War for 1901

The present provisions of law relating to the militia, and to the raising of volunteer forces, are quite imperfect and unsatisfactory. The militia law stands today virtually as it was enacted in 1792, and is practically obsolete. It is very desirable that Congress should now exercise the power conferred upon it by the Constitution to provide for organizing, arming, and disciplining the militia. The organization and armament of the National Guards of the several states, which are treated as militia in the appropriations made by Congress, should be made the same as those provided by Congress for the regular and volunteer forces. The relations of the National Guard organizations to the national forces, and the obligations and duties of those organizations in time of war, should be clearly defined, so that the confusion and distress regarding their action which accompanied the outbreak of the war with Spain may not again occur.

The reliance of the country for the large forces necessary in modern warfare must necessarily be chiefly upon volunteers. The method and procedure of raising volunteer forces should be prescribed in advance, so that instead of waiting to devise plans for a volunteer army until the excitement and haste of impending war makes perfection of design difficult and satisfactory execution impossible, Congress will have but to direct the execution of a well-understood plan by officers, each one of whom has long been familiar with the part he is to play. It is desirable that any plans adopted should provide for utilizing, in the earlier volunteer organizations called out, the training of those citizens who shall have served already in the regular and volunteer forces. If the earlier volunteer organizations can be constituted of these trained men, much valuable time and expense can be saved, and many dangers may be averted during the period the ordinary volunteers are receiving the necessary training. Provisions should also be made for the selection in advance of the officers of any volunteer force which may be raised. Careful selection is impossible at the outbreak of a war. It is entirely practicable in time of peace.

I recommend that the President be authorized to convene boards of officers (including the General Service and Staff College Board) for the examination of officers of the National Guard, and other citizens who may apply to be examined, as to their qualifications to hold volunteer commissions; that the persons passing such examinations shall receive certificates, stating the office for which they are found to be qualified, and upon the calling out of a volunteer force shall be entitled to receive commissions for such offices.

I recommend that the War Department be authorized to arm the National Guard with the present service small arms used by the regular army, navy, and marine corps; that the National Guard of the several states be treated as a first reserve, to be called into the service of the United States to execute the laws of the Union, suppress insurrections, and repel invasions, the term of service under any call to be limited to nine months; that the President be authorized, on the request of the governor of any state, to detail officers of the regular army for instruction, staff, and inspection duties with the National Guard of such state; that the War Department be authorized to furnish transportation, rations, and tentage to officers and men of National Guard organizations, who shall take part with the forces of the regular army in annual encampments and maneuvers at national military camps; that the Department be authorized to allow travel pay, commutation of rations and quarters, or commutation of quarters, to officers of the National Guard attending and regularly taking part in the courses of instruction at the General Service and Staff College at Fort Leavenworth. Both of these provisions should be within reasonable limits, proportional to the numbers of National Guard organizations in the several states.

I recommend that the President be now empowered to organize the volunteer forces whenever called out, in the manner provided for by the act of March 2, 1899, for the organization of the volunteer force which has recently returned from the Philippines, with such modifications as shall be necessary to give effect to the views above expressed.

The Militia System; the General Staff

Extract from the Report of the Secretary of War for 1902

Early in the last session a bill was prepared by the War Department, embodying the views expressed in my last report, upon the treatment of the National Guard of the several states by the Federal Government, the relation of the Guard to the militia and volunteer systems, and preparation in advance for the organization of volunteers in time of war. This bill was submitted to the chairman of the Committee on Military Affairs of the Senate, the chairman of the Committee on Militia of the House, and to a convention of officers of the National Guard organizations which met in Washington in January, 1902. The convention appointed a special committee to consider and report upon the proposed bill, and after some modifications it was reported favorably to the convention, which after thorough discussion adopted a resolution approving the measure and requesting its enactment by Congress. . . .

I earnestly urge that this measure be made a law. It is really absurd that a nation which maintains but a small regular army and depends upon unprofessional citizen soldiery for its defense should run along as we have done for one hundred and ten years under a militia law which never worked satisfactorily in the beginning, and which was perfectly obsolete before any man now fit for military duty was born. The result is that we have practically no militia system, notwithstanding the fact that the Constitution makes it the duty of the Federal Congress "to provide for organizing, arming, and disciplining the militia," and "for calling forth the militia to execute the laws of the Union, suppress insurrections, and repel invasions." The National Guard organizations of the several states have grown up in default of any national system and to meet local requirements. Their relations to the Federal Government have never been defined or settled. The confusion, controversy, and bad feeling arising from this uncertain status were painfully apparent at the beginning of the war with Spain; and it must always be the same until Congress shall exercise its constitutional power over the subject. Repeated efforts have been made to accomplish this result. . . .

. . . Almost every President, from Washington down, has urged the importance of this subject upon the attention of Congress. The chief reason why nothing has been done has been that no one system could be agreed upon. Everybody was agreed upon the general principle, but a majority of all the people interested were opposed to every particular concrete method suggested to give it effect.

The bill which has now passed the House is the result of extensive and painstaking conference among representatives of all the classes of citizens especially interested in the subject and especially qualified to express opinions upon it. It does not represent fully any one's view, but it contains many important provisions upon which a general agreement has been reached; and it will, I am sure, if enacted, be a great step in advance toward effective preparation for war otherwise than by the maintenance of a standing army.

The fundamental idea of the bill is to recognize the value to the National Government of the National Guard, which is capable of being utilized, first, as an active militia when called out by the President for the specific purposes enumerated in the Constitution; second, as an already organized volunteer force when its organizations respond as such to calls for volunteers for general military purposes under authority of Congress; and, third, as the great school of the volunteer soldier, the benefits of which are received by the country when the members of the Guard respond individually to calls for volunteers. . . .

The most important thing to be done now for the regular army is the creation of a general staff. . . . Since the report for 1899 was made many of the important measures then recommended for the greater efficiency of the army have been accomplished or are in course of accomplishment under authority conferred by legislation. Our military system is, however, still exceedingly defective at the top. We have a personnel unsurpassed anywhere, and a population ready to respond to calls for the increase of the personnel in case of need, up to the full limit at which it is possible to transport and feed an army. We have wealth and a present willingness to expend it reasonably for the procurement of supplies and material of war as plentiful and as good as can be found in any country. We have the different branches of the military service well organized, each within itself, for the performance of its duties. Our administrative staff and supply departments, as a rule, have at their heads good and competent men, faithful to their duties, each attending assiduously to the business of his department.

But when we come to the coördination and direction of all these means and agencies of warfare, so that all parts of the machine shall work true together, we are weak. Our system makes no adequate provision for the directing brain which every army must have, to work successfully. Common experience has shown that this cannot be furnished by any single man without assistants, and that it requires a body of officers working together under the direction of a chief and entirely separate from and independent of the administrative staff of an army (such as the adjutants, quartermasters, commissaries, etc., each of whom is engrossed in the duties of his own special department). This body of officers, in distinction from the administrative staff, has come to be called a general staff. There has been much misunderstanding as to the nature and duties of a general staff. . . .

. . . Neither our political nor our military system makes it suitable that we should have a general staff organized like the German general staff or like the French general staff; but the common experience of mankind is that the things which those general staffs do, have to be done in every well-managed and well-directed army, and they have to be done by a body of men especially assigned to do them. We should have such a body of men selected and organized in our own way and in accordance with our own system to do those essential things. The most intelligible way to describe such a body of men, however selected and organized, is by calling it a general staff, because its duties are staff duties and are general in their character.

The duties of such a body of officers can be illustrated by taking for example an invasion of Cuba, such as we were all thinking about a few years ago. It is easy for a President, or a general acting under his direction, to order that 50,000 or 100,000 men proceed to Cuba and capture Havana. To make an order which has any reasonable chance of being executed he must do a great deal more than that. He must determine how many men shall be sent and how they shall be divided among the different arms of the service, and how they shall be armed, and equipped; and to do that he must get all the information possible about the defenses of the place to be captured and the strength and character and armament of the forces to be met. He must determine at what points and by what routes the place shall be approached, and at what points his troops shall land in Cuba; and for this purpose he must be informed about the various harbors of the island

and the depth of their channels; what classes of vessels can enter them; what the facilities for landing are; how they are defended; the character of the roads leading from them to the place to be attacked; the character of the intervening country; how far it is healthful or unhealthful; what the climate is liable to be at the season of the proposed movement; the temper and sympathies of the inhabitants; the quantity and kind of supplies that can be obtained from the country; the extent to which transportation can be obtained, and a great variety of other things which will go to determine whether it is better to make the approach from one point or from another, and to determine what it will be necessary for the army to carry with it in order to succeed in moving and living and fighting.

All this information it is the business of a general staff to procure and present. It is probable that there would be in such case a number of alternative plans, each having certain advantages and disadvantages, and these should be worked out each by itself, with the reasons for and against it, and presented to the President or general for his determination. This the general staff should do. This cannot be done in an hour. It requires that the staff shall have been at work for a long time collecting the information and arranging it and getting it in form to present. Then at home, where the preparation for the expedition is to be made, the order must be based upon a knowledge of the men and material available for its execution; how many men there are who can be devoted to that purpose, from what points they are to be drawn, what bodies of troops ought to be left or sent elsewhere, and what bodies may be included in the proposed expedition; whether there are ships enough to transport them; where they are to be obtained; whether they are properly fitted up; what more should be done to them; what are the available stocks of clothing, arms and ammunition, and engineers' material, and horses and wagons, and all the innumerable supplies and munitions necessary for a large expedition; how are the things to be supplied which are not ready, but which are necessary, and how long time will be required to supply them.

All this and much more necessary information it is the business of a general staff to supply. When that has been done the order is made with all available knowledge of all the circumstances upon which the movement depends for its success. It is then the business of a general staff to see that every separate officer upon whose action the success of the movement depends understands his share in it and does not lag behind in the performance of that share; to see that troops and ships and animals and supplies of arms and ammunition and clothing and food, etc., from hundreds of sources, come together at the right times and places. It is a laborious, complicated, and difficult work, which requires a considerable number of men whose special business it is and who are charged with no other duties.

It was the lack of such a body of men doing that kind of work which led to the confusion attending the Santiago expedition in the summer of 1898. The confusion at Tampa and elsewhere was the necessary result of having a large number of men, each of them doing his own special work the best he could, but without any adequate force of officers engaged in seeing that they pulled together according to detailed plans made beforehand. Such a body of men doing general staff duty is just as necessary to prepare an army properly for war in time of peace as it is in time of war. It is not an executive body; it is not an administrative body; it acts only through the authority of others. It makes intelligent command possible by procuring and arranging information and working out plans in detail, and it makes intelligent and effective execution of commands possible by keeping all the separate agents advised of the parts they are to play in the general scheme. . . .

Organization of the General Staff

Extract from the Report of the Secretary of War for 1903

The important military event of the year affecting the regular army has been the reorganization of the system of military control under the General Staff Act approved February 14, 1903. This

Act abolished the separate office of General Commanding the Army, provided for a military Chief of Staff to the President, who, acting under the directions of the President, or of the Secretary of War representing him, should have supervision not only of all troops of the line but of the special staff and supply departments which had theretofore reported directly to the Secretary of War; and it created for the assistance of the Chief of Staff a corps of forty-four officers, who were relieved from all other duties. The function of this new corps is described by the statute in the following words:

> SEC. 2. That the duties of the General Staff Corps shall be to prepare plans for the national defense and for the mobilization of the military forces in time of war; to investigate and report upon all questions affecting the efficiency of the army and its state of preparation for military operations; to render professional aid and assistance to the Secretary of War and to general officers and other superior commanders, and to act as their agents in informing and coördinating the action of all the different officers who are subject, under the terms of this Act, to the supervision of the Chief of Staff; and to perform such other military duties not otherwise assigned by law as may be from time to time prescribed by the President.

. . . The regulations which govern the operation of the new corps were adopted on the third of August. They divide the corps into the War Department General Staff and the General Staff serving with troops (that is to say, in time of peace with the generals commanding geographical departments), and they prescribe the duties and relations of each of the two classes.

The tenth article of the regulations relating to the Chief of Staff states explicitly the new theory of control inaugurated by the General Staff Act. It will be remembered that our old plan of army administration was that there should be a General Commanding the Army in peace as well as in war, responsible for the efficiency, discipline, and conduct of the troops, but having no control over finances or the departments of supply and transportation; and that there should be a Secretary of War controlling the finances and the money-spending bureaus, but not commanding the army or responsible for the conduct of purely military affairs; and it will be remembered that the result of attempting to work upon that theory of dual and separate responsibility was almost constant discord and a consequent reduction of efficiency. The new theory is stated by the regulation. . . .

It will be perceived that we are here providing for civilian control over the military arm, but for civilian control to be exercised through a single military expert of high rank, who is provided with an adequate corps of professional assistants to aid him in the performance of his duties, and who is bound to use all his professional skill and knowledge in giving effect to the purposes and general directions of his civilian superior, or make way for another expert who will do so.

In this way it is hoped that the problem of reconciling civilian control with military efficiency with which we have been struggling for so many years will be solved. . . .

Joint Army and Navy Board

Extract from the Report of the Secretary of War for 1903

Following the same line of policy which led to the organization of the General Staff, the Secretaries of War and the Navy entered into an arrangement, with the approval of the President, which was published to the army in General Orders No. 107.

	HEADQUARTERS OF THE ARMY,
GENERAL ORDERS	ADJUTANT-GENERAL'S OFFICE
No. 107.	WASHINGTON, July 20, 1903

By direction of the Secretary of War, the following order is published to the army for the information and guidance of all concerned:

"July 17, 1903.
"The Department of War and the Department of the Navy have agreed upon the formation of a joint board to be composed

of four officers of the Army and four officers of the Navy, to hold stated sessions and such extraordinary sessions as shall appear advisable for the purpose of conferring upon, discussing, and reaching common conclusions regarding all matters calling for the coöperation of the two services. Any matters which seem to either Department to call for such consideration may be referred by that Department to the board thus formed. All reports of the board shall be made in duplicate, one to each Department. All reports and proceedings of the board shall be confidential. The senior member of the board present will preside at its meetings and the junior member of the board present will act as its recorder.

"On the recommendation of the provisional General Staff of the Army the following officers are detailed by the Secretary of War to serve upon the board:

"Major-General S. B. M. Young

"Major-General Henry C. Corbin

"Brigadier-General Tasker H. Bliss

"Brigadier-General Wallace F. Randolph

"On the recommendation of the General Board of the Navy the following officers are detailed by the Secretary of the Navy to serve upon the board:

"Admiral of the Navy George Dewey

"Rear-Admiral Henry C. Taylor

"Captain John E. Pillsbury

"Commander William J. Barnette

"ELIHU ROOT, *Secretary of War.*

"WILLIAM H. MOODY, *Secretary of the Navy.*

By command of Lieutenant-General Miles: W. P. HALL,

Acting Adjutant-General."

The common understanding and mutual assistance between the two services, which it is within the power of this board to bring about, may be made to cover a wide range of subjects of great public importance, including the parts to be taken by the military and naval forces, respectively, in case of military operations on the seaboards and on navigable lakes and rivers; artillery defense of naval stations and naval defensive aid to seacoast fortifications; the exchange of information obtained by one branch of the service and useful for both; the manufacture or purchase of cannon, projectiles, explosives, small arms, ammunition, and munitions of war generally available for both services; the purchase and transportation of supplies; the transportation of men upon changes of station; the study and discussion of joint military and naval problems. In all these, and in many other respects, much greater efficiency, at much less cost, can be obtained by coöperation and mutual understanding than by separate services working in entire independence of each other. If the two forces are ever to be called upon to coöperate, the time to determine what each shall do, and the time for each to learn what the other can do, is before the exigency arises. It is hoped that this joint board, which is so constituted as to command the assistance of the General Staff in both arms of the service for the working out of its problems, will contribute materially toward the end desired. . . .

28. Theodore Roosevelt: War and Defense in the "Imperial Years"

IN 1901 THE PRESIDENCY PASSED SUDDENLY INTO THE ENERGETIC HANDS of Theodore Roosevelt, who was, among many other things, our first amateur soldier in the Presidency. There were few subjects in which the late colonel of the Rough Riders took a livelier interest than those of military policy, organization, strategy, and tactics. In his first annual message, December 1901, he devoted an extended, and to modern eyes somewhat naïve and romantic, passage to the problems of war, peace, and military policy as he saw them, including a demand for the massive "upbuilding" of the Navy, redolent of Mahanite teaching. The Army, he then thought, was large enough, though wanting in efficiency. He backed Elihu Root's reforms, but did not see them with the urgency he attached to battleship building as the main guarantee of peace.

Six years later, in the annual message of December 1907, he was more concerned with the Army, and there appears a significant idea, which had made little headway in the Root era: "We should maintain in peace a fairly complete skeleton of a large army" against the possibility of a "great and long-continued war." But Roosevelt's major interest was in the demand for four new battleships. The 1907 message was long and detailed; it was the last before the election of his successor in 1908 and sought to establish the Roosevelt policies while he could still speak with authority. The demand for four battleships was an attempt to commit the United States to the new competition in dreadnaughts beginning in Europe. It failed. Congress gave him only two; and, under William Howard Taft, this was to be reduced to one a year, while the British and Germans went on laying them down by the half-dozen. Nor did Congress or the country show any interest in the "skeleton of a large army." The messages reveal much about American military thought in the pre-1914 era.

The First Annual Message, December 3, 1901

. . . The true end of every great and free people should be self-respecting peace; and this Nation most earnestly desires sincere and cordial friendship with all others. Over the entire world, of recent years, wars between the great civilized powers have become less and less frequent. Wars with barbarous or semi-barbarous peoples come in an entirely different category, being merely a most regrettable but necessary international police duty which must be performed for the sake of the welfare of mankind. Peace can only be kept with certainty where both sides wish to keep it; but more and more the civilized peoples are realizing the wicked folly of war and are attaining that condition of just and intelligent regard for the rights of others which will in the end, as we hope and believe, make world-wide peace possible. The peace conference at The Hague gave definite expression to this hope and belief and marked a stride toward their attainment.

This same peace conference acquiesced in our statement of the Monroe Doctrine as compatible with the purposes and aims of the conference.

The Monroe Doctrine should be the cardinal feature of the foreign policy of all the nations of the two Americas, as it is of the United States. Just seventy-eight years have passed since President Monroe in his Annual Message announced that "The Ameri-

From *Messages of the Presidents*, XIV, pp. 6664–6671, 7109–7117.

can continents are henceforth not to be considered as subjects for future colonization by any European power." In other words, the Monroe Doctrine is a declaration that there must be no territorial aggrandizement by any non-American power at the expense of any American power on American soil. It is in no wise intended as hostile to any nation in the Old World. Still less is it intended to give cover to any aggression by one New World power at the expense of any other. It is simply a step, and a long step, toward assuring the universal peace of the world by securing the possibility of permanent peace on this hemisphere.

During the past century other influences have established the permanence and independence of the smaller states of Europe. Through the Monroe Doctrine we hope to be able to safeguard like independence and secure like permanence for the lesser among the New World nations.

This doctrine has nothing to do with the commercial relations of any American power, save that it in truth allows each of them to form such as it desires. In other words, it is really a guaranty of the commercial independence of the Americas. We do not ask under this doctrine for any exclusive commercial dealings with any other American state. We do not guarantee any state against punishment if it misconducts itself, provided that punishment does not take the form of the acquisition of territory by any non-American power. . . .

. . .We do not wish to see any Old World military power grow up on this continent, or to be compelled to become a military power ourselves. The peoples of the Americas can prosper best if left to work out their own salvation in their own way.

The work of upbuilding the Navy must be steadily continued. No one point of our policy, foreign or domestic, is more important than this to the honor and material welfare, and above all to the peace, of our nation in the future. Whether we desire it or not, we must henceforth recognize that we have international duties no less than international rights. Even if our flag were hauled down in the Philippines and Puerto Rico, even if we decided not to build the Isthmian Canal, we should need a thoroughly trained Navy of adequate size, or else be prepared definitely and for all time to abandon the idea that our nation is among those whose sons go down to the sea in ships. Unless our commerce is always to be carried in foreign bottoms, we must have war craft to protect it.

Inasmuch, however, as the American people have no thought of abandoning the path upon which they have entered, and especially in view of the fact that the building of the Isthmian Canal is fast becoming one of the matters which the whole people are united in demanding, it is imperative that our Navy should be put and kept in the highest state of efficiency, and should be made to answer to our growing needs. So far from being in any way a provocation to war, an adequate and highly trained navy is the best guaranty against war, the cheapest and most effective peace insurance. The cost of building and maintaining such a navy represents the very lightest premium for insuring peace which this nation can possibly pay.

Probably no other great nation in the world is so anxious for peace as we are. There is not a single civilized power which has anything whatever to fear from aggressiveness on our part. All we want is peace; and toward this end we wish to be able to secure the same respect for our rights from others which we are eager and anxious to extend to their rights in return, to insure fair treatment to us commercially, and to guarantee the safety of the American people.

Our people intend to abide by the Monroe Doctrine and to insist upon it as the one sure means of securing the peace of the Western Hemisphere. The Navy offers us the only means of making our insistence upon the Monroe Doctrine anything but a subject of derision to whatever nation chooses to disregard it. We desire the peace which comes as of right to the just man armed; not the peace granted on terms of ignominy to the craven and the weakling.

It is not possible to improvise a navy after war breaks out. The ships must be built and the men trained long in advance. Some auxiliary vessels can be turned into makeshifts which will do in default of any better for the minor work, and a proportion of raw men can be mixed with the highly trained, their shortcomings being made good by the skill of their fellows; but the efficient fighting force of the Navy when pitted against an equal opponent will be found almost exclusively in the war ships that have been regularly built and in the officers and men who through years of faithful performance of sea duty have been trained to handle their formidable but complex and delicate weapons with the highest efficiency. . . .

. . . There should be no cessation in the work of completing our Navy. So far ingenuity has been wholly unable to devise a substitute for the great war craft whose hammering guns beat out the mastery of the high seas. It is unsafe and unwise not to provide this year for several additional battle ships and heavy armored cruisers, with auxiliary and lighter craft in proportion; for the exact numbers and character I refer you to the report of the Secretary of the Navy. But there is something we need even more than additional ships, and this is additional officers and men. To provide battle ships and cruisers and then lay them up, with the expectation of leaving them unmanned until they are needed in actual war, would be worse than folly; it would be a crime against the Nation.

To send any war ship against a competent enemy unless those aboard it have been trained by years of actual sea service, including incessant gunnery practice, would be to invite not merely disaster, but the bitterest shame and humiliation. Four thousand additional seamen and one thousand additional marines should be provided; and an increase in the officers should be provided by making a large addition to the classes at Annapolis. . . .

. . . We now have seventeen battle ships appropriated for, of which nine are completed and have been commissioned for actual service. The remaining eight will be ready in from two to four years, but it will take at least that time to recruit and train the men to fight them. It is of vast concern that we have trained crews ready for the vessels by the time they are commissioned. Good ships and good guns are simply good weapons, and the best weapons are useless save in the hands of men who know how to fight with them. The men must be trained and drilled under a thorough and well-planned system of progressive instruction, while the recruiting must be carried on with still greater vigor. Every effort must be made to exalt the main function of the officer—the command of men. The leading graduates of the Naval Academy should be assigned to the combatant branches, the line and marines. . . .

. . . It is not necessary to increase our Army beyond its present size at this time. But it is necessary to keep it at the highest point of efficiency. The individual units who as officers and enlisted men compose this Army, are, we have good reason to believe, at least as efficient as those of any other army in the entire world. It is our duty to see that their training is of a kind to insure the highest possible expression of power to these units when acting in combination.

The conditions of modern war are such as to make an infinitely heavier demand than ever before upon the individual character and capacity of the officer and the enlisted man, and to make it far more difficult for men to act together with effect. At present the fighting must be done in extended order, which means that each man must act for himself and at the same time act in combination with others with whom he is no longer in the old-fashioned elbow-to-elbow touch. Under such conditions a few men of the highest excellence are worth more than many men without the special skill which is only found as the result of special training applied to men of exceptional physique and morale. But nowadays the most valuable fighting man and the most difficult to perfect is the rifleman who is also a skillful and daring rider.

The proportion of our cavalry regiments has wisely been increased. The American cavalryman, trained to manoeuvre and fight with equal facility on foot and on horseback, is the best type of soldier for general purposes now to be found in the world. The ideal cavalryman of the present day is a man who can fight on foot as effectively as the best infantryman, and who is in addition unsurpassed in the care and management of his horse and in his ability to fight on horseback.

A general staff should be created. As for the present staff and supply departments, they should be filled by details from the line, the men so detailed returning after a while to their line duties. . . .

. . . Every effort should be made to bring the Army to a constantly increasing state of efficiency. When on actual service no work save that directly in the line of such service should be required. The paper work in the Army, as in the Navy, should be greatly reduced. What is needed is proved power of command and capacity to work well in the field. Constant care is necessary to prevent dry rot in the transportation and commissary departments. . . .

. . . Much good has already come from the act reorganizing the Army, passed early in the present year. The three prime reforms, all of them of literally inestimable value, are, first, the substitution of four-year details from the line for permanent appointments in the so-called staff divisions; second, the establishment of a corps of artillery with a chief at the head; third, the establishment of a maximum and minimum limit for the Army. It would be difficult to overestimate the improvement in the efficiency of our Army which these three reforms are making, and have in part already effected. . . .

The Seventh Annual Message, December 3, 1907

. . . Not only there is not now, but there never has been, any other nation in the world so wholly free from the evils of militarism as is ours. There never has been any other large nation, not even China, which for so long a period has had relatively to its numbers so small a regular army as has ours. Never at any time in our history has this Nation suffered from militarism or been in the remotest danger of suffering from militarism. Never at any time of our history has the Regular Army been of a size which caused the slightest appreciable tax upon the tax-paying citizens of the Nation. Almost always it has been too small in size and underpaid. Never in our entire history has the Nation suffered in the least particular because too much care has been given to the Army, too much prominence given it, too much money spent upon it, or because it has been too large. But again and again we have suffered because enough care has not been given to it, because it has been too small, because there has not been sufficient preparation in advance for possible war. Every foreign war in which we have engaged has cost us many times the amount which, if wisely expended during the preceding years of peace on the Regular Army, would have insured the war ending in but a fraction of the time and but for a fraction of the cost that was actually the case. As a Nation we have always been shortsighted in providing for the efficiency of the Army in time of peace. It is nobody's especial interest to make such provision and no one looks ahead to war at any period, no matter how remote, as being a serious possibility; while an improper economy, or rather niggardliness, can be practiced at the expense of the Army with the certainty that those practicing it will not be called to account therefor, but that the price will be paid by the unfortunate persons who happen to be in office when a war does actually come.

I think it is only lack of foresight that troubles us, not any hostility to the Army. There are, of course, foolish people who denounce any care of the Army or Navy as "militarism," but I do not think that these people are numerous. This country has to contend now, and has had to contend in the past, with many evils, and there is ample scope for all who would work for reform. But there is not one evil that now exists, or that ever has existed in this country, which is, or ever has been, owing in the smallest part to militarism. Declamation against militarism has no more serious place in an earnest and intelligent movement for righteousness in this country than declamation against the worship of Baal or Astaroth. It is declamation against a non-existent evil, one which never has existed in this country, and which has not the slightest chance of appearing here. We are glad to help in any movement for international peace, but this is because we sincerely believe that it is our duty to help all such movements provided they are sane and rational, and not because there is any tendency toward militarism on our part which needs to be cured. The evils we have to fight are those in connection with industrialism, not militarism. Industry is always necessary, just as war is sometimes necessary Each has its price, and industry in the United States now exacts, and has always exacted, a far heavier toll of death than all our wars put together. . . . The number of deaths in battle in all the foreign wars put together, for the last century and a quarter, aggregate considerably less than one year's death record for our industries. A mere glance at these figures is sufficient to show the absurdity of the outcry against militarism.

But again and again in the past our little Regular Army has rendered service literally vital to the country, and it may at any time have to do so in the future. Its standard of efficiency and instruction is higher now than ever in the past. But it is too small. There are not enough officers; and it is impossible to secure enough enlisted men. We should maintain in peace a fairly complete skeleton of a large army. A great and long-continued war would have to be fought by volunteers. But months would pass before any large body of efficient volunteers could be put in the field, and our Regular Army should be large enough to meet any immediate need. . . .

. . . It was hoped The Hague Conference might deal with the question of the limitation of armaments. But even before it had assembled informal inquiries had developed that as regards naval armaments, the only ones in which this country had any interest, it was hopeless to try to devise any plan for which there was the slightest possibility of securing the assent of the nations gathered at The Hague. No plan was even proposed which would have had the assent of more than one first class Power outside of the United States. The only plan that seemed at all feasible, that of limiting the size of battleships, met with no favor at all. It is evident, therefore, that it is folly for this Nation to base any hope of securing peace on any international agreement as to the limitations of armaments. Such being the fact it would be most unwise for us to stop the upbuilding of our Navy. To build one battleship of the best and most advanced type a year would barely keep our fleet up to its present force. This is not enough. In my judgment, we should this year provide for four battleships. But it is idle to build battleships unless in addition to providing the men, and the means for thorough training, we provide the auxiliaries for them, unless we provide docks, the coaling stations, the colliers and supply ships that they need. We are extremely deficient in coaling stations and docks on the Pacific, and this deficiency should not longer be permitted to exist. Plenty of torpedo boats and destroyers should be built. Both on the Atlantic and Pacific coasts, fortifications of the best type should be provided for all our greatest harbors.

We need always to remember that in time of war the Navy is not to be used to defend harbors and sea-coast cities; we should perfect our system of coast fortifications. The only efficient use for the Navy is for offense. The only way in which it can efficiently protect our own coast against the possible action of a foreign navy is by destroying that foreign navy. For defense against a hostile fleet which actually attacks them, the coast cities must depend upon their forts, mines, torpedoes, submarines, and torpedo boats and destroyers. All of these together are efficient for defensive purposes, but they in no way supply the place of a thoroughly efficient navy capable of acting on the offensive; for parrying never yet won a fight. It can only be won by hard hitting, and an aggressive sea-going navy alone can do this hard hitting of the offensive type. But the forts and the like are necessary so that the Navy may be footloose. In time of war there is sure to be demand, under pressure, of fright, for the ships to be scattered so as to defend all kind of ports. Under penalty of terrible disaster, this demand must be refused. The ships must be kept together, and their objective made the enemies' fleet. If fortifications are sufficiently strong, no modern navy will venture to attack them, so long as the foe has in existence a hostile navy of anything like the same size or efficiency. But unless there exists such a navy then the fortifications are powerless by themselves to secure the victory. For of course the mere deficiency means that any resolute enemy can at his leisure combine all his forces upon one point with the certainty that he can take it.

Until our battle fleet is much larger than at present it should never be split into detachments so far apart that they could not in event of emergency be speedily united. Our coast line is on the Pacific just as much as on the Atlantic. The interests of California, Oregon, and Washington are as emphatically the interests of the whole Union as those of Maine and New York, of Louisiana and Texas. The battle fleet should now and then be moved to the Pacific, just as at other times it should be kept in the Atlantic. When the Isthmian Canal is built the transit of the battle fleet from one ocean to the other will be comparatively easy. Until it is built I earnestly hope that the battle fleet will be thus shifted between the two oceans every year or two. The marksmanship on all our ships has improved phenomenally during the last five years. Until within the last two or three years it was not possible to train a battle fleet in squadron maneuvers under service conditions, and it is only during these last two or three years that the training under these conditions has become really effective. Another and most necessary stride in advance is now being taken. The battle fleet is about starting by the Straits of Magellan to visit the Pacific coast. Sixteen battleships are going under the command of Rear-Admiral Evans, while eight armored cruisers and two other battleships will meet him at San Francisco, whither certain torpedo destroyers are also going. No fleet of such size has ever made such a voyage, and it will be of very great educational use to all engaged in it. The only way by which to teach officers and men how to handle the fleet so as to meet every possible strain and emergency in time of war is to have them practice under similar conditions in time of peace. Moreover, the only way to find out our actual needs is to perform in time of peace whatever maneuvers might be necessary in time of war. After war is declared it is too late to find out the needs; that means to invite disaster. This trip to the Pacific will show what some of our needs are and will enable us to provide for them. The proper place for an officer to learn his duty is at sea, and the only way in which a navy can ever be made efficient is by practice at sea, under all the conditions which would have to be met if war existed. . . .

. . . It must be remembered that everything done in the Navy to fit it to do well in time of war must be done in time of peace. Modern wars are short; they do not last the length of time requisite to build a battleship; and it takes longer to train the officers and men to do well on a battleship than it takes to build it. Nothing effective can be done for the Navy once war has begun, and the result of the war, if the combatants are otherwise equally matched, will depend upon which power has prepared best in time of peace. The United States Navy is the best guaranty the Nation has that its honor and interest will not be neglected; and in addition it offers by far the best insurance for peace that can by human ingenuity be devised. . . .

29. Leonard Wood: Apostle of "Preparedness"

LEONARD WOOD WAS PERHAPS OUR OUTSTANDING SOLDIER IN THE PERIOD before the World War. The traditionalists always held against him the fact that he had entered the Army as a contract surgeon in the last Indian wars in the Southwest; he was, however, the first colonel of the Rough Riders and reached brigade command in Cuba. He distinguished himself as military governor in Cuba and later as commanding general in the Philippines; and as an eminent American soldier, he was invited to tour both the German and the French army maneuvers, thus acquiring a first-hand view of the great military systems he was to seek to emulate. As early as 1908 he had launched what was to prove a tireless campaign for "preparedness," which, rooted in Emory Upton's ideas, took the European and Japanese conscript military systems as its model and, in essence, sought to prepare the United States to wage a major war with them. Wood was Chief of Staff from 1910 to 1914—serving both Presidents Taft and Wilson—and his influence on the Army and on Army thinking was great. He was a voluminous speaker, letter-writer, and propagandist for his ideas but left little in the way of formal publication through which they can now be exposed. For that reason, a chapter from a small book, *Our Military History*, published in 1916, is presented here, out of strict chronological order, in order to introduce Wood in his own words, and because it seems to summarize the goals toward which he had been working through the pre–World War I years. His significant influence is more clearly seen in the staff documents that follow.

Our past military policy, so far as it concerns the land forces, has been thoroughly unsound and in violation of basic military principles. We have succeeded not because of it, but in spite of it. It has been unnecessarily and brutally costly in human life and recklessly extravagant in the expenditure of treasure. It has tended greatly to prolong our wars and consequently has delayed national development.

Because we have succeeded in spite of an unsound system, those who do not look beneath the surface fail to recognize the numerous shortcomings of that system, or appreciate how dangerous is our further dependence upon it.

The time has come to put our house in order through the establishment of a sound and dependable system, and to make such wise and prudent preparation as will enable us to defend successfully our country and our rights.

No such system can be established which does not rest upon equality of service for all who are physically fit and of proper age. Manhood suffrage means manhood obligation for service in peace or war. This is the basic principle upon which truly representative government, or free democracy, rests and must rest if it is successfully to withstand the shock of modern war.

The acceptance of this fundamental principle will require to a certain extent the moral organization of the people, the building up of that sense of individual obligation for service to the nation which is the basis of true patriotism, the teaching of our people to think in terms of the nation rather than in those of a locality or of personal interest.

This organization must also be accompanied by the organization, classification and training of our men and the detailed and careful organization of the material resources of the country with the view to making them promptly available in case of need and to remedying any defects.

In the organization of our land forces we must no longer place reliance upon plans based upon the development of volunteers or

From Leonard Wood, *Our Military History* (Chicago: Reilly & Britton, 1916), pp. 193–213. Reprinted by permission of Harrison Wood.

the use of the militia. The volunteer system is not dependable because of the uncertainty as to returns, and in any case because of lack of time for training and organization.

Modern wars are often initiated without a formal declaration of war or by a declaration which is coincident with the first act of war.

Dependence upon militia under state control or partially under state control, spells certain disaster, not because of the quality of the men or officers, but because of the system under which they work.

We must also have a first-class navy, well balanced and thoroughly equipped with all necessary appliances afloat and ashore. It is the first line of defense.

We need a highly efficient regular army, adequate to the peace needs of the nation. By this is meant a regular force, fully equipped, thoroughly trained and properly organized, with adequate reserves of men and material, and a force sufficient to garrison our over-sea possessions, including the Philippines and the Hawaiian Islands. These latter are the key to the Pacific and one of the main defenses of our Pacific coast and the Panama Canal, and whoever holds them dominates the trade routes of the greater portion of the Pacific and, to a large extent, that ocean. The army must be sufficient also to provide an adequate garrison for the Panama Canal, which is an implement of commerce and an instrument of war so valuable that we must not under any conditions allow it to lie outside our secure grasp.

The regular force must also be adequate to provide sufficient troops for our coast defenses and such garrisons as may be required in Porto Rico and Alaska. The regular force must also be sufficient to provide the necessary mobile force in the United States; by this is meant a force of cavalry, infantry, field artillery, engineers and auxiliary troops sufficient to provide an expeditionary force such as we sent to Cuba in 1898, and at the same time to provide a force sufficient to meet possible conditions of internal disorder. It must also furnish training units for the National Guard, or whatever force the federal government may eventually establish in place of it, and provide sufficient officers for duty under the detail system in the various departments, instructors at the various colleges and schools where military instruction is or may be established, attachés abroad and officers on special missions.

The main reliance in a war with a first-class power will ultimately be the great force of citizen soldiers forming a purely federal force, thoroughly organized and equipped with reserves of men and material. This force must be trained under some system which will permit the instruction to be given in part during the school period or age, thereby greatly reducing the time required for the final intensive period of training, which should be under regular officers and in conjunction with regular troops. In brief, the system must be one which utilizes as far as possible the means and opportunities now available, and interferes as little as possible with the educational or industrial careers of those affected. A system moulded on the general lines of the Australian or Swiss will accomplish this. Some modifications will be required to meet our conditions.

Each year about one million men reach the military age of 18; of this number not more than fifty per cent are fit for military service, this being about the average in other countries. Far less than fifty per cent come up to the standards required for the regular army, but the minor defects rejecting them for the regular army would not reject them for general military service. Assuming that some system on the general lines of the Australian or Swiss must be eventually adopted in this country, it would seem that about 500,000 men would be available each year for military training. If the boys were prepared by the state authorities, through training in schools and colleges, and in state training areas—when the boys were not in school—to the extent that they are in Switzerland or Australia, it would be possible, when they come up for federal training, to finish their military training—so far as preparing them for the duties of enlisted men is concerned—within a period of approximately three months. We should be able to limit the period of first line obligation to the period from eighteen to twenty-five, inclusive, or seven years, or we could make the period of obligatory service begin two years later and extend it to twenty-seven. This procedure would give in the first line approximately three and one-half millions of men at the age of best physical condition and of minimum dependent and business responsibility. From the men of certain years (classes) of this period, organizations of federal forces should be built up to the extent of at least twenty-five divisions. They would be organized and equipped exactly like the regular army and would be held ready for immediate service as our present militia would be were it under federal control.

Men of these organizations would not live in uniform but would go about their regular occupations as do the members of the militia to-day, but they would be equipped, organized and ready for immediate service. If emergency required it, additional organizations could be promptly raised from the men who were within the obligatory period.

There should be no pay in peace time except when the men were on duty and then it should be merely nominal. The duty should be recognized as a part of the man's citizenship obligation to the nation. The organizations to be made up of men within the period of obligatory service, could be filled either by the men who indicated their desire for such training or by drawing them by lot. This is a matter of detail. The regular army as organized would be made up as to-day; it would be a professional army. The men who came into it would be men who had received in youth this citizenship training. They would come into the regular army because they wanted to be professional soldiers. The regular army would be to a certain extent the training nucleus for the citizen soldier organizations and would be the force garrisoning our oversea possessions. It would be much easier to maintain our regular army in a highly efficient condition, as general military training would have produced a respect for the uniform and an appreciation of the importance of a soldier's duty.

The reserve corps of officers would be composed of men who had had longer and more advanced training, and could be recruited and maintained as indicated below, through further training of men from the military schools and colleges and those from the officers' training corps units of the nonmilitary universities and colleges. There would also be those from the military training camps and other sources, such as men who have served in the army and have the proper qualifications. This would give a military establishment in which every man would be physically fit to play his part and would have finished his obligation in what was practically his early manhood, with little probability of being called upon again unless the demands of war were so great as to require more men than those of the total first line, eighteen to twenty-five years, inclusive. Then they would be called by years as the occasion required, and would be available for service up to their forty-fifth year. It would give us a condition of real national preparedness, a much higher type of citizenship, a lower criminal rate and an enormously improved economic efficiency. Pending the establishment of such a system, every effort should be made to transfer the state militia to federal control. By this is meant its complete removal from state control and its establishment as a purely federal force, having no more relation to the states than the regular army has at present. This force under federal control will make a very valuable nucleus for the building up of a federal force of citizen soldiers. Officers and men should be transferred with their present grades and ratings.

The states have full authority to maintain a military force of their own and under their exclusive control, if they desire to do so. . . .

. . . As has been recommended by the General Staff, there should be built up with the least possible delay a corps of at least 50,000 reserve officers, on lines and through means recommended by the General Staff, and by means of a further development of the United States Military Training Camps for college students and older men, which have been in operation for a number of years. These plans include the coördination of the instruction at the various military college and schools and the establishment of well-thought-out plans for the nonmilitary colleges at which it may be decided to establish officers' training corps units on lines now under consideration.

This number of officers, fifty thousand, may seem excessive to some, but when it is remembered that there were one hundred and twenty-seven thousand officers in the Northern army during the Civil War, and over sixty thousand in the Southern, fifty thousand will not appear to be excessive. Fifty thousand officers will be barely sufficient properly to officer a million and a half citizen soldiers. We had in service, North and South, during the Civil War, over four million men, and at the end of the war we had approximately one and a quarter million under arms.

Under legislative provision enacted during the Civil War, commonly known as the Morrill Act, Congress established mechanical and agricultural colleges in each state, among other things prescribing military instruction and providing for this purpose officers of the regular army. There are nearly thirty thousand students at these institutions who receive during their course military instruction for periods of from one to two years. In some cases the instruction is excellent; in others it is very poor.

There are in addition a large number of military colleges and schools; at these there are some ten thousand students, so that there are approximately forty thousand young men receiving military instruction, nearly all of them under officers of the army. This means a graduating class of about eight thousand, of whom not more than forty-five hundred would be fit to undergo military training.

These men should be assembled in United States Military Training Camps for periods of five weeks each for two consecutive years, in order that they may receive that practical and thorough instruction which in the majority of instances is not possible during their college course. With these should be assembled the men who have taken the officers' training course at the various nonmilitary universities. This course, as outlined by the General Staff, will be thorough and conducted, so far as the purely military courses and duties are concerned, under the immediate control of officers of the army.

From all these sources we have practically an inexhaustible supply of material from which excellent reserve officers can be made. From the men assembled in camp each year, fifteen hundred should be selected and commissioned, subject only to a physical examination, as they are all men of college type, for one year as second lieutenants in the line and in the various staff corps and departments of the regular army. They should receive the pay and allowance of second lieutenants, or such pay and allowance as may be deemed to be appropriate.

The men who receive this training would furnish very good material for reserve officers of the grade of captain and major, whereas as a rule the men who have not had this training would qualify only in the grade of lieutenant.

From this group of men could well be selected, subject to the prescribed mental and physical examination, the greater portion of the candidates from civil life for appointment in the army. We have the material and the machinery for turning out an excellent corps of reserve officers. All that is needed is to take hold of it and shape it.

The prompt building up of a reserve corps of officers is one of the most vitally important steps to be taken. It is absolutely essential. It takes much time and care to train officers. Not only should students of the various colleges, universities and schools where military training is given, be made use of to the fullest extent, but the military training camps which have been conducted so successfully during the past few years should be greatly extended and made a part of the general plan of providing officers for the officers' reserve corps. It will be necessary to place the instruction at these camps on a different basis and to combine certain theoretical work with the practical work of the camp. This is a matter of detail which can be readily arranged. The results attained at these camps fully justify their being given the most serious attention and being made a part of the general plan for the training of officers.

30. The General Staff Outlines a "Well-Organized and Sufficient Army"

LEONARD WOOD HAD BEEN TRYING FOR YEARS, WITHOUT MUCH SUCCESS, to expand on Elihu Root's beginnings when his appointment as Chief of Staff gave him the opportunity for a frontal attack on the problem of military preparedness. He had the General Staff prepare a complete review of all aspects of military policy—the overseas responsibilities, the missions of the Army within the United States, the functions of the militia and the National Guard and their relation to the reserve question—all keyed to the rather new concept of a major war with a "first-class power." Thoroughly reflecting Wood's views, and doubtless largely of his drafting, the General Staff report on "The Organization of the Land Forces of the United States" appeared in 1912, as the Taft administration was nearing its pacific end. The report was not an analysis of any specific military need at the moment, but rather a generalized program for bringing the United States to a powerful military posture—unavoidably as effective for offense as for defense—on the world stage. Little of it was implemented at the time. But its ideas, arguments, and estimates reappeared in the massive "preparedness" legislation of 1916 and influenced the formation of the great army that was actually sent to Europe after 1917.

The Organization of the Land Forces of the United States.

I.

General Relations Between the Land and Naval Forces.

A general consideration of our responsibilities and our geographical position indicates that the maintenance of our policies and interests at home and abroad demand an adequate fleet and a well-organized and sufficient army. The function of the Navy is to secure and maintain the command of the sea. To accomplish this it must be free to seek and defeat the enemy. The use of any part of the fleet for local defense therefore defeats the chief object of naval power. The principal role of the Navy is offensive and the requirements of local defense must be met by other means. A fleet unsupported by an army is unable to secure the fruits of naval

From *War Department Annual Reports, 1912* (Washington, D.C.: Government Printing Office, 1913), pp. 71–83, 93–99, 126–128.

victory; a fleet defeated at sea is powerless to prevent invasion. The solution of the problem of national defense lies, therefore, in the provision of suitable land and sea forces and a due recognition of their coordinate relations.

II.

Relations Between the Land Forces at Home and Abroad.

Any plan for the organization of the land forces of the United States should be based upon a recognition of the fact that these forces are and must be divided into two distinct parts:

1. The Army on service beyond the territorial limits of the United States.

2. The Army within the territorial limits of the United States.

The Army on detached service beyond the territorial limits of the United States consists of the detachments required to meet the special military problems of the Philippines, Panama, Oahu, Alaska, Guantanamo, and Porto Rico. Each of these detachments has a distinct tactical and strategic mission and is to operate within a restricted terrain. All of them depend upon over-seas communication with the home country, and all of them may therefore be isolated for considerable periods, especially in the critical first stages of war. It is obvious that under these circumstances these detachments should be prepared to meet all military emergencies until reenforcements from the United States can reasonably be expected. They must, therefore, be organized with the view to being self-supporting until the Navy has accomplished its primary mission of securing the command of the sea.

The Army within the territorial limits of the United States is on an entirely different basis. It may or may not be given an adequate strength in time of peace, but it is supported by all of the resources of the Nation. It may be increased at the pleasure of Congress, and it may be reenforced by considerable forces of citizen soldiery. It follows from these considerations that the military establishment of the United States in time of peace should first provide effective and sufficient garrisons for the political and strategic outposts of the United States and that the residue at home should be organized with the view to ultimate expansion into such war forces as national interests may require. The essential difference between the forces at home and the forces abroad is thus seen to be that they have different capacities with reference to expansion at the outbreak of war. The Army at home is expansible to the highest degree, while the detachments abroad are not expansible at all in the brief but critical period that marks the first stage of modern war.

1. THE DETACHMENTS ON FOREIGN SERVICE.

The minimum garrisons required for the maintenance of national interests beyond the limits of the United States are as follows:

The Philippines.—4 regiments of Infantry at maximum statutory strength (150 men per company), 2 regiments of Cavalry at maximum statutory strength (100 men per troop), 2 battalions of Field and Mountain Artillery (6 batteries), 2 companies of Engineers, 2 companies of Signal troops (one of these a field company), 24 companies of Coast Artillery, 52 companies of Philippine Scouts, 1 ambulance company, 1 field hospital, with detachments pertaining to the Ordnance Department and enlisted men of the Hospital Corps on duty with organizations.

It is the duty of this force to support the authority of the United States throughout the archipelago, and in war it must be prepared to hold the defenses of Manila Bay at all costs until our fleet is free to operate in eastern waters. The garrison of mobile troops proposed for the Philippines comprises substantially the same enlisted strength as has been included in the garrison maintained there for the past few years. It is proposed to increase its economy and effectiveness by concentrating the bulk of this garrison in the vicinity of Manila. . . .

. . . *Oahu.*—The maintenance of this naval base is essential to the defense of our Pacific coast and to securing the full military value of the Panama Canal as a strategic highway between the two oceans. Pearl Harbor will be covered by seacoast fortifications, which are now nearing completion; but as the coast defenses of Pearl Harbor will be unable to prevent hostile landings on the 100 miles of coast which lie beyond the range of their guns, the security of the island and of the naval base ultimately depends upon maintaining a mobile force sufficient to defeat such hostile forces as may succeed in landing at any place on the island. Under conditions of modern warfare we can not count with certainty upon reenforcing the peace garrison of the island after a declaration of war or while war is imminent. The security of our naval base in the Pacific therefore demands that the garrison of Oahu must be able to hold out at all hazards until our fleet can arrive in Hawaiian waters. This may be taken as 40 days, assuming that the fleet is not employed on another mission and that the Panama Canal is open to its use.

The minimum peace garrison of Oahu is therefore placed as follows: 6 regiments of Infantry at maximum statutory strength (150 men per company), 1 regiment of Cavalry at maximum statutory strength (100 men per troop), 3 battalions of Field Artillery (9 batteries), 1 company of Engineers, 1 field company of Signal troops, 10 companies of Coast Artillery, 1 ambulance company, 1 field hospital.

Plans are being made for the expansion of the Hawaiian National Guard and the organization of volunteers from the American population. But the foundation of the defense must rest upon trained regulars who are familiar with the complicated terrain of the island. Our naval base in the Pacific will never be attacked except by troops of the highest skill and training and the attack will be made before extemporized troops can be prepared or hardened for full military effectiveness.

Panama.—Upon its completion, the Panama Canal will be our most important strategic position. By our control of this highway between the two oceans the effectiveness of our fleet and our general military power will be enormously increased. It is therefore obvious that the unquestioned security of the canal is our most important military problem. The permanent garrison must be strong enough to guard the locks and other important works and to prevent a naval attack which under modern conditions may even precede a declaration of war. We must therefore be able, even in peace, to man the seacoast guns that cover the approach to the canal, and we must have enough mobile troops to protect the rear of the forts and to defeat naval raids. A modern fleet can land a raiding party of several thousand bluejackets, and such a force landing out of range of the seacoast guns could penetrate to some vulnerable part of the canal within a few hours. The permanent garrison must therefore include a mobile force strong enough to anticipate and defeat naval raids at the beginning of hostilities, and to secure the canal until reenforcements can be expected from the United States.

The minimum peace garrison necessary for the defense of the canal is as follows: 3 regiments of Infantry at . . . maximum strength . . ., 1 battalion of Field Artillery (3 batteries), 1 squadron of Cavalry, 1 signal company, 1 engineer company, 1 ambulance company, 1 field hospital, 18 companies of Coast Artillery. . . .

. . . *Guantanamo.*—The policy of the United States contemplates the establishment of a naval base at Guantanamo. It is most necessary that the garrisons of coast artillery and mobile troops necessary for its land defense should be determined with the least possible delay.

Alaska.—The present garrison of Alaska comprises 1 regiment of Infantry and 2 companies of Signal troops. As troops can be withdrawn from Alaska only during a part of the year, this garrison can not be included among the troops available for general military purposes. The assignment of one infantry regiment as the garrison for Alaska is not with any idea of the defense of the Territory in the event of war, but simply to furnish a police force to quell local disorders.

With the settled conditions that now obtain in the government of Alaska it is believed that the time has come to relieve the Army from this police duty and that a force of constabulary should be organized and charged with the police of the Territory. The two companies of the Signal Corps should also be withdrawn and the lines turned over to the proper civil authorities.

Porto Rico.—The garrison of this island is the Porto Rico regiment of Infantry, comprising 2 battalions or 8 companies. Its enlisted men are native Porto Ricans. Its field officers are detailed from the United States Army, and its captains and lieutenants, some of whom are Porto Ricans, are specially commissioned for this regiment. This regiment might serve outside of Porto Rico under certain contingencies, but it can not be considered as available for general military purposes.

It is recommended that this regiment be completed so as to conform in organization to the infantry regiment recommended in this report and that promotion to the grade of major be authorized for the permanent officers of the regiment. . . .

III.

The Land Forces Within the Territorial Limits of the United States.

1. THE TRADITIONAL MILITARY POLICY OF THE UNITED STATES.

The problem of military organization has two aspects, a dynamic aspect and a political aspect. The measure of military force required to meet any given emergency is purely dynamic, while the form of military institutions must be determined on political grounds, with due regard to national genius and tradition. There can be no sound solution of the problem if either of these fundamental aspects be ignored. The military pedant may fail by proposing adequate and economical forces under forms that are intolerable to the national genius, while the political pedant may propose military systems which lack nothing except the necessary element of trained and disciplined military force. The practical military statesman must recognize both of these elements of the problem. He does not propose impracticable or foreign institutions, but seeks to develop the necessary vigor and energy within the familiar institutions that have grown with the national life. But the ultimate test is dynamic. In any military system the final test is capacity to exert superior military force in time to meet any given national emergency.

It is the traditional policy of the United States that the military establishment in time of peace is to be a small Regular Army and that the ultimate war force of the Nation is to be a great army of citizen soldiers. This fundamental theory of military organization is sound economically and politically. The maintenance of armies in time of peace imposes a heavy financial burden on the Nation, and the expenditure for this purpose should be kept at a minimum consistent with effectiveness for war. But reliance upon citizen soldiers is subject to the limitation that they can not be expected to meet a trained enemy until they, too, have been trained. Our history is full of the success of the volunteer soldier after he has been trained for war, but it contains no record of the successful employment of raw levies for general military purposes.

It is therefore our most important military problem to devise means for preparing great armies of citizen soldiers to meet the emergency of modern war. The organization of the Regular Army is but a smaller phase of this problem. It is simply the peace nucleus of the greater war army, and its strength and organization should always be considered with reference to its relation to the greater war force which can not be placed in the field until war is imminent. The problem is one of expansion from a small peace force to a great war force. Its solution therefore involves the provision of a sufficient peace nucleus, the partial organization and training of citizen soldiers in peace, and provisions for prompt and orderly expansion on the outbreak of war.

But the practical solution of the problem can not be met by the promulgation of a general theory. The Army at any time and place must be strong enough to defeat any enemy that may oppose it at that time and place. We are concerned more with the time required to raise the force of trained troops than with their ultimate numbers. If we need 60,000 soldiers in a given terrain within 30 days and can only deploy 50,000 soldiers in that time and place, we are not prepared for the emergency even if our plans provide for ten times that number at some period in the future. Whatever our military institutions may be, we must recognize the fundamental facts that victory is the reward of superior force, that modern wars are short and decisive, and that trained armies alone can defeat trained armies.

2. The Time Required to Raise Armies.

. . . In view of these considerations it is obvious that the citizen soldier must have some training in peace if he is to be effective in the sudden crisis of modern war. The organization in which he is to serve must exist and function in time of peace, and in view of the limited time available for training it should be a fundamental principle of American policy that no officer should be intrusted with the leadership of American soldiers who has not prepared himself for that responsibility in time of peace. The American soldier, whether regular or volunteer, is entitled to trained leadership in war.

It will never be possible for citizen soldiers to acquire thorough military training and experience in time of peace. Their training and hardening must be completed after mobilization, but the period required for such final training will be reduced exactly in proportion to the amount of training already received in time of peace. If the total peace training of a National Guard company is equivalent to two months in the field, it will be available for duty at the front two months earlier than a company of raw men, assuming other conditions equal in each case. But in any event during the period of final training, which will vary for different companies and regiments, the Regular Army must meet the situation at the front. If our citizen soldiery is put on a proper basis as to organization and training—a basis on which it does not now rest —its regiments will soon reenforce the line. Even with their limited peace training they will soon be effective for defense, and after a short period of field practice the best-officered organizations will begin to expand the Army for general military purposes.

3. Two Classes of Citizen Soldiery, Organized and Unorganized.

The traditional army of citizen soldiery should be considered as divided into two distinct classes, as follows:

1. The organized citizen soldiery, comprising those who are en-

rolled in definite military organizations and are partially trained in peace. This force is now known as the National Guard, and is organized under the militia clause of the Constitution.

2. The unorganized citizen soldiery. Included in this class is the Reserve Militia, which is made up of all the able-bodied citizens liable for militia duty, but who are not enrolled as members of the National Guard. . . .

. . . As the trained armies of modern nations will seek a decision in the early stages of war, and as extemporized armies will rarely be fit for use within the brief duration of such a conflict, it is obvious that our military policy should aim at increasing the peace strength and efficiency of the organized citizen soldiery. Provisions should be made for the organization of such new volunteer units as may be necessary on the outbreak of war, but it should always be the goal of sound policy to form the proper units in peace so that the war contingent of raw recruits can be absorbed into trained teams already in existence. This policy must be based upon the principle that a nation's military power is to be measured not by the total number of its male citizens capable of bearing arms, but by the number of trained soldiers with which it can meet a given emergency.

4. RELATION OF THE REGULAR ARMY TO THE NATION'S WAR POWER.

From a general consideration of our institutions and the requirements of modern war, it thus appears that the Regular Army is simply the peace nucleus of the greater war Army of the Nation. Its strength and organization should therefore be determined by its relation to the larger force. It must form a definite model for the organization and expansion of the great war Army, and it must also be prepared to meet sudden and special emergencies which can not be met by the Army of citizen soldiery. Some of the special functions of the Regular Army are indicated below:

1. The peace garrisons of the foreign possessions of the United States must be detachments of the Regular Army.

2. The peace garrisons of our fortified harbors and naval bases

with a sufficient nucleus of the mobile army elements of coast defense must be regular troops, definitely organized in time of peace.

3. The peace establishment of the Regular Army must be sufficient to prevent naval raids, which under modern conditions may precede a declaration of war. A successful raid of this character may determine the initiative by giving the enemy a convenient base for future operations.

4. The Regular Army must form a mobile reserve prepared to reenforce the foreign garrisons during periods of insurrection and disorder.

5. The Regular Army must be prepared to furnish expeditionary forces for minor wars or for the occupation of foreign territory where treaty rights or fundamental national policies are threatened.

6. The Regular Army must be prepared to cooperate with the Navy in the formation of joint expeditions in support of the foreign interests of the United States and for the protection of American citizens abroad.

7. At the outbreak of war regular forces should be concentrated and ready to seize opportunities for important initial successes. Such opportunities will frequently be offered before the mobilization of the Army of citizen soldiers can be completed.

8. At the outbreak of war special regular detachments should be ready to seize important strategic positions before they can be occupied or adequately defended by the enemy and before the concentration of the Army of citizen soldiers is complete. Initial operations of this kind, such as seizing the crossings of a river frontier or a port of embarkation, frequently determine the future conduct of war and assure an early decision. Capacity to take the initiative with an effective force is the best preventive of war.

9. By its definite organization in peace the Regular Army becomes the nucleus of the greater war Army. By its peace practice, its varied experience on foreign service, and its participation in expeditions, the Regular Army becomes the experimental model of the Volunteer Army. It solves practical problems of equipment,

armament, and supply, and makes its technical experience in these matters available for the larger force which is normally absorbed in peaceful occupations. It makes our war problem one of definite and orderly expansion instead of the vastly more difficult problem of extemporization.

10. The Regular Army will furnish a school of military theory and practice and will develop officers with special equipment and training for the higher staff duties in war.

11. Through its professional schools and General Staff the Regular Army will develop the unified military doctrine and policy which must permeate the entire National Army if it is to succeed in war.

12. Through its administrative and supply departments the Regular Army in peace will prepare in advance for the equipment, transportation, and supply of the great war Army of the Nation. . . .

6. THE JOINT USE OF REGULARS AND CITIZEN SOLDIERY.

In the defense of Great Britain regular divisions and territorial divisions will be combined in field armies for joint action. Any group of two or more divisions will form a field army. This permits the two forces to cooperate fully in the national defense and yet bases the ultimate grouping of the divisions on the undoubted differences of function of the two forces. This is pointed out because a different theory of organization has been proposed in this country, based on the idea of mixing regular troops and citizen soldiery in the same divisions. It has been proposed to form divisions comprising two brigades of Regulars and one brigade of citizen soldiers or one brigade of Regulars and two brigades of citizen soldiers, with various other combinations of these two classes of troops. A slight consideration will show the fundamental defects of this system. . . .

. . . We may therefore accept the following general principles as the basis of correct organization of our mobile forces:

1. The mobile elements of the Regular Army should have a divisional organization in time of peace. This requires that it be or-

ganized in tactical divisions, even if these divisions be incomplete and insufficient in number. Even a small army should be correctly organized as an army.

2. Every effort should be made to give a divisional organization to the organized citizen soldiery in time of peace. If our citizen soldiers ever go to war, they must be organized into divisions before they can be employed effectively against the enemy. In order to employ them promptly, every possible detail of this organization should be settled in time of peace.

Whenever it becomes necessary to reenforce the Regular Army and the National Guard by volunteer organizations, it is important that they should be prepared for effective service in the minimum of time. This requires that they be formed by trained officers acting under prearranged plans. It is believed that this can best be accomplished by forming the new organizations as United States Volunteers under a national volunteer law. . . .

. . . Each division district should contain a complete division and all of the plans for its mobilization, supply, and concentration should be prepared in peace and continually corrected to date. This can only be accomplished by assigning trained officers to arrange the details of organization under the supervision of the General Staff, which is intrusted by law with plans for war. Under present conditions it would be necessary to organize the fundamental war units after mobilization. The War College can and has prepared plans for such mobilization, but in the absence of a definite policy embodied in the law there is no assurance that such plans can be carried into effect. Solid and stable arrangements for mobilization can not be based on a hypothetical policy. Until there is a legalized system our actual mobilization will depend upon political conditions at the time of the crisis. Gaps in our legislation will be filled in haste and no human agency will be able to predict what the law will be. Our traditional theory of a small Regular Army and a great war army of citizen soldiers is not yet embodied as a definite institution. The mobilization of our citizen soldiery to-day would not result in a well-knit national army. It would be an uncoordinated army of 50 allies, with all of the inherent weaknesses of allied forces, emphasized by the unusual number of the allies. . . .

V.

The Necessity of a Reserve System.

1. Maintenance of Strength in War.

An army is an expensive machine maintained in order to support national interests in time of emergency. The economic efficiency of an army should therefore be measured by the effective fighting power which it is proposed to develop and maintain in war. It must not only be able to develop a high fighting efficiency at the outbreak of war, but it must be able to maintain that efficiency during the progress of the campaign. As soon as war begins military forces are subject to heavy losses, and unless means are definitely provided for replacing these losses the military machine will immediately deteriorate. The losses in war are not only the losses in battle, but losses due to disease and losses due to the hardship of campaign. The Prussian Guard Corps in its marches to Sedan lost 5,000 men on the march alone. It was necessary for the corps to arrive at the battle field in time, and that required a velocity of march that was more destructive than battle. It should be remembered that the soldiers in this force were trained soldiers and that the guard corps arrived and fought at Sedan in spite of its march losses. A force of soft or raw troops could not have arrived at all. Careful training is necessary to prepare troops for war; but it must be recognized that wastage will occur and that if a really effective force is to be maintained trained men must be supplied to replace this wastage.

It is the experience of modern warfare that any given unit loses at least 50 per cent of its strength in the first six months of war. If this loss is not replaced, there is 50 per cent deterioration in the power of the unit; and if it is replaced by raw men, the quality of the force as a highly trained team is destroyed.

This problem has an important economic aspect that has been

ignored throughout our military history. Military forces are maintained at great expense through long periods of peace in order to meet a brief emergency in war. Sound economics, therefore, demands that the peace expenditure be justified by unquestioned war efficiency. A company of Infantry with three officers should contain the maximum number of trained riflemen that three capable officers can command. This maximum appears to be about 150 men; but if the company starts in the campaign with 150 men, the natural wastage of war will immediately reduce it below that number. If the vacancies are not filled, it ceases to be an economical company, because under these conditions we have a less number of men than three trained officers should control; and, on the other hand, if the vacancies are filled by untrained men, the company ceases to be a trained team, as under these conditions the three officers can not effectively command 150 men in action.

The United States is the only nation that has no scientific means of meeting this situation. In all of our wars the companies first sent into the field have dwindled away in strength, and as these units have dwindled away new levies under untrained officers have been organized. The result has been that our wars have been long and protracted and attended by great sacrifices of blood and treasure. Each battle has generally been followed by a period of inactivity. Such an army has no power to keep up persistent military activity.

Without some solution of this problem there can be no definite military organization. The organization of divisions and other higher military units is based on the principle that the three arms should be combined in definite proportions. The Infantry division is differently organized in different countries, but in all countries it consists of from 10,000 to 15,000 infantrymen, with from 4 to 6 field guns per thousand rifles, and with similar definite proportions of cavalry, engineers, signal troops, and other auxiliaries. The infantry strength is the basis of organization. In every army except our own the number of infantrymen is definite and fixed, because means of replacing losses are provided in time of peace. With us, however, the infantry strength is an absolute variable.

We can only predict that the effective strength of each unit will fall after war begins. Under these conditions the division is not a continuing unit. Its components are fluid and indefinite, and there can be no stable organization under such conditions.

2. The Solution of the Problem.

The solution of this problem is very simple, and it is a significant fact that the same solution has been adopted in all modern armies. It is only necessary to provide that a man's army service shall consist of two periods, one period with the colors and the other a period of war obligation for a limited time after leaving active service. Under these circumstances when war is declared the active army is at once sent into the field and the former soldiers having a war obligation are assembled in depots, where they can be forwarded to the front as needed. At the same time raw recruits are enlisted and trained at the depot. As losses occur at the front, they are filled first by forwarding trained men from the depot, and if the number of these is sufficient new recruits are not forwarded until after they have had a sufficient period of training. The result is that even in a long war, which would ultimately require the services of thousands of raw recruits, it is so arranged that no man goes to the front until he is trained for active service and sufficiently hardened and disciplined to bear the stress of modern war. Under such a system the full energy of military activity can be maintained up to the limit of available recruits. Each unit works at its maximum efficiency, and the war power of the nation is developed with a minimum expenditure of life and money.

It thus appears that an army reserve is not a means of creating new forces or new units in time of war, but is a necessary means of maintaining the war strength of the peace establishment, such as it may be.

3. Power of Expansion.

But while one of the primary and necessary functions of a reserve system is to replace losses during the period required for the training of raw recruits, the principal function is to furnish the trained men necessary to pass from a peace to a war footing. If we have a reserve of trained men upon whom we can count in war, it is possible greatly to reduce the cost of the military establishment by giving it a minimum peace strength. Under our system our units are maintained in peace at considerably less than war strength, but there are no means of expanding to the war strength except by the absorption of untrained men. In every other modern army the economical peace strength is maintained without loss of war efficiency because trained reserves are available for a prompt expansion with trained men.

The effect of the reserve system on the cost of peace establishments can be illustrated in the following way: Let us suppose that we require a regular army of 100,000 men on the outbreak of war and that we propose to maintain this force in full effectiveness throughout the campaign. This requires that means should be provided for avoiding a deterioration of the force due to the absorption of raw recruits to replace the first losses of the campaign. It may be predicted that the losses will be 50 per cent, or 50,000 men, in the first six months, but before the expiration of six months, if we begin training recruits at once, some of the new men will be prepared to go to the front. We may, therefore, adopt a factor of safety of 25 per cent instead of 50 per cent and assume that the maintenance of 100,000 men will require an initial organized strength of 125,000 men if there be no reserves. Under conditions prevailing in the United States this force would cost probably $800 per man, or $100,000,000 per year.

But, if we had a system of reserves, the same effective war strength could be maintained at a greatly reduced cost. If the military establishment comprised 75,000 men with the colors and 50,000 men with the reserve, its cost would not exceed $65,000,-000 per year, and yet its war effectiveness would be just as great as the more expensive force without the reserves.

The economic effect of a reserve system, therefore, is to reduce the per capita cost of any given army at the same time assuring maximum effectiveness in war. If we do not have reserves, we are committed to a policy of maximum cost. It has been urged that a reserve system for the Regular Army is essentially foreign to our institutions and connected in some way with compulsory military service. It is true that the nations having a system of compulsory service also have a reserve system, but it is also true that Great Britain regards her regular army reserve as an indispensable part of her system of voluntary service. Great Britain did not adopt the reserve system until after her army broke down in the Crimean War because reserves were lacking. Her highly trained, long-service army almost immediately melted away. There was no way of renewing its strength except with untrained men. She found that without reserves her army was not adapted to the requirements of war.

The provision of a regular army reserve is purely a business proposition. The economic value of the reserve does not depend in any way upon its size. It is to be hoped that we can develop a sufficient reserve, but even a small reserve will reduce the per capita cost of the army and increase its effectiveness. . . .

4. Proposed Plan for a Regular Army Reserve.

In adopting a new policy in our Army it is important that present conditions should not be disturbed more violently than necessary. The present term of enlistment is three years and our men are accustomed to enlisting for that period of active service. It is therefore believed that in adopting a reserve system the normal period with the colors should be taken as three years. It is also important that the enlistment contract should be definite in so far as it affects the obligations assumed by the recruit. The important thing is to take a step toward the new policy, leaving its perfection to the experience of the future.

It is therefore recommended that the enlistment contract be for 6 years, with the understanding that the first three years are to be served with the colors and that during the last 3 years the man shall be furloughed to a reserve, where he shall be subject to duty in time of war only. It should be further understood that men so furloughed should not be included in the authorized peace strength of the Army. . . .

9. RESERVE OFFICERS.

The reserve system outlined above is designed to maintain the effective and economical enlisted strength, but it makes no provision for the increased number of officers that will become necessary in war. In modern military operations the loss of officers is fully as great as the loss of enlisted men, and further, under our system it will become necessary to detach officers from the regular establishment for staff duty and for employment with the citizen soldiery. The successful maintenance of large companies requires the presence of the full quota of officers and the whole machine breaks down if suitable men are not forthcoming.

The lack of some provision of this kind is one of the greatest defects in our military system. This defect has been recognized to a certain extent in the amended militia law, which provides that individuals who pass certain examinations may be placed on a list of persons available for appointment as volunteer officers in war. In the volunteer bill (S. 2518) now pending in the Senate it is provided that when officers are detached from the Regular Army on duty with the Volunteers their vacancies may be filled by the assignment of a corresponding number of Volunteer officers to the regular organizations. But neither of these provisions meets the specific requirement of providing a reserve of junior officers for the organizations in the Regular Army. And yet there is an abundance of such material which can easily be made available. We maintain military instructors at a great many schools and colleges in the country on the theory that such military training will become a military asset in war, and yet the young men who graduate at such institutions pass out into civil life without any definite place for them in our military establishment. They may in some cases go into the National Guard, some of them may enter the regular service, and some of them, no doubt, may find a place in the volunteer armies of the future, but the prospect of employing them is vague and contingent upon a great variety of uncertain conditions.

It is believed that it would be in the interest of sound policy to utilize young men of this type as reserve lieutenants in the Regular

Army. Upon their graduation opportunities could be given them to serve with regular organizations at camps of instruction or maneuvers. After such probationary service, if found to be properly qualified, they could be commissioned for a limited number of years under an obligation to serve in war. This class of reserve officers would be recruited mainly from the schools and colleges, but the appointments should be open to other suitable classes, such as former members of the Regular Army, Volunteers, and National Guard who comply with proper conditions to be determined by the Secretary of War. These reserve lieutenants would be analogous to the officers of the Medical Reserve Corps of the Army. They should be definitely commissioned, assigned to an arm, and authorized to wear the uniform of that arm. Their names should be carried in the Army Register, and under certain conditions they should be attached to definite organizations of the Regular Army, serving in the neighborhood of their homes. They should receive no pay except when called into the service, but should have the privilege of serving at maneuvers and of volunteering as members of expeditionary forces. They should also be regarded as a preferred class from which civilian appointments in the Regular Army should be made. The value of such a force in war would be incalculable. By having a full quota of officers it would always be possible to maintain the maximum economical strength of the Regular Army. They would replace losses due to the ordinary casualties in war and would enable the Regular Army to spare more officers for employment in the greater war force. On the outbreak of war the reserve lieutenants should mobilize with the reserves and should proceed to the front as the reserves are called to the front. At the depots they could assist in recruiting and in the training of recruits and would perform many functions which must be left to chance under our present system. It is also believed that such reserve commissions would be appreciated as an honor by the best type of young men and that it would be no more than a proper reward to them for giving a part of their college training to preparation for military service in war.

X.

Considerations Determining the Strength, Composition, and Organization of the Land Forces of the United States.

1. Political conditions affecting our country have changed very materially in the past 20 years, but it can hardly be said that the development of our land forces has kept pace with these changing conditions. Until quite recently our people have been almost wholly occupied with the task of overrunning our continental possessions and taking full possession of them. The Regular Army has been the forerunner of this movement, and has been organized, distributed, and trained for the requirements thus involved. This has kept the bulk of the Regular Army scattered in small units in our western country. Conquest and settlement have been fairly completed now, however, and the civil authorities are capable of maintaining orderly conditions as well in one part of our country as in another. If domestic questions were still the only ones that claimed serious attention it would seem that to deal with such questions only the Army should be distributed more equitably with respect to density of population.

But gradually our external problems have been assuming larger and larger proportions. While we were expanding other nations have been doing the like, and within the past few years it is found that practically the whole earth is now divided up among the principal nations and held by them either as actual possessions or as spheres of influence. Hitherto the interests of nations or of small groups of nations have been more or less local. But due to this world-wide expansion the contact between great nations and races has already become close. It tends to become continually closer, due to the increase of population and national needs, and due especially to the vastly increased facilities for intercommunication. With this close contact thus so recently established comes a competition, commercial, national, and racial, whose ultimate seriousness current events already enable us to gauge. Since our conflict with Spain in 1898 practically all of the principal nations of the earth have either been actively engaged in war or else brought to the verge of actual war. The evidence is clear that the nations and races capable of maintaining and protecting themselves are the only ones who can flourish in this world competition.

We have been drawn from our state of isolation and are inevitably involved in this competition. We must consider what preparation we will make to meet this change in our national situation. It may be said that we claim the undisturbed enjoyment of our possessions at home and the protection of our interests abroad. Our military requirements may then be summed up as follows: (1) To secure our home country from invasion; (2) to protect our foreign interests; (3) to maintain domestic peace and good order. Our forces should be proportioned, organized, and trained to meet these requirements.

2. Estimate of the Land Forces Needed in the United States.

Our requirements in the way of land forces are certain to change as the years go on, but in the light of present-day conditions it is estimated that at the outbreak of war with a first-class power we should be capable of mobilizing at once in the United States an effective force of 460,000 mobile troops and 42,000 Coast Artillery; that this is the minimum number of first-line troops necessary; and that to augment this force and replace its losses we should have plans made for raising immediately an additional force of 300,000 men.

To meet requirements less vital than a great national war—as for example, the sending of expeditionary forces to protect certain foreign interests—it may be presumed that we would draw upon the forces thus enumerated; and as in the light of our recent experiences we can not possibly foretell to what places expeditions may have to be sent nor what numbers will be required, all of these forces should be available for service anywhere.

3. Regular and Volunteer Troops.

The Regular Army contingent of this total mobile force at home should be sufficient to provide an expeditionary force capable of acting with the utmost promptness and decision, and sufficient to furnish a training nucleus for the volunteer troops in peace and a stiffening element in war. To meet conditions we can now foresee it is believed the Regular Army should comprise four complete divisions and that it should furnish as extradivisional troops, a division of Cavalry and the quota of Heavy Field Artillery, Engineers, Signal, and sanitary troops appropriate for one field army. On this basis the regular contingent of mobile troops within the United States proper when raised to war strength, would comprise about 112,000 men. The remaining 348,000 mobile troops would be made up of citizen soldiers organized in divisions and in field army auxiliaries. Each group of three division districts should furnish three complete divisions of citizen soldiers and the extradivisional troops considered appropriate for a field army of three divisions. On this basis the quota of 348,000 citizen soldiers might be raised from 12 division districts and they would be the equivalent of 4 normal type field armies. The regular and volunteer contingents taken together would then represent 5 field armies, but the exact number in which the various divisions and auxiliaries would actually be combined to make up field armies would depend entirely upon the necessities of the campaign in view.

The regular contingent of Coast Artillery troops in the United States should comprise 26,500 men when on war footing, leaving 21,000 to be furnished by the citizen soldiery. These figures are based on a complete regular personnel for mine companies and 50 per cent personnel of regulars for gun companies for authorized armament.

XI.

A Council of National Defense.

As war is but a phase of international politics, so military policy is but a phase of international policy. In its broadest sense the organization of the land forces is but a part of the national war organization, which includes the organization of the sea forces and of all other national resources.

A scientific solution of our military problem must include a determination and definition of national policy, and the provision of sufficient military and naval forces to support that policy against such adverse interests as may develop from time to time. As several departments of the Government are concerned in the settlement of this question, it is obvious that a sound policy must be predicated upon a comprehensive view of the whole problem with the view of coordinating and balancing its several elements.

In order to formulate a comprehensive policy for the consideration of Congress, it is believed that there should be a council of national defense similar to the one proposed in H. R. 1309. The function of this council, as defined in the bill, is to "report to the President, for transmission to Congress, a general policy of national defense and such recommendation of measures relating thereto as it shall deem necessary and expedient."

The members of the council, as provided in the bill, are as follows:

The President of the United States (ex officio president of the council).

The Secretary of State (to preside in the absence of the President).

The Secretary of War.

The Secretary of the Navy.

The chairman of the Committee on Appropriations of the Senate.

The chairman of the Committee on Foreign Affairs of the Senate.

The chairman of the Committee on Military Affairs of the Senate.

The chairman of the Committee on Naval Affairs of the Senate.

The chairman of the Committee on Appropriations of the House of Representatives.

The chairman of the Committee on Foreign Affairs of the House of Representatives.

The chairman of the Committee on Military Affairs of the House of Representatives.

The chairman of the Committee on Naval Affairs of the House of Representatives.

The Chief of the General Staff of the Army.

An officer of the Navy not below the rank of captain, to be selected by the Secretary of the Navy.

The president of the Army War College.

The president of the Navy War College.

It would seem that through the agency of this council the problem of national defense should receive the joint consideration of all of the branches of the Government which are responsible for its ultimate solution.

31. The General Board: A Navy to "Answer Any Challenge"

BY 1912 THE NAVY, LIKE THE ARMY UNDER LEONARD WOOD, WAS responding to the new concepts of defense responsibilities in a world of "first-class powers." No longer content with the old local or Western Hemisphere strategies, its goal became, as the Navy Department's annual report for 1913 put it, "to insure a fleet in 1920 of measurable equality with the fleets of the principal foreign powers"—disregarding the fact that the two "principal" foreign powers, Britain and Germany, were locked in a naval race irrelevant to American interests and likely to be decided before 1920. With its building programs cut back by the Taft administration, the Navy made a determined effort to secure a continuing naval policy and an initial authorization for four more dreadnaught battleships. For the first time, it published the annual "policy report" of its General Board. Over the signature of George Dewey, the victor at the battle of Manila Bay in the Spanish-American War, this revealed that since 1903 the Navy had taken as its objective a fleet of forty-eight battleships by 1920, to which it still clung despite all the vicissitudes of past (and putative future) changes in technology and in the international context. The Wilson administration, taking office in March 1913, did not adopt a continuing naval policy and cut the program back to only two new dreadnaughts. But the report, like Wood's General Staff report, remained to provide the basis for the naval expansion adopted in 1916.

From: President General Board;
To: Secretary of the Navy.
Subject: Naval policy.

1. The General Board invites the attention of the department to the fact that in the creation and maintenance of the fleet as an arm of the national defense, there is not now, and has never been in any true sense, a governmental or departmental naval policy. The fleet, as it exists, is the growth of an inadequately expressed public opinion; and that growth has followed the laws of expediency to meet temporary emergencies and has had little or no relation to the true meaning of naval power, or to the Nation's need therefor for the preservation of peace, and for the support and advancement of our national policies. The Navy, like our foreign policy and diplomacy, of which it is the arm and measure of strength, is broadly national, and has no relation to party or parties; and hence, should not be affected by changes of administration; but should develop and grow with the national growth on a fixed policy that should keep it equal to the demands that will be made upon it to support our just policies on challenge, and to preserve peace.

2. The General Board has from the time of its organization in March, 1900, studied the question of naval policy from the point of view of the Nation's need, free from other influences and having in mind solely the preservation of peace and the maintenance of the Nation's prosperity as it develops along the lines destiny has marked out, and according to the policies that have become national. In 1903 the General Board formulated its opinion as to what the naval development of the Nation should be, and established a policy for itself which it has consistently followed since, making recommendations to the department in accordance therewith from year to year. *This policy—as a policy—has remained a General Board policy only,* without adoption by the Government or even by the Navy Department, and without being understood by the people or Congress.

From *Annual Reports of the Navy Department, 1913* (Washington, D.C.: Government Printing Office, 1914), pp. 30–33.

In the opinion of the General Board any rational and natural development of the Navy looking to the continuance of peace and the maintenance of our national policies demands the adoption of, and the consistent adherence to, a governmental naval policy founded on our national needs and aims. To give life to such a policy requires the support of the people and of Congress; and this support can only be obtained by giving the widest publicity to the policy itself and to the reasons and arguments in its support, and taking the people and the Congress into the full confidence of the Government, inviting intelligent criticism as well as support.

3. The General Board does not believe the Nation stands ready to abandon or modify any of its well-established national policies, and repeats its position that the naval policy of the country should be to possess a fleet powerful enough to prevent or answer any challenge to these policies. The absolute strength necessary to accomplish this is a question that depends upon the national policies of prospective challengers and the force they can bring against us and, hence, is relative and varies with their naval policies and building program.

4. The General Board believes that only a lack of understanding of these views by the people at large prevents the adoption of a consistent naval policy; and recommends to the department a system of extended publicity in all matters relating to naval policy, acting through patriotic organizations, the press, or by whatever means a knowledge of the naval needs of the Nation may be brought home to the people of the country, with the meaning and reasons for them. The General Board believes that an understanding by the Nation of the Navy's rôle as a guarantor of peace and an upholder of those doctrines and polices which have become a part and parcel of our national existence will fix a naval policy that will meet those needs.

5. What that policy should be is stated broadly in paragraph 3 —the building and maintenance of a fleet powerful enough to prevent or answer any challenge to our national policies. To arrive at any concrete formulation of a naval policy, for recommending to

the department for presentation to Congress and the country, the General Board invites attention to the following fundamental facts:

(a) The "power" of the fleet consists of two elements, its personnel and its material.

(b) Of these two elements the personnel is of the greater importance.

(c) The measure of the matériel portion of a fleet's power is expressed in the number of its first-line battleships.

(d) The life and continued power to act of these first-line battleships are dependent on the assistance of a number of smaller fighting units of the fleet proper and of a number of auxiliaries in recognized proportion to the battleships.

6. From these fundamental facts two principles follow:

(1) That, in any consideration of naval policy to arrive at a fleet of a power suited to the Nation's needs, questions of personnel and material must go hand in hand, and the two must expand and grow together until the needed power is attained.

(2) That the basis of the material side of the fleet is the battleship of the first line, and that this basis, for life and action, requires to be supplemented by its military assistants—destroyers, scouts, submarines, aeroplanes—and by its auxiliaries—fuel ships, supply ships, repair ships, etc.—in proper proportionate numbers.

7. The General Board in its letter No. 420-422, of October 17, 1903, expressed an opinion of what the strength of the Navy should be in 1920, based on the second of the principles above stated, and placed the number of ships of the line which should form the basis of the fleet at 48. In paragraph 9 of the same letter it formulated the first principle in these words:

"These recommendations would be incomplete unless the General Board invited your attention to the futility of building vessels for the defense of the country without providing the personnel to man them. Whenever appropriations are made for new vessels the number of officers and enlisted men should be increased in due proportion."

From year to year, since the formation of those opinions in

1903, the General Board has consistently recommended a building program based on the policy of a 48-battleship strength in 1920, with necessary lesser units and auxiliaries; and these recommendations have varied only in the lesser units of the fleet, as developments and improvements have varied the relative value of those lesser units and the auxiliaries.

8. These recommendations of the board have been made in the pursuance of a fixed and definite "policy" adopted by the board for its guidance, after mature and deliberate consideration of all the elements involved and after a careful estimate and forecast of the future as to what would be the naval development of those foreign countries with which conflict might be probable, and what should be our own development to insure peace if possible, or superiority of force if war should be forced upon us. Expressed in concrete words, the *"policy"* of the board has been to provide the Nation with a fleet equal or superior to that of any probable enemy, as a guarantor of peace; and its forecast was that a fleet of 48 battleships, with the attendant lesser units and auxiliaries, ready for action by 1920 would accomplish this result.

9. The forecast of the board with regard to naval development in other countries has proved remarkably accurate. The absence of any definite naval policy on our part, except in the General Board, and the failure of the people, the Congress, and the Executive Government to recognize the necessity for such a policy, has already placed us in a position of inferiority which may lead to war; and this inferiority is progressive and will continue to increase until the necessity for a definite policy is recognized and that policy put into operation.

10. The General Board, while adhering to the policy it has consistently followed for the past 10 years, and believing that the naval needs of the Nation call for a fleet of 48 ships of the first line in 1920, with the attendant smaller units and auxiliaries in proper proportion, all with trained personnel, officers and enlisted men, active or reserve, recognizes conditions as they exist, and as clearly set forth in its memorandum of September 25, 1912, and the futility of hoping or expecting that the ships and men its policy

calls for will be provided by 1920. The board does believe, however, that this result may be eventually attained by the adoption by the Government of a definite naval policy, and the putting of it before Congress and the people clearly and succinctly. By this method responsibility for any rupture of our peaceful relations with other nations due to our naval weakness, or any national disaster in war due to the same cause, will be definitely fixed. The General Board believes that the people, with full understanding of the meaning of and the reasons for naval power, will instruct the legislative branch of the Government, and that that branch, with the same understanding, will provide the means. By the adoption and advocacy of a clearly defined, definite policy the department, with whom the responsibility first rests, will have done its part, and placed the responsibility with the people and the legislative branch of the Government. If the people, having been given the meaning of and the reasons for naval power, fail to instruct the Congress, the responsibility and the resulting material loss and national humiliation rests upon them; and if the Congress, having been instructed by the people, fails to provide the means, then the responsibility is theirs.

11. In this connection, and for the furtherance of the establishment and carrying out of a definite naval policy, the General Board invites especial attention to the proposed formation of a council of national defense. The formation of such a body would, in the opinion of the board, compel the adoption of a definite naval policy and assure the department of the aid of all other branches of the Government in carrying it out. Further, all other branches of the Government, more especially the legislative, would become instruments for disseminating knowledge of the naval needs of the Nation among the people in justifying the policy, thus giving the people that understanding which is needed for earnest support.

12. The General Board recognizes that full understanding and complete support from the people and from Congress can not be obtained immediately, nor in a few weeks or months, or possibly years. It believes, however, that it can eventually be obtained,

and that the best and surest method of doing this is for the department—which has knowledge and understanding of the questions involved—to adopt and maintain consistently from year to year a fixed governmental policy, taking the Congress and the people fully into its confidence, and disseminating generally through the press, through patriotic societies and organizations, and through any other available agencies its reasons and arguments in support of its policy.

13. As a basis for this governmental policy the General Board recommends:

(a) That the fleet shall consist of 48 battleships of the line, with the appropriate number of lesser units and auxiliaries to complete and maintain a fighting whole.

(b) That the personnel of the Navy, officers and enlisted men, shall grow and keep pace with the matériel fleet; and there shall at all times be on the lists, active and reserve, a sufficient number of officers and men to fully man the existing fleet for war.

(c) That the full strength of the fleet given in (a) shall be attained at the earliest date practicable by 1920 if possible. That, pending the full cooperation of the people and the Congress in carrying out this program, and as long as the full yearly increase the program calls for can not be obtained, the new construction each year shall be recommended in the proportions based on battleships to keep the fleet a complete fighting whole.

14. As a basis for departmental recommendation to Congress to carry out subhead (c) of the preceding paragraph, the General Board submits, as the results of its studies pursued since 1900, the following proportions of the various units needed for a complete fighting fleet: To 8 battleships there should be 32 destroyers; 16 submarines; 1 ammunition ship; 2 destroyer tenders; 4 fuel ships; 1 hospital ship; 1 repair ship; 2 submarine tenders; 1 supply ship; 1 transport. To these, with the present state of development, should be added at least 16 aeroplanes. With these proportions, to carry out the policy in full, there would be required to be laid down each year until the full fleet of 48 battleships was completed, 4 battleships, 16 destroyers, 8 submarines, 8 aeroplanes and 6 auxiliaries, the particular kind of auxiliaries to be laid down

each year to be of the character to keep the auxiliary fleet in the proportions given above.

(Note.—Until a sufficient number of aeroplanes for the existing fleet are obtained, the board recommends that no limitation be placed on the number to be built each year, since the aid for material states that the funds are available.)

15. The General Board recommends that the department place this program before Congress yearly until 1920, in pursuance of its definite policy. . . . .

GEORGE DEWEY.

32. The General Staff: "A Proper Military Policy"

IT IS SIGNIFICANT THAT THE ARMY AND NAVY PROGRAMS OF 1912 AND 1913 were elaborated at a time when there was no actual threat of war on the horizon. Both were abstract constructions, dealing in an abstract way with what at the time were only hypothetical possibilities. But in August 1914 World War I broke suddenly over Europe and over the whole age of which these programs were a reflection. For Americans, military policy at once became an urgent issue, and Leonard Wood's long campaign for preparedness began to bring impressive results. President Wilson remained cold to any strengthening of the defenses; but by 1915 the popular pressures for preparedness were making drastic revision of military policy unavoidable. The War College Division of the General Staff drafted a "Statement of a Proper Military Policy for the United States." While this was in large measure a rewrite of Wood's General Staff study of 1912, it was embellished with a more detailed discussion of the strategy of insular and continental defense and more precise estimates of the great hosts that foreign powers might fling into the Western Hemisphere—on the assumption, obviously, that the end of their own Great War in Europe would leave them with the means or wish to do so. Force-level and reserve requirements were pitched higher than Wood had stated them and the report boldly proposed to supersede the National Guard with a wholly Federal "Continental Army" of part-time soldiers. Congress was to reject the Continental Army, but in other respects the report provided the basis for the 1916 Defense Act.

Introduction.

The Military Problem Confronting the United States.

1. *The evolution of national military policies.*—National policies
are evolved and are expanded as the Nation grows. They reflect
the national sense of responsibility and also the national ambi-
tions. They constitute the doctrine underlying acts of statesmanship and diplomacy. A nation's military policy is the national doctrine of self-preservation. The world is never without virile, capable, and progressive nations, the circumstances of whose development have imbued them with the belief that their vital interests demand an active aggressive policy. They are forced to resort to universal service in the effort to fulfill, at any cost, what
they conceive to be their destiny. In the United States the development of the Nation has proceeded under an environment so favorable that there is no well-defined public opinion in regard to
what constitutes an adequate military policy. Heretofore isolation,
combined with the necessity of preserving the balance of power,
has been a sufficient guaranty against strong hostile expeditions
from Europe or Asia. The safeguard of isolation no longer exists.
The oceans, once barriers, are now easy avenues of approach by
reason of the number, speed, and carrying capacity of ocean-go-
ing vessels. The increasing radii of action of the submarine, the
aeroplane, and wireless telegraphy all supplement ocean transport
in placing both our Atlantic and Pacific coasts within the sphere
of hostile activities of oversea nations.

The great mass of the public does not yet realize the effect of
these changed conditions upon our scheme of defense.

Another thing that militates against the evolution of a sound
military policy for our country is the erroneous conclusion drawn
by the people from our past experiences in war. In developing
such a policy victory is often a less trustworthy guide than defeat.
We have been plunged into many wars and have ultimately
emerged successfully from each of them. The general public points
to these experiences as an indication that our military policy has

From *War Department Annual Reports, 1915* (Washington, D.C.: Government Printing Office, 1916) pp. 114–130.

been and still continues to be sound. That this is not really the belief of those in authority is shown by the fact that each war of importance has been followed by an official investigation of our military system and the policy under which it operated. The reports of these investigations give a startling picture of faulty leadership, needless waste of lives and property, costly overhead charges augmented by payment of bounties to keep up voluntary enlistments, undue prolongations of all these wars, and finally reckless expenditure of public funds for continuing pensions. These documents supply convincing proofs that all such shortcomings have been due entirely to a lack of adequate preparation for war in time of peace. But we have not yet learned our lesson. It has never been driven home by the bitterness of defeat. We have never known a Jena[1] or a Sedan. At no stage of our national life have we been brought face to face with the armed strength of a great world power free to land sufficient forces to gain a foothold at any desired portion of our coasts. That we have to some extent felt this danger is evidenced by our efforts to provide a navy as a first line of defense and to supplement it with the necessary harbor fortifications; but we have not yet realized that our ultimate safeguard is an adequate and well-organized mobile land force. Experience in war has shown the need of these three elements but the public has not yet demanded that they be perfected, coordinated, and combined in one harmonious system of national defense. *Not until this has been accomplished will a proper military policy for the United States be adopted.*

2. *Our abiding national policies.*—The majority of our people have always believed in asserting their own rights and in respecting those of others. They desire that the cause of right should prevail and that lawlessness should be crushed out. To live up to these high ideals imposes upon us new duties as a world power; duties that require something more positive than a policy of mere passive defense. In addition, there are two underlying and abiding national policies whose maintenance we must consider as necessary to our national life. These are the "Monroe doctrine"

[1] Battle of Jena (Germany), October 14, 1806, in which Napoleon defeated the Prussians [Ed.].

and the policy of avoiding "entangling alliances." They are distinctive and affect our international relations in a definite manner. In addition, policies may develop in the future as a result of international relations with respect to trade conditions.

A general consideration of our responsibilities as a nation and of our geographical position indicates that the maintenance of our abiding policies and interests at home and abroad involves problems of defense measures both on land and on sea. The solution of the general problem of national defense must be sought in the provision of adequate land and sea forces and a consideration of their coordinate relationship.

3. *Coordinate relationship of Army and Navy.*—Upon the Navy devolves the solution of the problem of securing and maintaining control of the sea. To accomplish this it must be free to take the offensive promptly—that is, to seek out and defeat the enemy fleet. The use of any part of the high-sea fleet for local defense defeats the chief object of the Navy and is a misuse of naval power. A fleet defeated at sea and undefended by an adequate army is powerless either to prevent invasion or even its own ultimate destruction by combined hostile land and naval forces. In illustration compare the cases of the Spanish fleet at Santiago and the Russian fleet at Port Arthur with the present example of the German, Austrian, and Turkish fleets under the protection of land forces.

Upon the Army devolves the task of gaining and maintaining on shore the ascendency over hostile land and naval operations. To accomplish this it must be able to seek out promptly and to defeat, capture, or destroy the invader wherever he may attempt either to secure a footing upon our territory or to enter the waters of our harbors with the objective of threatening the destruction of the seaport or of a fleet driven to seek refuge or repair therein.

The problems involved in operations against hostile land forces are complex and include only as an incident the protection of harbor defenses on the land side. The problems of harbor defense against attack from the sea are simple and passive in their nature.

4. *Coordinate relationship of statesman and soldier.*—In our

country public opinion estimates the situation, statecraft shapes the policy, while the duty of executing it devolves upon the military and naval departments.

Such a doctrine is sound in direct proportion to its success in producing a military system capable of developing fighting power sufficient to meet any given national emergency, at the proper time, supported by all the resources, technical and economic, of the country, in a word—preparedness. All the other world powers of to-day have realized the necessity of maintaining highly trained and organized military and naval forces in time of peace, and all, or nearly all, are allied in powerful coalitions.

Without superiority on the sea or an adequate land force there is nothing to prevent any hostile power or coalition of powers from landing on our shores such part of its trained and disciplined troops as its available transports can carry. The time required is limited only by the average speed of its vessels and the delay necessarily consumed in embarking and disembarking.

In order that the American people can intelligently decide on a doctrine of preparedness which shall constitute the military policy of the United States, and that Congress and the Executive may be able to carry out their decision, information concerning the military strength of other great nations and shipping available for transport purposes must be clearly set forth.

The work of the statesman and of the soldier and sailor are therefore coordinate; where the first leaves off the others take hold.

5. *Preparedness of the world powers for oversea expeditions.*— Control of the sea having been once gained by our adversary or adversaries, there is nothing to prevent them from dispatching an oversea expedition against us. In order to form an idea of the mobile force we should have ready to resist it an estimate must first be made of the approximate number of troops that other nations might reasonably be expected to transport and of the time required to land them on our coasts. . . .

. . . What the conditions were in August, 1914, is shown in the following table, which may be regarded as a reasonable estimate:

Preparedness of the great powers for over-sea expeditions.

Nation.	Strength of army.	Tonnage available of ships with capacity over—			First expedition using 50 per cent of tonnage given.		Second expedition using 75 per cent of tonnage given.		Time needed to—	
		3,000 tons.	2,000 tons.	1,000 tons.	Men.	Animals.	Men.	Animals.	Load, turn, and cross ocean with first expedition. Days.	Re-load, and cross and re-cross with second expedition. Days
Austria–Hungary	4,320,000		762,756		72,000	14,000	108,000	21,600	20.7	40.4
France	5,000,000		1,705,931		160,931	32,186	243,295	48,279	15.8	30.0
Germany	5,000,000	3,569,962	4,018,185		387,000	81,270	440,000	94,600	15.8	30.8
Great Britain	695,000	13,000,000			170,000	90,000			14.0	27.0
Italy	2,600,000		1,065,321	1,013,985	91,000	13,650	136,000	20,475	18.3	35.0
Japan	2,212,000				95,745	24,416	142,622	36,623	22.5	41.0
Russia	5,000,000		428,019		37,630	7,940	66,444	11,918	20.5	40.0

6. *Statement of the military problem.*—From what has been stated, we are forced to the conclusion that we must be prepared to resist a combined land and sea operation of formidable strength. . . .

. . . It has just been shown what the strength of these expeditions might be, as well as the time required for any one of them to develop its whole effective force. Hence it can be seen, when we take into consideration the possible two months' delay provided by the Navy, that our system should be able to furnish 500,000 trained and organized mobile troops at the outbreak of the war and to have at least 500,000 more available within 90 days thereafter. Here, however, it must be pointed out that two expeditions alone will provide a force large enough to cope with our 1,000,000 mobile troops, and consequently we must at the outbreak of hostilities provide the system to raise and train, in addition, at least 500,000 troops to replace the losses and wastage in personnel incident to war. To provide this organized land force is the military problem before us for solution. . . .

I. The Regular Army.

Relation Between Home and Oversea Garrisons.

10. The most rational method of determining the proper strength and organization of the Regular Army is based upon the fact that this force is and must be divided into two distinct parts —one for oversea service, the other for home service. Each of these parts must have its proper quota, both of mobile and Coast Artillery troops.

The troops on oversea service consist of the detachments required to meet the special military problems of the Philippines, Oahu, Panama, Alaska, Guantanamo, and Porto Rico. Each of these detachments has a distinct tactical and strategic mission, and is to operate within a restricted terrain. All of them are limited to oversea communication with the home country, and all of them may therefore be isolated for considerable periods, especially in the critical first stages of war. It is obvious that under these circumstances these detachments should be prepared to meet all military emergencies until reenforcements from the United States can reasonably be expected. They must, therefore, be maintained at all times at full statutory strength, and must, in addition, be organized with the view to being self-supporting, preferably during the continuance of war, or at least until the Navy has accomplished its primary mission of securing the command of the sea. . . .

General Requirements of Oversea Service.

11. *The Philippines.*—A decision to defend the Philippines against a foreign enemy is a matter of national and not of military policy. But in studying the military requirements of such defense it must be remembered that, under conditions of modern warfare, unless our Navy has undisputed control of the sea, we can not reenforce the peace garrison after a declaration of war or while war is imminent.

12. *Oahu.*—The maintenance of the naval base at Pearl Harbor, Oahu, is an essential factor in the military problem of holding the Hawaiian Islands. These islands constitute a vital element in the defense of the Pacific coast and in securing to ourselves the full value of the Panama Canal as a strategic highway between the two oceans.

The problem of holding the Hawaiian Islands can be solved by making Oahu, and therefore Pearl Harbor, secure against all comers. A satisfactory solution requires the joint action of the Army and Navy. Pearl Harbor and Honolulu are already protected from direct naval attack by fortifications now nearing completion. These, while deemed adequate to meet the conditions existing when they were designed, must now be strengthened to meet the recent increase in power of guns afloat; but no matter how complete these harbor fortifications on the southern coast of Oahu may be, they are unable to prevent attacks either on the remaining hundred miles of coast lying beyond the range of their guns or on the other islands of the group. Consequently there should be in addition a force of modern submarines and destroyers forming part of the permanent naval equipment of Pearl Harbor with sufficient radius of action to keep the Hawaiian waters thoroughly patrolled throughout their whole extent and to make them dangerous for enemy vessels. Should this force be worsted in combat and withdrawn before the arrival of our high-sea fleet, the complete control of the local waters might pass temporarily to the enemy, so that the ultimate security of both Honolulu, the naval base at Pearl Harbor, and indeed of the whole group, depends upon including in the Oahu garrison enough mobile troops to defeat any enemy that may land any-where on the island. It is clear that perfect coordination between the Army and Navy at this station is absolutely essential to suc-cess in holding this key to the Pacific. Unless we provide such dual defense of the Hawaiian Islands we can not be sure of re-taining control even of that part of the Pacific lying within the sphere of defense of our western coast. By making such provision the high-sea fleet is left free to seek out the enemy fleet in Pacific waters.

13. *Panama.*—The Panama Canal is a very important strategic position which it is our duty to hold. By our control of this high-way between the two oceans the effectiveness of our fleet and our general military power is enormously increased. It is there-fore obvious that the unquestioned security of the canal is for us a vital military need. The permanent garrison should be strong enough to guard the locks, spillways, and other important works and to prevent a naval attack which, under modern conditions, may even precede a declaration of war. We should therefore be able, even in peace, to man the seacoast guns and mine defense that cover the approach to the canal, and we must have enough mobile troops to defeat raids. A modern fleet might land a small raiding party of several thousand bluejackets at any one or more of a number of places, and such a force landing out of range of the seacoast guns could, if unopposed, penetrate to some vulner-able part of the canal within a few hours. The permanent garrison should therefore include a mobile force strong enough to antici-pate and defeat naval raids at the beginning of hostilities and to

protect the canal against more serious land operations liable to be undertaken later. If the enemy is operating on one ocean only, it might be possible to send reenforcements from the United States, but to count on such relief would be running too great chances. By authority of the Republic of Panama, this garrison is given facilities in time of peace to operate beyond the Canal Zone in order that the troops may be properly trained for their special mission and made familiar with the terrain over which they may be called upon to operate in defending the canal.

14. *Guantanamo*.—The policy of the United States contemplates the establishment of a naval base at Guantanamo. Garrisons of coast artillery and mobile troops are necessary for its defense and should be assigned to station there at the proper time.

15. *Alaska*.—The garrison of Alaska should be large enough to support the authority of the United States, and, in time of war, to maintain our sovereignty over a small selected area of the Territory. As work on the Alaskan Railroad progresses, the military needs of Alaska will increase.

16. *Porto Rico* is to be classified with the Philippines and Guam. Unlike Alaska and Hawaii, these island possessions have not been organized as Territories; nevertheless, they all belong to the United States and must be protected.

General Requirements of Home Service.

. . . 18. *General distribution of mobile troops in strategic areas.* —As previously explained, the influence of harbor defenses is limited to the areas within the range of their guns. To provide harbor defenses without mobile forces necessary to cover the unprotected intervals that lie between them would be comparable with attempting to make a house burglar proof by barring the doors and leaving the windows open. There is not a case in history where seacoast fortifications, efficiently manned, have been captured by direct attack from the sea. In all cases of capture mobile land forces have been employed for the purpose, and an enemy that hopes for success must undertake landing operations against us. We must therefore decide upon a rational distribution of our mobile forces to meet this contingency.

19. *Puget Sound area.*—Western Washington is bordered on the east by the steep and rugged Cascade Mountains, on the south by the Columbia River, and on the north by Juan de Fuca Strait and Canada. This corner of the United States is completely cut off from the rest of the country by great natural obstacles and presents an extensive front for attack by sea. While the maps show some twenty passes across the Cascade Mountains, communication with the east is almost entirely by three railroads, all crossing at points less than 50 miles apart and having tunnels or other vulnerable structures. The only practicable wagon road is effectually closed to traffic for between four and five months each year by heavy snows. Communication with the south is by one line of railroad, crossing the Columbia River by bridge at Vancouver. Communication between this section and the east and south is thus largely dependent upon a number of structures readily destroyed by high explosives, and impossible of restoration to traffic within a definite time. The two railroads along the Columbia River, at the point where it breaks through the mountains, could be easily wrecked so as to require considerable time to repair, and the gorge could be held by a small force against a large one coming from the east. If an enemy succeeds in entering western Washington and in seizing and destroying the important bridges and tunnels, he would be so securely established as to render it extremely difficult to dislodge him. In this rich region an invader could maintain himself indefinitely. The harbor defenses maintained in this region are reasonably strong. Ordinary precaution demands that a mobile force of reasonable strength be also maintained in this region.

20. *California area.*—There are five transcontinental lines of railway entering California. The Western Pacific and Southern Pacific by the passes through the Sierras northeast of Sacramento; the Atchison, Topeka & Santa Fe, and the San Pedro, Los Angeles & Salt Lake via Daggetts Pass northeast of Los Angeles; and the

Southern Pacific via the Salton Sea and Gorgonia Pass southeast of Los Angeles. There are no other passes through the Sierras that have been considered practicable. There is no railroad running south into Lower California. Only one railroad, the Southern Pacific, runs north into Oregon. As in the Puget Sound region, communication with the east is largely dependent upon structures readily destroyed by explosives and impossible of restoration to traffic within a definite time; California and the greater centers of population are separated by wide expanses of sparsely settled country. To transport promptly large bodies of troops into California would be difficult if not impossible in face of opposition at the passes. The invader would have a most fertile region at his back, while the reverse would be the situation with us.

The harbor defenses maintained in this region are reasonably strong, but they are of little use unless supported by a reasonably strong mobile force maintained in this region.

To rely, for defense, during the first stages of a war upon a mobile force shipped in from the east is to invite disaster.

21. *Atlantic area.*—In case of war with a first-class power on the Atlantic, that portion of our country lying between and including Maine and Virginia would undoubtedly be the primary object of an invader. While all other points along the Atlantic and Gulf coasts and all points on our land frontiers would undoubtedly be in danger, the danger would be secondary to that of the North Atlantic States above named. Here, also, the harbor defenses are reasonably strong, and here, also, a mobile force should be kept sufficient in size to hold important points until the citizen soldiery can be mobilized.

While many other regions are important, the three regions described—Puget Sound, California, and the North Atlantic States—contain the critical areas.

22. *Middle West area.*—The center of population of the United States is in the middle west, and here should be located a mobile force for use in case of need, on either the Pacific or Atlantic coast, the northern or southern border.

Necessary Strength of Mobile Troops for Oversea Service.

23. Constant study of the problem which confronts each of our oversea garrisons in connection with the advance made in arms, transportation, tactics, lines of information, methods of communications, undersea craft, and aerial operations, has led to the conclusions that the strength of the overseas garrisons, herein given is the minimum below which they should not be allowed to fall at any time. . . .

. . . 30. The following table gives a summary of the minimum garrison to be maintained on over-sea service:

Table of garrisons for over-sea stations.

Localities.	Regiments of Infantry.	Regiments of Cavalry.	Batteries of Field Artillery.	Battalions of Engineers.	Battalions, Signal Corps.[1]	Aero squadrons.	Companies of Coast Artillery Corps.
Philippines	9	3	18	[2] 1⅓	1½	1	26
Oahu	9	1	12	2	1½	1	14
Panama	9	1	6	2	1½	1	21
Alaska	1						
Porto Rico	[3] 1						
Total	29	5	36	5⅓	4½	3	61

[1] Includes 1 telegraph company in each garrison.
[2] 1 company mounted for Cavalry brigade.
[3] Native.

Combatants—	Officers and men.
Mobile	74,500
Coast Artillery Corps	7,500
Total	82,000

Necessary Strength of Mobile Troops for Home Service.

31. Careful studies made at the War College, extending over a period of years, lead to the conclusion that the strength of the Infantry, Cavalry, Field Artillery, Engineers, and signal troops of the Regular Army maintained at home in time of peace, and the

distribution of administrative units of these arms in the principal strategic areas, should be as given in the following table:

Combatant troops.

	Infantry regiment.	Cavalry regiment.	Field Artillery regiment.	Engineer battalions.	Battalions Signal Corps.	Aero squadrons.
Puget Sound area	9	3	¹ 3½	2⅓	¹ 1½	1
California	9	4	3½	2⅓	1½	1
North Atlantic States	9	4	3½	2⅓	1½	1
Middle West	9	3	3½	2⅓	1½	1
Mexican border		6	1	⅔	1	1
Total	36	20	15	10	7	5

¹ Each Cavalry brigade to have 1 battalion horse artillery; 1 company mounted Engineers; 1 company Signal Corps.

Approximate total, 121,000 officers and men.

These troops should be organized in higher tactical units and distributed in strategic areas substantially as follows:

Puget Sound area.... One division (less divisional Cavalry) and one Cavalry brigade (of 3 regiments).

California .... One division and one Cavalry brigade.

North Atlantic States. One division and one Cavalry brigade.

Middle West .... One division (less divisional Cavalry) and one Cavalry brigade.

Mexican border—

West of El Paso... One Cavalry brigade.

East of El Paso... One Cavalry brigade.

Necessary Strength of Coast Artillery Troops Required for Service Overseas and at Home.

32. The strength of the Coast Artillery depends upon the number of guns and mine fields installed and projected and upon the assistance to be received from Organized Militia units. An estimate prepared in the Office of the Chief Coast Artillery gives the following strength, in companies, required under the supposition

that all mine fields and all oversea guns and one-half the guns at home are manned from the Regular Army:

	Companies.
Philippines	26
Oahu	14
Panama	21
United States	228
Total	289
Total companies (gun and mine)	289
Officers and men	34,413

. . . These figures may be summarized as follows:

Oversea:		
Mobile (combatant)	74,500	
Coast Artillery Corps	7,500	
		82,000
In United States:		
Mobile (combatant)	121,000	
Coast Artillery Corps	27,000	
		148,000
Total:		
Mobile (combatant)	195,500	
Coast Artillery Corps	34,500	
		230,000

To this total should be added officers and men for the Sanitary, Quartermaster, Ordnance Department, etc., appropriate to a force of this strength, amounting approximately to 30,000 officers and men. Including Philippine Scouts, 21,000, the grand total becomes 281,000. . . .

II. The Organized Militia.

35. The act of Congress approved April 25, 1914, commonly known as the volunteer law, defines the land forces of the United States as "the Regular Army, the organized land militia while in

the service of the United States, and such volunteer forces as Congress may authorize."

The Organized Militia, in addition to its use as a State force, is available for use by the Federal Government, as provided in the Constitution, viz, to execute the laws of the Union, suppress insurrection, and repel invasion.

36. *Constitutional functions of the Organized Militia.*—Its constitutional functions are the following:

(*a*) A State force to preserve order within the State limits, in order to avoid calling upon the Regular Army or the Organized Militia of other States to discharge such function.

(*b*) A Federal force when called forth by the President, as prescribed by Congress, for any of the three purposes authorized by the Constitution.

37. *Some uses of the Organized Militia as a Federal force.*— Having been called forth as militia, they may be used as follows:

(*a*) As Coast Artillery supports and reserves.

(*b*) To guard and protect certain bridges, canal locks, arsenals, depots of supplies, docks, navy yards, and other vulnerable points in the home territory.

(*c*) To guard lines of communication within the limits of the United States.

38. *Limitations.*—It is stated later in this report that 12 months at 150 hours per month, "is considered the minimum length of time of actual training considered necessary to prepare troops for war service." Due to constitutional limitations, Congress has not the power to fix and require such an amount of training for the Organized Militia. No force can be considered a portion of our first line whose control and training is so little subject to Federal authority in peace. No force should be considered a portion of our first line in war unless it be maintained fully organized and equipped in peace at practically war strength. This would exclude the Organized Militia from consideration for service in the first line mainly because of the impossibility of giving it in peace the training required for such function. It may be necessary to continue Federal support of the Organized Militia in order that some

organized force may be immediately available for the purposes set forth in paragraphs 3 and 4. . . .

III. Reserves.

40. Reserves include: (*a*) Well-instructed soldiers of the Regular Army furloughed to what is herein termed the regular reserve, (*b*) citizen soldiers, (*c*) reserve officers.

41. *The regular reserve.*—As the United States should have a mobile force of 500,000 soldiers available at home at the outbreak of war, the Army, with the regular reserve, should amount to this strength. In order to develop the necessary regular reserve with the Army at the strength advocated in this policy, enlistments would have to be for about eight years—two with the colors and six in reserve. That would, in eight years, result in approximately the following mobile forces at home available at the outbreak of war:

(1) Mobile regular troops (combatant) with the colors	121,000
(2) The regular reserve	379,000
Total	500,000

During the first weeks of war in this country the military situation will probably be critical. At that time every fully trained soldier should be put in the field. To do that with the small military establishment herein advocated it is necessary that during peace the Army be kept at war strength, and that the regular reserve be organized and not kept back to replace losses expected during war. Such losses should be replaced from depot units.

42. *Citizen soldiers.*—In addition to the 500,000 fully trained mobile troops mentioned above, at least 500,000 more—a total of 1,000,000 men—should be prepared to take the field immediately on the outbreak of war and should have had sufficient previous military training to enable them to meet a trained enemy within three months. Twelve months' intensive training is the minimum that will prepare troops for war service. Therefore the 500,000 partly trained troops above referred to require nine months' military training before war begins. Military efficiency of reserves re-

quires that Regular Army officers be assigned thereto for training purposes—at least one to every 400 men—and that organizations and specially designated noncommissioned officers of the Army be utilized in instructing reserves as far as practicable.

Based upon experience with Tables of Organization, 1914, the War College Division has recently prepared a new plan of organization for the Army. The Regular Army and the reserves should be organized according to this plan. Organizations should be formed of men from the districts to which their respective organizations are assigned for recruiting. For this purpose, each organization should be assigned to a district from which recruits most suitable for the service required of the organization may be obtained—mounted units to horse-raising districts, technical troops to manufacturing districts, etc. As a rule the size of districts should be about in proportion to population of the qualifications—age, etc.—required. Organizations in war should be kept at full strength from the depot units which they should have in their respective recruiting districts.

43. *Reserve officers.*—Officers for staff and organizations of reserves, and officers for temporary appointment in the Regular Army as provided for in section 8 of the volunteer law (act of Congress approved Apr. 25, 1914), should be selected and trained in time of peace. The President should be authorized to issue, by and with the advice and consent of the Senate, commissions as reserve officers to citizens of the United States who, upon examination prescribed by the Secretary of War, demonstrate their physical, mental, moral, and professional fitness therefor, and who duly obligate themselves to render military service to the United States while their commissions are valid. Such commissions should be valid five years, and renewable under such regulations regarding examinations and qualifications as the Secretary of War may from time to time prescribe.

IV. Volunteers.

44. In addition to any forces that may be maintained and trained in time of peace, provision must be made for vastly increasing such forces in time of war. These must come from the

untrained body of citizens and provisions for raising them is contained in the act of Congress approved April 25, 1914.

45. This act meets the military needs for raising volunteer troops as far as concerns the enlisted personnel, except in two particulars, which are: First, that under the existing laws certain organizations of the militia, with numbers far below the full strength, can enter the volunteer force in advance of other similar volunteer organizations from the same State; and second, no volunteers of any arm or branch can be raised until all the militia of that particular arm or branch have been called into the service of the United States. . . .

V. Reserve Matériel.

46. Of all the features disclosed by the war in Europe none stands more clearly revealed than the power to be derived from national economic organization behind the armed forces of a nation.

47. In a war of gigantic proportions the chances of success are immeasurably lessened by wastage, abuse, and confusion. Steps should be taken looking toward a national organization of our economic and industrial resources as well as our resources in fighting men.

48. In its report the commission appointed by the President to investigate the conduct of the War Department in the War with Spain used the following language:

> One of the lessons taught by the war is that the country should hereafter be in a better state of preparation for war. Testimony has been taken on this subject and suggestions have been made that large supplies of all the matériel not liable to deterioration should be kept on hand, to be continuously issued and renewed, so that in any emergency they might be available. Especially should this be the case with such supplies, equipment, and ordnance stores as are not in general use in the United States and which can not be rapidly obtained in open market.

49. The lack of such articles as shoes, wagons, harness, rifles, saddles, medical chests, and so on, will render ineffective an army just as certainly as will the lack of ammunition. . . .

. . . 52. A fully trained force, to be effective during the critical period when war is imminent and during the first few weeks of a war, must not be hampered by lack of necessary supplies and equipment. For this reason, supplies of all kinds which can not be obtained in the open market at any time must be kept on hand, in use and in store, at home and oversea, sufficient to equip without delay all troops whose training warrants sending them promptly into the field.

53. It is probable that as soon as war becomes imminent, the Continental Army—500,000 mobile troops—will also be called out. As this partially trained force can not be expected to take the field within three months' time, it is practicable to refrain, after the third year, from keeping on hand or in store for it any articles of equipment except those necessary to complete its training and those which can not be procured within three months.

54. The total number of harbor defense troops necessary is about 50,000. Due to conditions of service, it is believed that ultimately supplies of all kinds for 60,000 should be kept on hand.

55. In any great war, volunteers must be called out in addition to the troops above enumerated.

56. It would be unwise to have on hand at the beginning of a war merely the supplies sufficient to place in the field our first contingent of troops and to complete the training of the Continental Army, and to be unprepared to supply to even a limited extent the Volunteer Army we should have to raise, not to mention replacements of arms, ammunition, clothing and equipment of all kinds for those already in the field; but on account of the great sum of money which will be necessary in entering upon a program for collecting and storing military supplies it is believed that the subject of equipment for a Volunteer Army and replacements for the Regular and Continental Armies should be provided for by obtaining options with domestic manufacturers to furnish the required supplies, all of domestic manufacture, in accordance with tentative contracts to be made by the supply departments with such manufacturers in time of peace. By so doing we will be taking the initial steps toward organizing the industrial

and economic resources of the country as well as its resources in fighting men.

57. Referring to Part II, approximately the following troops will be available at the close of the successive years:

	Fully-trained mobile troops.	Partially-trained Continental Army.	Harbor-defense troops.	Total.
First year	160,000	185,000	30,000	375,000
Second year	219,000	351,000	40,000	610,000
Third year	320,000	500,000	50,000	870,000
Fourth year	383,000	500,000	52,000	935,000
Fifth year	439,000	500,000	54,000	993,000
Sixth year	489,000	500,000	56,000	1,045,000
Seventh year	534,000	500,000	58,000	1,092,000
Eighth year	574,000	500,000	60,000	1,134,000

A study of these figures and of the difficulties we have experienced in the past in the matter of supplies lead to the conclusion that the program adopted for procuring reserve supplies should be such that at the close of each year we should have in use and in store, at home and oversea, supplies of all kinds necessary to equip:

	Infantry divisions.	Cavalry divisions of 9 regiments.	Harbor-defense troops.
First year	13	3	30,000
Second year	22	5	40,000
Third year	32	6	50,000
Fourth year	34	7	52,000
Fifth year	36	8	54,000
Sixth year	37	9	56,000
Seventh year	38	10	58,000
Eighth year	40	10	60,000

33. The General Board: A Navy Second to None

IN 1913 THE NAVY, METHODICALLY PURSUING ITS GOAL OF FORTY-EIGHT battleships by 1920, had asked the new Wilson administration for four ships but had been given only two. By 1915, under the impact of World War I, the General Board's estimate of the naval need had considerably expanded; and so had the administration's. When the board submitted, as usual, a one-year construction program for fiscal 1917, Navy Secretary Josephus Daniels, to the Navy's delight, asked it to expand this into a five-year continuing construction program. The board now took as its goal a Navy ultimately "equal to the most powerful maintained by any other nation of the world," which practically meant matching Britain's Royal Navy—an objective not before officially stated. The board's five-year program called for beginning, over this period, no less than ten new dreadnaught battleships and six of the battle cruiser type, with lesser craft—cruisers, destroyers, and submarines—in "proportion." Experience was later to suggest that the indicated proportions were grossly out of line with the real naval needs of the time; and the General Board's discussion of the early lessons of the war may today indicate the fallibility of all military thinking when it seeks to penetrate the future. But by early 1916 President Wilson had been converted to preparedness and was speaking for a Navy "incomparably the greatest in the world." That summer Congress not only adopted the Navy program but compressed it from five years into three.

. . . The General Board submits the following report. It does not include in this report a building program for the fiscal year of 1917 for reasons that appear in succeeding paragraphs.

2. In July last the General Board was called upon to express its opinion to the department "as to what the Navy must be in the future in order to stand upon an equality with the most efficient and most practically serviceable"; and to submit "a program . . . formulated in the most definite terms . . . planned for a consistent

From *Annual Reports of the Navy Department, 1915* (Washington, D.C.: Government Printing Office, 1916), pp. 73–76, 79–81.

and progressive development of this great defensive arm of the nation."

3. Accordingly, under date of July 30 the General Board reported as follows:

"In compliance with the oral order of the Secretary of the Navy to express its opinion at the earliest practicable date as to a policy which should govern the development of the Navy and a building program, the General Board reports as follows:

Policy.

"The Navy of the United States should ultimately be equal to the most powerful maintained by any other nation of the world. It should be gradually increased to this point by such a rate of development year by year, as may be permitted by the facilities of the country, but the limit above defined should be attained not later than 1925."

At the same time the General Board submitted a building program for the fiscal year 1917 only, which in its opinion would be adequate to the requirements of the nation if continued in subsequent years on a similar scale.

4. In a letter dated October 7, 1915, the Secretary of the Navy directed the General Board to prepare "a building program for the Navy that will continue over a period of five years, with an expenditure of about $100,000,000 each year for five years, on new construction only." This the General Board did under date of October 12, 1915 . . . with special consideration as to the first years schedule [See Appendix B below.]

5. The General Board is convinced of the great advantages, both military and economic, which will follow upon the acceptance of the general principle of a building program extending over a period of years. This is the first time that any administration has decided to present to Congress a continuing shipbuilding program. On one hand a continuing program enables the Navy Department to plan with greater foresight than is possible with an annual noncontinuing program. The military end to be reached at the close of such a period is thus made clearly evident by the

Navy Department to Congress and to the country. On the other hand, a degree of financial security is offered the industries of the country by the foreknowledge which they thus obtain as to probable naval expenditures. This will encourage them to invest money in enlarging their plants for naval shipbuilding and all its allied industries. At the same time, the strong probability of continued work throughout the period of the program, will tend to reduce contract prices.

6. The General Board believes that the course of the present war in Europe affords convincing reasons for modifying the opinion which it has expressed for the past 11 years as to the proper size of the Navy. A navy in firm control of the seas from the outbreak of war is the prime essential to the defense of a country situated as is the United States bordering upon two great oceans. A navy strong enough only to defend our coast from actual invasion will not suffice. Defense from invasion is not the only function of the Navy. It must protect our sea-borne commerce and drive that of the enemy from the sea. The best way to accomplish all these objects is to find and defeat the hostile fleet or any of its detachments at a distance from our coast sufficiently great to prevent interruption of our normal course of national life. The current war has shown that a navy of the size recommended by this board in previous years can no longer be considered as adequate to the defensive needs of the United States. Our present Navy is not sufficient to give due weight to the diplomatic remonstrances of the United States in peace nor to enforce its policies in war.

Lessons of the Current War.

7. Considering a building program for the Navy Department the General Board has noted the progress of the war abroad in order to profit by its lessons in making recommendations to the department as to the type and relative numbers of ships to be laid down.

8. The superiority of the naval forces of the entente allies has been so great as to remain without serious challenge. By this great superiority they have securely held the objective of all naval ef-

fort; namely, the control and utilization of ocean communication on behalf of their own trade and commerce and military transportation, while denying such utilization to their enemies.

9. Owing to the disparity of the opposing naval forces, the main naval strength of the central powers has not yet undertaken the task of meeting that of the enemy, and the naval events of the war have been confined to a double series of minor incidents. In the first series fall the world-wide attacks upon the commerce of the entente allies by a small number of hostile raiders, which have finally been destroyed or driven from the seas by systematic pursuit.

10. In the second series falls the work of the submarines. The deeds of the submarines have been so spectacular that in default of engagements between the main fleets undue weight has been attached to them. It is desirable to arrive at a true estimate of their importance, which, although undeniable, is less than the public believes. The North Sea, across which the combatants face each other, is not of great extent, and its comparatively limited area offers a field not too large for the submarine to maneuver in any part of it.

11. Consequently, at the beginning of the war, in the North Sea and elsewhere about Great Britain, and later in the Mediterranean, where conditions were not entirely dissimilar, the German submarines obtained some striking successes against the allies before the latter, who held the general control of the sea, discovered the proper method of guarding against attack by their invisible enemy. Both in the North Sea and in the Mediterranean the submarine upon its first appearance scored heavily. Its high score was obtained by surprise; it was not due to inherent combatant superiority.

12. After six months of war the submarine form of attack drew renewed attention by its direction against hostile commerce. American public attention was redoubled toward this side of the war owing to the humanitarian interests involved, and to the diplomatic questions which were raised thereby. To hastily formed public opinion, it seemed that submarines were ac-

complishing great military results because little else of importance occurred in the maritime war to attract public attention. Yet at the present time, when the allies have learned in great measure how to protect their commerce, as they learned a few months previously to protect their navies from the submarine menace, it is apparent that the submarine is not an instrument fitted to dominate naval warfare. It appears from British returns that the first eight months of this submarine warfare against British commerce resulted in the loss of 183 merchant vessels and 175 trawlers. The total British merchant tonnage lost was not greatly in excess of one-half a million; the total loss under all flags was about 650,000 tons. In the same time the total arrivals and departures in British ports averaged from 1,350 to 1,400 per week, or nearly 50,000 in all. Allied commerce is continuing under a loss in no way vital. The submarine is a most useful auxiliary, whose importance will no doubt increase, but at present there is no evidence that it will become supreme.

13. As to types of ships, the conclusion to be drawn so far from the history of the current war is that the battleship is still the principal reliance of navies, as it has been in the past.

Need of Fast Ships.

14. The United States Navy has hitherto been somewhat ill balanced as to the different types of ships represented in it, as battleships need auxiliaries of every sort, both combatant and administrative, for their support in battle and in being. These auxiliaries have not been authorized in proper proportion.

15. With its two extensive coast lines the United States offers great opportunities to an enemy to descend by surprise upon its shores. To meet such attack the tendency of the country is to place too much reliance upon localized defenses, such as fortifications, mines, and submarines. These are essential, but these alone can not accomplish the desired purpose. The aim should be to meet the enemy at a distance and defeat him before he reaches the neighborhood of the coasts. For this purpose the country must rely upon the seagoing fleet. To forestall the attack of the enemy

our main fighting force must be concentrated at a strategic center, ready to move and defeat the hostile main body before it has entered an area where its presence is seriously dangerous to this country's interests. When concentrated the main fleet can expect to move in time to forestall the enemy's intentions only if it has an adequate information service to provide early and continuous intelligence of the enemy's movements. An efficient scouting force composed of battle cruisers and scouts must be thrown far beyond the main body to assure this indispensable service of information, which can not otherwise be secured. In default of information the main fleet can only act blindly.

The Use to Be Made of Scouts.

16. In the general development of our naval strength, the time has now come to provide for battle cruisers and scouts. The main duty of both types is to get information. For this purpose numbers are necessary, and to provide these numbers without undue cost we have recourse to the scout type, wherein the size is as small as will afford adequate speed and radius for the accomplishment of the work. A scout in the pursuance of her duties should rather avoid than seek battle. Yet she must seek and maintain contact with the enemy, and, therefore, can not dispense with a small armament for her protection when unavoidably forced into an engagement by ships which she can not evade.

The Use to Be Made of Battle Cruisers.

17. The battle cruiser, also chiefly meant to secure information, nevertheless has a somewhat different rôle from that of the scout. In addition to high speed and endurance the battle cruiser has high offensive powers, so that if necessary she may fight for information and break through a hostile screen. Another important duty of the battle cruiser is to support the protective screen of lighter craft about her own fleet, which is formed to detect the approach of the enemy and guard the main body from surprise.

18. The battle cruiser can do all that the scout can do and

more, but her greater powers entail greater cost. If the financial question were not involved, all ships built to seek information would be of the battle-cruiser type.

19. By her size, speed, and armament, the battle cruiser is well able to perform other combatant services than her primary one of offering security and information to the main body of battleships. She may be used to protect national sea routes, both military and commercial, and attack those of the enemy. As high speed is particularly important in torpedo warfare, she may aid the battleships in a general action by taking up a favorable torpedo position where her own heavy guns will also be effective.

20. Precedent to a general naval action we may normally expect the seas to be swept by the lighter and faster craft of both belligerents seeking to damage hostile trade, to discover the intentions of the enemy and to draw him into ex-centric and unwise movements. Such has been the principal employment of battle cruisers in the present war. They have been in contact with the enemy and their performances have attracted much public attention; but as yet the main forces of battleships have not been engaged and the control of the sea remains in the hands of the powers having the superior battle fleet.

21. As in the case of submarines, so in the case of battle cruisers, the particular course of the present war does not justify the prevalent exaggerated idea of their importance.

Need of Fleet Auxiliaries.

22. The general board has little to add to its report of last year concerning other types of ships recommended. The general board has thought necessary to recommend a reasonable increase of fleet auxiliaries which are necessary to the movements and maintenance of the fleet.

Personnel.

23. The General Board recommends that legislation be sought for the fiscal year 1917 which will authorize an active personnel, officers and enlisted force, capable of—

(*a*) Keeping in full commission all battleships under 15 years of age from date of authorization, all destroyers and submarines under 12 years from date of authorization, half of the cruisers, all gunboats, and all necessary auxiliaries that go with the active fleet.

(*b*) Providing partial complements for all other ships in the Navy that would be placed in active use in time of war.

(*c*) Providing the necessary personnel for training and for shore stations. . . .

GEORGE DEWEY

Appendix B.

. . . The General Board has drawn up a program which "will continue over a period of five years, with an expenditure of about $100,000,000 each year for five years on new construction only"; the program to "be so arranged as to provide the fleet with the necessary fighting units and auxiliaries as will make it as powerful and well balanced as possible at the end of this period."

2. Omitting certain ships now nearing the end of their usefulness, the General Board estimates that at the end of the fiscal year 1921 the effective strength of the present Navy, including all ships now authorized, will be as follows:

TABLE I.—*Ships of the present fleet remaining serviceable in 1922.*

Dreadnaughts, first line	17
Predreadnaughts, second line	13
Superannuated predreadnaughts, third line	9
Battle cruisers	0
Scouts	21
Destroyers	58
Fleet submarines	3
Coast submarines	72
Fuel ships, coal	10
Fuel ships, oil	3
Repair ships	2
Supply ships	4
Transports	4

Hospital ship	1
Mine ships	3
Destroyer tenders	2
Fleet submarine tender	1
Ammunition ships	0
Harbor-defense monitors	6
Harbor-defense battleships	8
Gunboats	22
River gunboats	2

...4. The General Board is of the opinion that the $500,000,000 mentioned in the above reference should be so expended that at the end of the quinquennial period a well-balanced fleet will have been authorized in which the ships of the several types will exist in the proportions suited to the geographic and strategic situation of the United States.

5. To accomplish this end the General Board recommends the authorization within the next five fiscal years, 1917–1921, of ships as given in the following table. To this table of ships has been added the sum of $7,000,000 for aircraft service and $11,000,000 for a reserve of ammunition. The last item is to establish a sufficient reserve for ships now in service or authorized. The necessity for it exists now without any reference to future ship building.

6. In order to admit of the expenditure of the sum of $500,000,-000 upon the most favorable terms the General Board suggests that the appropriation for "new construction only" should be for $100,000,000 each year as a continuing appropriation. The General Board further recommends that the appropriation acts should authorize new construction each year during the quinquennial period about in accordance with the following table, but for the first year, 1917, it definitely recommends the items as given.

7. The General Board believes that this schedule provides the most needed ships at the earliest dates. Under such an arrangement the annual expenditures for new construction only would run in detail approximately as shown in Appendix B.

TABLE II.—*Classification of new construction with estimated cost.*

Number and class.	Unit price.	Total.
10 dreadnaughts	$18,800,00	$188,000,000
6 battle cruisers	17,500,000	105,000,000
10 scouts	5,000,000	50,000,000
50 destroyers	1,360,000	68,000,000
9 fleet submarines	1,500,000	13,500,000
58 coast submarines	650,000	37,700,000
3 fuel ships, oil	1,355,000	4,065,000
1 repair ship	2,051,000	2,051,000
1 transport	2,000,000	2,000,000
1 hospital ship	2,450,000	2,450,000
2 destroyer tenders	2,000,000	4,000,000
1 fleet submarine tender	1,510,000	1,510,000
2 ammunition ships	1,500,000	3,000,000
2 river gunboats	300,000	600,000
		481,876,000
Aircraft service		7,000,000
Reserve ammunition		11,000,000
Grand total		499,876,000

8. The expenditures in Appendix B and the unit prices set forth in Table II are in accordance with estimates made by the Bureau of Construction and Repair, Navy Department, based upon current prices of labor and material. They are subject to change before the expiration of the quinquennial period. The board believes that prices of material are not unlikely to diminish in the future, particularly upon the conclusion of the present European war.

9. With a view of obtaining as large an addition to the Navy as possible from the total appropriation, the above building program should be revised and, if necessary, modified from year to year not only to take advantage of further developments of the present war and its professional lessons, but also to profit by the probable fall in prices.

TABLE III.—*Building program, 1917 to 1922.*

	First year (1917).	Second year (1918).	Third year (1919).	Fourth year (1920).	Fifth year (1921).
Dreadnaughts	4	2	2	2	
Battle cruisers	3		1	2	
Scouts	4	2	1	3	
Destroyers	10	10	10	14	6
Fleet submarines	2	2	2	2	1
Coast submarines	20	10	10	10	8
Fuel ships, oil	1			2	
Repair ship				1	
Transports				1	
Hospital ship	1				
Destroyer tender	1			1	
Fleet submarine tender				1	
Ammunition ship	1			1	
River gunboat	2				
Aircraft service	$3,000,000	$1,000,000	$1,000,000	1,000,000	$1,000,000
Reserve ammunition	$11,000,000				

34. Hugh Scott Calls for Compulsory Military Service

THE DEFENSE ACT OF 1916 HAD BARELY BEEN SIGNED WHEN CRISIS arose on the Mexican border. General Pershing was ordered into Mexico in pursuit of the bandit general, Pancho Villa, while the National Guard was mobilized along the Rio Grande as a backstop. The Defense Act, conceived as a long-range answer to the problems of military policy, cannot fairly be judged by its failure in the first weeks of its existence; but the failure itself was inescapable. The Regular Army lacked almost everything—airplanes, artillery, motor transport, machine guns, and even manpower—that Europe was demonstrating to be essential to modern war. The National Guard was mobilized, but it proved almost impossible to fill its ranks. The whole Mexican experience was invaluable as a dress rehearsal for a major war, but its chief lesson seemed to be that the 1916 act could not work. In the fall, Hugh Scott, Leonard Wood's successor as Chief of Staff, reviewed the somewhat sorry history and concluded that compulsory military service was the only rational answer in a complicated new era in which the American people no longer accepted the "fundamental doctrine that every man owes a military as well as a civil obligation to his Government." A new age of military-political-social relationships was dawning even within the democracies. It was not well understood by any of the military men or politicians. But in the following year, the imperatives of this new age were to become clearer when we scrapped the 1916 system in order to organize a conscript mass-army to throw into the scales against the German Empire.

WAR DEPARTMENT,
OFFICE OF THE CHIEF OF STAFF,
Washington, September 30, 1916.
SIR: I have the honor to submit my annual report.

Military Policy.

In compliance with instructions of the Secretary of War, the War College Division of the General Staff Corps prepared a Statement of a Proper Military Policy for the United States, which was submitted to the Secretary of War, September, 1915. . . .

. . . This report was based upon the actual needs of the country, as they existed at that time, leaving to Congress the ways and means to provide the men. The first 500,000 mentioned was to be composed of the Regular Army and its reserve, the reserve to be produced by a term of enlistment of eight years, two with the colors and six with the reserve. The second 500,000 mentioned above was to be composed of citizen soldiers, to be given nine months' military training in time of peace and three months' addi-

From *War Department Annual Reports, 1916*, I (Washington, D.C.: Government Printing Office, 1917), pp. 155–162.

tional training on or before the outbreak of war before they would be prepared for war service.

The General Staff prepared a plan of organization for the first 500,000 which called for 7 infantry divisions of 9 regiments each, and 2 cavalry divisions of 9 regiments each, with necessary field artillery, engineer and signal troops to complete the divisions. In addition, there was to be provided a total of 263 companies of coast artillery. . . .

Congress accepted the recommendation of the General Staff in regard to the number of organizations, but at practically two-thirds of the strength recommended. . . .

. . . The recommendation of the General Staff that a citizen volunteer army of 500,000 men, with a minimum of nine months' training in time of peace, be created was not accepted by Congress. This recommendation was attacked on various grounds as being radical, unnecessary, and impracticable, and as being particularly aimed at the Organized Militia, which the General Staff recommended be maintained as it existed at the date of the report. . . .

. . . In the consideration of this question, the constitutional limitations regarding the militia occupied most of the attention of Congress to the exclusion of the standard of training necessary to prepare troops for service in the first line. Congress believed, as shown by the national defense act, that the constitutional questions that were raised were not serious enough to interfere to any extent with the transformation of the Organized Militia into a citizen force substantially in number as recommended by the General Staff, and the bill, as passed, provides that at the end of five years the National Guard will consist of about 17,000 officers and 440,000 men, the period of enlistment in the National Guard being six years, three with the colors and three with the reserve of the National Guard. A liberal provision is made in the bill for the payment. . . .

. . . The debate in Congress and the discussion in the press of the country indicated that there is a very widespread, serious and vital misconception in this country in regard to the time it takes to train the individual soldier and the organization of which he is an element.

In the belief that soldiers can be very quickly trained and armies improvised, we not only run counter to the military opinion and practice of practically all the other great nations of the world, but we run counter as well to our own experience as a nation in war. The time required for the training of armies depends largely on the presence or absence of trained officers and noncommissioned officers. If there be a corps of trained officers and noncommissioned officers and a tested organization of higher units with trained leaders and staff officers, the problem of training is largely limited to the training of the private soldier. This has been satisfactorily accomplished in Europe as is being demonstrated in the present war by giving the soldiers in time of peace two years of intensive training with the colors and additional training in the reserve.

It should be obvious to any unprejudiced mind that if we are to *defeat* highly trained and splendidly disciplined armies of our possible enemies, our own forces when called upon for battle should have training and discipline at least equal to that of our opponent. While we have splendid material for soldiers, for us seriously to claim that the average American youth can be trained and disciplined in less time than the average English, French, German, or Japanese youth argues a decided lack of understanding on the part of our people of the progress and character of the English, French, German, or Japanese people. . . .

. . . If we can not increase the period of training for the National Guard to the minimum laid down as essential by the General Staff, and it is very doubtful if we will be able to do so and keep the force recruited to the maximum authorized by Congress, we are confronted by a serious situation. The difficulty that is being now experienced in obtaining recruits for the Regular Army and for the National Guard in service on the [Mexican] border and at their mobilization camps raises sharply the question of whether we will be able to recruit the troops authorized by Congress in the national-defense act, both Regular Army and National Guard.

It is, in my judgment, a cause for very sober consideration on the part of every citizen of the country when the fact is fully understood that the units of the National Guard and the Regular Army have not been recruited to war strength in the crisis which we have just passed through. The number of units in both organizations are relatively small and the total number of men needed to recruit them to war strength certainly not great—almost negligible, in fact, when considered in relation to the total male population in the United States of military age; that is, men between 18 and 45 years. Many of the elements which favor recruiting under a volunteer system in this country existed at the time of the call for mobilization for the militia. Among others may be enumerated:

a. The agitation for preparedness that has swept over the country, due largely to the lessons of the European war.

b. The public press of the country generally, regardless of party, had given liberal space in the news and editorial columns in favor of military preparation for months previous to the call.

c. Preparedness parades in which thousands had participated had recently been held in many of the principal cities of the country.

d. Congress had but recently, in response to public sentiment, passed a new national-defense act, which will ultimately almost double the size of our small Regular Army and almost quadruple the size of the Organized Militia.

e. In response to the same national sentiment, Congress has passed, since the National Guard was called to active service, a naval bill giving the largest naval increase in the history of the country.

These facts are mentioned to show that public interest in the Army and Navy, and the national defense generally, had been aroused to a comparatively high degree; yet, in what is considered by the Government a grave emergency the National

Guard is mobilized for service on the southern frontier to protect the lives of American men, women, and children, recruiting is found so difficult that many of its organizations have not yet, over three months after the call, been raised to even minimum peace strength, and likewise the units of the Regular Army have not been recruited to the minimum peace strength authorized in the new national-defense act. . . .

. . . In my judgment, the country will never be prepared for defense until we do as other great nations do that have large interests to guard, like Germany, Japan, and France, where everybody is ready and does perform military service in time of peace as he would pay every other tax and is willing to make sacrifices for the protection he gets and the country gets in return. The volunteer system in this country, in view of the highly organized, trained, and disciplined armies that our possible opponents possess, should be relegated to the past. There is no reason why one woman's son should go out and defend or be trained to defend another woman and her son who refuses to take training or give service. The only democratic method is for every man in his youth to become trained in order that he may render efficient service if called upon in war.

Universal Military Training.

. . . Universal military training has been the corner stone upon which has been built every republic in the history of the world, and its abandonment the signal for decline and obliteration. This fact was fully recognized by the makers of our Constitution and evidenced in our early laws. A regular army was regarded as inconsistent with the principles of free government, dangerous to free institutions, and apart from the necessities of the times. All were imbued with a patriotism which would make them stand shoulder to shoulder in upholding the laws, and in the defense of the common country, sharing equally the blessings of peace and the hardship of war. The law required every able-bodied male between 18 and 45 years to keep himself provided with rifle and ammunition and to attend muster, and was in effect compulsory military service. They were called together for training at muster time only, for the outdoor life of the early settlers was considered sufficient training for any military duty they were then liable to be called upon to perform. Unfortunately the doctrine of States rights crept in to prevent the enforcement of Federal law, and each State was left to build up its militia. The Regular Army existed as a small force to protect the western march of civilization from Indian foray, and notwithstanding its brilliant record, the attitude of a great mass of our people continued hostile to the soldier, so much so that several States and Congress have in recent times had to pass laws to insure respect to the uniform and its wearers in public places. Some of our States, while extending the right to vote to aliens of a few months' residence who have declared their intention to become citizens, deny it absolutely to persons in the military and naval service of the United States, putting them in a class with the criminal and insane.

It is vital that our ideas with reference to military service be regenerated. For our small army we go into the labor market for recruits. When the demand for labor is lax, the stipend of the soldier attracts; when the daily wage goes up, recruiting is at its lowest ebb. There is no appeal to patriotism, no appeal for the individual to obtain military training as the highest duty of his citizenship. Enlistment is held out as a job in which the individual gets small pay but is well cared for, with an outdoor, wholesome life and retirement on three-quarters pay and allowances after thirty years of service, and it is accepted as a job. . . .

. . . A few years ago we reached across the seas and assumed responsibilities of insular possessions and alien races. In the interest of advancing civilization we have built the Panama Canal. We have given a fiat to the world that on this hemisphere at least must survive the principle that rulers derive their just powers from the consent of the ruled. We claim an enlightened civilization of over a hundred million people and stand the richest country in the world. As a nation we are devoted to the peaceful avocations of industrial and commercial life. We treat others as we desire to be treated. Few have knowledge of war and fewer still any training for its rigors. We are entering fully into the affairs of the world and as the greatest of nations we must be ready to uphold and protect our institutions.

It is fundamental with a free people that equal opportunities and protection under the law brings equal responsibility in upholding and maintaining the law. Each owes to the body politic his duty not only in civil affairs but also in the defense of the nation. But with us thousands have been inculcated with the belief that wars were to be ended and that the United States should, as the exponent of the highest civilization, set an example in a minimum of military preparedness, and some even advocated the Army and Navy be disbanded. The country became apathetic in the training of its people for national defense. But the awful cauldron of war into which Europe was suddenly plunged has served to awaken us in a measure to a realization that we must believe in ourselves, and as the exponents of a democracy that should regenerate the political systems of the world, we must be ready to hold our place in the councils of the world, and to do this we must be physically fit, or we shall be brushed aside by the vigorous manhood of other races who sacrifice self that the nation may live.

During the months of May and June hundreds of thousands marched in so-called preparedness parades to the plaudits of onlookers. But when the militia was called out in June to protect our border, it was with the utmost difficulty that its units were recruited to the small number required, and some were never filled. The spirit was rife to let somebody else do it. Not only is there evidence of the volunteer spirit being moribund, but the States have for years been unable to make an efficient showing with the militia, even with the generous assistance of the General Government in qualified instructors and supplies. It would seem that the self-reliance of the individual, like that of the States, had given way to dependence upon others. The fine volunteer spirit of the States militia was injured in the demand for Federal pay in time of peace. It sounded the knell of patriotic military training for individuals and commercialized the highest duty that a State can demand from its people. We have fallen away from the teaching of the Fathers, for there is no longer instilled into our people the fundamental doctrine that every man owes a military as well as a civil obligation to his Government. . . .

35. Peyton C. March: Lessons of World War I

NEITHER THE ARMY NOR THE NAVY PREPAREDNESS PROGRAM OF 1916 was in fact well calculated to prepare the nation for the crisis that actually arose in 1917. Both were keyed to long-range possibilities rather than to the immediate context of international politics. Neither program was expected to yield practical results until four or five years after its institution; but with the declaration of war on Germany in April 1917, we had to have results as soon as possible. Both programs were swept aside. The Army's concept of a great volunteer reserve system was promptly replaced with conscription—called "universal service"—while the Navy dropped its goal of a battlefleet "second to none" in order to build the small craft and merchant ships necessary to defeat the U-boats. The plans of 1916 provided a basis for the tremendous effort of 1917–1918, but had little direct relation to what in fact had to be done. With the 1918 armistice, American military thought was once more confronted by the problem of the unpredictable future. General Pershing and the other field commanders had little to say about this, but the wartime Chief of Staff, Peyton C. March, discussed the "lessons of the war" in the following concluding section of his annual report for 1919. In so doing, he laid down the general lines on which the Defense Act of 1920—which was to serve through the succeeding fifteen years as the basis of American defense policy— was to be constructed.

The lessons of this war are many and important. Probably no great industry or activity exists in the country which has not gained, during the mobilization of the resources of the Nation

From *War Department Annual Reports, 1919* (Washington, D.C.: Government Printing Office, 1920), pp. 471–478.

which was accomplished during the war, experience which, when analyzed and studied, will be of great and lasting benefit to it and to the Nation. Undoubtedly the country has incurred much expense, and has lost many lives on account of the improvisations which were inevitable on account of its lack of preparedness for war, and it is essential that the lessons which have crystallized out of the experience of the War Department, as of the other great agencies directly concerned in the war, be heeded and profited by if this tremendous toll of wealth and of life is not to have been in vain.

In the preceding pages of this report there have been outlined some of the steps in the evolution and development of the organization and of the methods used in planning and in executing the military program, including the organizing, training, transporting, and supplying of the Army. This development has been gradual; each step has taught its lesson, and the lesson should not require repetition in any future war.

Before the war the theory was frequently advanced that future wars would, due to the terrible efficiency of modern instruments of warfare, be short and decisive. In this war the scientific and technical skill of the world has been concentrated for four years on the problems of devising either new death-dealing devices or means of protection against them. The history of the war, however, has shown that this theory is untenable. It has shown that, on the contrary, a modern war is a war of nations rather than of armies; that it involves a mobilization of the entire resources of these nations, and that it will, therefore, require for its decision a length of time not incomparable with that of previous wars.

Necessity for General Staff control.—This consideration accentuates the necessity, already referred to in this report, of a War Department organization in future which is adequate to the efficient formulation and execution of a military program which will require a definite and effective articulation of the War Department with all the agencies involved in the mobilization of the industries, activities, utilities, and resources of the Nation. I have set forth in this report the fundamental principles upon which, in my opinion, such an organization must be based. I am convinced that without a properly organized and efficient General Staff charged with the responsibility for, and empowered with the authority to formulate and to execute, the Army program, it will, in any future war, as in this and in every other war in our history, be impossible for the activities of the various agencies, services, and bureaus of the War Department to be controlled and directed, with promptness and effectiveness, to the attainment of the common end. It can be stated without qualification that the success of an army in modern war is impossible without such a General Staff.

Under the terms of the treaty of peace,[1] the German general staff is abolished. Had the Germans won the war they would, in all probability, have prescribed somewhat similar terms for the United States. It was necessary that the legislative restrictions hitherto imposed upon the organization and activities of the General Staff be removed, upon the declaration of war, in order that the military program might be carried out, and the Army organized, trained, and commanded with the expedition and the efficiency that the country demanded. Unless these restrictions are permanently removed and the General Staff is established upon a proper basis, the experience gained during this war will have been largely without avail, restrictions not incomparable with those that might have been expected from a German victor will have been imposed upon the General Staff, and it is inevitable that a future war will find this country as unprepared as it was for this war—with consequences which may endanger the Nation.

Necessity for reserves of clothing and equipment.—On the declaration of war the mobilization and the training of the Army suffered inevitable and serious delay due to the lack of an adequate reserve supply of winter clothing and other equipage and equipment required for training, which could not be manufactured in a short time. It was necessary to improvise this equipment. It became necessary to send to France entire brigades of Artillery with such meager and totally inadequate training as could be gained

[1] Article 160, Treaty of Versailles [Ed.].

from drill with wooden logs mounted on ash carts. It should never be necessary for this lesson as to the necessity for an adequate reserve of material to be learned again. Fortunately, it will be practicable, from the tremendous amounts of material of all kinds that were coming into quantity production on the signing of the armistice, four years after the beginning of the war, and a year and a half after our entry into it, to make reasonable provision in this regard for the future.

Supply and training of officers and replacements.—Reference has also been made to the necessity of making adequate and special provision in any future contingency for the organization and training, in the early stages of mobilization, of officers, and of replacements and special troops. In this war it was necessary to train approximately 180,000 officers who had had little, if any, previous military training. The Regular Army consisted of less than 6,000 officers, of whom more than 1,000 had less than two years' service. It was necessary to use a large number of these trained officers for the various staff and other duties required to mobilize the Army; the training of the officers and men required for the new Army could not, for months, be effective. There can be no avoiding a recurrence of this situation except to provide an adequate reserve of trained officers and men.

Due to our lack of preparedness, the execution of our military program necessitated the sending to France and into battle of some organizations and replacements without proper training; undoubtedly the lack of proper equipment and instructors for training resulted, in some cases, in a loss of lives that might have been avoided with well trained and disciplined officers and men. This action was taken only because of the firm conviction that it was imperative. There was no alternative if the war was to be won without a prolonged struggle resulting in an aggregate loss of life far exceeding that which actually occurred. The disadvantages were great and were fully considered. Events have proved that they were the price of victory. It is a price that it should never be necessary to pay again.

The war has taught many lessons; the principles of warfare,

however, remain unchanged. It was not won, as some had predicted it would be, by some new and terrible development or modern science; it was won, as has every other war in history, by men, munitions, and morale.

Viewed as a whole it has many of the characteristics of a single great battle. Like a battle it began with a period of maneuvering for position, which developed into a period of close contact and attrition, and like a battle it terminated in a short period of decision in which the victory was won by an offensive operation which, by the utilization of a strong and effective reserve, became overwhelming in its effect. It differs from any previous battle chiefly in the magnitude of the forces, material, and time involved. With the entire man power and resources of great nations mobilized and engaged the period of contact and attrition occupied years instead of hours or days as in previous battles. Only the determination, the valor, and the sacrifices of our allies throughout this terrible period of ordeal by battle made it possible for us to furnish the final reserve which, with its impetuous vigor and its irresistible force, enabled the allied army to pass from the defensive to the offensive and made possible an early and decisive victory.

Development of special services.—The changes in warfare as the result of this war are in its practice only and not its principles. These changes have been, to a large degree, due to the development of the numerous and important special services which have been made necessary as the result of the concentration of the best technical and military skill of the world upon the application to military purposes of the most recent engineering and scientific developments. The remarkable development in aeroplanes, tanks, motor transport, railroad artillery, caterpillars, trench mortars, machine guns, gas warfare, radio and sound and flash ranging apparatus,[2] and photography have modified in many respects the details and conditions of warfare, and have made possible operations of an unprecedented magnitude. In the Meuse-Argonne Battle the American expenditure of artillery ammunition is estimated at

[2] Devices to determine ranges by use of gun-flashes, sound and radio bearings [Ed.].

more than 4,000,000 rounds; in the battle of Gettysburg, the Union Army expended less than 40,000 rounds. Thus the development of motor transport has rendered practicable expenditures of artillery and machine-gun ammunition in amounts practically limited only by the production and transportation capacity of the country. In all of these developments the contribution of the American engineers has been conspicuous; the Liberty 12-cylinder aeroplane engine, the Browning machine gun, and the American gas-warfare equipment are noteworthy examples.

Important as has been the effect of these mechanical developments and special services, their true value has been as auxiliaries to the Infantry. Nothing in this war has changed the fact that it is now, as always heretofore, the Infantry with rifle and bayonet that, in the final analysis, must bear the brunt of the assault and carry it on to victory. The war has taught the necessity of the appreciation by all officers of the interdependence of all arms of the service in battle. They are to fight together; they must be trained and taught together if the common knowledge of the powers and limitations of each arm, and the mutual confidence, without which efficient teamwork in battle is impossible, is to be attained.

Necessity for combined tactical training in large units.—The important lesson to be learned in this connection is that a reasonable efficiency in peace time training for war can never be secured until the present system of small, isolated battalion and company posts, which is a relic of the days of Indian fighting, is replaced by a system which enables entire divisions to be trained together and to be consolidated frequently for the maneuvers of larger units. By such a system only can commanding, staff, and line officers be developed and trained for the duties they will have to perform in modern warfare. That this is true has long been recognized by the responsible military authorities. For the first time in our history conditions now permit of its accomplishment; no one thing is more essential to the future efficiency of the military establishment than that this opportunity be taken advantage of.

The war has shown that the American ideas of the training of the soldier were sound and that the American-trained soldier has no superior. It has also shown that the principles underlying the instruction in our service schools for officers are sound. The results attained both in staff work and in the command and leading of troops in combat are remarkable, in view of the fact that opportunities for the training of officers in the actual command of, or in the actual performance of staff duties in, divisions and larger units have prior to this war been practically nonexistent. These results are largely attributable to the instruction given in the various service schools before the war, and they have emphasized the necessity for the continuation and development of these schools in the future.

As the result of the war the Army has many problems that must be solved. For every branch of the service there are questions of organization, equipment, and training. These are largely matters of detail which will involve a careful and well-considered study of the experience gained both in this country and overseas. These studies are already well under way. They will require much time and consideration for their preparation; there is no urgent necessity for their early completion.

There are, however, larger problems of the organization of the Army as a whole, affecting to a vital degree its efficiency, which press for early action.

There are also problems arising from the experience of the war which affect the military policy of the Nation itself.

Military policy as effected by the war.—The idea that a force of one and one-half million men could be transported within six months 3,000 miles across a submarine-infested ocean and there maintained was one unconceived of not only in our own war plans but in those of any other country. Perhaps no lesson of the war has been of more universal interest. We are not alone in having learned it; it is one that must inevitably affect to a material degree all future military plans, both offensive and defensive, throughout the world.

At the beginning of the war this country occupied a position apart in world affairs. This position but reflected its geographical isolation from the continental great powers. As the result of the war, however, the position of this country has, in many important respects, undergone marked changes of far-reaching effect. Its geographical position, upon which it has long relied largely for its military defense, may no longer be regarded as isolated from the military operations of any possible powerful enemy. Its present international position must be recognized as being attended by tremendously increased responsibilities.

Our former position, international and geographical, had resulted in a long-continued national policy which precluded the adoption of a military policy upon which the country could depend with safety in time of war. It entered the war, therefore, practically unprepared for war. Its military power consisted almost entirely of its potential resources of man power, wealth, and munitions. These resources, while inexhaustible, were undeveloped and unavailable—to such a degree that the enemy considered it impossible for them to be rendered effective in time to permit the participation of the United States to become a potent factor in the prosecution of the war.

The national mobilization of these resources, including the complete and successful diversion to essential war work of practically every industry and activity of the country, between April 6, 1917, and November 11, 1918, rendered the participation of this country a decisive factor in the winning of the war for civilization and constitutes a national achievement of which we may well be proud. It is essential, however, that consideration be given to the fact that this mobilization of our resources, and this achievement, required a year and a half for its accomplishment and that it was possible only due to the extraordinary and unprecedented conditions that obtained during that period. It was possible for us to create, organize, train, equip, and transport an army, and to direct all of the activities of the Nation to its support and maintenance, only because of the assistance of our Allies, especially in supplying tonnage and equipment and in rendering available to us all the results of three years' experience in the war, and only because of the fact that by their heroic efforts and sacrifices, on land and sea, they protected us during this period of one and one-half years from the ruthlessness of the common enemy. Surely we can never expect to prepare for defense against the attack of a powerful and determined enemy again under such favorable conditions to ourselves.

The war has shown that this country can, in an emergency, be self-sustaining in all respects for an indefinite period. This is probably true of no other great power; certainly it is true of no insular power. This fact bears upon our policy of national defense. It follows that under any possible naval situation, even with our Navy and our fleets denied access to the seas by any conceivable combination of the other great navies of the world, this country could not be defeated and forced to capitulate by naval operations alone.

This, involving, as it does, our unlimited resources of man power and wealth, constitutes our greatest national military asset, provided, and only provided, we are prepared to prevent the landing on our shores of an enemy of the size which our own performance has demonstrated to the world can be landed by a first-class power under certain conditions. These conditions are that it shall have control of the sea and control of proper bases for debarkation. Without the possession of such bases in France we could not have landed our army irrespective of the fact that the Allies had control of the sea.

It is, accordingly, one of the very important lessons of this war that reasonable prevision and a sound military policy demand that there shall be at all times available for immediate use a sufficient trained and organized force to insure, in connection with our fixed coast defenses, that no probable or possible enemy can ever seize a great strategic base on our coast. With such a base in his possession it is not inconceivable that he could, within a short time, land a sufficient number of fully-equipped troops to seize and hold, by establishing a line of defense not incomparable in length with that held by the Germans on the western front, an area including such an appreciable portion of the resources and wealth of the country as to result in consequences of incalculable moment to the Nation.

Obviously such an attacking force, irrespective of its power on the sea, as represented by the strength of its Navy, and of its power on the land, as represented by the strength of its Army, will be at its weakest during the period it is attempting to land its army on our shores. During this period only will it be possible to nullify any numerical superiority of troops that he may bring to bear by the resistance of a trained and organized force of relatively small size. Only by the provision of such a force can we be assured that we shall be able to utilize to full advantage our greatest military asset, by gaining the time required to develop our resources and to organize an army which will be adequate to any contingency. The size of such a force, which is essential if the country is to be afforded that degree of protection which a sound military policy requires, must be determined by a consideration of our extended coast line, by the necessary dispersion of the force due to the distance from coast to coast, and by the necessity of providing for the safety of the Panama Canal and our other insular possessions.

Peace strength of Army.—The minimum force which, in my opinion, is adequate for this purpose is one field army of five corps, skeletonized to about 50 per cent of its strength, in such a way as to include a nucleus for all organizations which require extended training and instruction in time of peace, and as to be capable of ready expansion, in time of war to full strength without seriously impairing its efficiency for service.

Universal military training.—With such a force, and with a system of universal training which will insure an adequate reserve of officers and men to enable it, in case of emergency, to be expanded by Congress to such an extent as may be required, no foreign country could, in view of our performance in this war, disregard our rights or our military power. Such a system of universal training, which can be arranged so as to afford a negligible interference with the industrial and educational activities of the individual or of the nation, will, by developing physically, mentally, and morally the youth of the country, make them better citizens as well as better soldiers. The force which I have indicated as being the minimum required by a sound military policy for the adequate protection of the country, could, without increase and without serious impairment to its efficiency, be utilized in time of peace to furnish, in great part at least, the trained, professional military specialists required to conduct efficiently such a system of intensive universal military training.

I have outlined some of the considerations which, in my opinion, must, in connection with the study of the experiences of the war, be regarded as bearing directly upon our national military policy.

Definite military policy now possible.—For the first time in its history this country is now, as the result of the war, in a position to formulate a definite military policy. All studies which have been made in this connection prior to the war have, necessarily, been academic. There has existed no supply of trained officers or men or of equipment and stores commensurate with the requirements of such a policy. No definite or adequate policy could be formulated which did not contemplate universal military service in time of war as the source of a national army; no precedents existed which warranted the assumption that such a system would be accepted by the country. Any war plans that might be prepared could only provide, on paper, for the disposition to be made of armies and supplies that did not exist, which could not be made available in case of an emergency and which could only be created by slow and evolutionary processes the nature of which could not be foreseen. Such plans were necessarily academic. To-day the entire situation is changed. The country has universally accepted and demanded, as the only rational and equitable solution of the problem that the great army required for our participation in this war be raised by the draft, and the nation-wide support of the draft act and the general satisfaction with its operation and its results can leave no doubt but that it may be accepted as the future policy of the country in time of war.

There are to-day in the country nearly 4,000,000 men and 200,-000 officers physically and mentally fit and trained for war. No such reserve exists in any other country. It may be relied upon to meet the requirements of any possible contingency that may arise within the next five years. There is also a reserve of artillery, ammunition, motor transport, machine guns, rifles, and other military essentials that will amply provide for any possible requirement in the near future.

There exist complete cantonments, flying fields, firing and training centers, storehouses, and port terminals which will in general provide for any probable future requirements of peace or of war; steps have been taken to provide an adequate transport reserve, operating commercially but under American title and available on short notice for use in an emergency; the industries of the country have been trained to produce, with the minimum of delay, in time of necessity, the war materials which they are best adapted to produce, great plants have been constructed for the manufacture of explosives, and there exists an army of skilled workmen trained in the manufacture of every kind of military matériel. All this constitutes a national military asset of incalculable but in part of temporary value. It makes possible now, as never before, the formulation of a definite military policy, which, by a reasonable and moderate utilization of the present and the future resources of the country, will insure, beyond all peradventure, that the future of the Nation will be safeguarded for all time. Had such a force and such a system of training as is above outlined been in existence in this country at the outbreak of the war, it is probable that Germany would not have dared, by the violation of the rights of this country under international law, to have brought the United States into the war. In fact, had such a force and system been in existence in England in 1914, it is, in the light of subsequent events, by no means improbable that Germany would never have begun the war at all.

During the period, of approximately one and one-half years, of our participation in the war, the War Department expenditures were approximately $14,000,000,000 and the total war expenditures of the country were approximately $24,000,000,000. The interest on either of these amounts would maintain indefinitely the scheme above outlined. Not only would it provide an army which would, in any case, have resulted in a material saving in the cost, not only in money but in lives as well, of the war to this country, but it would also provide for a system of universal military training which, in addition to being a military asset of incalculable value, would constitute a most potent factor in Americanizing and educating the great alien and illiterate population which otherwise, under the influence of unscrupulous and disloyal agitators, may become a national menace. That such an investment would be sound from the standpoint of national military policy is, in my opinion, indisputable; I am convinced that from the standpoint of national business and economic policy it is equally sound.

I have indicated in this report some of the lessons of the war which appear to be of special significance at this time. Such action as it has been possible to take, under existing legislation, to profit by these lessons, has already been taken.

Legislation proposed.—Since the submission of my previous report the study of the plan for the reorganization of the Army in the light of the experience that has crystallized out of the war, to which reference was made in that report, has been completed and, in the form of proposed legislation, has been submitted to you, with the recommendation that it be transmitted for the consideration of Congress. . . .

P. C. March,
General, Chief of Staff.

36. Charles Evans Hughes Proposes the Limitation of Navies

The Navy's first response to the problems of the post-war world was simply to resume construction of the big battleship and battle-cruiser program authorized in 1916 but laid aside in order to fight the war. The Naval Act of 1916 had, however, carried a clause requesting the President to summon a disarmament conference when the European war should be over and directing the cancellation of any of the newly authorized vessels should a disarmament agreement require it. While the Navy revived the 1916 authorizations, the Harding administration, guided by its able Secretary of State, Charles Evans Hughes, revived this disarmament clause. The result was the Washington Conference on the Limitation of Armaments, which sat during the winter of 1921–1922. Hughes startled the conference and the world by presenting at the opening session a detailed plan for the limitation of navies, explaining the principles on which it was based, calling by name for the scrapping of a large number of old or as yet uncompleted battleships, and imposing rigid limits on future construction. Hughes's opening address is given here, as representing a high point in American Naval thought and policy. A number of adjustments had to be made in the plan originally proposed, but its essential elements were successfully incorporated into the Washington Naval Treaty of 1922. Establishing the "treaty ratios," calling for American parity with Great Britain and a 5–3 superiority over Japan, it provided the foundation for Naval policy over the next dozen years.

. . . The President invited the Governments of the British Empire, France, Italy, and Japan to participate in a conference on the subject of limitation of armament, in connection with which Pacific and Far Eastern questions would also be discussed. It would have been most agreeable to the President to have invited all the Powers to take part in this Conference, but it was thought to be a time when other considerations should yield to the practical requirements of the existing exigency, and in this view the invitation was extended to the group known as the Principal Allied and Associated Powers, which, by reason of the conditions produced by the war, control in the main the armament of the world. The opportunity to limit armament lies within their grasp.

It is recognized, however, that the interests of other Powers in the Far East made it appropriate that they should be invited to participate in the discussion of Pacific and Far Eastern problems, and, with the approval of the five Powers, an invitation to take part in the discussion of those questions has been extended to Belgium, China, the Netherlands, and Portugal.

The inclusion of the proposal for the discussion of Pacific and Far Eastern questions was not for the purpose of embarrassing or delaying an agreement for limitation of armament, but rather to support that undertaking by availing ourselves of this meeting to

From *Conference on the Limitation of Armament*, 67th Congress, Session 2, Senate Documents, pp. 41–49.

endeavor to reach a common understanding as to the principles and policies to be followed in the Far East and thus greatly to diminish, and if possible wholly to remove, discernible sources of controversy. It is believed that by interchanges of views at this opportune time the Governments represented here may find a basis of accord and thus give expression to their desire to assure enduring friendship.

In the public discussions which have preceded the Conference, there have been apparently two competing views: one, that the consideration of armament should await the result of the discussion of Far Eastern questions, and another, that the latter discussion should be postponed until an agreement for limitation of armament has been reached. I am unable to find sufficient reason for adopting either of these extreme views. I think that it would be most unfortunate if we should disappoint the hopes which have attached to this meeting by a postponement of the consideration of the first subject. The world looks to this Conference to relieve humanity of the crushing burden created by competition in armament, and it is the view of the American Government that we should meet that expectation without any unnecessary delay. It is, therefore, proposed that the Conference should proceed at once to consider the question of the limitation of armament.

This, however, does not mean that we must postpone the examination of Far Eastern questions. These questions, of vast importance, press for solution. It is hoped that immediate provision may be made to deal with them adequately, and it is suggested that it may be found to be entirely practicable through the distribution of the work among designated committees to make progress to the ends sought to be achieved without either subject being treated as a hindrance to the proper consideration and disposition of the other.

The proposal to limit armament by an agreement of the Powers is not a new one, and we are admonished by the futility of earlier efforts. It may be well to recall the noble aspirations which were voiced twenty-three years ago in the imperial rescript of His Majesty the Emperor of Russia [Nicholas II]. It was then pointed out with clarity and emphasis that "The intellectual and physical strength of the nations, labor and capital, are for the major part diverted from their natural applications and unproductively consumed. Hundreds of millions are devoted to acquiring terrible engines of destruction, which, though to-day regarded as the last word of science, are destined to-morrow to lose all value in consequence of some fresh discovery in the same field. National culture, economic progress, and the production of wealth are either paralyzed or checked in their development. Moreover, in proportion as the armaments of each Power increase, so do they less and less fulfill the object which the Governments have set before themselves. The economic crises, due in great part to the system of armaments *à outrance* and the continual danger which lies in this massing of war materials, are transforming the armed peace of our days into a crushing burden, which the peoples have more and more difficulty in bearing. It appears evident, then, that if this state of things were prolonged it would inevitably lead to the calamity which it is desired to avert, and the horrors of which make every thinking man shudder in advance. To put an end to these incessant armaments and to seek the means of warding off the calamities which are threatening the whole world—such is the supreme duty which is today imposed on all States."

It was with this sense of obligation that His Majesty the Emperor of Russia proposed the Conference, which was "to occupy itself with this grave problem" and which met at The Hague in the year 1899.[1] Important as were the deliberations and conclusions of that Conference, especially with respect to the pacific settlement of international disputes, its result in the specific matter of limitation of armament went no further than the adoption of a final resolution setting forth the opinion "that the restriction of military charges, which are at present a heavy burden on the world, is extremely desirable for the increase of the material and moral welfare of mankind," and the utterance of the wish that the governments "may examine the possibility of an agreement as to

[1] Twenty-six nations participated. The United States and Mexico were the only American powers represented [Ed.].

the limitation of armed forces by land and sea, and of war budgets."

It was seven years later that the Secretary of State of the United States, Mr. Elihu Root, in answering a note of the Russian Ambassador suggesting in outline a program of the Second Peace Conference, said: "The Government of the United States, therefore, feels it to be its duty to reserve for itself the liberty to propose to the Second Peace Conference, as one of the subjects for consideration, the reduction or limitation of armaments, in the hope that, if nothing further can be accomplished, some slight advance may be made toward the realization of the lofty conception which actuated the Emperor of Russia in calling the First Conference." It is significant that the Imperial German Government expressed itself as "absolutely opposed to the question of disarmament" and that the Emperor of Germany [Wilhelm II] threatened to decline to send delegates if the subject of disarmament was to be discussed. In view, however, of the resolution which had been adopted at the First Hague Conference, the delegates of the United States were instructed that the subject of limitation of armament "should be regarded as unfinished business, and that the Second Conference should ascertain and give full consideration to the results of such examination as the Governments may have given to the possibility of an agreement pursuant to the wish expressed by the First Conference." But by reason of the obstacles which the subject had encountered, the Second Peace Conference at The Hague, although it made notable progress in provision for the peaceful settlement of controversies, was unable to deal with limitation of armament except by a resolution in the following general terms: "The Conference confirms the resolution adopted by the Conference of 1899 in regard to the limitation of military expenditure; and inasmuch as military expenditure has considerably increased in almost every country since that time, the Conference declares that it is eminently desirable that the Governments should resume the serious examination of this question."

This was the fruition of the efforts of eight years. Although the effect was clearly perceived, the race in preparation of armament, wholly unaffected by these futile suggestions, went on until it fittingly culminated in the greatest war of history; and we are now suffering from the unparalleled loss of life, the destruction of hopes, the economic dislocations and the widespread impoverishment which measure the cost of the victory over the brutal pretensions of military force.

But if we are warned by the inadequacy of earlier endeavors for limitation of armament, we cannot fail to recognize the extraordinary opportunity now presented. We not only have the lessons of the past to guide us, not only do we have the reaction from the disillusioning experiences of war, but we must meet the challenge of imperative economic demands. What was convenient or highly desirable before is now a matter of vital necessity. If there is to be economic rehabilitation, if the longings for reasonable progress are not to be denied, if we are to be spared the uprisings of peoples made desperate in the desire to shake off burdens no longer endurable, competition in armament must stop. The present opportunity not only derives its advantage from a general appreciation of this fact, but the power to deal with the exigency now rests with a small group of nations, represented here, who have every reason to desire peace and to promote amity. The astounding ambition which lay athwart the promise of the Second Hague Conference no longer menaces the world, and the great opportunity of liberty-loving and peace-preserving democracies has come. Is it not plain that the time has passed for mere resolutions, that the responsible Powers should examine the question of limitation of armament? We can no longer content ourselves with investigations, with statistics, with reports, with the circumlocution of inquiry. The essential facts are sufficiently known. The time has come, and this Conference has been called, not for general resolutions or mutual advice, but for action. We meet with full understanding that the aspirations of mankind are not to be defeated either by plausible suggestions of postponement or by impracticable counsels of perfection. Power and responsibility are here and the world awaits a practicable program which shall at once be put into execution.

I am confident that I shall have your approval in suggesting that in this matter, as well as in others before the Conference, it is desirable to follow the course of procedure which has the best promise of achievement rather than one which would facilitate division: and thus, constantly aiming to agree so far as possible, we shall, with each point of agreement, make it easier to proceed to others.

The question, in relation to armament, which may be regarded as of primary importance at this time, and with which we can deal most promptly and effectively, is the limitation of naval armament. There are certain general considerations which may be deemed pertinent to this subject.

The first is that the core of the difficulty is to be found in the competition in naval programs, and that, in order appropriately to limit naval armament, competition in its production must be abandoned. Competition will not be remedied by resolves with respect to the method of its continuance. One program inevitably leads to another, and if competition continues, its regulation is impracticable. There is only one adequate way out and that is to end it now.

It is apparent that this can not be accomplished without serious sacrifices. Enormous sums have been expended upon ships under construction and building programs which are now under way can not be given up without heavy loss. Yet, if the present construction of capital ships goes forward, other ships will inevitably be built to rival them and this will lead to still others. Thus the race will continue so long as ability to continue lasts. The effort to escape sacrifices is futile. We must face them or yield our purpose.

It is also clear that no one of the naval Powers should be expected to make these sacrifices alone. The only hope of limitation of naval armament is by agreement among the nations concerned, and this agreement should be entirely fair and reasonable in the extent of the sacrifices required of each of the Powers. In considering the basis of such an agreement and the commensurate sacrifices to be required, it is necessary to have regard to the existing naval strength of the great naval Powers, including the extent of construction already effected in the case of ships in process. This follows from the fact that one nation is as free to compete as another, and each may find grounds for its action. What one may do another may demand the opportunity to rival, and we remain in the thrall of competitive effort. I may add that the American delegates are advised by their naval experts that the tonnage of capital ships may fairly be taken to measure the relative strength of navies, as the provision for auxiliary combatant craft should sustain a reasonable relation to the capital ship tonnage allowed.

It would also seem to be a vital part of a plan for the limitation of naval armament that there should be a naval holiday. It is proposed that for a period of not less than ten years there should be no further construction of capital ships.

I am happy to say that I am at liberty to go beyond these general propositions, and, on behalf of the American delegation acting under the instructions of the President of the United States, to submit to you a concrete proposition for an agreement for the limitation of naval armament.

It should be added that this proposal immediately concerns the British Empire, Japan, and the United States. In view of the extraordinary conditions due to the World War affecting the existing strength of the navies of France and Italy, it is not thought to be necessary to discuss at this stage of the proceedings the tonnage allowance of these nations, but the United States proposes that this matter be reserved for the later consideration of the Conference.

In making the present proposal the United States is most solicitous to deal with the question upon an entirely reasonable and practicable basis, to the end that the just interests of all shall be adequately guarded and that national security and defense shall be maintained. Four general principles have been applied:

(1) That all capital ship building programs, either actual or projected, should be abandoned;

(2) That further reduction should be made through the scrapping of certain of the older ships;

(3) That, in general, regard should be had to the existing naval strength of the Powers concerned;

(4) That the capital ship tonnage should be used as the measurement of strength for navies and a proportionate allowance of auxiliary combatant craft prescribed.

The principal features of the proposed agreement are as follows:

Capital Ships:

United States:

The United States is now completing its program of 1916 calling for 10 new battleships and 6 battle cruisers.

One battleship has been completed. The others are in various stages of construction; in some cases from 60 to over 80 per cent of the construction has been done. On these 15 capital ships now being built over $330,000,000 have been spent. Still, the United States is willing in the interest of an immediate limitation of naval armament to scrap all these ships.

The United States proposes, if this plan is accepted—

(1) To scrap all capital ships now under construction. This includes 6 battle cruisers and 7 battleships on the ways and in course of building, and 2 battleships launched.

The total number of new capital ships thus to be scrapped is 15. The total tonnage of the new capital ships when completed would be 618,000 tons.

(2) To scrap all of the older battleships up to, but not including, the *Delaware* and *North Dakota.* The number of these old battleships to be scrapped is 15. Their total tonnage is 227,740 tons.

Thus the number of capital ships to be scrapped by the United States, if this plan is accepted, is 30, with an aggregate tonnage (including that of ships in construction, if completed) of 845,740 tons.

Great Britain:

The plan contemplates that Great Britain and Japan shall take action which is fairly commensurate with the action on the part of the United States.

It is proposed that Great Britain—

(1) Shall stop further construction of the 4 new *Hoods*, the new capital ships not laid down but upon which money has been spent. These 4 ships, if completed, would have tonnage displacement of 172,000 tons.

(2) Shall, in addition, scrap her predreadnaughts, second-line battleships, and first-line battleships up to but not including the *King George V* class.

These, with certain predreadnaughts which it is understood have already been scrapped, would amount to 19 capital ships and a tonnage reduction of 411,375 tons.

The total tonnage of ships thus to be scrapped by Great Britain (including the tonnage of the 4 *Hoods*, if completed) would be 583,375 tons.

Japan: ·

It is proposed that Japan—

(1) Shall abandon her program of ships not yet laid down, viz., the *Kii, Owari, No. 7* and *No. 8*, battleships, and *Nos. 5, 6, 7,* and *8*, battle cruisers.

It should be observed that this idea does not involve the stopping of construction, as the construction of none of these ships has been begun.

(2) Shall scrap 3 capital ships: the *Mutsu* launched, the *Tosa* and *Kaga* in course of building; and 4 battle cruisers: the *Amagi* and *Akagi* in course of building, and the *Atoga* and *Takao* not yet laid down but for which certain material has been assembled.

The total number of new capital ships to be scrapped under this paragraph is seven. The total tonnage of these new capital ships when completed would be 289,100 tons.

(3) Shall scrap all predreadnaughts and battleships of the second line. This would include the scrapping of all ships up to but not including the *Settsu;* that is, the scrapping of 10 older ships, with a total tonnage of 159,828 tons.

The total reduction of tonnage on vessels existing, laid down, or for which material has been assembled (taking the tonnage of the new ships when completed), would be 448,928 tons.

The three Powers:

Thus, under this plan there would be immediately destroyed, of the navies of the three Powers, 66 capital fighting ships, built and building, with a total tonnage of 1,878,043.

It is proposed that it should be agreed by the United States, Great Britain, and Japan that their navies, with respect to capital ships, within three months after the making of the agreement shall consist of certain ships designated in the proposal and numbering for the United States 18, for Great Britain 22, for Japan 10.

The tonnage of these ships would be as follows: of the United States, 500,650; of Great Britain, 604,450; of Japan, 299,700. In reaching this result, the age factor in the case of the respective navies has received appropriate consideration.

Replacement:

With respect to replacement, the United States proposes—

(1) That it be agreed that the first replacement tonnage shall not be laid down until 10 years from the date of the agreement;

(2) That replacement be limited by an agreed maximum of capital ship tonnage as follows:

For the United States 500,000 tons.

For Great Britain 500,000 tons.

For Japan 300,000 tons.

(3) That, subject to the 10-year limitation above fixed and the maximum standard, capital ships may be replaced when they are 20 years old by new capital ship construction;

(4) That no capital ship shall be built in replacement with a tonnage displacement of more than 35,000 tons.

I have sketched the proposal only in outline, leaving the technical details to be supplied by the formal proposition which is ready for submission to the delegates.

The plan includes provision for the limitation of auxiliary combatant craft. This term embraces three classes; that is: (1) auxiliary surface combatant craft, such as cruisers (exclusive of battle cruisers), flotilla leaders, destroyers, and various surface types; (2) submarines; and (3) airplane carriers.

I shall not attempt to review the proposals for these various classes, as they bear a definite relation to the provisions for capital fighting ships.

With the acceptance of this plan the burden of meeting the demands of competition in naval armament will be lifted. Enormous sums will be released to aid the progress of civilization. At the same time the proper demands of national defense will be adequately met and the nations will have ample opportunity during the naval holiday of 10 years to consider their future course. Preparation for offensive naval war will stop now. . . .

PART FIVE

World Power:
To 1947

37. The Morrow Board: Military Policy in the Air Age

AMONG ITS OTHER DEFECTS, THE DEFENSE ACT OF 1920 MADE NO adequate provision for the revolutionary appearance of the military airplane. At the time of its enactment, controversy was already acute over the strategic function of "air power," over the relation of aviation —and more particularly the young aviators—to the old arms and services, over the future of the new air industry, and over the correct organization and direction of the air component in the total national defense structure. These issues received no answer in the 1920 act. Passionately debated, they were to preoccupy most American military thinking for the next two decades.

Brigadier General William (Billy) Mitchell, who had been General Pershing's air commander in France, made himself the flamboyant spokesman of air power, and kept matters in a high state of turmoil, until in September 1925 he deliberately invited court martial with a vituperative attack upon both the Army and Navy high commands. That Mitchell would be convicted was inevitable. Possibly with an eye to softening the political consequences, President Coolidge appointed a board to report, not on the Mitchell case, but on "the best means of developing and applying aircraft in national defense." Headed by Dwight W. Morrow, an eminent banker, diplomat, and public servant, it included a retired general and admiral but was otherwise civilian in composition; it took testimony, however, from many military officers as well as civilian officials and industrialists. The report illustrates the extent to which the airplane had challenged all the accepted bases of national strategy and military policy. Its subject was merely the use of aircraft in the national defense. But the board found itself going

rather deeply into the foundations of military thinking in what was—
not only on account of the airplane—a new technologized and industrialized age of war.

[The board first met on September 17, 1925.] Thereafter we
held public hearings for four weeks, having before us in person
99 witnesses, of whom more than half were actual flying men. We
designedly gave the greater portion of the time to hearing those
men who had actual air experience. This seemed desirable because there has been a widespread impression among flying men
that their point of view and professional opinions have not been
enough considered, that large matters of policy have been determined by men without flying experience. Through the hearty cooperation of the War and Navy Departments we were able to
make clear to the flying men that the opinions desired of them
were their personal opinions, whether or no those opinions coin-
cided with the opinions of the departments.

In addition to the flying men, we have heard from the Secretary
of War, the Secretary of the Navy, the Postmaster General, and
the Secretary of Commerce, as well as from their technical advisers and the heads of their bureaus and departments. We have
heard representatives of the National Advisory Committee for
Aeronautics. We have heard the chairman of the Appropriations
Committee of the House of Representatives. We have heard the
leaders of the aircraft industry. . . .

. . . We have kept steadily in mind the mission which you gave
us. We are not primarily concerned with questions of Army discipline. These are problems with which armies always have had to
deal and always will have to deal. They must be dealt with
through the ordinary channels. They do not fundamentally affect
the problem upon which you [President Coolidge] have asked us
to report.

The one thing that stands out clearly at the very outset of a
consideration of the problem is the great conflict in the testimony.

From *Aircraft in National Defense,* 69th Congress, Session 1, Senate Documents, pp. 2–29.

This conflict extends not only to matters of opinion, where it is necessarily to be expected—indeed, where to some extent it is to be desired—but also to what seem to be differences in statement of fact. . . . We are told that the United States Army has available for use 1,396 good airplanes, and that it has available for use only 34 good airplanes; that America stands far behind Japan in number of airplanes, and that Japan stands far behind America in number of airplanes; that anti-aircraft fire has no effect upon air attack, and that anti-aircraft fire is one of the greatest menaces to air attack; that the United States is at the present time open to air attack from overseas from all sides, and that the distance from which an effective air attack can be launched is not more than 200 miles; that the air mail service between Chicago and New York does not yet commercially pay, and that an air service between New York and Peking should be established and that the saving in the transportation of commercial paper alone would pay its expenses from the beginning.

With the outbreak of the World War there was removed from aircraft development one of the great limiting factors, to wit, the question of expense. No cost was too great for anything that might contribute to the winning of the war. . . . A colossal effort was made, and a colossal industrial machine created from practically nothing. More than 16,000 airplanes, with motors, were delivered by American manufacturers. In addition approximately 25,000 motors were produced and at the time of the armistice were being provided at the rate of 4,000 per month. Competent authorities believe that by March, 1919, the country could have been producing 10,000 Liberty motors a month. In aircraft, as in many other lines of America's endeavors, things that were gotten ready for possible campaigns in 1919 and 1920 were fortunately not needed. How much that unused preparation contributed to the shortening of the war no one can tell.

With the coming of the armistice, the United States began to liquidate a vast war machine, at the same time endeavoring to retain and further extend the scientific and technical knowledge which the war experience had brought. The severe liquidation brought a violent wrench to all industries, including those furnishing aircraft. Moreover, the reduced army of peace meant reduction in rank and curtailment of opportunity for all officers in the Army. It is not unnatural that the controversy which arose between the newer and the older arms of that service should have raged with some bitterness. Various causes have been assigned for that controversy—the prejudice of the older arms of the service against the new arm, the lack of discipline of the new arm, the fact that the casualties in the new arm are much greater than in any other arm of the service, the sensational character of the airman's work even without exaggeration, the readiness with which that work may be exploited by those seeking sensation, the violent propaganda of interested parties. Any and all of these causes have been put forward. It is impossible to attribute the controversy to any single cause, particularly in view of the fact that it has gone on in much the same terms in every country that participated in the war. The conflict is one between the old and the new, emphasized by the sharp adjustments required in a period immediately following a great war. Such conflicts of thought have gone on from the beginning. They will go on until the end. It is in many ways desirable that they should go on, even in armies, subject always, of course, to that essential discipline without which an army becomes a mob. What is needed is a more generous appreciation by each side of the difficulties of the other side. On each side there is need of patience with what seems the unreasonableness of the other side. The fundamental problem may not be settled. It may, however, be understood if men will approach it with less feeling and more intelligence.

In taking up the actual problems with which our study has been concerned it has seemed to us useful to divide our report into two parts. In Part One we put forward a series of questions covering some matters in controversy, which, despite the conflict in testimony, admit of answers. Having answered such questions as the evidence before us requires, we then consider in Part Two some positive action that we think should be taken to improve the Air Services—I, with reference to the Army; II, with reference to the

Navy; and III, with reference to industry as the source of supply for aeronautic matériel.

In suggesting remedies we rest upon the sound principle that no solution proposed at this time can be lasting. It is, therefore, of the first importance to lay the emphasis upon the best method of achieving the desired result. To that end we rely chiefly upon the appointment of an additional Assistant Secretary of War, Assistant Secretary of the Navy, and Assistant Secretary of Commerce, to devote themselves under the direction of their respective heads, primarily to aviation and jointly to coordinate so far as may be practicable the activities of their three departments with respect to aviation.

Part One

The questions to which we attempt answers are as follows:

First. In determining an aviation policy for the United States Government, what should be the relation between the military and civilian services?

Our answer to this question is that they should remain distinctly separate.

The historic tradition of the United States is to maintain military forces only for defense and to keep those forces subordinate to the civilian government. This policy has been amply justified by our experience. It has been proposed that we should establish a Department of Aeronautics, which should control all or a portion of our military air power as well as our civilian air activities. Such a departure would be quite contrary to the principles under which this country has attained its present moral and material power. If the civilian air development should have anything like the wide ramifications that are predicted for it, such a new policy might have a profound effect upon the historic attitude of our Nation toward military and civilian activities. The peace-time activities of the United States have never been governed by military considerations. To organize its peace-time activities, or what it is thought may ultimately be one large branch of them, under military control or on a military basis would be to make the same mistake which, properly or improperly, the world believes Prussia to have made in the last generation. The union of civil and military air activities would breed distrust in every region to which our commercial aviation sought extension.

Nor do we see any force in the argument that the building up of a large air power—partly military and partly civilian—would be a peace movement. In the Conference on the Limitation of Naval Armaments the nations which took part made a real sacrifice of weapons which they believed to be effective. There was a real effort to secure peace by relying upon mutual agreements and good faith. Those who believe in the preponderating effect of air power, however, are not talking of disarmament when they suggest the sacrifice of battleships. They are talking of discarding the weapon which they think is becoming useless and substituting therefor what they believe to be a more deadly one. Whole cities are to be quickly demolished and their inhabitants destroyed by high explosives and poisonous gases. The argument is thus stated: "The influence of air power on the ability of one nation to impress its will on another in an armed contest will be decisive." Wars against high-spirited peoples never will be ended by sudden attacks upon important nerve centers such as manufacturing plants, depots, lighting and power plants, and railway centers. The last war taught us again that man can not make a machine stronger than the spirit of man. The real road to peace rests not upon more elaborate preparations to impress wills but rather upon a more earnest disposition to accommodate wills.

By our fortunate geographical position we have heretofore been freed from the heavy burden of armament which necessity seems to have imposed upon the nations on the Continent of Europe. If one thing has stood out sharply in the past century it has been the great danger of the defensive movements of a nation being interpreted by their neighbors as offensive movements. This has naturally, perhaps inevitably, thrown most of the countries within the European orbit into the vicious circle of competitive armaments. We are all in accord that the United States must at all times maintain an adequate defensive system, whether it be surface ships, submarines, land armies, or air power. But let us not deceive ourselves. This new weapon, with its long range of power not only for defense but also for offense, is subject to the psychological rules which govern all armament. Armaments beget armaments. It has been our national policy heretofore to oppose competitive armaments. The coming of a new and deadlier weapon must not result in any change in this policy. The belief that new and deadlier weapons will shorten future wars and prevent vast expenditures of lives and resources is a dangerous one which, if accepted, might well lead to a readier acceptance of war as the solution of international difficulties. The arrival of new weapons operating in an element hitherto unavailable to mankind will not necessarily change the ultimate character of war. The next war may well start in the air but in all probability will wind up, as the last war did, in the mud.

Second. How can the civilian use of aircraft be promoted?

This brings us directly to the part of our inquiry which has perhaps attracted the least popular attention but which may well be the most important question which aviation presents in its far-reaching consequences to our people.

The rapid development of aircraft under the impetus of the war has not unnaturally led to the strange assumption in many people's minds that this new conquest of science is to be dedicated mainly to war purposes. No witness who appeared before your board made a more striking impression than the modest gentleman from Dayton, Ohio, who, with his brother, more than 20 years ago, started men flying. We can not refrain from quoting to you the words with which Orville Wright began his testimony:

> Not being a student of naval or military affairs, I shall not presume to make any suggestions as to the use of aircraft in warfare. I offer only a few suggestions, and none of them new, along the lines of civil aviation, in which I believe the National Government can and should take part immediately.

A great opportunity lies before the United States. We have natural resources, industrial organizations, and long distances free from customs barriers. We may, if we will, take the lead in the world in extending civil aviation. In this field international competition is to be desired by all. . . .

. . . The principal conditions standing in the way of progress and acting in restraint of the more rapid investment of private capital in the field of air transport are:

(1) The excessive burden placed upon private capital if it is to be required to pioneer in the development of flying equipment best suited to air transport and at the same time supply all the collateral requirements including airways and air navigation facilities, especially as such facilities are, by their very nature, open to the use of all, and no proprietary rights can be retained by the parties undertaking the original investment and the expense of maintenance. The parallel with maritime transport in this particular is exact.

(2) A fear of the hazards of the air which makes it difficult to secure passengers, and a general idea of the airplane as a military or sport vehicle, unreliable for other use.

(3) A general uncertainty on the part of potential operators regarding the extent of the traffic available.

(4) The lack of a definite legal status and of a body of basic air laws.

(5) The absence of Government inspection and certification of flying equipment and licensing of pilots, and the lack of control over methods of maintenance and operation in so far as they have a direct bearing on safety.

(6) The slowness of the development of insurance facilities.

To the end that this important field should receive the attention that it deserves, we recommend that provision be made for a Bureau of Air Navigation under an additional Assistant Secretary of Commerce. . . .

Third. What should be the military air policy of the United States?

Any consideration of the air policy of the United States, especially as regards the military air strength which we should develop, with its influence on the National Budget, should be based on a careful consideration of—

(1) The general military policy of the United States,

(2) The air strength of those foreign States which, having in view our geographical position, could menace our security.

Our naval strength is now determined by international agreement. So far as naval warfare is concerned, the strengths of the air arms of the naval forces of world powers will presumably be in close relation to the naval strengths authorized under the convention regarding the limitation of armaments. Here our obvious general policy should be to maintain our naval aviation in due relation to the fleet.

Our national policy calls for the establishment of the air strength of our Army primarily as an agency of defense. Protected, as the United States is, by broad oceans from possible enemies, the evidence submitted in our hearings gives complete ground for the conclusion that there is no present reason for apprehension of any invasion from overseas directly by way of the air; nor indeed is there any apparent probability of such an invasion in any future which can be foreseen.

It furthermore appears that in order to place any considerable enemy air force in a position for effective operation against our cities, ground armies, or military positions, it would be necessary to transport such force by water-borne shipping—airplane carriers and cargo ships—and establish a land base from which such operations could be carried on. This could not be effected so long as our fleet is undefeated on the sea.

A careful study by the Army and Navy high commands of the factors entering into the question of the air strength, should indicate the total strength needed in order to insure the proper measure of national security, while at the same time holding a consistent relation to our traditional policy of maintaining armed forces for defense rather than for aggression, and to the need of wise economy in all demands on the public purse. . . .

Fourth. Is the United States in danger by air attack from any potential enemy of menacing strength?

Our answer to this question is no.

This conclusion is based on the facts as they now are. No airplane capable of making a transoceanic flight to our country with a useful military load and of returning to safety is now in existence. Airplanes of special construction and in special circumstances have made nonstop flights over land of 2,520 and 2,730 miles. Neither of the airplanes which made these flights carried any military load. Both flights were made under as nearly ideal weather conditions as possible, the purpose being record-breaking performances. The mere fact of the distance covered in these flights is, therefore, no criterion of the ability of airplanes to make transoceanic flights of equal distance under war conditions and with an effective military load. Although there is some variance in the testimony on this point it seems to be the consensus of expert opinion that the effective radius of flight for bombing operations is at present between 200 and 300 miles. By effective radius of flight of a bombing airplane is meant the distance from point of departure to an objective which this airplane could bomb and then return to its starting point. This distance, for large bombing operations, includes allowance for possible adverse weather conditions, for the capacity of personnel as contrasted with the capacity of the airplane itself, for some reduction in speed and range in the case of a squadron as compared with a single plane, and for time lost over the objective. All of this results in a very considerable reduction in radius for effective operation as compared with that which might be based on a single trial flight under favorable conditions. With the advance in the art it is to be expected that there will be substantial advance in the range and capacity of bombing airplanes; but, having in view present practical limitations, it does not appear that there is any ground for anticipation of such development to a point which would constitute a direct menace to the United States in any future which scientific thought can now foresee. . . .

. . . . The fear of such an attack is without reason.

In the foregoing we are speaking of an attack upon the continental United States, and are ignoring an attack from Mexico or Canada. To create a defense system based upon a hypothetical air attack from Canada, Mexico, or any other of our near neighbors would be wholly unreasonable. For a century we have, under treaty, left the Great Lakes unguarded by a naval force; by mutual consent the long Canadian frontier is free from armament on either side. The result has justified such a course.

Fifth. Should there be a department of national defense under which should be grouped all the military defensive organizations of the Government?

We have, at an earlier point, considered a separate department of the air under which it has been proposed there should be grouped both military and civilian aviation activities. Such a proposition we have disapproved for the reason that civilian and military activities should, in our opinion, be kept separate. The present question involves different considerations. It is, in fact, largely a question of administrative machinery. Entirely apart from the problems that have been raised by the new and enlarged uses of military aviation, the question has been often before considered of uniting the Army and the Navy under a Secretary of National Defense. President Harding made such a proposal to Congress, but so far as we have been able to discover, this proposal did not meet with favor either in Congress or in the Army and the Navy.

The argument in favor of such a course has been and is that there is now overlapping of the Army and Navy. There is some strength in the argument. Such consolidation might secure more cooperative training in times of peace and perhaps some economies in buying. The amount of overlapping is, however, less than is generally assumed. Moreover, an element of competition in certain matters has its advantages.

The argument against such a course is the added complexity in organization which would inevitably result. The Army and Navy organizations urge with force that each of them is entitled to a member of the Cabinet in order that its special views may be properly presented to the President and to the Congress. If the two present service organizations were consolidated under a single secretary it would at once become necessary to create a super general staff. No secretary of national defense could operate the two organizations without subsecretaries and technical advisers. This super general staff, which would be in addition to the present service staffs, would necessarily comprise Army and Navy advisers who had been educated not only in their own particular schools but who would be required to have taken courses in the schools of the service to which they did not belong. It is difficult to see how any such super-organization would make for economy in time of peace or efficiency in time of war.

During a war period the President as the Commander in Chief of both services must act as the director of national defense. President Lincoln in the Civil War and President Wilson in the World War had to assume such a position. Moreover, when the President assumes such a position the necessity of linking the defensive agencies of the Government does not stop with the Army and the Navy. The Council of National Defense, which during the World War was organized to coordinate our industries and resources, included the Secretaries of War, Navy, Interior, Agriculture, Commerce, and Labor. There are thus swept into the actual department of national defense, acting under the President many other organizations whose activities during peace time have nothing directly to do with defense. The memory of the Great War is so recent that we hardly need call attention to the fact that railroads, coal supply, agricultural activities, important war industries, dealings with labor, all by special legislation had to be brought into coordination with the work of the Army and the Navy.

We do not recommend a Department of National Defense, either as comprising the Army and the Navy or as comprising three coordinate departments of Army, Navy, and Air. The disadvantages outweigh the advantages.

Sixth. Should there be formed a separate department for air, coordinate with the present Departments of War and Navy?

Our answer is no.

The quoted opinion of General Pershing and the direct testimony of General Summerall, General Hines, and General Ely, of Admiral Sims, Admiral Eberle, Admiral Robison, Admiral

Coontz, and Admiral Hughes stressed the need of the Army and of the Navy for their own air services. Modern military and naval operations can not be effectively conducted without such services acting as integral parts of a single command. Moreover, the .training of these air services that are to act with the Army and with the Navy must be under the continuous direction and control of the command which is ultimately to use them. In these conclusions and principles we concur. The question left to consider is whether the country has need of a separate independent air force in addition to the air power required for use with the Army and the Navy. We do not consider that air power, as an arm of the national defense, has yet demonstrated its value—certainly not in a country situated as ours—for independent operations of such a character as to justify the organization of a separate department. We believe that such independent missions as it is capable of can be better carried out under the high command of the Army or Navy, as the case may be. . . .

Part Two

Having answered the foregoing questions as the evidence before us requires, we shall now consider some positive action that we think should be taken to improve the air services, (I) with reference to the Army, (II) with reference to the Navy, and (III) with reference to the industry as the source of supply for aeronautic matériel.

I. *The Army*

Our consideration of the Army Air Service can be conveniently treated under three headings, first, its strength; second, its condition in respect of personnel and matériel and the criticisms thereof; third, recommendations for its improvement.

The Army Air Service is a branch of the Army which in its general status is similar to other major branches of the Army, such as Artillery, Infantry, and Cavalry. It has in general the same degree of independence and is subject to the same degree of supervision and control under the Secretary of War and the War Department General Staff as the other branches. It has two major functions—one to render service in an auxiliary rôle in time of war to other combatant branches of the Army and the other that of an air force acting alone on a separate mission.

Its present authorized strength is 1,247 officers and 8,760 enlisted men out of a total authorized strength for the entire Military Establishment of 12,000 officers and 124,988 men. The actual strength on June 30, the close of the last fiscal year, was 912 officers and 8,825 men, at which time the actual strength of the whole Army, including the Air Service, was 11,647 officers and 115,130 men.

In assessing the matériel strength of the Air Service the board has encountered much difficulty, particularly in attempting to compare this strength with that of the other principal military powers.

Regarding the strength of our own service, the most authoritative figures placed before us are those of General Patrick, the Chief of the Army Air Service, in which he defined "standard" planes as those "that could be used in emergency or if we suddenly went to war." Under this definition he places our strength on June 30 last, at 396 standard planes. He also states that there were on June 30 last in commission or in reserve an additional 1,000 "of a similar type but of less value—but planes that might be used in war times." He further has stated that since June 30 last there have been received or are on order or are covered by present purchase plans for the Air Service 439 additional standard planes. . . .

The air strength of any particular power should be considered in relation to its anticipated value in the scheme of national defense of that power and in relation, likewise, to the remainder of the military establishment. France, for example, has an army more than five times as large as our own, while the army of the British Empire is more than twice our own. Our strength of air arm in proportion to general military establishment compares favorably with that of any other power. Geographical position with reference to other nations is bound to affect necessary air strength as it affects the rest of the Army.

We turn to the second consideration—that is, the condition of personnel and matériel in the Air Service and the criticisms thereof. . . .

If we have found difficulty in arriving at fair bases of comparison in dealing with figures of strength, it is even more difficult to assess our exact place in comparison with other powers in the more intangible fields of military and technical development. It must be recognized, however, that our military and naval Air Services hold a major share of the world's records. The round-the-world flight was made by American Army pilots. Other notable feats have been at least as numerous in our services as in those of other powers. The quality of our personnel and of our equipment in general can safely face comparison with that of any other power.

It must be recognized that our Army Air Service personnel has been subjected in the years since the war to an extremely difficult and trying ordeal. The general effects of the reduction of the Army after the world-wide war endeavor have been traced in an earlier section of this report. The effect of the violent change from war to peace conditions, involving as it did great reductions in rank, was a difficult ordeal for all branches of the service, and particularly so for the newest branch, which as an arm had little experience of peace conditions.

One effect of these readjustments has been to create a feeling of unrest and dissatisfaction and of impatience against the control of the War Department General Staff. These feelings have been aggravated by questions of rank and promotion, resentment of control by non-flying officers, shortage of officers of flying experience in the higher grades, apprehension of wholesale transfers to the Air Service of senior officers from other branches of the Army, and dissatisfaction with the single promotion list.

We do not believe that the release of the Air Service from the same degree of control by the General Staff as that imposed on other coordinate branches of the Army is justified. Such a move would strike at the basic principle of unity of command and would depart from the organization of the Army created by Congress in 1903, developed and perfected through 17 years of peace and war, and again revised by Congress in the national defense act of 1920. These changes in organization first established and then strengthened the General Staff, whose business is to exercise supervision over training, discipline, and inspections, to formulate policies, and to advise the Secretary of War. It does not administer. Its chief duties are concerned with preparation for war. . . .

. . . Turning now from personnel to matériel, there is found among the criticisms adduced in evidence before us the recurrence of the terms "obsolete," "obsolescent," and "unsafe."

The question of when an airplane for military purposes becomes "obsolete" is entirely a matter of judgment. In appraising the judgment exercised on this question two points must be kept in mind. First, that in a national emergency until the industry has been mobilized on a large production basis, every existing airplane which is safe, regardless of age and type, will probably be used for some military purpose; and second, that the useful life of a plane in active military service even in time of peace is very limited.

The term "obsolescent" may be applied to any type of plane as well as to any type of automobile as soon as it has been put in service. By such time a new and better model is likely to be in the stage of design or development. This is a condition of progress and is especially notable in a new and fast developing science or art such as aviation.

The rapidity of development in the new science must of necessity in any country result in there being but a small proportion of absolutely new and up-to-date planes out of the total possessed by any service.

The fact that any plane is "obsolete" or "obsolescent" does not necessarily mean that it is "unsafe." Lack of safety may result from faulty aerodynamic or general design, from structural weakness, from unreliability of power plant, or from deterioration through use or age. We find no evidence tending to show basically faulty aerodynamic design, or lack of structural strength as dependent upon design or construction. Nor unreliability of American airplane engines as compared with those of foreign design and manufacture.

The safety of planes, in so far as their deterioration through use or age is concerned, is dependent on rules and regulations for inspection and operation, and their strict enforcement. General Patrick stated before us on October 13 that "the planes we have in service are inspected most rigidly before they are taken into the air. No man is allowed to take into the air a plane that is regarded in any way as unsafe." Casualties have occurred. Moreover, with the art of military flying depending as it does so largely on elements of physical condition, training, skill, and judgment on the part of the pilot, casualties will occur, no matter what the equipment or how careful the inspection. The records show that the accident rate per number of miles flown has been steadily decreasing and that it compares favorably with the accident rate in other air services.

In particular, much criticism has been directed against the DH plane [the De Havilland bomber, a biplane], of which a large number were on hand at the close of the war. Our policy for the continued use of this plane is paralleled by that of the British Air Service, in which at the close of the war great numbers of this type were on hand and are still in use. A late report shows that the British Royal Air Force in their trans-Africa flight, recently completed, used DH planes substantially like ours and equipped with American-built Liberty engines. Our DH planes now in service have been modified in design or have been reconditioned, and the same is true of war-built Liberty engines before being placed in use. This particular type of plane, though referred to by some critics as "flaming coffins," has in the last three years been flown approximately 1,000,000 miles "cross country" on the Army airways without a casualty. . . .

. . . After careful consideration of the foregoing facts and criticisms as adduced in evidence we come to the third heading;—recommendations for legislative and administrative changes in the Army Air Service. We submit the following recommendations:

(1) To avoid confusion of nomenclature between the name of the Air Service and certain phases of its duties, we recommend that the name be changed to Air Corps. The distinction between service rendered by air troops in their auxiliary rôle and that of an air force acting alone on a separate mission is important.

(2) In order that the Air Corps (Air Service) should receive constant sympathetic supervision and counsel, we recommend that Congress be asked to create an additional Assistant Secretary of War who shall perform such duties with reference to aviation as may be assigned to him by the Secretary of War. . . .

. . . (3) It seems desirable to give to aviation some special representation on the General Staff. There has not as yet been opportunity for many aviation officers of suitable rank to be qualified for membership on the General Staff. We therefore recommend that the Secretary of War create, administratively, in each of the five divisions of the War Department General Staff, an air section, to be headed by a General Staff or acting General Staff officer detailed from the Air Corps (Air Service); such section, under the same supervision as other sections of its division, to consider and recommend proper action on such air matters as are referred to the division. . . .

II. The Navy

In a manner similar to that made use of in the instance of the Army, we may conveniently consider naval aviation under three headings: First, its strength and accomplishments; second, its condition in respect of personnel and matériel and the criticisms thereof; third, recommendations for its improvement.

Naval aviation is not a separate branch of the Navy, as the Air Service is of the Army. Its personnel and equipment are distributed throughout and form an integral part of the fleet. It is administered through the Bureau of Aeronautics in the Navy Department, which in turn is subject to the general supervision of the Chief of Naval Operations in much the same manner that the Army Air Service is supervised by the General Staff. On matters of personnel it is subsidiary to the Bureau of Navigation.

On June 30 last there were 398 service airplanes in naval aviation. Of this total 218 were with the fleet. The remainder were in reserve. In addition there were about 200 airplanes used for training or experimental purposes. In personnel there were 623 officers and 3,330 men whose major duties were concerned with aviation. Of these officers, 377 were qualified pilots. These numbers are included in the total naval strength of 8,389 officers and 84,332 men. . . .

In estimating naval air strength the following two factors must further be considered: First, the ability of the ships of the Navy other than aircraft carriers to utilize airplanes. To further this end catapults for the launching of airplanes are now installed on 25 to 30 combatant ships and are being provided for on others. Each of these ships carries from two to four airplanes. No foreign navy has accomplished anything substantial in this direction. Second, our strength in airplane carriers. We now have only one airplane carrier, the *Langley*, which is a converted collier and has been used chiefly for experimental purposes. The *Lexington* and the *Saratoga*, which will be the largest and fastest airplane carriers in the world, will be commissioned in 1927. The treaty for the limitation of naval armaments governs our ultimate comparative strength in this class of vessel.

Our Navy was the first among those of the world to adapt the airplane to use on and over the sea. This was accomplished through the development of seaplanes and flying boats. In these types of airplanes we have continued to hold our lead. The Navy early developed the catapult for the launching of planes from ships. No other navy has as yet produced a successful counterpart. We have done more extended cruising with large seaplanes than any other navy. Our naval aviators hold at least their share of world's records and have to their credit many outstanding accomplishments, such as the first trans-Atlantic flight.

We find nothing but praise of the personnel engaged in naval aviation. The matériel at its disposal is likewise generally of high grade, as is shown by the almost total absence of criticism of matériel by the naval witnesses who appeared before us. From these facts and from considerations similar to those outlined in the instance of the Army we believe that the quality of our naval personnel and of its equipment is at least the equal of and in certain directions undoubtedly superior to that of any other power.

There is a controversy in regard to the ability of airplanes under war conditions to sink the largest naval vessel. In our records will be found a complete summary of naval experimentation on this subject over the past 15 years. This is a highly technical question, and, in our opinion, any present answer must partake more of prophecy than of fact.

There is unrest and dissatisfaction among the aviation personnel in the Navy. They all agree in desiring to remain a part of the Navy. They feel that their devotion to aviation has prejudiced their chances for promotion and their opportunity for high command. They feel that the requirements for all officers to qualify in all branches ought not to be applied to aviators in its full rigor, as constant practice is essential to continued successful flying. These are among the most difficult questions we have been called upon to consider. There is justification, of course, for the contention of the higher officers that to be competent to command ships or fleets an officer must have sea experience. On the other hand, we feel that there should be a recognition of the principle that an officer with both air and sea experience should, other things being equal, be better fitted for command than an officer who has had sea experience only. We believe the solution lies in a broad and generous recognition of Admiral Mahan's maxim that a naval officer should have a general knowledge of all branches of his profession and a specialized knowledge of one. Beyond this, however, it must be clearly recognized that special provision for promotion must be made for those officers who, through no fault of their own, have been confined solely to aviation duty.

As in the Army, we find the direct command of flying men by non-flying officers is objected to. This difficulty has arisen partly through the operation of causes discussed in the preceding paragraph, but more largely through the fact that there are no officers in the higher ranks of the Navy with long experience in aviation. There appears to us justice in this contention, and we are recommending temporary advanced rank, following therein the same principle as in the case of the Army. . . .

. . . After careful consideration of the foregoing, we recommend as follows:

First. The appointment of an additional Assistant Secretary of the Navy under the conditions and for the purposes discussed elsewhere in this report.

Second. The carrying as extra numbers, and at their own request, of officers (line or staff) of the grade of captain, commander, and lieutenant commander, who have specialized in aviation so long as to jeopardize their selection for the next higher grade and thus insure such promotion as would be otherwise due. . . .

. . . Sixth. To the end that naval aviators should have the opportunity to present naval aviation problems to those responsible for the shaping of the policies and for the handling of the personnel of the Navy, we recommend that representation should be given naval aviators in details in both the Office of the Chief of Naval Operations and the Bureau of Navigation. We recognize that there are fundamental distinctions between the organization of the high command in the Army and the Navy. With a proper spirit of cooperation, however, we feel that the naval high command will find real opportunity to utilize the special knowledge and counsel of the naval aviator. This is analogous to the infiltration of Air Corps officers into the General Staff of the Army. Here, as in the Army, the particular men chosen must be of the temper of mind to appreciate not only the special needs of aviation but the needs of the Navy as a whole.

Seventh. Selections for command or for general line duty on aircraft carriers and tenders, or for command of flying schools, or for other important duties requiring immediate command of flying activities should be confined to those officers, who, while otherwise qualified, are also naval aviators; and such a policy should be followed as will provide a sufficient body of officers thus doubly qualified from which to select. . . .

III. The Aircraft Industry

The importance of the aircraft industry in relation to national defense is obvious. The size of the air force needed in the event of a great war will always be far beyond anything that it is economically feasible to keep up in any country in times of peace. The rapidity of the development of the art of airplane design, rendering flying equipment inferior for service use against a major power within a few years after design, prohibits the gradual manufacture and accumulation of matériel and its storage for use in any future emergency. The airplanes to equip the expanded force in case of war must therefore be built when war is actually at hand, and the speed of their manufacture is a vital factor in military effectiveness. The relative wastage of equipment in war, too, is beyond anything known in peace, and production must be kept continuously at the highest pitch in order to supply the demands of the forces in the field.

The experience of the late war gives concrete illustration of the war-time and postwar problems of an aircraft industry and shows that in respect of the production of airplanes an international conflict coming without appreciable warning divides roughly into three successive parts. The first, lasting but a few weeks, is that in which dependence has to be placed on factory equipment and factory personnel actually in the service, before there has been time to get any program of expansion under way. It is succeeded by a somewhat longer period, during which the aircraft industry, using its existing facilities to the utmost and expanding them as rapidly as possible, delivers new airplanes to the service at a moderate but steadily increasing rate. In the third and final period the production of the aircraft industry proper is augmented by the incursion into the airplane field of a wide variety of plants normally engaged in manufacturing such things as pianos, furniture, automobile bodies, fancy hardware, and other articles not vitally necessary in the prosecution of war. When that stage is reached the rate at which airplanes can be produced in a highly industrialized country like the United States is very great.

The permanent aircraft industry is most important during the first and second stages and as a source of engineering development and supervisory talent at all times. For a few months, and they would be among the most important months of any war, it would have to carry the full burden of supplying equipment. After others had begun to take a share of that burden the industry would still have the responsibility for the design of improved machines. The furniture manufacturer can not be expected to start experimental work or to do anything more than build from complete sets of drawings furnished to him. Anything that strengthens the industry as a whole, and especially anything that conduces to the strengthening of the design and engineering departments of the companies building aircraft, must be considered as a contribution toward the national defense.

There are certain obvious difficulties which preclude accurate appraisal of the capacities of the airplane industries of the United States and of the principal powers. Even in respect of many of the airplane-manufacturing plants in the United States data as to existing capacity submitted to us were found unreliable, data as to potential capacity were even more so, and corresponding data in respect of the aircraft industries of the principal powers were in most cases pure speculation.

We have taken into consideration (1) data obtained by the Industrial War Plans Division of the office of the Chief of Air Service, United States Army, as a result of the survey of the aircraft industry which was made during 1925 in conjunction with the Aeronautical Chamber of Commerce; (2) the data submitted by individual companies of the industry in response to requests from us; (3) the data as to World War production of airplanes compiled in the office of the Chief of Air Service; (4) the data obtained by personal visits to various plants by representatives of the Industrial War Plans Division. Upon the basis of this data, we estimate that the aircraft industry of the United States can be counted upon to contribute to the air strength of the United States during the first 12 months of a major emergency calling for the mobilization of the entire industrial resources and man power of the country, approximately 15,000 airplanes. This production would, of course, come in gradually, starting at a moderate figure and increasing steadily throughout the year. While the first year's requirement of our military and naval services might not be met by this production (dependent upon the rapidity with which the other phases of our military and naval programs go forward), it is not apparent that any other power could make appreciably greater progress toward meeting its aggregate requirements within the first 12 months of a war. During the second year of the war new plants constructed or converted for mass production during the first year should be capable of bearing an increasingly greater proportion of the total war load, and it is probable that, at the end of 18 months, if not sooner, our aggregate monthly production would be measurably greater than that of any other nation. In this connection it should be borne in mind that our geographic situation makes dire urgency of aircraft at the beginning of the war far less important for us than for European countries.

If a certain amount of business is needed to keep an essential industry in a sound condition, the amount of support that the Government must, directly or indirectly, provide decreases as the business coming from other sources is increased. It is, therefore, in the interests of economy and of efficient national defense that these other sources should be developed. . . .

It seems to us probable, however, that for some time to come the strength of the aircraft industry in the United States will depend primarily on the number of new airplanes ordered by the services. The determination of new policies will be of no avail to the manufacturers without orders for work to be done in the factories. This does not mean that the size of a government's air force should be determined by the need of industry. On the contrary, the size of the air force must be determined solely on the basis of the large policy of national defense.

The gradual depletion of the war stock requires increase in the amount of new equipment ordered annually. In that respect the industry's situation is assured of improvement. Whatever the size of the orders placed, however, they can be made to yield the best result both for the services and for the manufacturers if there is some continuity of policy and some clear aim.

It appears impracticable to make definite plans for the size of the air force at some period 10 years or more distant, and for the amount and type of equipment to be bought each year to reach that goal. Conditions change too rapidly. It does, however, seem feasible to lay down a general policy.

It appears that it should be possible, at this stage of the development of the art, to select a given type of machine as a standard for two or three years, with the understanding that, barring some extraordinary development, no change would be made within that time. The industry would then be assured of a continuous series of orders for a standard design, while an excessive multiplication of types of equipment in service would be avoided. Those advantages seem to outweigh the small gain in performance of the individual airplane that might at times result from a willingness to put a new type into service every few months. There should be a standard rate of replacement, selected to give a complete turnover of service equipment at definite intervals, so that the number of new pursuit machines ordered, for example, might show no extreme fluctuations from year to year. . . .

38. The Baker Board: Military and Air Policy in the 1930's

THE MORROW BOARD REPORT IN 1925 FAILED TO END THE CONTROVERSIES over air policy. The Navy came to a reasonably satisfactory adjustment with its aviators and its air component; but the Army Air Corps, denied its independence and what it believed to be adequate appropriations, remained dissatisfied and resentful. In 1933 a staff study under Major General Hugh A. Drum worked out a new, semi-autonomous organization for the Air Corps together with a substantially increased program for airplane procurement. This was, however, in the depths of the depression; and the Drum proposals had not been adopted when a new crisis arose. At the beginning of the winter of 1933–1934 President Roosevelt abruptly cancelled the contracts of the private air-mail carriers and ordered the Army Air Corps to take over the mail service. A shocking series of casualties ensued. It appeared that the Army pilots had neither the training nor the equipment requisite for the duty; this was no reflection on them, but it did raise a question as to the Air Corps' claims to possess a reliable and world-ranging air power.

Once again a high-level board was appointed to review the whole problem of air policy, this time by the War Department itself. It called upon its wartime secretary, Newton D. Baker, to head the committee, consisting, in addition to Mr. Baker, of five general officers from the active list and five civilian scientists, engineers, and air executives. Their report, of July 1934, was another significant contribution to military thought; it also had the practical effect of stilling most of the controversy and putting the Air Corps on a more satisfactory foundation. The Baker Board endorsed the Drum Plan to establish a "General Headquarters Air Force," as a largely independent organization directly answerable only to the Chief of Staff, and to give the corps an authorized standard strength of 2,320 airplanes. Congress failed, as usual, to support the authorization. But the new organization was that with which the United States Army Air Force entered World War II and was the basis of the command system under which the war was fought.

1. Scope of the Inquiry and Historical Background

This committee is the fifteenth committee or board which, during the past 16 years, has studied the major problems and improvement of national-defense aviation, including the Army Air Corps. Every major difficulty has been repeatedly considered. It is the hope of this committee that the present study, which has comprised extensive hearings of representatives of all phases of aviation and which has considered and reviewed all prior studies, may be accepted as the basis for the development of the Army

From *Final Report of the War Department Special Committee on Army Air Corps* (Washington, D.C.: Government Printing Office, 1934), pp. 61–75.

Air Corps for the next 10 years and thus terminate the continuing agitation and uncertainty which has been so detrimental to harmonious development and improvement.

2. Aviation Development Since 1926 and Comparison with Foreign Aviation

Since the report of the Morrow Board and the congressional act of 1926, aviation in the United States has made outstanding and satisfactory progress. This is true in all lines of aviation, not only from the viewpoint of design, development and manufacture, but also relative to the facilities for operating transcontinental and other extensive airways systems. *In general aviation the United States leads the world; it is superior in commercial aviation, its naval aviation is stronger than that of any other power, and with more financial support its Army aviation can be raised to a world position equal to that held by our Navy.*

This success is attributed to national interest and assistance which fostered sound legislation, organization and financial support, and visioned and provided the essential facilities for future development.

3. National Considerations

a. National Defense Policy

Our national defense policy contemplates aggressive action against no nation; it is based entirely upon the defense of our homeland and overseas possessions, including protection of our sea- and air-borne commerce. We do not advocate any increase in our armaments beyond the minimum deemed essential for this purpose. The immediate needs of our Army are a professional standing Army adequate to block hostile invasion and to protect our overseas possessions during the time necessary to mobilize a citizen army. These army covering and overseas forces should comprise ground and air units, be immediately available and characterized by great mobility and striking power; their existence is as important and vital as naval forces.

Aviation has increased the power of the offense where countries at war border upon or are very close to each other, and has enhanced the power of the defense where contestants are widely separated—consequently, it is advantageous to our national policy. However, it has vital limitations and inherent weaknesses. It cannot invest or capture and hold territory—operating bases, land or floating, are absolutely essential to its operations and they have to be protected from land, air and sea attacks—operations of large air forces are dependent on at least fairly good weather—under present developments, in distant overseas flights, all available load capacity has to be devoted to fuel, leaving little space for military munitions. To date no type of airplane has been developed capable of crossing the Atlantic or Pacific with an effective military load, attacking successfully our vital areas, and returning to its base. Aviation is so expensive a weapon that no nation can afford to base its organization and supply thereof on visionary approaches, but rather on proven facts and possibilities. The "Air invasion of the United States" and the "Air defense of the United States" are conceptions of those who fail to realize the inherent limitations of aviation and to consider ocean barriers. Aircraft in sufficient numbers to threaten serious damage can be brought against us only in conjunction with sea forces or with land forces which must be met by forces identical in nature and equally capable of prolonged effort.

b. Organizational Questions

Has the introduction of aviation as an agent of national defense developed any grounds for a revision in our existing national defense organization? The committee has carefully studied this question and all associated proposals.

It is convinced of the soundness of our traditional policy of maintaining separate civil and war functions, and attributes to a large degree our present world supremacy in civil aviation to our adherence thereto.

The committee has studied the various considerations and arguments advanced during the last 16 years in behalf of the proposal to concentrate all national defense aviation under one Executive Department, i.e., a Department of Air, or a Department of National Defense with three separate subdivisions—Army, Navy and Air. Thorough study and analysis of the various European organizations indicate clearly that they accord with conditions and circumstances peculiar to Europe but have no general application to the United States or Japan, which maintain their air components as integral parts of their Army and Navy. The possibilities of economy in such a consolidation were explored with conclusions that the existing organization would be less expensive. Joining the foregoing considerations with vital and far-reaching military objections, the committee is convinced that the adoption of any plan along the lines indicated above would be a serious error, jeopardize the security of the Nation in an emergency, and be an unnecessary burden on the taxpayer.

Consideration has also been given to other organizational proposals such as: (1) Consolidating all civil (Federal) and Army aviation functions under one head, Navy aviation to remain separate as a part of the Navy; (2) creation of a Federal commission, permanent in character, to regulate national aviation. The committee feels that such approaches are merely compromises to accomplish in part the plans indicated in preceding subparagraphs. For reasons already given it cannot recommend such changes. If the proposal for a permanent Federal commission is limited to civil aviation the committee believes there may be a useful field for it, although the Bureau of Air Commerce, Department of Commerce, and the National Advisory Committee for Aeronautics now handle efficiently practically all Federal civil aviation problems. The committee realizes that the full development of aviation has not been reached and its possibilities in the future are extensive, and appreciates fully the hold aviation has on the public. However, it does not believe such considerations warrant sacrificing sound national defense principles and doctrines or placing unnecessary financial burdens.

In view of the results achieved in aviation as indicated in paragraph 2 of these conclusions the committee sees no reason for any change in organization, but does see a greater necessity for immediate financial support of the Army component.

c. Aviation Industry

The Air Corps units of the Army's covering and overseas forces must be ready at all times for war service. The next great war is likely to begin with engagements between opposing aircraft, either sea-based or land-based, and early aerial supremacy is quite likely to be an important factor. This involves many considerations, but primarily a superior supply of efficient airplanes and accessories. *An adequate aircraft industry, therefore, is essential to national defense.* Military aviation in time of war must rely largely upon airplanes built in time of war and consequently the general condition and the peace-time productive capacity of the aircraft industry are of national concern. For the first few and vitally important months of the war, the permanent aircraft industry would carry the full burden of supplying equipment and thereafter would provide in addition for the emergency industry a necessary engineering and supervisory talent.

It is difficult to determine the maximum productive capacity of the American aircraft industry in time of war, and no reliable data are available as to the maximum productive capacity of other nations. It is believed, however, that no other power could exceed the productive capacity of the highly industrialized United States. While the development of commercial aviation in the United States has been more rapid than in any other country, the number of civil and commercial airplanes produced is, however, not sufficient to maintain a satisfactory nucleus of an aircraft industry.

In the opinion of the committee a major measure to insure the existence of a satisfactory nucleus of an aircraft industry in the United States is the establishment, with the President's approval, of an annual program of procurement for the Army and the Navy. If these programs are based on a normal annual replacement of the Army's airplane strength, as recommended herein, plus that of the Navy, the committee believes that the airplane industry of the United States can be maintained on a sound basis and adequate from a national defense viewpoint.

The Government should encourage development of design and

engineering staffs of the various airplane manufacturers by a more liberal policy of design competitions and the placing of orders for experimental prototypes on a basis on which the Government bears in full the proper cost of development. Such experimental contracts should also provide for changes and additions ordered by the Government at proper increases in contract prices.

In view of the importance of the aviation industry to national defense, the committee believes the Government should not enter into competition with private industry by the manufacture of airplanes in Government factories. In the same connection, the committee believes it would be advisable for the Department of Commerce to encourage further the airplane export business.

The Air Corps Act of 1926, in the opinion of the committee, is a farsighted piece of legislation resulting from a thorough study of the subject by the Morrow Board and the Congress and at this time should not be changed. It is the view of this committee, based upon the testimony of witnesses who appeared before it, that the act permits three methods of purchasing aircraft, engines and accessories. These methods are: Purchase after design competition, purchase by negotiation, and purchase by open competition. It is the opinion of the committee that it is necessary to have these three methods of purchasing aircraft if we hope to maintain our efficiency in the air from the viewpoint of national defense. Consequently, the committee believes that the Secretary of War should have authority to use any one or any combination of the three methods of purchasing indicated above.

The committee recommends, as did the Morrow Board and Lampert committee, that proprietary design rights be fully recognized. It is further recommended that the Secretary of War give such instructions to the Department.

4. National Defense Functions, Army-Navy, Including Aviation Functions of Each

The common mission assigned to the Army and Navy and the definition of their primary and secondary functions, including aviation functions, are in general sound. Certain differences in the field of aviation and particularly in relation to aviation programs and allocations of industry for war-time production remain to be solved. These differences are not insurmountable if approached from a broad national viewpoint. The joint agencies set up by the War and Navy Departments, such as the Joint Board, the Aeronautical Board and the Army and Navy Munitions Board are adequate for the purpose, and the new and difficult questions brought up by the rapidly developing air component of each service can be settled as have other important questions.

The committee recommends:

(1) That in the determination of priorities by joint agencies, the requirements for the primary missions of both services should have precedence over requirements for secondary missions of either service. Financial programs should be based on the foregoing policy.

(2) That the War Department take up with the Navy Department the advisability of bringing all the joint agencies of the two Departments under the authority of the Joint Board functioning as a superior board for the two Departments.

5. Army Organization—Army Air Corps' Place Therein

a. General Considerations

The application of the principle, "Unity of Command," is as essential in the War Department as in an Army in the field. The military adviser to the President, as Commander in Chief, and to the Secretary of War as head of the War Department, is the Chief of Staff. The duties placed on this office by law, as well as by sound organization, require the Chief of Staff to command and control, from a purely military viewpoint, the Army and all its various parts. Consequently the committee cannot accept the various proposals seeking to separate the Air Corps from the supervision and control of the Chief of Staff. These include: (1) The reestablishment of the office of the Assistant Secretary of War for Air, and (2) placing the Air Corps under the direct control of the Secretary of War.

The Secretary of War and Chief of Staff have as planning advisers the War Department General Staff and the various chiefs of arms and services and, as directors of execution, the various Army, Corps Area and overseas commanders and many of the chiefs of the various arms and services of the War Department. The General Staff is an essential planning and coordinating element in this organization. It comprises specially trained and selected officers from all arms and services, including the Air Corps, whose tours are limited, insuring a constant turn-over. The committee is not greatly impressed with the validity of the several imputations against the General Staff. Control is always repressive when misunderstood or inimical to personal interests. The committee believes the number of Air Corps officers on the General Staff should be increased, with the object of more equitable representation and the inculcation of a broader undertsanding. Until more Air Corps officers are qualified legally for this detail, it would appear desirable to meet this recommendation by temporary attachment.

b. Administrative Organization of the Air Corps Within the Army

The primary functions of the Air Corps are twofold, i.e. (a) fighting, to be carried out by combat units, and (b) development, procurement and supply of equipment and trained personnel. The committee is convinced that these two functions should be separate and distinct, as in the other arms and services of the Army. There should be a commander of the combat units reporting directly to the Chief of Staff in peace and to the commander of the Army in war. The Chief of Air Corps, as a staff officer of the War Department, should handle the development, procurement and supply functions in the same manner as other chiefs of arms and services of the War Department. His primary qualifications should be to direct efficiently the business and commercial side of the Air Corps development and procurement problems— the ability to pilot an airplane should not be considered as a major prerequisite for this office.

The War Department policy to organize the tactical combat

units of the Air Corps located in the continental United States into a General Headquarters Air Force is advocated by the committee. It believes this force, when adequately equipped and organized, will be able to carry out all the missions contemplated for a separate or independent air force, cooperate efficiently with the ground forces and make for greater economy. It should be organized without delay and commanded by a leader with suitable general officer's rank who has had broad experience as an airplane pilot—his headquarters should be with his troops, away from Washington, and his jurisdiction should include all questions of organization, training and maneuvers, and maintenance and operation of technical equipment and inspection thereof, relative to the General Headquarters Air Force. In order to increase the readiness for field service of tactical units, mobile service and maintenance units should be created in the Air Corps to take over the administration, operation and maintenance of fields, permanent, temporary and emergency.

With a view to facilitating the combat operations of the General Headquarters Air Force, provisions should be made for adequate landing fields in all strategic areas and the maneuvers of the Air Force should include concentrations thereon and operations therefrom.

6. Air Corps Interior Organization and Strength

The existing strength in personnel and airplanes is inadequate to meet the Army requirements of the national defense. There is faulty distribution and utilization of existing airplanes in that an undue proportion are rendered unavailable for combat training and fighting purposes.

The personnel of the Air Corps should be brought up to the strength now authorized by law, but not at the expense of the rest of the Army.

The strength in airplanes recommended by the latest (1933) War Department study, viz 2,320 airplanes, is the minimum considered necessary to meet our peace-time Army requirements.

The committee believes some increase may be necessary from time to time to provide for larger reserves and as may be justified by War Department studies.

The meteorological organization should be strengthened within the Air Corps itself.

The engineering and procurement divisions of the office of the Chief of Air Corps should be perfected in organization. Officers should be developed who are specially qualified in engineering and for dealing with industry. To this end further provision should be made for sending selected officers to the best schools of technology and business administration.

7. Personnel Questions, Regular Officers of the Army, Including the Air Corps

a. The committee is convinced that the problems relating to officers, not only in the Air Corps but in the whole Army, are basic to existing difficulties. Once a reasonable solution is secured in this respect, correct and expeditious solutions to most others may be expected. Over age in grade, stagnation in promotion, and the "hump" are problems involving the whole Army. Officer shortage, rank commensurate with responsibilities and separate and single promotion lists are problems closely associated with the foregoing and will, no doubt, be solved when the former are definitely settled.

The committee did not find in the Air Corps the universally low morale claimed in some quarters. Testimony clearly indicates a fine morale on foreign service and among the young officers who carried the air mail. Uncertainty as to the promotion situation of the future and the lack of definite procurement programs and adequate flying hours have had an effect on morale.

Special steps are apparently required to overcome a tendency of the air soldiers and ground soldiers to grow apart in a professional way. It appears most desirable that steps be instituted which will amalgamate the air and ground components into a homogeneous army in which all parts play their respective roles. The ground soldier should be experienced in aviation and prepare himself for its further development in the future. The air soldier should know the ground branches and prepare himself to function as a higher commander of all branches of the Army. This conforms to the general policy followed by our Navy.

In furtherance of the foregoing general conclusions, the committee submits the following recommendations:

(1) Definite decision which will remove all uncertainty as to the future national defense position of the Army Air Corps, should be announced and adhered to for some reasonable period.

(2) There should be adopted a system of selection and retirement for officers of the whole Army similar to that now provided for the Navy and Marine Corps.

(3) Pending the time when action under the previous suggestion results within the Air Corps in rank commensurate with responsibility, place in force the provisions of the Air Corps Act of 1926, providing for temporary advance in rank.

(4) Special efforts should be made to fill all vacancies in the Air Corps by requesting Congress to grant additional funds for the 403 officers authorized in 1926.

(5) Extend for a period of 5 years the provisions of the Air Corps Act of 1926 covering the field from which the Chief of Air Corps may be selected.

(6) Require that the cadets of the United States Military Academy shall have air experience of a minimum of 20 hours as a part of the regular course at the Academy.

(7) a. Require each officer hereafter commissioned in the Army in peace, regardless of the source from which commissioned, to serve 2 years in a combat arm other than the Air Corps. Upon completion of this 2 years' detail, each officer physically qualified and not previously graduated as a pilot, to take the regular established course at the Air Corps Primary and Advanced Training School.

b. From those graduated from the Air Corps Primary and Advanced Training School assign permanently to the Air Corps those who request such assignments. Should the number so assigned be insufficient to meet the authorized strength, continue the present system of filling tactical units by Reserve officers on extended active duty, by detail of flying cadets and of enlisted pilots. The tour of extended active duty for Reserve officers and flying cadets should be extended so as to minimize the turn-over in tactical units.

(8) All Air Corps officers of 15 or less years' service should be qualified pilots. A standard qualification should be established administratively for all Air Corps officers of 15 or less years' service in the Air Corps who are placed on flying duty. This standard qualification should include annual flying as pilots of not less than 100 hours, including a reasonable percentage of cross-country, instrument, night and formation flying. Exceptions to these requirements should be made only by the approval of the Secretary of War in each specific case. Those not qualified to meet the standard qualifications should be utilized or disposed of in accordance with the following paragraph.

(9) After 15 years of service, all Air Corps officers should be tested periodically by a qualified board, to determine their qualifications as flying officers. Those capable of meeting the conditions given in (8) above, and others as deemed desirable, should be declared eligible as pilots for flying command duty, that is, to command combat squadrons and groups.

Those found disqualified as pilots for flying command duty, unless coming within the provisions of existing retirement and class B laws, should be divided into two groups—(a) those capable and qualified for nonpiloting duty in the Air Corps; (b) those not capable or qualified for piloting or non-piloting duty with the Air Corps.

The non-piloting group referred to above should include those deemed qualified for such duties as high command and staffs in the Air Corps, senior officers of the engineering group and procurement-supply group of the Air Corps. They should be required to continue aerial experience and fulfill the legal requirements to draw flying pay.

Those disqualified for Air Corps duty as per (b) above should be given the option of transferring, if qualified, to a ground branch of the Army or retiring with 2½ percent of their base pay per year of commissioned service up to 75 percent.

(10) It is believed desirable for the War Department to establish some system or policy which will insure that all officers of the Army of more than 15 years' service, especially those qualified for General Staff duty, receive experience with both ground and air branches of the Army. This should be secured not only by the staff and school system now in force, but also by temporary tours of duty with troops of other arms.

(11) Flying pay should be based primarily on hazard in performance and provision for adequate insurance for dependents. Actuarial experience data indicate that the present basis does not meet these desiderata. As all services should be treated alike, the committee believes that this question should be referred to an interdepartmental board comprising representatives of all interested governmental departments.

(12) Grant wide discretion in the application of regulations and policies affecting foreign service and detached duty to those Air Corps officers required for the development, construction, procurement, and test of technical air equipment.

8. Personnel Questions, Enlisted Men, Air Corps

In connection with the conclusions previously expressed above relative to covering and overseas forces, the committee is of the opinion that there is a marked shortage of enlisted men for the whole Army. Relative to the Army Air Corps, the committee found its enlisted strength has been brought up to adequate numbers by the transfer of several thousand enlisted men from other arms and services, thereby seriously weakening these other arms and services. The committee believes there should be a readjustment of the assignment of grades and ratings to specific tasks in the Air Corps.

9. Training Air Corps

Training of the individual at the primary and advanced flying school at the Air Corps training center is thorough and efficient except that too little attention has been paid to cross-country, instrument, night and radio beam flying, to mastery of avigation and communication instruments, and to the study of meteorology.

Unit training is not satisfactory at this time due to the lack of sufficient and suitable equipment, to frequent turnover of personnel, the absence of definite tactical doctrines and uniformity in unit training and lack of experience under field-service conditions.

In order to obtain close supervision and control over Air Corps training the committee recommends that responsibility for unit training and the training of individuals assigned to tactical units and their staffs of the General Headquarters Air Force be removed from corps area commanders and be placed on the Commanding General, General Headquarters Air Force. It is also recommended that the directive for such training be prepared by the Commanding General, General Headquarters Air Force, subject to approval by the War Department.

Responsibility for the operation of and training given at the Air Corps schools and the training of detached Air Corps officers (other than those on duty with tactical units) should remain with the Chief of the Air Corps.

The present policy of requiring Air Corps officers to attend the Command and General Staff School and the Army War College should be continued.

Frequent scheduled training of Air Corps tactical units in conjunction with ground troops should be provided.

In order that Air Corps pilots be thoroughly trained in all essentials, an average of 300 flying hours per pilot per year should be provided.

Increased provision should be made in training directives to provide for all individual officers and for tactical units sufficient time to perfect all pilots in the ability to successfully avigate on cross-country flights in all kinds of weather, by day and by night, by the use of instruments, the radio beam, and to efficiently utilize all types of communication equipment available.

In order that experience may be gained in cold weather, high and low altitude, and unfamiliar weather operations, and in the

difficulties incident thereto in engine starting, fuel, oil and servic-
ing problems, the committee recommends that frequent training
of tactical units be held in different parts of the United States under winter conditions; and, in addition thereto, that at least one
composite squadron be given opportunity for frequent training in
Alaska in all-year weather.

Sufficient airplanes should be maintained with tactical units
to provide adequate training facilities. The practice of detaching
airplanes for other purposes should be reduced to a minimum.

The committee recommends that more adequate provision be
made for ammunition and live bombs for training.

As a result of the advance in speed and general performance of
airplanes, the committee recommends the detail of one or more
flight surgeons to study and report upon the physiological effect
on pilots resulting from the high accelerations and altitudes.

As a measure of economy, the committee recommends the purchase of small, inexpensive standard commercial airplanes adequate for training of pilots with units in cross-country and night
flying.

To assist in correcting the present unsatisfactory condition of
unit training, the committee recommends the early creation of the
Air Corps Board and that when created this board give prompt
attention to the formulation of uniform tactical doctrines for all
types of Air Corps units.

The committee recommends that every available opportunity
be utilized to concentrate Air Corps tactical units by wings in the
minimum possible number of posts and stations.

The committee recommends the creation of a model Air Corps
unit at the Air Corps Tactical School for demonstration and exercises in the training of student officers and for cooperation with
the Air Corps Board in the development of tactical doctrines.

10. Equipment Questions of the Air Corps and of the Army as a Whole

The Army Air Corps has been successful in the development of
military airplanes of superior performance. From the national de-

fense viewpoint of the United States, as well as tactical requirements, its technical equipment, including airplanes, is equal or superior, with few exceptions, to that of any other nation. However, the clear mandate of the Congress in the Air Corps Act of 1926, which contemplates 1,800 serviceable airplanes, has not been made effective due to lack of appropriations. The shortage in the above program at the present time exceeds 300 airplanes. Of the airplanes in actual operation many cannot be considered modern efficient weapons of war due to their age, general unsuitability and improper type distribution. This shortage is further emphasized when the recommendation of the committee for the immediate completion of the full 2,320-airplane program is considered.

It is believed that further progress may be made in the periodic standardization of different types of airplanes, the shortening of the time between design and quantity production, and that considerable economies may be secured thereby.

The evidence presented to the committee indicates clearly that the whole Army, as well as the Air Corps, is short of modern armament, equipment, and transportation, as well as an adequate munition reserve. The War Department has developed units for all branches of the Army of modern armament, equipment, and transportation, and only needs sufficient funds with which to equip the Army.

The committee believes that more definite and continuing appropriations should be available for research and development programs. These programs of research should include studies and development relative to liquid-cooled aircraft engines of higher speed and higher horsepower; improved fuel for aircraft engines; basic aircraft materials; instruments for avigation and blind landings; communication equipment; armament, including combat equipment; mobile field and ground equipment; safety devices, including meteorological forecasts and study of air-mass analyses; facilities for improving the take-off and landing characteristics; and the construction of research equipment, including a wind tunnel for the study of the aerodynamic characteristics of wings and of control surfaces at an air speed of 500 miles per hour.

The committee invites special attention to section XII of the body of this report, where the detailed consideration of the above subjects is set forth.

11. Finance

A considerable part of the present unsatisfactory situation in the Air Corps is due to lack of appropriations. The responsibility for this is divided between the Bureau of the Budget and the Congress, with the ultimate responsibility in the Congress.

The general procedure of preparing estimates and processing the Budget from the War Department through the Bureau of the Budget to the Congress is sound and tends to economy. Throughout the process, the estimating agencies, including the Air Corps, are given full opportunity to present their requirements and defend their estimates. Coordination in the process of preparing the final estimate for all military activities is and should be placed in the office of the Secretary of War. Any restrictions on him as to the use of his advisers on the General Staff, or of any other of his officers or agencies he chooses is basically unsound from every point of view.

Failure to complete the 5-year aircraft program was largely due to failure of the Bureau of the Budget and the Congress to approve a financial program and coordinate it with the program for procurement of personnel and matériel prescribed by the law.

A balanced program covering all expenditures for military activities should be prepared and coordinated in the War Department. A separate budget uncoordinated by the War Department with other expenditures for military activities should not be provided for the Air Corps.

There should be submitted by the War Department a definite plan for the improvement of the whole Army, including the Army Air Corps. The plan for the Army Air Corps should be along the lines recommended by the latest (1933) War Department study. This plan should be accompanied by the War Department's estimate of the financial program necessary to carry it out; and this combined plan should be reviewed by the proper authority and if not approved the War Department should be given a directive as to basic changes to be made. The revised plan, including an approved financial program, thus coordinated, should then be presented to the Congress.

12. National Guard and Reserve Aviation

These components of the national defense are carrying out their peace-time missions in an excellent spirit and with the best results obtainable under restrictions which have been imposed by economy.

Practically all of the matters presented calling for remedial action are traceable to lack of funds.

The committee believes that special consideration should be given, when adequate funds can be made available, to increasing the flying equipment and to supplying combat types of airplanes and greater facilities for the training of the civilian components.

13. Civil Aviation in Relation to National Defense

Encouragement should be given to the further development of airways, air-navigation facilities, and ground facilities. Increased airway facilities covering the United States will be of value to the Air Corps from the standpoint of national defense, and with increased operation a larger reserve will be developed from which may be drawn trained personnel and flight equipment.

Air Corps airplanes should be equipped as far as desirable with suitable navigation instruments, and Air Corps pilots should be trained in the use of special instruments for operation on the national airways.

Commercial air transport pilots should be encouraged to become members of the Army Air Corps Reserve.

There should be a close liaison beween commercial and military aviation, in order to familiarize the Air Corps with the latest developments in use in commercial air transport.

The Army Air Corps should wherever possible use converted commercial air transports of acceptable performance for cargo and transport airplanes.

14. Air Mail Lessons

The committee has considered in great detail the operations of the air mail by the Army Air Corps. This experience has been invaluable and taught many lessons. These lessons have been embodied in the body of this report and in the conclusions mentioned above.

Respectfully submitted.

NEWTON D. BAKER.

H. A. DRUM, *Maj. Gen., U.S. Army.*

KARL T. COMPTON.

GEORGE W. LEWIS.

C. E. KILBOURNE, *Brig. Gen., U.S. Army.*

GEO. S. SIMONDS, *Maj. Gen., U.S. Army.*

JAMES H. DOOLITTLE.

EDGAR S. GORRELL.

J. W. GULICK, *Brig. Gen., U.S. Army.*

BENJ. D. FOULOIS, *Maj. Gen.,*
Chief of Army Air Corps.

CLARENCE D. CHAMBERLIN.

ALBERT E. BROWN, *Maj., G.S. (Inf.) U.S. Army,*
Recorder.

I believe in aviation—both civil and military. I believe that the future security of our Nation is dependent upon an adequate air force. This is true at the present time and will become increasingly important as the science of aviation advances and the airplane lends itself more and more to the art of warfare. I am convinced that the required air force can be more rapidly organized, equipped and trained if it is completely separated from the Army and developed as an entirely separate arm. If complete separation is not the desire of the committee, I recommend an air force as a part of the Army but with a separate budget, a separate promotion list and removed from the control of the General Staff. These are my sincere convictions. Failing either, I feel that the Air Corps should be developed and expanded under the direction of the General Staff as recommended above.

JAMES H. DOOLITTLE.

39. The Protective Mobilization Plan

THE BAKER BOARD HAD APPROACHED THE PROBLEMS OF WAR AND defense in the traditional theoretical way. National policy, as it said, "is based entirely upon the defense of our homeland and overseas possessions, including protection of our sea- and air-borne commerce" against generalized and unpredictable perils that the future might bring. But by the mid-1930's the perils, though still not precisely foreseeable, were becoming real and urgent. With the Japanese on the march in Manchuria, Hitler in power in Germany, and both the League of Nations and the Washington Naval Treaty system approaching collapse, the possibility of another "major emergency" was growing much more immediate than it had seemed when the traditional defense policies were developed in the 1920's. Both the Army and the Navy began to revise their war planning. The Army found that it had almost nothing to plan with; the 1920 concepts were at best out of date and had virtually disappeared for want of appropriations. In 1937 the Army began to develop a new "protective mobilization plan," making the best use of the slim resources likely to become available to it and at the same time recognizing the industrial and popular forces that had been introduced into warfare. In their annual reports for 1938 the Secretary of War, William H. Woodring, and the Chief of Staff, Malin Craig, described the situation and indicated the origins and outlines of the protective mobilization plan. Summarizing the best Army thought of the time, the P.M.P. was to provide the framework of Army planning down to the Lend-Lease Act of 1940, if not to the attack on Pearl Harbor.

Annual Report of the Secretary of War, William Woodring

Mr. PRESIDENT:

During my tenure of office as Assistant Secretary of War from 1933 to 1936 I became convinced that the then current War Department plan for mobilization in the event of major emergency contained discrepancies between the programs for procurement of

From *Annual Report of the Secretary of War, 1938* (Washington, D.C.: Government Printing Office, 1939), pp. 1–6, 29–35.

personnel and procurement of supplies which were so incompatible that the plan would prove ineffective in war time. The basic War Department mobilization plan had its genesis in the days of the World War. It was a plan worked out conscientiously by officers of high military attainments, who, as the result of their wartime experience, naturally thought in terms of the vast armies of millions mobilized for World War service. It was a plan that contemplated the use of great surpluses of supplies accumulated after the World War—supplies which by 1936 had become greatly depleted or obsolete. Furthermore, it was a plan that called for the maintenance of huge reserve supplies requiring expenditures of sums which the Congress never found it feasible to appropriate.

My duties as Assistant Secretary of War specifically charged me by law with responsibility for "the assurance of adequate provision for the mobilization of matériel and industrial organizations essential to war-time needs." It became evident to me that the War Department mobilization plan then current was gravely defective in that supplies required during the first months of a major war could not be procured from industry in sufficient quantities to meet the requirements of the mobilization program.

When I assumed the duties of Secretary of War, the General Staff had under consideration a revision of the basic War Department mobilization plan. Apart from the problem of supply procurement, the question had arisen in the War Department as to whether even the rate of personnel procurement contemplated by the original plan could be realized. My conviction on the inadequacy of the initial plan from the supply procurement standpoint was so strong that one of the first directives issued by me as Secretary of War was that the General Staff restudy the whole intricate problem of emergency mobilization with a view to complete replacement of the then current War Department mobilization plan with a program that would prove completely adequate and thoroughly practicable.

The result of that study is now found in what we term the protective mobilization plan of 1937. The 1937 plan has not been perfected; details remain to be worked out and are being worked out thoroughly and diligently. But we have every reason to believe that the protective mobilization plan is feasible and will meet our national defense requirements.

I believe the reduction of our mobilization program to sensible workable proportions to be one of the highest attainments of the War Department since the World War.

In general, the protective mobilization plan visualizes in the event of a major war immediate employment of an initial protective force of approximately 400,000 men. This force will comprise existing units of the Regular Army and National Guard at existing strength, augmented by such recruitment of personnel with prior military training as the exigencies of the military situation will permit. Under the protection of this initial defensive force there will be progressively mobilized, trained, and equipped such larger national armies as the defense of the United States demands.

In our mobilization planning and our military preparations we contemplate no aggression against any power on earth; we visualize only the possible necessity for armed defense of our own domains. The title "Protective mobilization plan" is fully indicative of our intent.

Not since the War of 1812 has a foreign invader set foot upon our soil. We are therefore too prone, I believe, to visualize preparation for a future war in the light of our preparation for war in 1917. We must not be deluded by recollection of huge cantonments where divisions had opportunity to undergo training for several months before engaging in combat. We cannot have any assurance that the military situation will permit the establishment of training centers where potential commissioned personnel may undergo instruction for comparatively long periods. Upon our entrance into the World War American industry by reason of wartime productive activities since 1914 was geared up, at least partially, to meet our own American war-time requirements. We cannot expect in the future immediate overnight transformation of American industry from a peace-time to a war-time basis. In a defensive situation we can place no dependence upon allied forces holding the battle lines while we make belated preparations for mobilization of personnel and of industry.

At the very outbreak of war the 400,000 officers and soldiers of the initial protective force must be so trained and so equipped that there can be no question whatsoever as to their ability to withstand any onslaught until such time as their thin ranks can be augmented by units of the Organized Reserves component of the Army of the United States. We place a tremendous responsibility on these first 400,000 defenders. If they fail in their protective mission the fate of the reinforcing citizens' armies is sealed.

An immediate objective of the War Department must be complete adequacy of personnel and matériel for the initial protective force. Fortunately, we require little in the form of increased personnel. Our main problem is to assure the complete equipment of our Regular Army and National Guard units and the organization of the initial protective force into a balanced force fully capable of shouldering its heavy burden. We must also provide and maintain in reserve those critical supply items which must be placed in the hands of the reinforcing units immediately upon their mobilization—those items of equipment which industry physically cannot produce until long, if not fatal, periods of time have elapsed.

Your incumbency as President of the United States[1] has been characterized by continuous improvement in our Military Establishment. When, in 1933, I first entered upon my official duties in the War Department I was discouraged to find that despite the insistent warnings of the military authorities, much of our Army existed in little more than name only. Our territorial posts were inadequately garrisoned—dangerously so. The number of Regular troops in the continental United States barely sufficed for what might be termed military "housekeeping" and overhead duties. Training was being conducted with outmoded equipment. In the development of air power, motorization, and mechanization, the rest of the world was setting a fast pace; the United

[1] Franklin Delano Roosevelt [Ed.].

States was floundering along in the ruck. What troops we had were housed to a great extent in flimsy structures erected during the World War and designed for temporary occupancy.

I can now report a far more encouraging situation than that which obtained 5 years ago. The enlisted strength of the Regular forces has been increased to a figure which permits more adequate garrisons for our critical outlying defenses and the maintenance of units within the United States at strengths which assure more efficient training. It should not be overlooked that the increase in enlisted personnel incidentally has served in no small measure to solve the unemployment problems of many ambitious youthful citizens.

Congress has authorized an increase of the commissioned personnel of the Regular Army from 12,000 to 14,659. Under that authority a few hundred additional officers have already been commissioned. We hope to attain the newly authorized strength by gradual increments over a period of 5 years. The augmentation of commissioned personnel provides additional officers for the Air Corps, for now undermanned tactical units, and for an overworked Medical Department. Eventually it will provide additional officers for instructional duty with the civilian components and activities, and to some small extent may permit the War Department to meet continuous requests for needed increases in the instructional staffs of existing Reserve Officers' Training Corps units.

The last Congress likewise authorized an increase in National Guard strength which will permit the enrollment of 205,000 during 1939.

Of great significance to the national defense was the enactment by the last Congress of a measure providing, at small cost, an Enlisted Reserve for the Regular Army. It is hoped that this Reserve eventually will reach 75,000, thus enabling units of the permanent establishment, immediately upon the outbreak of an emergency, to augment their reduced peace-time ranks by the inclusion of physically fit young soldiers who have had the advantage of one or more terms of enlistment in the Regular Army.

At the close of the World War this Nation was fortunate in having as a potential military asset more than 4,000,000 experienced World War veterans. The ravages of time have sadly reduced that number. Seventy-five thousand enlisted reservists cannot replace 4,000,000 war veterans. But these 75,000 reservists will constitute a reservoir of manpower of immeasurable value to a military force, the mission of which is wholly defensive. By the establishment of this Enlisted Reserve, the Government has wisely decreed that the military door shall not be shut in the face of the well-trained and capable discharged soldier, who, though seeking to make his mark in civil life, is willing again immediately to take his place in the ranks of the Regular Army in a period of major emergency.

Continuous progress in individual and organizational proficiency has characterized the activities of the Organized Reserves. In the event of a grave national emergency, upon the officers of this component of the Army of the United States eventually will fall the brunt of our military effort. The comparatively small sums expended for betterment of our Organized Reserves will pay manifold dividends if this reserve element of the national defense is ever summoned to the colors for war duty.

Popular interest in the citizens military training camps continues unabated. Neither funds nor facilities have permitted acceptance of the many thousands who have annually applied for enrollment in this popular democratic institution for the instruction of our youths.

The War Department is in receipt of continuous requests for increases in authorized enrollments in the advanced course of the Reserve Officers' Training Corps, for augmentation of the instructional staffs with existing units, and for the establishment of new units, attesting the popularity, the efficiency and the military value to the Nation of this activity conducted in our educational institutions.

I must not leave the impression that only in matters pertaining to personnel has the Army's efficiency been promoted. There has been provided a powerful defensive arm in the form of the General Headquarters Air Force. In creating this extremely important arm, it was necessary to do more than merely procure increased numbers of airplanes. A balanced air force had to be established—balanced in personnel, ground installations, training, and supplies. In the gradual development of this air force we constantly strove to keep abreast of rapid development of aviation equipment and technique and simultaneously to provide military aircraft of unexcelled quality. Considering our initial deficiencies, it is my opinion that we have builded wisely and well in developing our General Headquarters Air Force. The efficiency attained by that force in the few short years of its history is a most noteworthy achievement. We have a substantial framework for the extension which now appears essential.

The motor has replaced the horse as the tractive power in the supply trains of practically all our Regular Army and National Guard units. Likewise, much of the field artillery of both the permanent establishment and the National Guard has been motorized. This motorization permits both tactical mobility and economy of operation. In the procurement of antiaircraft artillery progress has been achieved, as is also true of mechanized vehicles. The Springfield rifle, of honored and most hallowed history, is being replaced by the new semi-automatic rifle which promises much for troops through speedier training and greater effectiveness of fire.

This vitalized national defense force of 1938 continues to experiment with changes in organizational strength with a view to assuring greater mobility and tactical effectiveness without lessening fire power.

Funds have been made available in recent years for comprehensive command post exercises and for large-scale maneuvers by combined arms of all the components of the Army of the United States. These exercises, so long neglected, are essential for promoting high standards of training in a modern army. Combining as they do participating personnel from the Regular Army, the National Guard, and the Organized Reserves, they go far toward fostering that most desirable conception of a single Army of the

United States in which all soldiers, be they of the permanent establishment or of the civilian components, play essential and indispensable roles.

Army housing conditions are undergoing constant improvement. Dilapidated posts, which a few years ago were eye-sores to the citizens of the neighboring municipalities, are being transformed into modern installations in which our people can have every pride. Soldiers and officers are being removed from quarters which, after years of neglect, had become little more than hovels. In the long run these sums spent on improvement of Army housing will prove a measure of very real and lasting economy. There can be no thriftiness in the fitful patching up of structures which have long outlived their usefulness.

True it is that this progress has not been made without the expenditure of considerable sums. But engulfed in succeeding so-called economy waves, the Army, its equipment, and its plants had become so run-down that the neglect of years could be rectified only by increased appropriations. In passing, I should report that considerable use has been made of so-called emergency funds in the betterment of our defensive installations. Such expenditures have served to relieve unemployment and to put both labor and capital to work. The War Department, I believe, has made wise and judicious use of these emergency funds, to the permanent economic advantage of the Nation.

I recognize that this report constitutes a summary of developments covering a period of years rather than the single fiscal year 1938. In view of the prevalent world-wide disquietude, I believe it opportune and advantageous at this time to present this summation. Improvements to our national defense installations, begun in 1933, continued during the period covered by this report. For specific recital of developments within the Army of the United States during the fiscal year 1938 I respectfully refer you to the detailed annual report of the highly capable Chief of Staff, Gen. Malin Craig.

I would be remiss did I leave the impression that we now have a completely modernized and thoroughly efficient defensive establishment. There remain deficiencies in organization, equipment, and personnel which must be corrected before we can be assured of maintenance of a military force fully adequate for our defensive needs. Specific requirements of the Military Establishment are covered in the annual report of the Chief of Staff, with whose recommendations I fully concur.

In concluding this report, I have but brief recommendations to make. I consider them recommendations of utmost importance. I reiterate that an immediate objective of the War Department must be perfection in the units which comprise our initial protective force—our peace-time establishment.

We must recognize that our initial protective force, less than half of which comprises full-time personnel of the Regular Army scattered throughout the continental United States and in our outlying territories, is a very small foundation upon which we may find it necessary to erect a towering war-time edifice. It follows that it must be a strong foundation, a perfect foundation, a foundation upon which we are at all times promptly and fully prepared to build any larger defensive structure deemed essential.

The units garrisoning our outlying defenses are components of that initial protective force. Reinforcement of those garrisons in the event of a sudden war might prove of extreme difficulty if not an impossibility. Sudden war would find the troops in the Panama Canal Department in an especially precarious situation. The defenses of the Panama Canal must be strengthened. All locks and dams on that vital waterway must be made bombproof. The possibility of sabotage by crews of ships transiting the canal must be completely eliminated. We must greatly augment our air forces and our antiaircraft artillery installations in the Panama Canal Zone. The Panama Canal must be made impregnable.

I also urgently recommend that early provision be made for the critical items with which to equip those units which, in the event of war, will follow the initial protective force into the field. We place upon the initial protective force and the larger national armies subsequently to be raised grave responsibilities; we must give them the means to accomplish the war-time mission imposed upon them by the Protective Mobilization Plan.

Annual Report of the Chief of Staff, Malin Craig

The Honorable, The SECRETARY OF WAR.

My DEAR MR. SECRETARY: I submit the following report on the state of the Military Establishment at the close of the fiscal year 1938.

The Military Establishment set up by the National Defense Act in 1920 differs fundamentally from those maintained elsewhere by the larger powers. In a special sense it is an Army of the people. Its professional component, the Regular Army, is only its nucleus. Around it the civilian components can be assembled and integrated only after an emergency arises.

The National Defense Act fixed an upper limit for the strength of this nucleus at 280,000 enlisted men. This strength it has never attained. On the contrary, in subsequent years its strength was allowed to fall to 118,500. Successive studies have indicated the grave inadequacy of this latter figure. It is a source of gratification to record that legislation enacted at the last session of Congress authorized the attainment of 165,000 enlisted men.

Our Regular Army at this latter strength ranks only eighteenth among the standing armies of the world. This marked inferiority in strength suggests that it is all the more imperative that the armament of this force be equal to that which it may be called upon to face. Here, too, we fell behind. We failed to keep pace with the development in defensive weapons that has occurred since the World War.

Among the more notable innovations in that war was the development of the airplane and the tank—arms that are essentially offensive. There was necessarily a lag in time before there could be developed weapons effective for defense against these new arms. Efficient antiaircraft and antitank armament did not appear until after the close of the war. Contemporaneously also there appeared new and greatly improved types of small arms and of various classes of howitzers.

Until the past year the limited amounts appropriated annually for armament were devoted largely to the procurement of aircraft. To a lesser extent they were applied to the procurement of tanks and similar combat vehicles. Substantially little was devoted to the new defensive weapons. Fortunately, considerably larger appropriations for rearmament were made at the last session of Congress. They will suffice for the attainment of the objective of the Baker Board, and they will permit a marked reduction in the extreme shortages of semiautomatic rifles and antiaircraft armament and the initiation of the procurement of an efficient antitank weapon.

The current operations in Spain[2] and China[3] illustrate from day to day the greatly increased power of these new defensive weapons. They have restored to the defense the superiority it seemed to lose with the advent of the new offensive arms. It is largely because of these new defensive weapons that we find current operations confirming anew the testimony of history that the Infantry is the core and the essential substance of an army. It alone of all the arms approximates a military entity. It alone can win a decision. Each of the other arms is but an auxiliary—its utility measured by the aid that it can bring to the Infantry.

It is a source of gratification to record also that during the past year our people seem to have come to a clearer understanding of the fact that our Army is purely defensive in type and nonprovocative in outlook. The charge that it is militaristic, that its activities menace peace, is now rarely heard. The facts are, of course, quite the reverse. Our Army has never in the slightest degree contributed to the occurrence of any of our wars. Throughout its entire history it has remained consistently within the field assigned to it by the Constitution—always wholly subordinate to the civil authorities. It has jealously guarded itself against political connections of any nature. It has remained true to its traditions—withdrawn and aloof in peace; a forward, dependable bulwark in war.

In the paragraphs which follow I shall endeavor to describe the present status of the Military Establishment and its more important deficiencies.

2 The Spanish Civil War (1936–1939) [Ed.].

3 The Japanese invasion of China, beginning in 1931 [Ed.].

Strength of the Regular Army

a. Enlisted men.—In the fiscal year 1938, budgetary limitations restricted the average enlisted strength of the Army to 162,000. Appropriations for the fiscal year 1939 provide for an average strength of 165,000. Heretofore, this strength has been regarded as the minimum required to provide adequate overseas garrisons and the force needed at home to perform the many tasks that devolve upon the Regular Army as the nucleus of the Military Establishment. It has been found, however, that a slightly larger enlisted strength will be necessary, primarily because of the increased needs of the Air Corps and of antiaircraft defense. Recent legislation authorizes an enlisted strength of 21,500 for the Army Air Corps. It is hoped that the necessary additional funds will be provided to bring the Air Corps enlisted strength to this figure in the fiscal year 1940. The requirements of the whole Army in that fiscal year will aggregate a total of about 168,000 enlisted men.

b. Officers.—The enactment of Public, No. 485, Seventy-fifth Congress, third session, authorizing a commissioned strength of 14,659 is an important step toward the provision of a more adequate commissioned personnel for the Army. The first increment of the increase under this general authorization is provided in the Appropriation Act for the fiscal year 1939. This act carries, in addition to increments under the Thomason and Engineer Acts, an increase of 200 officers in the Air Corps and 75 officers in the Medical Department. . . .

National Guard

Progress in the training of the National Guard is gratifying, and its readiness for combat is believed to be at the highest point of its post-war history.

Further progress has been made in obtaining equipment required for the National Guard, particularly in respect to antiaircraft armament. The appropriations for the fiscal years 1938 and 1939 will permit procurement of the major ordnance items of antiaircraft equipment required for the 10 existing National Guard antiaircraft regiments.

At its last session Congress authorized an increase of 5,000 in the National Guard, bringing its total authorized strength to 205,000. The ultimate objective is 210,000.

A few States have not provided all units with proper and adequate armory facilities. In general, however, there has been a marked improvement in such facilities and it is hoped that the deficiencies that exist will be corrected in the near future.

Organized Reserves

This component of the Army has made commendable progress during the past year. A total of 27,685 officers received active duty training compared with 24,285 during the previous fiscal year. In addition 4,704 Reserve officers were performing duties of an administrative nature with the Civilian Conservation Corps on June 30, 1938.

At the close of this fiscal year there were 100,116 Reserve officers on the rolls of the War Department eligible for assignment, active duty, and promotion, an increase of 3,571 above last year's strength. While improvement has been noted in the discharge of command and staff functions, I consider that higher standards could be attained if a greater number of Reserve officers were sent to the general and special service schools and, therefore, renew my previous recommendations that not less than 300 be sent annually. Because of increases in the strength of assignable officers and recent radical changes in the technique of warfare, 14-day training should be made available for more Reserve officers than heretofore. The rapidity with which modern wars are launched shows clearly that the time available for training after the outbreak of any emergency will be brief in comparison with our past experience. For this reason thorough training of our Organized Reserves in time of peace is imperative.

Reserve Officers' Training Corps

The interest in this activity is increasing steadily. Applications on file have more than doubled during the past year. The new programs of instruction for R. O. T. C. courses, inaugurated at the beginning of the academic year 1937–38, are regarded as a distinct improvement. The continued increase in junior and basic course enrollments has resulted in requests for a corresponding increase in advanced course enrollments. These requests could not be met because of limitation of funds. It is desirable that additional funds be provided to permit an increase of about 25 percent in advanced course enrollments, or a total of about 18,000.

Shortages in Regular Army commissioned personnel have precluded meeting the requirements for R. O. T. C. instructors. Untill these shortages are met, it will not be practicable to establish new units.

Citizens' Military Training Camps

A total of 57,073 applications was received for training at citizens' military training camps; 36,259 were authorized to attend, 33,445 reported, 32,522 were enrolled, and 21,239 completed the month of training. This is an increase of 3 percent over the number completing the training last year.

This form of training continues to be popular. In addition to the benefits derived by the trainees, and the opportunity given them to qualify for a commission in the Officers' Reserve Corps, it is of value in the training of the Reserve officer instructors in the problems of actual command.

Regular Army Reserve

In authorizing the reestablishment of the Regular Army Reserve, Congress, at its last session, restored an essential element of the national defense structure. This Reserve will be made up of men who upon completion of an enlistment in the Regular Army elect to return to civil life but are willing to enroll in the Reserve and thereby assume the obligation to return to active service in an emergency. Since they are thoroughly trained they can be utilized immediately in front line units. Enlistment in this Reserve began on July 1, 1938. The expected strength of 75,000 will not be reached for several years because only men who have completed an active tour of service will be eligible for the Reserve. The yearly increment will thus depend upon the number of qualified men leaving the service during the year.

Civilian Conservation Corps

Working harmoniously with the other Government agencies cooperating in this activity, the War Department continued to perform its administrative functions with respect to the Civilian Conservation Corps. The authorized enrolled strength was 300,-000. The maximum number of camps in operation during the year was 1,849 and the minimum 1,501.

Organization

The major factor that determines the composition and organization of a military unit is the character of its equipment. So changes in weapons or in other types of military equipment must find their reflection in corresponding changes in organization. The subject is one of continuing study. It is in recognition of the evolution in equipment that has occurred since the World War that there was instituted the test of the greatly modified Infantry division described in my last report. The first phase of the test has been completed, but further experimentation will be had before an attempt is made to reach definite conclusions as to the type of divisional organization to be adopted. For the same reason a field service test was conducted in the Eighth Corps Area during the past year of an experimental Cavalry division. The reports of the test are still undergoing study.

Other changes in organization that have occurred in the Regular Army include the addition of two batteries of field artillery to the mechanized brigade at Fort Knox, the organization of an additional regiment of antiaircraft (Fort Winfield Scott) and the organization of an additional signal company (Fort Des Moines).

In the National Guard, progress is continuing in the organization of the additional units permitted by the second increment of 5,000 men. . . .

Armament, Motorization, Mechanization, Equipment

Further progress has been made in providing the Army with modern equipment. In certain essential and critical items of equipment discussed in detail below there are, however, marked shortages:

a. Antiaircraft.—The extreme shortage of antiaircraft material has been relieved in part by the Appropriation Act of 1939. In consequence it will now be possible to provide the major items of ordnance equipment for the 15 active antiaircraft regiments of the Regular Army and National Guard, and to accumulate in war reserve stocks of certain critical items. Further appropriations, however, will be required for armament, searchlights, and fire control equipment.

b. Antitank weapons.—An imperative need is that of antitank armament. Our Army at present is wholly lacking in an effective weapon of this type. One has been developed by the Ordnance Department and will be supplied to the limited extent permitted by the appropriation for the fiscal year 1939.

c. Mechanization.—The light tank program of the Regular Army has been completed. A modern medium tank has been developed and a program for meeting requirements in this weapon will be initiated in the fiscal year 1939.

The initial equipment of the mechanized Cavalry brigade, including its artillery component, has been completed. Future programs will provide for essential replacements and expansion.

d. Field Artillery material.—The program to equip the active units of the Regular Army with the modernized 75-mm gun is nearing completion. The modification of artillery matériel for high speed transport is completed with active units, and considerable numbers of guns in reserve have been thus modified. The development of a new 105-mm howitzer for divisional artillery is well under way.

e. Airplane procurement.—Great progress has been made toward the attainment of the Baker Board objective. Funds provided in fiscal year 1939 will permit the completion of this objective. The Air Corps is now being equipped with airplanes and matériel that are the equal, if not superior, to any military planes in design, speed, endurance and suitability for the military use for which intended. This was convincingly demonstrated in February of this year by the record breaking flight to Argentina by six United States Army bombers of the Second Bombardment Group, to participate in the inaugural ceremonies at Buenos Aires. These airplanes with normal crews, equipment, and training gave a demonstration of speed, range, and navigation accuracy unexcelled by any military planes in the world.

f. Miscellaneous equipment.—The .30 caliber semiautomatic rifle is now under manufacture in quantity at a greatly reduced price, and its issue to units is proceeding under a program which will equip both the Regular Army and the National Guard. Substantial reductions are being made yearly in the shortages in other infantry weapons, searchlights, radio equipment, and gas masks.

g. Motorization.—With the funds made available for the fiscal year 1939, the motorization program will become approximately 67 percent complete for the Regular Army and 50 percent for the National Guard.

h. Seacoast defense.—The program of modernization and augmentation of the seacoast defenses of the continental United States, Hawaii, and Panama, which was begun in the fiscal year 1937, has progressed satisfactorily. Additional funds for this purpose will be available during the coming fiscal year.

Munitions

Following the adoption of the Protective Mobilization Plan, an exhaustive study was made of the War Reserves for the accomplishment of that plan. Articles of a purely military character cannot be obtained promptly from commercial sources upon the outbreak of war. They must be procured in time of peace and held in War Reserve. The quantities of each of these items that should be provided in War Reserve are those that will be needed to meet the requirements of the plan during the period that will elapse before industry can obtain a rate of production adequate to meet the then current military needs.

The total cost of the War Reserves required for the Protective Mobilization Plan is considerably less than that of the plan that it superseded. Nevertheless, our present War Reserves are far short of requirements in a number of critical items. The situation will be improved to some extent through the funds that will be available during the ensuing fiscal year, but large shortages will still remain. The removal of these shortages is a matter of major military importance. . . .

40. The Lessons of World War II

THOUGH MILITARY PLANNING IN 1938 WAS A GOOD DEAL MORE SOPHIS-ticated than in 1915, it was no more successful in bringing the United States to a military posture effective against the impending crisis. When dire emergency broke at last with the French collapse in June 1940, the Army lacked almost everything necessary to enable it to fight a major war under the new conditions; and if the Navy was in somewhat better shape, it still had many deficiencies. The nation still had some eighteen months to gear itself for the great conflict; they were by no means wasted. But when in December 1941 the Japanese precipitated us into the war we still, as in 1917, had little more than token forces available; and another year was to elapse before we could make any real contribution to the struggle. It was not until two and a half years after the bombing of Pearl Harbor that we were, with the Normandy landing and the great advances across the Pacific, to throw a decisive weight into the scales of victory.

It is quite impossible to document the innumerable trends of thought, theory, and practical decision that shaped the war effort. But in their final reports at the end of the war the three service chiefs of staff reviewed their experience and two of them—Marshall and Arnold —went at some length into the military problems of the future as they saw them.

Report of General of the Army George C. Marshall, Chief of Staff

For the Common Defense

To fulfill its responsibility for protecting this nation against foreign enemies, the Army must project its planning beyond the immediate future. In this connection I feel that I have a duty, a responsibility, to present publicly at this time my conception, from a military point of view, of what is required to prevent another international catastrophe.

For years men have been concerned with individual security. Modern nations have given considerable study and effort to the establishment of social security systems for those unable or unwise enough to provide for themselves. But effective insurance against the disasters which have slaughtered millions of people and leveled their homes is long overdue.

We finish each bloody war with a feeling of acute revulsion against this savage form of human behavior, and yet on each occasion we confuse military preparedness with the causes of war and then drift almost deliberately into another catastrophe. This error of judgment was defined long ago by Washington. He proposed to endow this nation at the outset with a policy which should have been a reasonable guarantee of our security for centuries. The cost of refusing his guidance is recorded in the sacrifice of life and in the accumulation of mountainous debts. We have continued impractical. We have ignored the hard realities of world affairs. We have been purely idealistic.

We must start, I think, with a correction of the tragic misunderstanding that a security policy is a war policy. War has been defined by a people who have thought a lot about it—the Germans. They have started most of the recent ones. The German soldier-philosopher Clausewitz described war as a special violent form of political action. Frederic of Prussia, who left Germany the

From "Biennial Report of the Chief of Staff, July 1, 1943 to June 30, 1945" and "Third Report of the Commanding General of the Army Air Forces, November 12, 1945," *The War Reports* (Philadelphia: J. B. Lippincott Company, 1947), pp. 289–296, 452–470.

belligerent legacy which has now destroyed her, viewed war as a device to enforce his will whether he was right or wrong. He held that with an invincible offensive military force he could win any political argument. This is the doctrine Hitler carried to the verge of complete success. It is the doctrine of Japan. It is a criminal doctrine, and like other forms of crime, it has cropped up again and again since man began to live with his neighbors in communities and nations. There has long been an effort to outlaw war for exactly the same reason that man has outlawed murder. But the law prohibiting murder does not of itself prevent murder. It must be enforced. The enforcing power, however, must be maintained on a strictly democratic basis. There must not be a large standing army subject to the behest of a group of schemers. The citizen-soldier is the guarantee against such a misuse of power.

In order to establish an international system for preventing wars, peace-loving peoples of the world are demonstrating an eagerness to send their representatives to such conferences as those at Dumbarton Oaks and San Francisco[1] with the fervent hope that they may find a practical solution. Yet, until it is proved that such a solution has been found to prevent wars, a rich nation which lays down its arms as we have done after every war in our history, will court disaster. The existence of the complex and fearful instruments of destruction now available make this a simple truth which is, in my opinion, undebatable.

So far as their ability to defend themselves and their institutions was concerned, the great democracies were sick nations when Hitler openly massed his forces to impose his will on the world. As sick as any was the United States of America. We had no field army. There were the bare skeletons of three and one-half divisions scattered in small pieces over the entire United States. It was impossible to train even these few combat troops as divisions because motor transportation and other facilities were lacking and funds for adequate maneuvers were not appropriated. The air forces consisted of a few partially equipped squadrons serving continental United States, Panama, Hawaii, and the

[1] At which the United Nations was founded [Ed.].

Philippines; their planes were largely obsolescent and could hardly have survived a single day of modern aerial combat. We lacked modern arms and equipment. When President Roosevelt proclaimed, on 8 September 1939, that a limited emergency existed for the United States we were, in terms of available strength, not even a third-rate military power. Some collegians had been informing the world and evidently convincing the Japanese that the young men of America would refuse to fight in defense of their country.

The German armies swept over Europe at the very moment we sought to avoid war by assuring ourselves that there could be no war. The security of the United States of America was saved by sea distances, by Allies, and by the errors of a prepared enemy. For probably the last time in the history of warfare those ocean distances were a vital factor in our defense. We may elect again to depend on others and the whim and error of potential enemies, but if we do we will be carrying the treasure and freedom of this great Nation in a paper bag.

Returning from France after the last war, with General Pershing, I participated in his endeavors to persuade the nation to establish and maintain a sound defense policy. Had his recommendations been accepted, they might have saved this country the hundreds of billions of dollars and the more than a million casualties it has cost us again to restore the peace. We might even have been spared this present world tragedy. General Pershing was asked against whom do we prepare. Obviously that question could not be answered specifically until nearly 20 years later when Adolf Hitler led the replenished armies of defeated Germany back into world conflict. Even as late as 1940 I was asked very much the same question before a committee of Congress. Not even then could I say definitely exactly where we might have to fight, but I did recall that in past wars the United States forces had fought in Latin America, in France, in Belgium, in Germany, in Russia, in Siberia, in Africa, in the Philippines, and in China, but I did not anticipate that in the near future American soldiers would fight in the heart of Burma and in the islands of the vast Pacific, and would be garrisoning areas across the entire land and water masses of the earth. From this lesson there is no alternative but that this nation must be prepared to defend its interest against any nation or combination of nations which might sometime feel powerful enough to attempt the settlement of political arguments or gain resources or territory by force of arms.

Twice in recent history the factories and farms and people of the United States have foiled aggressor nations; conspirators against the peace would not give us a third opportunity.

Between Germany and America in 1914 and again in 1939 stood Great Britain and the U.S.S.R., France, Poland, and the other countries of Europe. Because the technique of destruction had not progressed to its present peak, these nations had to be eliminated and the Atlantic Ocean crossed by ships before our factories could be brought within the range of the enemy guns. At the close of the German war in Europe they were just on the outer fringes of the range of fire from an enemy in Europe. Goering stated after his capture that it was a certainty the eastern American cities would have been under rocket bombardment had Germany remained undefeated for two more years. The first attacks would have started much sooner. The technique of war has brought the United States, its homes and factories into the front line of world conflict. They escaped destructive bombardment in the second World War. They would not in a third.

It no longer appears practical to continue what we once conceived as hemispheric defense as a satisfactory basis for our security. We are now concerned with the peace of the entire world. And the peace can only be maintained by the strong.

What then must we do to remain strong and still not bankrupt ourselves on military expenditures to maintain a prohibitively expensive professional army even if one could be recruited? President Washington answered that question in recommendations to the first Congress to convene under the United States Constitution. He proposed a program for the peacetime training of a citizen army. At that time the conception of a large professional Regular Army was considered dangerous to the liberties of the

Nation. It is still so today. But the determining factor in solving this problem will inevitably be the relation between the maintenance of military power and the cost in annual appropriations. No system, even if actually adopted in the near future, can survive the political pressure to reduce the military budget if the costs are high—and professional armies are very costly.

There is now another disadvantage to a large professional standing army. Wars in the twentieth century are fought with the total resources, economic, scientific, and human of entire nations. Every specialized field of human knowledge is employed. Modern war requires the skills and knowledge of the individuals of a nation.

Obviously we cannot all put on uniforms and stand ready to repel invasion. The greatest energy in peacetime of any successful nation must be devoted to productive and gainful labor. But all Americans can, in the next generations, prepare themselves to serve their country in maintaining the peace or against the tragic hour when peace is broken, if such a misfortune again overtakes us. This is what is meant by Universal Military *Training*. It is not universal military *service*—the actual induction of men into the combatant forces. Such forces would be composed during peacetime of volunteers. The trainees would be in separate organizations maintained for training purposes only. Once trained, young men would be freed from further connection with the Army unless they chose, as they now may, to enroll in the National Guard or an organized reserve unit, or to volunteer for service in the small professional army. When the Nation is in jeopardy they could be called, just as men are now called, by a committee of local neighbors, in an order of priority and under such conditions as directed at that time by the Congress.

The concept of universal military training is not founded, as some may believe, on the principle of a mass army. The Army has been accused of rigidly holding to this doctrine in the face of modern developments. Nothing, I think, could be farther from the fact, as the record of the mobilization for this war demonstrates. Earlier in this report I explained how we had allocated manpower to exploit American technology. Out of our entire military mobilization of 14,000,000 men, the number of infantry troops was less than 1,500,000 Army and Marine.

The remainder of our armed forces, sea, air, and ground, was largely fighting a war of machinery. Counting those engaged in war production there were probably 75 to 80,000,000 Americans directly involved in prosecution of the war. To technological warfare we devoted 98 percent of our entire effort.

Nor is it proposed now to abandon this formula which has been so amazingly successful. The harnessing of the basic power of the universe will further spur our efforts to use brain for brawn in safeguarding the United States of America.

However, technology does not eliminate the need for men in war. The air forces, which were the highest developed technologically of any of our armed forces in this war, required millions of men to do their job. Every B-29 that winged over Japan was dependent on the efforts of 12 officers and 73 men in the immediate combat area alone.

The number of men that were involved in the delivery of the atomic bomb on Hiroshima was tremendous. First we had to have the base in the Marianas from which the plane took off. This first required preliminary operations across the vast Pacific, thousands of ships, millions of tons of supply, the heroic efforts of hundreds of thousands of men. Further, we needed the B-20's and their fighter escort which gave us control of the air over Japan. This was the result of thousands of hours of training and preparation in the U. S., and the energies of hundreds of thousands of men.

The effect of technology on the military structure is identical to its effect on the national economy. Just as the automobile replaced the horse and made work for millions of Americans, the atomic explosives will require the services of millions of men if we are compelled to employ them in fighting our battles.

This war has made it clear that the security of the Nation, when challenged by an armed enemy, requires the services of virtually all able-bodied male citizens within the effective military age group.

In war the nation cannot depend on the numbers of men willing to volunteer for active service; nor can our security in peace.

In another national emergency, the existence of a substantial portion of the nation's young manpower already trained or in process of training, would make it possible to fill out immediately the peacetime ranks of the Navy, the Regular Army, the National Guard, and the Organized Reserve. As a result our armed forces would be ready for almost immediate deployment to counter initial hostile moves, ready to prevent an enemy from gaining footholds from which he could launch destructive attacks against our industries and our homes. By this method we would establish, for the generations to come, a national military policy: (1) which is entirely within the financial capabilities of our peacetime economy and is absolutely democratic in its nature, and (2) which places the military world and therefore the political world on notice that this vast power, linked to our tremendous resources, wealth, and production, is immediately available. There can be no question that all the nations of the world will respect our views accordingly, creating at least a probability of peace on earth and of good will among men rather than disaster upon disaster in a tormented world where the very processes of civilization itself are constantly threatened.

The decision in this matter is so grave in consequences that it demands complete frankness on my part. Therefore I must say that many of the objections which have been made to Universal Military Training appear to be influenced by ulterior motives, or to ignore completely the tragedies of the past and present which we are seeking to avoid for the future. They often seem to give undue importance to restrictions on our freedom of life, trivial in comparison with the awful tragedies we are seeking to avoid and the great blessings we hope to secure for succeeding generations.

The timing of our decision on the question of Universal Military Training is urgent. The officials of the State Department have been strongly of the opinion that a decision in this matter prior to the final peace negotiations would greatly strengthen the hand of the United States in securing acceptance of a genuine organization to handle international differences.

The terms of the final peace settlement will provide a basis for determining the strength of the regular or permanent postwar military forces of the United States, air, ground, and naval, but they cannot, in my opinion, alter the necessity for a system of Universal Military Training.

The yardstick by which the size of the permanent force must be measured is maximum security with minimum cost in men, materiel, and maintenance. So far as they can foresee world conditions a decade from now, War Department planners, who have taken every conceivable factor into consideration, believe that our position will be sound if we set up machinery which will permit the mobilization of an army of 4,000,000 men within a period of 1 year following any international crisis resulting in a national emergency for the United States.

The Regular Army must be comprised largely of a strategic force, heavy in air power, partially deployed in the Pacific and the Caribbean ready to protect the Nation against a sudden hostile thrust and immediately available for emergency action wherever required. It is obvious that another war would start with a lightning attack to take us unaware. The pace of the attack would be at supersonic speeds of rocket weapons closely followed by a striking force which would seek to exploit the initial and critical advantage. We must be sufficiently prepared against such a threat to hold the enemy at a distance until we can rapidly mobilize our strength. The Regular Army, and the National Guard, must be prepared to meet such a crisis.

Another mission of the Regular Army is to provide the security garrisons for the outlying bases. We quickly lost the Philippines, Guam, and Wake Islands at the beginning of this war and are still expending lives and wealth in recovering them.

The third mission of the permanent Army is to furnish the overhead, the higher headquarters which must keep the machine and the plans up to date for whatever national emergency we may face in the future. This overhead includes the War Department, the War College, the service schools, and the headquarters of the military areas into which continental United States is subdivided to facilitate decentralized command and coordination of the peacetime military machine. This was about all we had on the eve of this war, planners and a small number of men who had little to handle in practice but sound ideas on how to employ the wartime hosts that would be gathered in the storm. Had it not been for the time the British Empire and the Soviets bought us, those plans and ideas would have been of little use.

The fourth and probably the most important mission of the Regular Army is to provide the knowledge, the expert personnel, and the installations for training the citizen-soldier upon whom, in my view, the future peace of the world largely depends.

Of the citizen army, the National Guard is in the first category of importance. It must be healthy and strong, ready to take its place in the first line of defense in the first weeks of an emergency, and not dependent upon a year or more of training before it can be conditioned to take the field against a trained enemy. It is not feasible under the conditions of peace for the National Guard within itself to provide the basic, the fundamental training which is an imperative requirement for its mission. Therefore, in my opinion, based on a long and intimate experience with the Guard from 1907 until 1941, the essential requirement for such a system under modern conditions is Universal Military Training from which to draw the volunteers for the ranks of the Guard. Without such a firm foundation, I am clearly of the opinion that a sufficiently dependable force for our postwar needs cannot be maintained.

The second important component of the citizen army is the Organized Reserve through which full mobilization of the nation's resources to war footing is accomplished. . . . Only by universal military training can full vigor and life be instilled into the Reserve system. It creates a pool of well-trained men and officers from which the National Guard and the Organized Reserves can draw volunteers; it provides opportunities for the

Guard and Reserve units to participate in corps and Army maneuvers, which are vital preparations to success in military campaigns. Without these trained men and officers, without such opportunities to develop skill through actual practice in realistic maneuvers, neither the Regular Army, the National Guard, nor the Reserve can hope to bring high efficiency to their vital missions. . . .

Report of General of the Army H. H. Arnold,
Commanding General, Army Air Forces

Air Power and the Future

1. The Characteristics of Modern War

Wars are fought today not solely by Ground, Naval and Air Forces but by all citizens united in a joint effort which touches every phase of national and private life. The danger zone of modern war is not restricted to battle lines and adjacent areas but extends to the innermost parts of a nation. No one is immune from the ravages of war.

With present equipment, an enemy Air Power can, without warning, pass over all formerly visualized barriers or "lines of defense" and can deliver devastating blows at our population centers and our industrial, economic or governmental heart even before surface forces can be deployed. Our own Air Force, when mobilized and deployed, would have a similar capability and might attack an enemy within hours instead of the days, weeks, or months, required by our surface forces.

Future attack upon the United States may well be without warning, except what may be obtained from an active national intelligence agency.

In any future war the Air Force, being unique among armed services in its ability to reach any possible enemy without long delay, will undoubtedly be the first to engage the enemy and, if this is done early enough, it may remove the necessity for extended surface conflict.

It is entirely possible that the progressive development of the air arm, especially with the concurrent development of the atomic explosive, guided missiles, and other modern devices will reduce the requirement for or employment of mass armies and navies. These latter forces must have sufficient rapidity of movement or be sufficiently dispersed at all times to avoid location and destruction by future airborne power.

Air superiority accordingly is the first essential for effective offense as well as defense. A modern, autonomous, and thoroughly trained Air Force in being at all times will not alone be sufficient, but without it there can be no national security.

2. Teachings of World War II

As a nation we were not prepared for World War II. Yes, we won the war, but at a terrific cost in lives, human suffering, and material, and at times the margin of winning was narrow. History alone can reveal how many turning points there were, how many times we were near losing, and how our enemies' mistakes often pulled us through. In the flush of victory, some like to forget these unpalatable truths.

Our enemies' blunders, not likely to be repeated in the future, contributed materially to Allied victory. Among them were the following:

a. Germany's underestimate of the power, technological resources, and the determination of the Royal Air Force in the Battle of Britain.

b. The failure of Germany to invade England, which would have been possible after Dunkerque.

c. Underestimation of the temper and power of the United States.

d. The failure of Germany to appreciate the threat of the United States heavy bombers, and to understand and adopt the strategic uses of Air Power.

e. Germany's incapacity to understand the Soviet Union's determination to maintain its integrity, and to realize the power with which it would back that determination.

f. The failure of Japan to invade Hawaii after the Pearl Harbor attack.

g. The failure of Japan to secure bases in Australia.

Although we were woefully unprepared as a nation, we still had the time so essential to build a military force, time given us by our Allies fighting with their backs to the wall, and by the distance of oceans. That precious time without doubt will not be given us again.

Today many modern war devices of great destructive power can be built piecemeal and under cover. Sub-assemblies might be secretly made in underground laboratories, and assembled into an annihilating war machine. War may descend upon us by thousands of robots passing unannounced across our shorelines—unless we act now to prevent them.

Today, Japanese and German cities lie in ruins, but they merely suggest the vast destruction that can be done with the weapons of tomorrow. The first target of a potential aggressor might well be our industrial system or our major centers of population. If the United States is to be secure in the future, we must never relinquish the means of preventing such a blow.

The AAF's [Army Air Force's] size and power have been achieved only by tremendous efforts and expenses which, to a large extent, might have been unnecessary if as a nation we had been realistic about war from 1930 to 1940.

What we shall lose in size as a peacetime Air Force, we must compensate for in the lessons we have learned in two world wars. Equally with the problems of today, the problems which may have to be faced in 1975 or 1985 will require imagination, boldness, and the utilization of available skills, manpower, resources.

It is recalled that at the outset of this war, some of the leading aircraft manufacturers in the country stated that they could not make the necessary number of airplanes in the time set. They also believed that only aircraft companies could manufacture aircraft because of the precision methods required. As it turned out, automobile, refrigerator, radio and other manufacturers quickly learned to produce aircraft and related equipment with precision methods.

Certain strategic and critical materials necessary to the AAF might be difficult to procure in time of war. Such materials must be procured in time of peace and a sufficient stockpile maintained.

The training of personnel in time of war, like the production of materials, can only be done in a wholesale manner by utilizing all available facilities and experienced operators wherever found. While we trained men in new skills, we also went to the shops, garages, laboratories, and factories of the Nation and adapted old skills to new military jobs. Ingenuity of this kind kept us going through a very critical period.

As we think of the future, we would do well to remember that any United States preparation for preserving the peace would be incomplete without participation by other nations of this hemisphere. The American Republics must work together in ever closer unity. To this end, military equipment, training and indoctrination should be standardized as much as possible among these nations, especially in the technical field of aviation.

Since the birth of this Nation, the people of the United States, peace-loving and hoping for world-wide acceptance of our concept of democracy, have never sponsored a strong peacetime military organization. History has demonstrated that we have thereby neither avoided war nor deterred others from going to war.

We cannot measure the price which we have paid in lives and effort for the wars in which we have participated. We cannot know for certain to what extent the maintenance of a strong peacetime military organization would have reduced the price we have paid in past wars, nor to what degree such an organization would have worked toward the maintenance of world peace. We do know, however, that the course which we have followed in the past has not achieved the goal which we sought. Might it not now be wise to try the alternative course of action in the hope that it will bring us what we seek—world peace and our own security?

3. AIR POWER AND AIR FORCE

Air Power includes a nation's ability to deliver cargo, people, destructive missiles and war-making potential through the air to a desired destination to accomplish a desired purpose.

Air Power is not composed alone of the war-making components of aviation. It is the total aviation activity—civilian and military, commercial and private, potential as well as existing.

Military Air Power—or Air Force—is dependent upon the air potential provided by industry which, in turn, thrives best in an atmosphere of individual initiative and private enterprise. Government can do much to increase this air potential by judicious use of its coordinating and planning powers.

An Air Force is always verging on obsolescence and, in time of peace, its size and replacement rate will always be inadequate to meet the full demands of war. Military Air Power should, therefore, be measured to a large extent by the ability of the existing Air Force to absorb in time of emergency the increase required by war together with new ideas and techniques.

National safety would be endangered by an Air Force whose doctrines and techniques are tied solely to the equipment and processes of the moment. Present equipment is but a step in progress, and any Air Force which does not keep its doctrines ahead of its equipment, and its vision far into the future, can only delude the nation into a false sense of security.

Further, our concept of the implements of Air Power should not be confined to manned vehicles. Controlled or directed robots will be of increasing importance, and although they probably will never preclude some form of human guidance, reliance upon direct manual skills in pilotage will gradually decrease.

In practical terms for the immediate future, the doctrine of Air Force growing out of the larger concept of Air Power can be expressed as a determination:

1. To maintain a striking air arm in being.

2. To keep the AAF and the aviation industry able to expand harmoniously as well as rapidly.

3. To maintain well-equipped overseas bases.

4. To support an alert and aggressive system of commercial air transportation—one of the foundations of American Air Power.

5. To remember that it is the team of the Army, Navy and Air Forces working in close cooperation that gives strength to our armed services in peace or war.

6. To make available to the United Nations Organization, in accordance with the provisions of its Charter, adequate and effective Air Force contingents for possible use by the Security Council in maintaining international peace and security.

7. To promote scientific research and development, and to maintain a close contact with industry.

In accordance with its plan for transition from war to peace, the AAF will reduce its officer and enlisted personnel to less than one fifth of its war strength. There will also be an orderly reduction in the number of installations, and the surplus airplanes will be disposed of in a manner which will not disorganize the aircraft industry. Prompt and speedy disposal of surpluses is a keystone to our postwar progress and a healthy aviation industry.

Equally important at the present time is the retention of sufficient personnel, equipment and facilities to maintain adequate Occupation Air Forces and to provide for the supply and rotation of personnel in Europe and the Pacific, the streamlining of domestic commands for peacetime functions and the adjustment of air transport to military needs.

The discharge of AAF personnel is in accordance with the policies of the War Department. No officer or enlisted man will be retained in uniform longer than he is absolutely needed; no office will be continued longer than it has essential work to do.

Our Air Force must be flexible in its basic structure and capable of successfully adapting itself to the vast changes which are bound to come in the foreseeable future. Whatever its numerical size may be, it must be second to none in range and striking power.

4. Air Operations and Strategic Theory

The Strategic Theory, upon which were based the major air operations in World War II, was not new. Its application, however, was new, and in the course of the war the original concept was greatly extended.

The Strategic Theory, as applied to the United States air warfare concept, postulates that air attack on internal enemy vitals can so deplete specific industrial and economic resources, and on occasion the will to resist, as to make continued resistance by the enemy impossible.

To accomplish the strategic purpose, it is necessary to destroy only a small proportion of industry, probably not more than a fraction of the total required to conduct modern warfare on a large scale. Indiscriminately widespread destruction of enemy industry is simply a waste of effort.

Examination of any national economy will disclose several specific industries or other national activities without which the nation cannot effectively carry on modern warfare. It is conceivable that there will always be one industry, such as the oil industry in Germany, so necessary to all phases of the national war-making ability that its destruction would be fatal to the nation.

The real effect of our strategic air assaults, unlike that of tactical air attack, was seldom immediately apparent. Its effect was more like that of cancer, producing internal decay ultimately resulting in death.

Strategic air assault is wasted if it is dissipated piecemeal in sporadic attacks between which the enemy has an opportunity to readjust defenses or to recuperate.

The following principles should guide those who are responsible for planning and conducting strategic air warfare:

a. Through a world-wide intelligence system, maintain constantly up-to-date information regarding all phases of the national life, economy and philosophy of potential enemy states.

b. Maintain an analysis, continuously being revised to meet new conditions, to show the importance of all industries and other activities of potential enemies and to evaluate the relative importance of each of the units in each activity.

c. To meet any emergency with the rapidity which survival in future wars will necessitate, prepare and maintain plans, in consonance with the latest information to provide for destruction of the decisive units of the key industries and other activities of each potential enemy nation.

d. After a soundly conceived and carefully prepared strategic campaign has been launched, carry it through inexorably and without interruption. Diversion of effort to purposes of momentary importance will endanger the success of a whole air campaign.

Operations of an Air Force can no longer be considered as being local in extent or limited in range. Bombers can now range the world, and we must have the necessary facilities such as well-equipped bases, meteorological information, communications and other devices including radar, to provide for such employment.

Long-range escort fighters, at one time considered impossible, are both practical and essential to bombing operations.

Accurate day and night operations in all weather are essential in maintaining pressure on the enemy, magnifying his requirements for defense, interfering with his production, and attacking movements of troops and supplies which have been driven to rely on protection of darkness and bad weather.

The searching and destructive power of aerial operations is so great that few targets on earth are safe in spite of armor or anti-aircraft guns or camouflage. Dispersion, active defenses and passive defenses, such as going underground, multiply the cost and provide protection only with tremendous expenditure of effort by the enemy.

Regardless of the role that surface forces may play, the establishment of air superiority is a prerequisite to any successful ground or naval action.

The basic planning, development, organization and training of the Air Force must be well rounded, covering every modern means of waging air war, and the techniques of employing such means must be continuously developed and kept up to date. The Air Force doctrines likewise must be flexible at all times and entirely uninhibited by tradition.

Air Force is a complex combination of many types of airplanes, weapons, personnel, units and tactics, supported by the industrial and scientific resources of the nation. New weapons and new developments, including the use of atomic energy, have not basically altered this principle of modern war. This country must plan and build its military establishment with full knowledge that the methods of waging war now are changing at a rate never equalled in history.

Air operations, once surface forces are near engagement, become more intimately related to the surface operations. In determining doctrine, organization and provision of equipment careful consideration must be given to this fact.

Both photographic and visual air reconnaissance are essential to the efficient conduct of modern war. These are necessary to guard against surprise and to avoid wasteful expenditures in useless attacks on targets already destroyed, as well as to preclude omission of important military objectives and to provide briefing material for attack. Evaluation of the ultimate effect on enemy resources also comes in part from these activities.

Airborne troops have become one of the most effective units of a modern fighting force and the development of equipment and techniques for their employment must be given continuous and imaginative attention. . . .

7. New Concepts

A future Air Force developed in the light of the basic principles I have mentioned, together with provision for training and for constant supporting Intelligence, will enable the United States to face the future with confidence. Such an Air Force will constitute a base from which required departures can be made with least loss of time or effectiveness.

We must look at the future of aerial warfare in the light of the following considerations:

1. Aircraft, piloted or pilotless, will move at speeds far beyond the velocity of sound, well over 700 miles per hour.

2. Improvements in aerodynamics, propulsion, and electronic control will enable unmanned devices to transport means of destruction to targets at distances up to many thousands of miles. However, until such time as guided missiles are so developed that there is no further need for manned aircraft, research in the field of "conventional" aircraft of improved design must be vigorously pursued.

3. Small amounts of explosive materials, as in atomic bombs, will cause destruction of many square miles.

4. Defense against present-day aircraft may be perfected by target-seeking missiles.

5. Only aircraft or missiles moving at extreme speeds will be able to penetrate enemy territory protected by such defenses.

6. A communications system between control center and each individual aircraft will be established.

7. Location and observation of targets, take-off, navigation and landing of aircraft, and communications will be independent of visibility or weather.

8. Fully equipped airborne task forces will be able to strike at far distant points and will be totally supplied by air.

(A) *Influence of Atomic Energy on Air Power.* The influence of atomic energy on Air Power can be stated very simply. It has made Air Power all-important. Air Power provides not only the best present means of striking an enemy with atomic bombs, but also the best available protection against the misuse of atomic explosives.

Use of atomic energy for propelling aircraft has also been suggested. This development seems rather far in the future, so that it is difficult today to predict the types of aircraft—or space craft—which may later be propelled in this fashion. The immediate danger to civilization raised by the very existence of atomic bombs is so great that we shall do better to concentrate our attention on the role of present-day power as a means of employing atomic bombs offensively, for instance for possible enforcement of decisions of the Security Council of the United Nations, and as a safeguard against their irresponsible use in aggression.

The chief difference between an atomic bomb and the largest conventional type of bomb lies in the immense destructive power of a single atomic missile. This means that measures intended for protection against an atomic bomb attack must be highly efficient from the very start of a war if they are to be any good at all. Our experience in this war has shown that it is most difficult to attain this goal.

Further, the great unit cost of the atomic bomb means that as nearly as possible every one must be delivered to its intended target. This can be done in one of several ways, all of which involve air power. For example, the following evolution may be suggested:

a. Today, our Army Air Forces are the recognized masters of strategic bombing. Until others can match the present efficiency of our own anti-aircraft defenses, we can run a large air operation for the sole purpose of delivering one or two atomic bombs. Our experience in the war suggests that the percentage of failures in an operation of this kind would be low.

b. When improved antiaircraft defenses make this impracticable, we should be ready with a weapon of the general type of the German V-2 rocket, having greatly improved range and precision, and launched from great distances. V-2 is ideally suited to deliver atomic explosives, because effective defense against it would prove extremely difficult.

c. If defenses which can cope even with such a 3,000-mile-per-hour projectile are developed, we must be ready to launch such projectiles nearer the target, to give them a shorter time of flight and make them harder to detect and destroy. We must be ready to launch them from unexpected directions. This can be done from true space ships, capable of operating outside the earth's atmosphere. The design of such a ship is all but practicable today; research will unquestionably bring it into being within the foreseeable future.

Three types of defense against the atomic bomb can be conceived: first, we should attempt to make sure that nowhere in the world are atomic bombs being made clandestinely; second, we should devise every possible active defense against an atomic bomb attack, once launched; and third, we might redesign our country for minimum vulnerability to atomic bomb attack. All three could, of course, be combined.

Complete dispersal of our cities and moving vital industries underground on a sufficiently large scale would be overwhelmingly expensive. In addition to the expense, the unsolved technological problems would present the greatest difficulty.

Unceasing patrol of the entire world, possibly under the guidance of the United Nations Organization, would do much to prevent the illegal manufacture of atomic bombs in their present form. This, however, would be only a partial solution of the problem. In any event, air patrol, supplemented under international agreements by ground inspection, should be employed to the maximum possible extent. The Air Forces used for patrol of this kind might very well be those air contingents which are made available to the Security Council for possible enforcement action.

Although there now appear to be insurmountable difficulties in an active defense against future atomic projectiles similar to the German V-2 but armed with atomic explosives, this condition should only intensify our efforts to discover an effective means of defense.

Meanwhile, the only known effective means of delivering atomic bombs in their present stage of development is the very heavy bomber, and that is certain of success only when the user has air superiority. This fact, although perhaps true only temporarily, points up the urgent necessity for the maximum effort on air defense, both in the air and on the ground. For the moment at least, absolute air superiority in being at all times, combined with the best antiaircraft ground devices, is the only form of defense that offers any security whatever, and it must continue to be an essential part of our security program for a long time to come.

While this country must employ all of its physical and moral force in the cause of peace, it must recognize that real security against atomic weapons in the visible future will rest on our ability to take immediate offensive action with overwhelming force. It must be apparent to a potential aggressor that an attack on the United States would be immediately followed by an immensely devastating air-atomic attack on him.

The atomic weapon thus makes offensive and defensive Air Power in a state of immediate readiness the primary requisite of national survival. . . .

10. Public Understanding of Air Power

It is the American people who will decide whether this Nation will continue to hold its air supremacy.

In the final analysis, our air striking force belongs to those who come from the ranks of labor, management, the farms, the stores, the professions, the schools and colleges and the legislative halls.

Air Power will always be the business of every American citizen. The Army Air Forces recognizes its duty in formulating intelligent programs of education to the end that the public will understand aviation in all of its forms as well as realize the danger of unpreparedness in the air.

Propaganda has no place in this program. Public relations must give the public a thorough understanding of the general problems of war mobilization of aviation, and especially of military Air Power. The Air Force public relations policy and the educational program should be steered along sound lines by a directorate or committee composed of individuals trained not only as writers and reporters but also as technical specialists.

11. Integration of Air Power into National Defense

The greatest lesson of this war has been the extent to which air, land and sea operations can and must be coordinated by joint planning and unified command. The attainment of better coordination and balance than now exists between services is an essential of national security.

Unity of command is not alone sufficient. Unity of planning, unity of common item procurement and unity of doctrines are equally necessary. In addition, Ground, Naval and Air Forces must each have an equal voice as well as an equal responsibility in all plans and policies. Maximum efficiency and economy cannot be attained when one type of force is subservient to another in planning or operational councils. The full capabilities of the subservient force will never be exploited efficiently and serious blunders are bound to follow.

In order to secure the maximum effectiveness with the greatest economy, our fighting forces must be organized so as to provide soundly integrated command of three autonomous services, each of which has an equal and direct share of the total responsibility.

The Joint Chiefs of Staff organization presided over by the

Chief of Staff to the President, as developed during World War II, proved itself sound, and made coordination of effort possible not only among our own armed services but also with our Allies. This organization should be continued in time of peace when the absence of the compulsions of war make cooperation and coordination of effort much more difficult to achieve.

The following requirements, in my opinion, must accordingly be met:

A. Organization. (1) One integrated, balanced United States military organization that will establish, develop, maintain and direct at the minimum expense the forces, including the mobile striking forces, required for peace enforcement and for national security with the capability for the most rapid expansion in case of all-out war.

(2) Retention of the Joint Chiefs of Staff organization with a Chief of Staff to the President.

(3) The size and composition of our striking forces to be based on:

(a) Capabilities and limitations of possible enemies.

(b) Effectiveness and employment of modern weapons of war.

(c) The geographical position of the United States, its outlying bases and such other bases as it might control or use.

(4) Maximum economy and efficiency to be secured by:

(a) Ruthless elimination of all arms, branches, services, weapons, equipment or ideas whose retention might be indicated only by tradition, sentiment or sheer inertia.

(b) Ruthless elimination of duplication throughout the entire organization.

B. Principles. (1) The above organization, to attain its objectives, must adhere rigidly to the following principles:

(a) Development of the Intelligence necessary for the effective application of our military force to whatever job it may be called upon to do.

(b) Continuous planning for both offensive and defensive

operations against all potential enemies, taking into account their capabilities and possible intentions.

(c) Planning for, and direction of technical research to ensure that the most modern weapons are being developed, tested and service tested in order to retain for the United States military equipment its present preeminent position.

(d) Development and application of the most effective tactics and techniques.

(e) Realistic recommendations for Congressional appropriations for military purposes and for the distribution of these appropriations where they will produce the maximum benefit to the national security.

The Air Forces must also assume their full responsibility, under the provisions of the Charter of the United Nations Organization, to hold immediately available national Air Force contingents for combined enforcement action. These forces must be of sufficient strength, and their degree of readiness must be such as to make effective use of their inherent striking power and mobility.

World War II brought unprecedented death and destruction to war-making and peace-loving nations alike, and as any future war will be vastly more devastating, the mission of the armed forces of the United States should be not to prepare for war, but to prevent war to insure that peace be perpetuated.

41. Harry S. Truman Faces a Revolutionary Future

IN HIS SECOND ANNUAL MESSAGE, JANUARY 6, 1947, PRESIDENT TRUMAN raised the two massive questions that the war had presented to American military thought. One concerned the control of atomic energy and the strategy of nuclear weapons; the other concerned the reorganization of the traditional military establishments and, indeed, of the whole defense structure to take account not only of nuclear weapons but also of many other revolutionary changes that the great struggle had introduced into all the problems of war and international politics. No lasting solution was to be found for either, at the time, although the National Security Act of 1947, which only partially followed the President's recommendations, was to provide a temporary answer for the second.

ATOMIC ENERGY

The United States has taken the lead in the endeavor to put atomic energy under effective international control. We seek no monopoly for ourselves or for any group of nations. We ask only that there be safeguards sufficient to insure that no nation will be able to use this power for military purposes. So long as all governments are not agreed on means of international control of atomic energy, the shadow of fear will obscure the bright prospects for the peaceful use of this enormous power.

In accordance with the Atomic Energy Act of 1946, the Commission established under that law is assuming full jurisdiction over domestic atomic energy enterprise. The program of the Commission will, of course, be worked out in close collaboration with the military services in conformity with the wish of the Congress, but it is my fervent hope that the military significance of atomic energy will steadily decline. We look to the Commission to foster the development of atomic energy for industrial use and scientific and medical research. In the vigorous and effective development of peaceful uses of atomic energy rests our hope that this new force may ultimately be turned into a blessing for all nations.

MILITARY POLICY

In 1946 the Army and Navy completed the demobilization of their wartime forces. They are now maintaining the forces which we need for national defense and to fulfill our international obligations.

We live in a world in which strength on the part of peace-loving nations is still the greatest deterrent to aggression. World stability can be destroyed when nations with great responsibilities neglect to maintain the means of discharging those responsibilites.

From *Public Papers of the Presidents of the United States, Harry S. Truman, 1947* (Washington, D.C.: Government Printing Office, 1963), pp. 10–12.

This is an age when unforseen attack could come with unprecedented speed. We must be strong enough to defeat, and thus forestall, any such attack. In our steady progress toward a more rational world order, the need for large armed forces is progressively declining; but the stabilizing force of American military strength must not be weakened until our hopes are fully realized. When a system of collective security under the United Nations has been established, we shall be willing to lead in collective disarmament, but, until such a system becomes a reality, we must not again allow ourselves to become weak and invite attack.

For those reasons, we need well-equipped, well-trained armed forces and we must be able to mobilize rapidly our resources in men and material for our own defense, should the need arise.

The Army will be reduced to 1,070,000 officers and men by July 1, 1947. Half of the Army will be used for occupation duties abroad and most of the remainder will be employed at home in the support of these overseas forces.

The Navy is supporting the occupation troops in Europe and in the Far East. Its fundamental mission—to support our national interests wherever required—is unchanged. The Navy, including the Marine Corps, will average 571,000 officers and men during the fiscal year 1948.

We are encountering serious difficulties in maintaining our forces at even these reduced levels. Occupation troops are barely sufficient to carry out the duties which our foreign policy requires. Our forces at home are at a point where further reduction is impracticable. We should like an Army and a Navy composed entirely of long-term volunteers, but in spite of liberal inducements the basic needs of the Army are not now being met by voluntary enlistments.

The War Department has advised me that it is unable to make an accurate forecast at the present time as to whether it will be possible to maintain the strength of the Army by relying exclusively on volunteers. The situation will be much clearer in a few weeks, when the results of the campaign for volunteers are known. The War Department will make its recommendations as to the need for the extension of Selective Service in sufficient time to enable the Congress to take action prior to the expiration of the present law of March 31st. The responsibility for maintaining our armed forces at the strength necessary for our national safety rests with the Congress.

The development of a trained citizen reserve is also vital to our national security. This can best be accomplished through universal training. I have appointed an Advisory Commission on Universal Training to study the various plans for a training program, and I expect that the recommendations of the Commission will be of benefit to the Congress and to me in reaching decisions on this problem.

The cost of the military establishment is substantial. There is one certain way by which we can cut costs and at the same time enhance our national security. That is by the establishment of a single Department of National Defense. I shall communicate with the Congress in the near future with reference to the establishment of a single Department of National Defense.

National security does not consist only of an army, a navy, and an air force. It rests on a much broader basis. It depends on a sound economy of prices and wages, on prosperous agriculture, on satisfied and productive workers, on a competitive private enterprise free from monopolistic repression, on continued industrial harmony and production, on civil liberties and human freedoms—on all the forces which create in our men and women a strong moral fiber and spiritual stamina.

But we have a higher duty and a greater responsibility than the attainment of our own national security. Our goal is collective security for all mankind.

If we can work in a spirit of understanding and mutual respect, we can fulfill this solemn obligation which rests upon us.

The spirit of the American people can set the course of world history. If we maintain and strengthen our cherished ideals, and if we share our great bounty with war-stricken people over the world, then the faith of our citizens in freedom and democracy will be spread over the whole earth and free men everywhere will share our devotion to those ideals. . . .

42. Congress Provides for the National Security

THE NATIONAL SECURITY ACT OF 1947 OFFERS A CONVENIENT DIVIDING point in American military thinking. It summarized the lessons of the past, in so far as they could then be understood, and provided the foundation from which military thought and policy were to advance into a difficult, complex, and, in many ways, unanticipated future. The act failed to fulfill the recommendations either of General Marshall (universal military training, which he made the central element in his thought, was never adopted) or of General Arnold, some of whose visions of air power in the new age were to be disappointed. Within two years the act was to undergo the first of several amendments; and today's giant Department of Defense bears little resemblance to the modest coordinating "office" that was all that the act gave to the new Secretary of Defense when it created the post. The act did, however, establish the Air Force as an independent service under its own department and sought to mesh it with the older services into a coherent, overall structure of defense policy-making. The act's principles, if not its details, have guided the evolution of American military thought since then.

Declaration of Policy

SEC. 2. In enacting this legislation, it is the intent of Congress to provide a comprehensive program for the future security of the United States; to provide for the establishment of integrated policies and procedures for the departments, agencies, and functions of the Government relating to the national security; to provide three military departments for the operation and administration of the Army, the Navy (including naval aviation and the United States Marine Corps), and the Air Force, with their assigned com-

From *United States Statutes at Large*, 80th Congress, Session 1 (1947), LXI, pp. 496–507.

bat and service components; to provide for their authoritative co-ordination and unified direction under civilian control but not to merge them; to provide for the effective strategic direction of the armed forces and for their operation under unified control and for their integration into an efficient team of land, naval, and air forces.

Title I—Coordination for National Security

National Security Council

SEC. 101. (a) There is hereby established a council to be known as the National Security Council (hereinafter in this section referred to as the "Council").

The President of the United States shall preside over meetings of the Council: *Provided,* That in his absence he may designate a member of the Council to preside in his place.

The function of the Council shall be to advise the President with respect to the integration of domestic, foreign, and military policies relating to the national security so as to enable the military services and the other departments and agencies of the Government to cooperate more effectively in matters involving the national security.

The Council shall be composed of the President; the Secretary of State; the Secretary of Defense . . . the Secretary of the Army . . . the Secretary of the Navy; the Secretary of the Air Force . . . the Chairman of the National Security Resources Board . . . and such of the following named officers as the President may designate from time to time: The Secretaries of the executive departments, the Chairman of the Munitions Board . . . and the Chairman of the Research and Development Board . . . but no such additional member shall be designated until the advice and consent of the Senate has been given to his appointment to the office the holding of which authorizes his designation as a member of the Council.

(b) In addition to performing such other functions as the President may direct, for the purpose of more effectively coordinating the policies and functions of the departments and agencies of the

Government relating to the national security, it shall, subject to the direction of the President, be the duty of the Council—

(1) to assess and appraise the objectives, commitments, and risks of the United States in relation to our actual and potential military power, in the interest of national security, for the purpose of making recommendations to the President in connection therewith; and

(2) to consider policies on matters of common interest to the departments and agencies of the Government concerned with the national security, and to make recommendations to the President in connection therewith.

(c) The Council shall have a staff to be headed by a civilian executive secretary who shall be appointed by the President. . . .

(d) The Council shall, from time to time, make such recommendations, and such other reports to the President as it deems appropriate or as the President may require.

Central Intelligence Agency

SEC. 102. (a) There is hereby established under the National Security Council a Central Intelligence Agency with a Director of Central Intelligence, who shall be the head thereof. The Director shall be appointed by the President, by and with the advice and consent of the Senate, from among the commissioned officers of the armed services or from among individuals in civilian life. . . .

(b) (1) If a commissioned officer of the armed services is appointed as Director then—

(A) in the performance of his duties as Director, he shall be subject to no supervision, control, restriction, or prohibition (military or otherwise) other than would be operative with respect to him if he were a civilian in no way connected with the Department of the Army, the Department of the Navy, the Department of the Air Force, or the armed services or any component thereof; and

(B) he shall not possess or exercise any supervision, control, powers, or functions (other than such as he possesses, or is authorized or directed to exercise, as Director) with respect to the armed services or any component thereof, the Department of the Army, the Department of the Navy, or the Department of the Air Force, or any branch, bureau, unit or division thereof, or with respect to any of the personnel (military or civilian) of any of the foregoing. . . .

. . . (d) For the purpose of coordinating the intelligence activities of the several Government departments and agencies in the interest of national security, it shall be the duty of the Agency, under the direction of the National Security Council—

(1) to advise the National Security Council in matters concerning such intelligence activities of the Government departments and agencies as relate to national security;

(2) to make recommendations to the National Security Council for the coordination of such intelligence activities of the departments and agencies of the Government as relate to the national security;

(3) to correlate and evaluate intelligence relating to the national security, and provide for the appropriate dissemination of such intelligence within the Government using where appropriate existing agencies and facilities: *Provided,* That the Agency shall have no police, subpena, law-enforcement powers, or internal-security functions: *Provided further,* That the departments and other agencies of the Government shall continue to collect, evaluate, correlate, and disseminate departmental intelligence: *And provided further,* That the Director of Central Intelligence shall be responsible for protecting intelligence sources and methods from unauthorized disclosure;

(4) to perform, for the benefit of the existing intelligence agencies, such additional services of common concern as the National Security Council determines can be more efficiently accomplished centrally;

(5) to perform such other functions and duties related to intelligence affecting the national security as the National Security Council may from time to time direct.

(e) To the extent recommended by the National Security

Council and approved by the President, such intelligence of the departments and agencies of the Government, except as hereinafter provided, relating to the national security shall be open to the inspection of the Director of Central Intelligence, and such intelligence as relates to the national security and is possessed by such departments and other agencies of the Government, except as hereinafter provided, shall be made available to the Director of Central Intelligence for correlation, evaluation, and dissemination: *Provided, however,* That upon the written request of the Director of Central Intelligence, the Director of the Federal Bureau of Investigation shall make available to the Director of Central Intelligence such information for correlation, evaluation, and dissemination as may be essential to the national security.

(f) Effective when the Director first appointed under subsection (a) has taken office—

(1) the National Intelligence Authority . . . shall cease to exist . . .

National Security Resources Board

SEC. 103. (a) There is hereby established a National Security Resources Board (hereinafter in this section referred to as the "Board") to be composed of the Chairman of the Board and such heads or representatives of the various executive departments and independent agencies as may from time to time be designated by the President to be members of the Board. The Chairman of the Board shall be appointed from civilian life by the President, by and with the advice and consent of the Senate. . . .

. . . (c) It shall be the function of the Board to advise the President concerning the coordination of military, industrial, and civilian mobilization, including—

(1) policies concerning industrial and civilian mobilization in order to assure the most effective mobilization and maximum utilization of the Nation's manpower in the event of war;

(2) programs for the effective use in time of war of the Nation's natural and industrial resources for military and

civilian needs, for the maintenance and stabilization of the civilian economy in time of war, and for the adjustment of such economy to war needs and conditions;

(3) policies for unifying, in time of war, the activities of Federal agencies and departments engaged in or concerned with production, procurement, distribution, or transportation of military or civilian supplies, materials, and products;

(4) the relationship between potential supplies of, and potential requirements for, manpower, resources, and productive facilities in time of war;

(5) policies for establishing adequate reserves of strategic and critical material, and for the conservation of these reserves;

(6) the strategic relocation of industries, services, government, and economic activities, the continuous operation of which is essential to the Nation's security.

(d) In performing its functions, the Board shall utilize to the maximum extent the facilities and resources of the departments and agencies of the Government.

Title II—The National Military Establishment

Establishment of the National Military Establishment

SEC. 201. (a) There is hereby established the National Military Establishment, and the Secretary of Defense shall be the head thereof.

(b) The National Military Establishment shall consist of the Department of the Army, the Department of the Navy, and the Department of the Air Force, together with all other agencies created under title II of this Act.

Secretary of Defense

SEC. 202. (a) There shall be a Secretary of Defense, who shall be appointed from civilian life by the President, by and with the advice and consent of the Senate: *Provided,* That a person who has within ten years been on active duty as a commissioned officer in a Regular component of the armed services shall not be eligible for appointment as Secretary of Defense. The Secretary of Defense shall be the principal assistant to the President in all matters relating to the national security. Under the direction of the President and subject to the provisions of this Act he shall perform the following duties:

(1) Establish general policies and programs for the National Military Establishment and for all of the departments and agencies therein;

(2) Exercise general direction, authority, and control over such departments and agencies;

(3) Take appropriate steps to eliminate unnecessary duplication or overlapping in the fields of procurement, supply, transportation, storage, health, and research;

(4) Supervise and coordinate the preparation of the budget estimates of the departments and agencies comprising the National Military Establishment; formulate and determine the budget estimates for submittal to the Bureau of the Budget; and supervise the budget programs of such departments and agencies under the applicable appropriation Act:

Provided, That nothing herein contained shall prevent the Secretary of the Army, the Secretary of the Navy, or the Secretary of the Air Force from presenting to the President or to the Director of the Budget, after first so informing the Secretary of Defense, any report or recommendation relating to his department which he may deem necessary: *And provided further,* That the Department of the Army, the Department of the Navy, and the Department of the Air Force shall be administered as individual executive departments by their respective Secretaries and all powers and duties relating to such departments not specifically conferred upon the Secretary of Defense by this Act shall be retained by each of their respective Secretaries.

(b) The Secretary of Defense shall submit annual written reports to the President and the Congress covering expenditures, work, and accomplishments of the National Military Establishment, together with such recommendations as he shall deem appropriate.

(c) The Secretary of Defense shall cause a seal of office to be made for the National Military Establishment, of such design as the President shall approve, and judicial notice shall be taken thereof.

Military Assistants to the Secretary

Sec. 203. Officers of the armed services may be detailed to duty as assistants and personal aides to the Secretary of Defense, but he shall not establish a military staff.

Civilian Personnel

Sec. 204. (a) The Secretary of Defense is authorized to appoint from civilian life not to exceed three special assistants to advise and assist him in the performance of his duties. . . .

Department of the Army

Sec. 205. (a) The Department of War shall hereafter be designated the Department of the Army, and the title of the Secretary of War shall be changed to Secretary of the Army. Changes shall be made in the titles of other officers and activities of the Department of the Army as the Secretary of the Army may determine. . . .

. . . (d) The Secretary of the Army shall cause a seal of office to be made for the Department of the Army, of such design as the President may approve, and judicial notice shall be taken thereof.

(e) In general the United States Army, within the Department of the Army, shall include land combat and service forces and such aviation and water transport as may be organic therein. It shall be organized, trained, and equipped primarily for prompt and sustained combat incident to operations on land. It shall be responsible for the preparation of land forces necessary for the effective prosecution of war except as otherwise assigned and, in accordance with integrated joint mobilization plans, for the expansion of peacetime components of the Army to meet the needs of war.

Department of the Navy

Sec. 206. (a) The term "Department of the Navy" as used in this Act shall be construed to mean the Department of the Navy at the seat of government; the headquarters, United States Marine Corps; the entire operating forces of the United States Navy, including naval aviation, and of the United States Marine Corps, including the reserve components of such forces; all field activities, headquarters, forces, bases, installations, activities, and functions under the control or supervision of the Department of the Navy; and the United States Coast Guard when operating as a part of the Navy pursuant to law.

(b) In general the United States Navy, within the Department of the Navy, shall include naval combat and services forces and such aviation as may be organic therein. It shall be organized, trained, and equipped primarily for prompt and sustained combat incident to operations at sea. It shall be responsible for the preparation of naval forces necessary for the effective prosecution of war except as otherwise assigned, and, in accordance with integrated joint mobilization plans, for the expansion of the peacetime components of the Navy to meet the needs of war.

All naval aviation shall be integrated with the naval service as part thereof within the Department of the Navy. Naval aviation shall consist of combat and service and training forces, and shall include land-based naval aviation, air transport essential for naval operations, all air weapons and air techniques involved in the operations and activities of the United States Navy, and the entire remainder of the aeronautical organization of the United States Navy, together with the personnel necessary therefor.

The Navy shall be generally responsible for naval reconnaissance, antisubmarine warfare, and protection of shipping.

The Navy shall develop aircraft, weapons, tactics, technique, organization and equipment of naval combat and service elements; matters of joint concern as to these functions shall be coordinated between the Army, the Air Force, and the Navy.

(c) The United States Marine Corps, within the Department of the Navy, shall include land combat and service forces and such aviation as may be organic therein. The Marine Corps shall be organized, trained, and equipped to provide fleet marine forces of combined arms, together with supporting air components, for service with the fleet in the seizure or defense of advanced naval bases and for the conduct of such land operations as may be essential to the prosecution of a naval campaign. It shall be the duty of the Marine Corps to develop, in coordination with the Army and the Air Force, those phases of amphibious operations which pertain to the tactics, technique, and equipment employed by landing forces. In addition, the Marine Corps shall provide detachments and organizations for service on armed vessels of the Navy, shall provide security detachments for the protection of naval property at naval stations and bases, and shall perform such other duties as the President may direct: *Provided*, That such additional duties shall not detract from or interfere with the operations for which the Marine Corps is primarily organized. The Marine Corps shall be responsible, in accordance with integrated joint mobilization plans, for the expansion of peacetime components of the Marine Corps to meet the needs of war.

Department of the Air Force

SEC. 207. (a) Within the National Military Establishment there is hereby established an executive department to be known as the Department of the Air Force, and a Secretary of the Air Force, who shall be the head thereof. The Secretary of the Air Force shall be appointed from civilian life by the President, by and with the advice and consent of the Senate. . . .

. . . (c) The term "Department of the Air Force" as used in this Act shall be construed to mean the Department of the Air Force at the seat of government and all field headquarters, forces, reserve components, installations, activities, and functions under the control or supervision of the Department of the Air Force.

(d) There shall be in the Department of the Air Force an Under Secretary of the Air Force and two Assistant Secretaries of the Air Force, who shall be appointed from civilian life by the President by and with the advice and consent of the Senate.

(e) The several officers of the Department of the Air Force shall perform such functions as the Secretary of the Air Force may prescribe.

(f) So much of the functions of the Secretary of the Army and of the Department of the Army, including those of any officer of such Department, as are assigned to or under the control of the Commanding General, Army Air Forces, or as are deemed by the Secretary of Defense to be necessary or desirable for the operations of the Department of the Air Force or the United States Air Force, shall be transferred to and vested in the Secretary of the Air Force and the Department of the Air Force: *Provided*, That the National Guard Bureau shall, in addition to the functions and duties performed by it for the Department of the Army, be charged with similar functions and duties for the Department of the Air Force, and shall be the channel of communication between the Department of the Air Force and the several States on all matters pertaining to the Air National Guard. . . .

(g) The Secretary of the Air Force shall cause a seal of office to be made for the Department of the Air Force, of such device as the President shall approve, and judicial notice shall be taken thereof.

United States Air Force

SEC. 208. (a) The United States Air Force is hereby established under the Department of the Air Force. The Army Air Forces, the Air Corps, United States Army, and the General Headquarters Air Force (Air Force Combat Command), shall be transferred to the United States Air Force.

(b) There shall be a Chief of Staff, United States Air Force, who shall be appointed by the President, by and with the advice and consent of the Senate, for a term of four years from among the officers of general rank who are assigned to or commissioned in the United States Air Force. Under the direction of the Secretary of the Air Force, the Chief of Staff, United States Air Force, shall exercise command over the United States Air Force and shall be charged with the duty of carrying into execution all lawful orders and directions which may be transmitted to him. The functions of the Commanding General, General Headquarters Air Force (Air Force Combat Command), and of the Chief of the Air Corps and of the Commanding General, Army Air Forces, shall be transferred to the Chief of Staff, United States Air Force. When such transfer becomes effective, the offices of the Chief of the Air Corps, United States Army, and Assistants to the Chief of the Air Corps, United States Army . . . and Commanding General, General Headquarters Air Force . . . shall cease to exist. While holding office as Chief of Staff, United States Air Force, the incumbent shall hold a grade and receive allowances equivalent to those prescribed by law for the Chief of Staff, United States Army. The Chief of Staff, United States Army, the Chief of Naval Operations, and the Chief of Staff, United States Air Force, shall take rank among themselves according to their relative dates of appointment as such, and shall each take rank above all other officers on the active list of the Army, Navy, and Air Force: *Provided,* That nothing in this Act shall have the effect of changing the relative rank of the present Chief of Staff, United States Army, and the present Chief of Naval Operations.

(c) All commissioned officers, warrant officers, and enlisted men, commissioned, holding warrants, or enlisted, in the Air Corps, United States Army, or the Army Air Forces, shall be transferred in branch to the United States Air Force. All other commissioned officers, warrant officers, and enlisted men, who are commissioned, hold warrants, or are enlisted, in any component of the Army of the United States and who are under the authority or command of the Commanding General, Army Air Forces, shall be continued under the authority or command of the Chief of Staff, United States Air Force, and under the jurisdiction of the Department of the Air Force. . . .

. . . (f) In general the United States Air Force shall include aviation forces both combat and service not otherwise assigned. It shall be organized, trained, and equipped primarily for prompt and sustained offensive and defensive air operations. The Air Force shall be responsible for the preparation of the air forces necessary for the effective prosecution of war except as otherwise assigned and, in accordance with integrated joint mobilization plans, for the expansion of the peacetime components of the Air Force to meet the needs of war. . . .

War Council

SEC. 210. There shall be within the National Military Establishment a War Council composed of the Secretary of Defense, as Chairman, who shall have power of decision; the Secretary of the Army; the Secretary of the Navy; the Secretary of the Air Force; the Chief of Staff, United States Army; the Chief of Naval Operations; and the Chief of Staff, United States Air Force. The War Council shall advise the Secretary of Defense on matters of broad policy relating to the armed forces, and shall consider and report on such other matters as the Secretary of Defense may direct.

Joint Chiefs of Staff

SEC. 211. (a) There is hereby established within the National Military Establishment the Joint Chiefs of Staff, which shall consist of the Chief of Staff, United States Army; the Chief of Naval Operations; the Chief of Staff, United States Air Force; and the Chief of Staff to the Commander in Chief, if there be one.

(b) Subject to the authority and direction of the President and the Secretary of Defense, it shall be the duty of the Joint Chiefs of Staff—

(1) to prepare strategic plans and to provide for the strategic direction of the military forces;

(2) to prepare joint logistic plans and to assign to the military services logistic responsibilities in accordance with such plans;

(3) to establish unified commands in strategic areas when such unified commands are in the interest of national security;

(4) to formulate policies for joint training of the military forces;

(5) to formulate policies for coordinating the education of members of the military forces;

(6) to review major material and personnel requirements of the military forces, in accordance with strategic and logistic plans; and

(7) to provide United States representation on the Military

Staff Committee of the United Nations in accordance with the provisions of the Charter of the United Nations.

(c) The Joint Chiefs of Staff shall act as the principal military advisers to the President and the Secretary of Defense and shall perform such other duties as the President and Secretary of Defense may direct or as may be prescribed by law.

Joint Staff

SEC. 212. There shall be, under the Joint Chiefs of Staff, a Joint Staff to consist of not to exceed one hundred officers and to be composed of approximately equal numbers of officers from each of the three armed services. The Joint Staff, operating under a Director thereof appointed by the Joint Chiefs of Staff, shall perform such duties as may be directed by the Joint Chiefs of Staff. The Director shall be an officer junior in grade to all members of the Joint Chiefs of Staff.

Munitions Board

SEC. 213. (a) There is hereby established in the National Military Establishment a Munitions Board (hereinafter in this section referred to as the "Board").

(b) The Board shall be composed of a Chairman, who shall be the head thereof, and an Under Secretary or Assistant Secretary from each of the three military departments, to be designated in each case by the Secretaries of their respective departments. The Chairman shall be appointed from civilian life by the President, by and with the advice and consent of the Senate. . . .

(c) It shall be the duty of the Board under the direction of the Secretary of Defense and in support of strategic and logistic plans prepared by the Joint Chiefs of Staff—

(1) to coordinate the appropriate activities within the National Military Establishment with regard to industrial matters, including the procurement, production, and distribution plans of the departments and agencies comprising the Establishment;

(2) to plan for the military aspects of industrial mobilization;

(3) to recommend assignment of procurement responsibilities among the several military services and to plan for standardization of specifications and for the greatest practicable allocation of purchase authority of technical equipment and common use items on the basis of single procurement;

(4) to prepare estimates of potential production, procurement, and personnel for use in evaluation of the logistic feasibility of strategic operations;

(5) to determine relative priorities of the various segments of the military procurement programs;

(6) to supervise such subordinate agencies as are or may be created to consider the subjects falling within the scope of the Board's responsbilities;

(7) to make recommendations to regroup, combine, or dissolve existing interservice agencies operating in the fields of procurement, production, and distribution in such manner as to promote efficiency and economy;

(8) to maintain liaison with other departments and agencies for the proper correlation of military requirements with the civilian economy, particularly in regard to the procurement or disposition of strategic and critical material and the maintenance of adequate reserves of such material, and to make recommendations as to policies in connection therewith;

(9) to assemble and review material and personnel requirements presented by the Joint Chiefs of Staff and those presented by the production, procurement, and distribution agencies assigned to meet military needs, and to make recommendations thereon to the Secretary of Defense; and

(10) to perform such other duties as the Secretary of Defense may direct.

(d) When the Chairman of the Board first appointed has taken office, the Joint Army and Navy Munitions Board shall cease to exist and all its records and personnel shall be transferred to the Munitions Board.

(e) The Secretary of Defense shall provide the Board with such personnel and facilities as the Secretary may determine to be required by the Board for the performance of its functions.

Research and Development Board

SEC. 214. (a) There is hereby established in the National Military Establishment a Research and Development Board (hereinafter in this section referred to as the "Board"). The Board shall be composed of a Chairman, who shall be the head thereof, and two representatives from each of the Departments of the Army, Navy, and Air Force, to be designated by the Secretaries of their respective Departments. The Chairman shall be appointed from civilian life by the President, by and with the advice and consent of the Senate. . . . The purpose of the Board shall be to advise the Secretary of Defense as to the status of scientific research relative to the national security, and to assist him in assuring adequate provision for research and development on scientific problems relating to the national security.

(b) It shall be the duty of the Board, under the direction of the Secretary of Defense—

(1) to prepare a complete and integrated program of research and development for military purposes;

(2) to advise with regard to trends in scientific research relating to national security and the measures necessary to assure continued and increasing progress;

(3) to recommend measures of coordination of research and development among the military departments, and allocation among them of responsibilities for specific programs of joint interest;

(4) to formulate policy for the National Military Establishment in connection with research and development matters involving agencies outside the National Military Establishment;

(5) to consider the interaction of research and development and strategy, and to advise the Joint Chiefs of Staff in connection therewith; and

(6) to perform such other duties as the Secretary of Defense may direct.

(c) When the Chairman of the Board first appointed has taken office, the Joint Research and Development Board shall cease to exist and all its records and personnel shall be transferred to the Research and Development Board.

(d) The Secretary of Defense shall provide the Board with such personnel and facilities as the Secretary may determine to be required by the Board for the performance of its functions. . . .

PART SIX

The Military Revolution: Since 1948

43. Douglas MacArthur: War in Transition

Douglas MacArthur was the most brilliant American soldier of his era and one of the ablest. Graduating first in the West Point class of 1903, he was to leave a deep impress, throughout a long and continually spectacular career, on American military thought. A product of the pre-1914 school of war, he served with eminence through all the great struggles that followed and was finally called upon to command in the Korean War, the most recent of the major military conflicts of the twentieth century. With Korea, war was already in a state of transition. It was fought, basically, with the weapons and tactics of the two world wars, but in political and strategic contexts already profoundly altered by both the nuclear weaponry and the anticolonial revolution. The summary relief of MacArthur from command in the spring of 1951 itself attests to the strains that this situation was creating; and MacArthur's testimony before the Senate Armed Services and Foreign Relations Committees' inquiry into "the military situation in the Far East" illustrates the confusions between the old concepts of war and the new. The general was, of course, defending a personal case and might have spoken somewhat differently under different circumstances. But these were the views expressed by one of our most experienced and distinguished soldiers on the fundamental problems of war and peace as they appeared to him in the transition period represented by the Korean War.

Senator SALTONSTALL . . . on April 15, the Assistant Secretary of State, Dean Rusk, in a television and press broadcast, stated, in part—and this is the pertinent part of his speech, as I read it:

What we are trying to do is to maintain peace and security without a general war. We are saying to the aggressors, "You will not be allowed to get away with your crime. You must stop it."

At the same time, we are trying to prevent a general conflagration which would consume the very things we are now trying to defend.

I would appreciate it very much, with your knowledge of the Far East, if you will give me your opinion of that statement, and if that is a practical policy.

General MACARTHUR. That policy, as you have read it, seems to me to introduce a new concept into military operations—the concept of appeasement, the concept that when you use force, you can limit that force.

The concept that I have is that when you go into war, you have exhausted all other potentialities of bringing the disagreements to an end.

As I understand what you read, that we would apply to the military situation in Korea certain military appeasements—that is, that we would not use our Air Forces to their maximum extent, only to the limited area of that Korea; that we would not use our Navy, except along the border lines of Korea.

To me, that would mean that you would have a continued and indefinite extension of bloodshed, which would have limitless—a limitless end.

You would not have the potentialities of destroying the enemy's military power, and bringing the conflict to a decisive close in the minimum of time, and with a minimum of loss.

It seems to me the worst possible concept, militarily, that we would simply stay there, resisting aggression, so-called, although I do not know what you mean by "resisting aggression."

The very term of "resisting aggression," it seems to me that you

From *The Military Situation in the Far East*, 82d Congress, Session 1, Senate Armed Services and Foreign Relations Committees, pp. 39–40, 45, 66–69, 144–148, 208–211.

destroy the potentialities of the aggressor to continually hit you.

If that is the concept of a continued and indefinite campaign in Korea, with no definite purpose of stopping it until the enemy gets tired or you yield to his terms, I think that introduces into the military sphere a political control such as I have never known in my life or have ever studied.

Senator SALTONSTALL. In other words, you feel that the Korean situation, having gone into an armed conflict, it should be brought to an end in the quickest possible way through a military victory.

General MACARTHUR. I do, Senator, exactly; and I believe if you do not do that, if you hit soft, if you practice appeasement in the use of force, you are doomed to disaster.

I believe that if you continue that way, you are inviting the very thing that you desire to stop—the spread of the conflict. . . .

. . . Senator GREEN. There is one other phase to the question which applies to both Korea and China, which you touched upon, and that is this: You have dealt with these questions in both countries on a purely military basis. But isn't our Government required to give consideration and decide upon it on both a military and a political basis? Can you separate them so distinctly and say that a military victory is a political victory?

General MACARTHUR. I think that it is quite impossible to draw a line of differentiation and say this is a political and this is a military situation.

The American Government should have such coordination so that the political and military are in coordination.

The general definition which for many decades has been accepted was that war was the ultimate process of politics; that when all other political means failed, you then go to force; and when you do that, the balance of control, the balance of concept, the main interest involved, the minute you reach the killing stage, is the control of the military. A theater commander in any campaign, is not merely limited to the handling of his troops; he commands that whole area politically, economically, and militarily. You have got to trust at that stage of the game when politics fails, and the military takes over, you must trust the military, or otherwise you will have the system that the Soviet once employed of the political commissar, who would run the military as well as the politics of the country.

Now, the differentiation that exists between the political features and the military features, I am not able to discuss because I have not been here in Washington. Others will be able to tell you more about that than I, but I do unquestionably state that when men become locked in battle, that there should be no artifice under the name of politics, which should handicap your own men, decrease their chances for winning, and increase their losses.

Senator GREEN. Well, but the point is a little different from that. A military victory, a quick military victory, does not necessarily mean anything but the defeat and disintegration of the armies, but it does not affect the population. If you would defeat the Communist armies, it does not necessarily mean that you can defeat communism in China.

General MACARTHUR. Senator, as far as the United Nations in Korea is concerned, it is limited to Korea. They are trying to clear Korea. I don't understand that in any decisions or discussions that have arisen we are trying to do more than stop the Chinese from aggression in Korea. I believe when we do that we have to put sufficient military forces upon them to do it.

I do not believe we can put that sufficient military force upon them if we limit ourselves to the inhibitions we do now, just in the area of Korea. I believe the minute that we put those pressures on them that the Red Chinese, if they have any sensibilities of discretion at all, would enter into a cease-fire parley. . . .

. . . Senator MORSE. . . . I am to understand, from your testimony, that you discount the danger of Russia coming into the war, either with a bombing operation, or on a full-scale basis, including manpower, if we should bomb bases in Manchuria?

General MACARTHUR. That is stating it in a little different way than the way I stated it, Senator.

I stated that under the present conditions, the losses we are sustaining, of Americans in Korea, cannot go on indefinitely, without bleeding this country white.

Senator MORSE. I agree.

General MACARTHUR. I say that if you are trying to buy time, you are doing it the worst way you can. You are buying time at the expense of American blood. I think that is too expensive.

There is no certainty that Russia will come in.

There is no certainty that she will not come in.

There is no certainty that anything that happens in Korea will influence her.

That is speculative.

You have to take a certain degree of risk on these things, one way or another.

All I know is that our men are going by the thousands over there, every month, and if you keep this thing on indefinitely, nothing could happen that would be worse than that.

Therefore, I suggest that some plan be carried out that will bring this dreadful slaughter to a definite end; that we shall not continue to buy time, as you put it, sacrificing thousands of American boys every month.

It is too expensive, from my point of view.

Senator MORSE. I do not quarrel with you on that.

General MACARTHUR. Now, as far as buying time is concerned, you make the assumption that we increase our strength as compared with the enemy's.

That is too speculative.

If we add 50 divisions to our forces, he might add 60. He can do it just as quickly as we can.

The relativity of the forces that are involved—these basic questions are too complicated to be answered in the categorical way that you present the questions. Your questions are really argument, and I cannot meet them except what I have said before— that we do face an actual condition in Korea in which we are losing thousands and thousands and thousands of men in an indecisive way.

I do not believe that that is warranted by any concept that relatively we might increase our strength as compared with a foe who has not as yet indicated that he really intends to strike.

We do not know.

This is speculative; but I do know, when we have got a war on our hands, and when we are suffering the way we do, we should try to bring it to an end.

I do say that the worst thing that we can do is go on indecisively sacrificing these men, with no definite end in sight.

Now, my proposition is, in my opinion, the best way, and as far as I know, the only way in which a solution has been offered, and on January 12, the Joint Chiefs of Staff apparently thought so, too.

Now, if there is any way in which—if there is any proposition that has been made, any place, here or any other place, to bring this thing to a conclusion, without abject appeasement and surrender on the enemy's terms, I would be the first one to want to try it.

The only way I know, when a nation wars on you, is to beat her by force. I do not know of any argument that will bring an end to this thing.

War, in itself, is the application of superior force, and as we chose that path, and have entered upon that path, it seems to me that we must end it in some way.

Now, there are only three ways that I can see, as I said this morning: Either to pursue it to victory; to surrender to an enemy and end it on his terms; or, what I think is the worst of all choices, to go on indefinitely and indefinitely, neither to win nor lose, in that stalemate; because what we are doing is sacrificing thousands of men while we are doing it.

If you could just say that this line stops aggression, and we didn't lose the men, that would be a different thing; but every day over there you have this terrific and savage conflict, the most savage I ever fought in; and you are losing the very flower of our youth, and if you keep on month after month, and month after month, why, these losses are going to mount up to figures which would stagger the imagination.

Now, in that third process of merely continuing, as has been projected in some circles, that leads to an indefinite sacrifice of lives.

Senator MORSE. Will the general let me say that——

General MACARTHUR. Now, war never before in the history of the world has been applied in a piecemeal way, that you make half war, and not whole war.

Now, that China is using the maximum of her force against us is quite evident; and we are not using the maximum of ours against her, in reply.

The result is—we do not even use, to the maximum, the forces at our disposal, the scientific methods, and the result is that for every percentage you take away in the use of the Air and the Navy, you add a percentage to the dead American infantrymen.

It may seem emotional for me to say that, but I happen to be the man that had to send them into it. The blood, to some extent, would rest on me; and with the objectives, I believe I could stop them—it seems terrific to me that we should not attempt something.

The inertia that exists. There is no policy—there is nothing, I tell you, no plan, or anything.

When you say, merely, "we are going to continue to fight aggression," that is not what the enemy is fighting for.

The enemy is fighting for a very definite purpose—to destroy our forces in Korea.

We constantly, every day, run that risk, without the potential of defeating him, and stopping him—to come again.

He attacks today. We resist it. We fall back. We form a new line, and we surge back.

Then, he is right back, within a week, maybe, up to the battle front with his inexhaustible supply of manpower. He brings in another hundred thousand, or another half-million men, and tosses them at these troops constantly.

That is a new concept in war.

That is not war—that is appeasement.

Senator MORSE. General, let me say that I haven't any doubt about the fact that my questions are argumentative. I do not see any way of avoiding it when we are confronted here with analyzing the two sides in a great argument, namely your proposals or program in Asia, and the proposals of those in the administration who have differed from you.

All I am seeking to do is to bring out into this record with crystal clearness—and you certainly are making it crystal clear—the basis for your point of view that we ought to follow the suggestions that you made in your speech.

I want you to understand as I ask you my questions, that is the only motivation behind those questions.

Now my next question is if following the bombing in China of the Manchurian bases Russia should carry out her aid and assistance agreement with Red China and proceed to help Red China with an all-out bombing attack of her own, would we then in our present state of defense lose more men than we would lose if we buy time, as is alleged, for some little time in the future until we get our own defenses in a stronger position?

In other words my question is what is your judgment as to the effect in terms of American losses that an all out war with Russia and Asia at the present time would cost?

General MacArthur. My own belief is that what will happen in Korea and Asia will not be the deciding factor in whether the Soviet attacks us or not. If he is determined to attack us, sooner or later he will, and there is nothing that I can see that would prevent it, but I do say that the constant sacrifice of blood, of American blood in Korea today, is of so serious a nature that we must face that problem irrespective of what the future, the speculative future may have in store.

Senator Morse. Do you consider, General, that we are in fact today at war with Communist China?

General MacArthur. I don't see how it's possible that Communist China could be more at war with us than she is today.

Senator Morse. That seems to me to be——

General MacArthur. Now we are not at war with her. We are very limited in our repulse of her efforts, and all I say is that after due warning to China that she cannot continue in this almost fantastic favoritism of war to her, that if she continues, if she will not sit around a peace table and discuss this matter rationally, that we should take all the necessary economic and military sanctions that are necessary to force her to stop.

Senator MORSE. Which would include a declaration of war against her?

General MACARTHUR. That is beyond my technical province. That we would use the necessary force to require her, to force her to stop her predatory actions in Korea, I would say "Yes."

If that meant that you would have to acknowledge the state of war that she has declared on us, and admit it, of course the answer is "Yes."

Senator MORSE. If we gave her an opportunity——

General MACARTHUR. I think that we should say explicitly, Senator, that if this thing was not brought to an end within a reasonable time, that this would mean the culmination of the all-out forceful effort to knock her out. . . .

. . . Senator FULBRIGHT. Well, would you consider that the authorities in China could make a peace with you without the approval of the Kremlin?

General MACARTHUR. A peace with me?

Senator FULBRIGHT. Well, with the United Nations, or with the United States.

General MACARTHUR. I believe that there would be great possibilities of it. I don't know what the action or the impulse would be from the Kremlin. I know no more about that than you do.

I believe that the plan that I have put forward offers the only hope that I know of to stop that insensate slaughter in Korea, to give Korea and its nation a chance to survive.

I believe we accepted that moral obligation, and I believe we should go through with it.

Senator FULBRIGHT. Well, General, with all due deference, I think our first and continuing responsibility is to this country, rather than Korea.

I would not jeopardize this country——

General MACARTHUR. I agree with you in that, too, Senator; but I believe that they are parallel.

I believe the interests of this country are involved in saving the lives of its sons, rather than embarking upon an indefinite, indecisive campaign which will sacrifice thousands and thousands of additional American lives.

And there is no sophistry of or philosophy of discussion that would change the view I have on that.

I believe there is an excellent chance to do it. I believe there is no chance, if you decide otherwise, before you give an opportunity to practice, and attempt the only solution that I know of which will bring a hope for a successful conclusion.

Now, no man in the world is more anxious to avoid the expansion of war than I am. I am just 100 percent a believer against war. I believe the enormous sacrifices that have been brought about by the scientific methods of killing have rendered war a fantastic solution of international difficulties.

In war, as it is waged now, with the enormous losses on both sides, both sides will lose. It is a form of mutual suicide; and I believe that the entire effort of modern society should be concentrated on an endeavor to outlaw war as a method of the solution of problems between nations.

Now, you have an actual fact in Korea. You do have war. The great question is how are you going to end it.

Are you going to let it go on indefinitely, destroying the fabric of society, or are you going to make an effort to end it?

Are you going to let it go on indefinitely, on the plea that a still greater calamity might follow?

You certainly have a tremendous calamity on your hands right now.

You may avoid a future calamity.

It is my belief that if you bring the Korean War to a successful conclusion, you will put off the possibility and diminish the possibility of a third world war.

It is my own belief, if you continue this thing indefinitely, it will eventually overtake you. It will spread. I believe that the plan and the policy I have offers the greatest hope for not having a third world war.

Now those are my opinions. I am not trying to force their acceptance.

As I said when I appeared before this committee, I am not a

voluntary witness, but those are my views and I repeat, there is no sophistry of argument of philosophical trends that will alter those basic facts, and those basic facts are all that I have tried to offer to this committee or to the Congress. . . .

. . . Senator FULBRIGHT. . . . There is one other idea, General, that I think many of us are confused about. That is the idea that anything short of a complete victory in an all-out effort to end it by force of arms in the Orient would be called appeasement.

In other words, the word "appeasement" has come to have a sort of all-inclusive meaning. It does not seem to me that a negotiated peace, for example, is necessarily appeasement. Do you think so?

General MACARTHUR. Senator, I have my own definition of appeasement that might disagree with yours. I believe when you enter into war, you should use sufficient force to impose your will upon the enemy. The only purpose we have in the Korean conflict is to make the enemy stop his depredations. It isn't his conquest. It hasn't got an ounce of imperialism in it at all.

I believe that we do have the power to do so without sacrificing any of our other interests, and I do not believe in doing so that we in the slightest degree prejudice the beginning of another world war. On the contrary, I have said repeatedly I believe that it would have the opposite effect.

Senator FULBRIGHT. Well, I understood at one time that you were willing to have a cease-fire in Korea. Wasn't that short of an all-out victory?

General MACARTHUR. I would be glad to have a cease-fire in Korea on honorable terms at any time. I have had no other thought and hope in the last 10 months than to bring it to an honorable end with the least bloodshed that is possible.

Every recommendation I have made is to that end and to that purpose and none other. The glorification of a so-called over-all victory or conquest, as you put it, has never even entered my thoughts. What I am anxious to do is to bring the enemy to a round-table discussion on an honorable basis which will cause him to stop his depredation.

He is the aggressor without cause or reason. He is the one that sprung that foul blow on us. It's to stop that that we fight, and I say that anything that does not tend to stop that is in my lexicon appeasement.

Senator FULBRIGHT. Well, I think that puts a little different light on it from what I had understood before. I mean that the only way would be, in effect, unconditional surrender. By the way, did you feel that the policy of——

General MACARTHUR. I don't know what you mean by "unconditional surrender," Senator. The only thing that the United Nations and the United States as its agent has ever demanded is a liberated, unified Korea.

Never by word or deed they indicated that they had any other concept. The enemy, on the other hand, has openly announced its purposes which involve the complete destruction of our forces, the complete occupation of Korea, the forcing upon Korea of a totalitarian system of government.

All of those things have been announced, but the only purpose that we have as I see it, is to stop the depredation of the Chinese Communist forces in North Korea, and their allies, the North Koreans.

I have endeavored to the best of my ability to suggest a discussion of honorable terms to end this war. We have been met at every turn by that, by the introduction of other political efforts, the recognition of Red China, which has nothing to do with the Korean conflict, the turning over of Formosa, which has nothing to do with the Korean conflict. Those are the insistence of the enemy before he sits down.

Those, if they were accepted, would again fit my definition of appeasement.

Senator FULBRIGHT. Well, do you feel our Government has accepted those principles that you have just mentioned?

General MACARTHUR. Do I feel that our Government has accepted them?

Senator FULBRIGHT. Yes.

General MACARTHUR. No, sir. Those are the demands of the

enemy, and as I said today, the Joint Chiefs of Staff within the month have recommended that in the discussion of cease-fire terms, that neither of those appeasement policies should be acceptable even for discussion. What the attitude of our Government is, I don't know, but I would doubt very much that it would consider such terms.

Senator FULBRIGHT. Well, that is my impression.

General MACARTHUR. What is that?

Senator FULBRIGHT. That is my impression, sir.

General, would you care to say whether or not you feel that war with Russia is inevitable? I mean that question comes to all of us here, not only this year, but in this conflict that has grown up with Russia, it must be settled by war. Do you have a feeling or view about that?

General MACARTHUR. No, sir; I do not feel that war is inevitable. I believe that the great masses of the world, what you might call the ordinary men of the world, are invincibly against war.

I believe that is so among the Russian masses, just as it is among our own people.

I believe that the great tragedy of the world today is that we have not been able to establish the mechanics to carry out the will of the common people that war shall be nonexistent.

I believe that the same impulses against the destructiveness of war exist in common by all people.

Now, war, you have got to understand the history of war; you have got to understand that in the beginning it was a sort of gladiatorial contest in which when the opposing parties disagreed, they would agree to abide by the decisions of this gladiatorial contest. I suppose the beginning was the David and Goliath story of the Bible. It progressed from that into small professional armed forces, which would fight in some obscure corner of the world, but the results of that would be accepted in the chancellories of the world, and the peace would be written.

Gradually, with the scientific methods which have made mass destruction reach appalling proportions, war has ceased to be a sort of the roll-of-the-dice to determine what the winner should be—which should be the winner, and dictate the terms.

It has become an all-out effort. It has involved every man, child and woman in the whole world. The integration of the world into this compressed community now which exists has involved everybody.

I tell you it has outlawed the very basic concepts, gentlemen, upon which war was used as a final word when politics failed to settle international disputes. It is inherently a failure now.

The last two wars have shown it. The victor had to carry the defeated on his back. I have been carrying with all the resources possessed, and with the noble help of this country, that defeated country in Japan, trying to save her from destruction, and win her back into decency.

We paid, perhaps, $2 billion in that effort. We have been doing the same thing with Germany. We did win the war, but we did have to carry the loser.

If you have another world war, you are going to get such destruction and destructiveness, I think it was a philosopher who said—since we are talking about philosophers—under such conditions only those will be happy that are dead.

Now, the masses of the world are far ahead of their leaders, I believe, in this subject. I believe it is the massed opposition of the rank and file against war that offers the greatest possible hope that there shall be no war.

I believe it is the confession of defeatism in our civilization to say that war is inevitable. I believe the greatest mistake that was made in the League of Nations was not to tackle that fundamental problem.

It represents the highest hopes and concepts of mankind, and its mission was to keep the peace, but it developed into a body which had all the weaknesses of a legislative group, which could not speak with the authority of elected representatives; it had all the weaknesses of a judicial forum which did not have the moral and spiritual code which gave conviction to the world at large in its decision, and executively, it had all the weakness that it did not have the agencies under its control to carry out its decisions. It still remains a hope. . . .

. . . Senator JOHNSON. . . . Since we are living now, and will continue to live for years to come, in a world of uncertainties, I wonder if you do not think that some system of universal training which would guarantee that all of our young men would be made available for service, and they would be trained young men, should be invoked so that when the Nation was threatened we would be prepared?

General MACARTHUR. As I said, Senator, I am for preparedness, and the maximum preparedness, and the maximum utilization of all of our resource.

Now, whether universal military training accomplishes that fact would have to be pretty carefully considered by me.

There are other demands upon our manpower. Whether the total effort to train these great masses of millions of men, whether in actual combat those men would go into the niches for which they have been trained, I don't know. I have not studied the bill. I have not studied the potentialities of it.

It is not a question, I think, that can be settled by merely whether you are for or whether you are not for it. I am for the utilization of the total manpower that we have.

But whether the program of universal military training all youths along practically the same line, which I understand is the point considered, whether that will reduce and produce the greatest military effectiveness, I would not attempt to say until I had studied the problem very, very thoroughly.

I believe there are many complicated considerations. I believe the fitting in of the manpower, of the expert efficiency of the country, is a very intricate problem that can't be settled in such a broad general way as that.

I believe the greatest possible consideration has got to be given to the demands of industry. I believe that if you are going to prepare the youth, that you have got to understand that modern warfare has as its basis industry.

I believe that you have got to understand that the money that is involved is not limitless; that you have got to get the maximum efficiency for every penny you spend.

Now, I would not have the slightest hesitation in completely approving that, if I thought that was the best way to get the effectiveness.

Now, at the present moment, of course, this is a future plan you are working on; at the present moment, as I understand it, it is not applicable. There are other and more acute demands.

I should advise most seriously, if I were considering the problem, that I would wait and get through with the emergency that faces us now, and then on what has resulted and what exists then, I would sum up the facts, and make my decision.

If universal military training is the best way to do it, I would unhesitatingly advocate it. The question is the survival of the Nation, and I believe it is every citizen's duty to give that need in time of necessity that is required by the Nation. . . .

. . . You know the acuteness of modern war is increasing very vividly. It took a long time in the old days before the war machines really began to roll. But with the integration of the world, increase in scientific methods of destruction, the blow falls much quicker; that is, you don't get the time now to prepare that you had in the past. The first blow in the next war may well be the decisive blow. The first blows or the potency of the first blows— and that first blow, you understand, there is no method by which you can avoid the surprise attack of an enemy these days. He hits and then he announces, or he hits and he doesn't announce. And if you are not ready at that time you might well be overwhelmed before many factors, which I won't attempt to go into, gave you a certain period of time in which you could build up to meet the attack. But with every passing year that diminishes. Therefore, the corollary is with every passing year, as long as you have a maverick running loose in the world, it means that your necessity for preparedness increases unless you can find the formula to settle the whole matter. . . .

44. Dwight D. Eisenhower: A "New Look" in National Defense

PRESIDENT EISENHOWER WAS THE SECOND WEST POINT GRADUATE AND career soldier to occupy the White House (the first was U. S. Grant). Shaped, like MacArthur, in the two world wars, he was ten years younger; and when he became Constitutional Commander-in-Chief in 1953, his age, his temperament, and his new responsibilities combined to give a more modern tinge to his thought on military problems. By 1953 it was apparent that the defense structure set up by the National Security Act of 1947 was, despite subsequent amendment, inadequate to meet the rapidly changing demands of international politics and military technology. The Eisenhower administration developed a reorganization plan for the national defenses—the "new look"—which went into effect in June 1953. In the memoirs of his Presidency, published ten years later, Eisenhower explained the reorganization and the reasoning behind it. The following passage indicates how far American military thought had moved from the concepts of 1914 and 1915 into a new age, dominated by unusable—because suicidal—nuclear weapons, by the politics of "cold war," and by the enormous enhancement of American overseas responsibilities. The actual revisions in the defense structure may have been of mainly technical significance, but a comparison of the rationale of the Eisenhower reforms with that of the Root reforms—barely half a century before—is enough to show the transformations that had been wrought in the whole approach and climate of American military thought.

. . . I have often been told that deep-seated concern over the possibilities of nuclear war persuaded many people to vote for me in 1952 who under other circumstances might have opposed the candidacy of a professional military man. Whatever the impact on the political campaign, however, my military background assured at least that as President I would hold certain definite convictions on national security. With some oversimplification, it seemed to me, as I took over the office, that five basic considerations pro-

From *Mandate for Change, 1953–1956,* by Dwight D. Eisenhower. Copyright © 1963 by Dwight D. Eisenhower. Reprinted by permission of Doubleday & Company, Inc., pp. 445–458.

vided logical guidelines for designing and employing a security establishment.

I had long been convinced that the composition and structure of our military establishment should be based on the assumption that the United States on its own initiative would never start a major war. This meant that the nation had to maintain forces of greater strength and effectiveness than would be necessary if our purposes had been aggressive. So long as we were to allow an enemy the initiative, we would have to be capable of defeating him even after having sustained the first blow—a blow that would almost certainly be a surprise attack and one that would make Pearl Harbor, by comparison, look like a skirmish. Nevertheless, the assumption did not, in my view, presuppose that America's response to attack would have to accord with the exact nature of the aggression. For example, an invasion of Europe in overwhelming strength by conventional forces did not mean that our reaction had to be limited to force of the same kind.

The second guideline was that since modern global war would be catastrophic beyond belief, America's military forces must be designed primarily to deter a conflict, even though they might be compelled later to fight.

A third was that national security could not be measured in terms of military strength alone. The relationship, for example, between military and economic strength is intimate and indivisible. What America needed, I felt, was a fully adequate military establishment headed by men of sufficient breadth of view to recognize and sustain appropriate relationships among the moral, intellectual, economic, and military facets of our strength. This meant also that they should have the capacity to dispose our forces intelligently, in such a fashion as best to serve peacetime objectives and yet to be of maximum effectiveness in case of attack. They would, of course, have to realize that the diabolical threat of international Communism—and our problems in meeting it—would be with us for decades to come.

A fourth consideration was that our armed forces must be modern, designed to deter or wage the type of war to be expected in the mid-twentieth century. No longer could we afford the folly, so often indulged in in the past, of beginning each war with the weapons of the last.

The fifth important guideline was that United States security policy should take into account the need for membership in a system of alliances. Since our resources were and are finite, we could not supply all the land, sea, and air forces for the entire Free World. The logical role of our allies along the periphery of the Iron Curtain, therefore, would be to provide (with our help) for their own local security, especially ground forces, while the United States, centrally located and strong in productive power, provided mobile reserve forces of all arms, with emphasis on sea and air contingents.

In the early months of my administration the Korean War still dragged on; it would be difficult to effect major changes immediately. But thorough study could be undertaken without delay. An immediate task was to ensure an effective advisory mechanism concerned with all phases of national defense. The basic organ, the National Security Council, was already in existence. To ensure a breadth of viewpoint in considering security problems, I invited the Secretary of the Treasury, the Director of the Budget, and the Director of the United States Information Agency to participate, in addition to the statutory members, in the advisory work of the council.

The brave statement "America can afford anything it needs for national security" was and is true; in the earliest days of my administration I made this plain. But I also emphasized that America could not afford to waste money in any area, including the military, for anything that it did *not* need. I knew from experience that there was much duplication among the three services in research and development, in procurement, and even in roles and missions—these last always at least partly self-assigned.

To aid in the elimination of waste and duplication in the armed services, I felt that some reorganization of the Pentagon was desirable. The result was a reorganization plan which had three basic objectives: (1) to strengthen civilian control by establishing clearer lines of responsibility; (2) to improve administrative procedure in the Department of Defense by eliminating unwieldy boards and committees and substituting instead responsible executive officials; (3) to provide mechanisms for better strategic planning. The plan was prepared with the benefit of a report from a study committee which Secretary [of Defense Charles E.] Wilson had established as early as January 30, 1953.

This reorganization emphasized the position of the Secretary of Defense as my channel for communicating decisions to the defense establishment; likewise, it clearly recognized the legal responsibilities of the Joint Chiefs of Staff as advisers to the President and to the Secretary of Defense in purely military matters.

The last part of the reorganization plan involved strengthening the structure of the staff whose mission it was to serve the Joint Chiefs of Staff and, indirectly, the President and the Secretary of Defense. This Joint Staff was composed of officers assigned from the military services. They were, inescapably, too much under the divisive influence of the separate services from which they came. My objective was to take at least one step in divorcing the thinking and the outlook of the members of the Joint Staff from those of their parent services and to center their entire effort on national planning for the over-all common defense of the nation and the West. To accomplish this I directed that the selection of every military officer for service on the Joint Staff should require the approval of the chairman of the Joint Chiefs.

Opposition developed in Congress to this plan because of a fear that we were setting up a "Prussian-style general staff." This notion was scarcely based on any real knowledge of Germany's pre-World War I staff concepts, and after I had succeeded in clarifying the matter for the Legislative leaders, Reorganization Plan Number Six went into effect on June 30, 1953. . . .

. . . Conventionally the armed forces of the United States are thought of in terms of the specific services: the Army, the Navy, the Air Force, the Marine Corps, and sometimes the Coast Guard. But a better approach in analyzing strategic requirements is to make what has been called in military terminology a "horizontal analysis," which simply means to examine our armed might in the light of tasks which must be performed and the forces and weapons available to perform them, regardless of parent service.

Thus modern combat forces (as contrasted with logistical support forces) can be classified as follows:

(1) *Nuclear retaliatory or strike forces,* designed primarily for instant destruction of the enemy by large-scale nuclear attack. In the days of my first administration the bulk of this power was invested in the Air Force's Strategic Air Command, the backbone of which was the heavy intercontinental bomber, with the B-52 in the process of replacing the B-36. In addition, the Navy, with its attack carriers, made a contribution, particularly in the Far East.

(2) *Forces deployed overseas.* These forces, including land and tactical air forces, were stationed principally in Europe and the Far East. Their duty was to bolster our allies' defenses in those areas and to insure that the boundaries between freedom and slavery would not be moved to our disadvantage. In Europe these forces came under the command of the man in a U.S. post called CINCEUR, or Commander-in-Chief, Europe (who was also Supreme Commander for the Allied powers of Europe). The United States contribution was made up of the U. S. Seventh Army, the Ninth Air Force, and the Sixth Fleet, the last normally stationed in the Mediterranean.

In the Far East, at the close of the Korean fighting, was the U. S. Eighth Army in Korea, and the U. S. Fifth Air Force, the Seventh Fleet, and units of all services, stationed on the offshore island chain.

(3) *Forces to keep the sea lanes open in the event of emergency.* These forces, primarily Navy and Marine, were deployed in the Atlantic and Pacific.

(4) *Forces to protect the United States from air attack.* These consisted primarily of air-defense units, both Army and Air Force, assigned to the Continental Air Defense Command, with headquarters in Colorado. This command later became a combined command between the United States and the Canadians, and its title was changed to North American Air Defense Command.

(5) *Reserve Forces.* These forces, located primarily within the

continent of the United States, were normally left under the control of their respective service chiefs for training purposes. They consisted of Army divisions, Air Force and Navy wings and fleets, and supporting units.

Keeping these missions in mind, then, we might define the New Look, as first, a reallocation of resources among the five categories of forces, and second, the placing of greater emphasis than formerly on the deterrent and destructive power of improved nuclear weapons, better means of delivery, and effective air-defense units.

Other active combat units, including those deployed overseas and forces to keep the sea lanes open, were to be modernized and maintained at a maximum mobility and effectiveness, but with decreases in numerical strength. Supporting reserves in the United States, while important, were given a lower priority.

The New Look called for a new outlook by the men concerned. This was not easy to acquire, for, as it turned out, the reallocations resulted in an increase in the Air Force, whereas the bulk of the reductions were primarily in the Army and secondarily in the Navy. This came about partly because during the Korean War the Army had expanded far beyond its necessary peacetime size.

This change in emphasis came at a time when the administration was exerting every effort to cut the costs of government everywhere; therefore the two separate efforts came to be associated in many minds. . . .

. . . I directed that this concept of defense should be implemented with minimum delay. However, in order to attain the necessary wholehearted cooperation of the senior military officers, I did, from time to time, meet with the Joint Chiefs and other defense officials to review progress.

One important meeting of this kind was held in my office in early December 1954. I pointed out to the group, once again, that long-term security required a sound economy, that no predicted critical danger date could be taken as a decisive factor in the nation's defense planning, and that the only way the United States could be quickly knocked out was by surprise attack on its mainland. I went over, once more, all of the missions for which the armed forces would be responsible and the priorities that had been established.

I indicated the necessity of making a realistic appraisal of what the maintenance of an adequate but not extravagant defense establishment over an extended period of time (say, half a century) could mean to the nation, and urged that we do our best to create a national climate favorable to dynamic industrial effort. I said that, since there could not possibly be any large-scale deployment of military forces from the continental United States to overseas theaters during the first few months of a nuclear war, our requirements in ground forces, other than those already overseas, should be limited to reserves of sufficient strength to meet a "brush-fire" war in one—or at most, two—localities. If conflicts started in a number of places simultaneously, then we would automatically be in a major war, which was a different problem entirely. In this instance, I repeated, our objectives in the first phase of such a global war would have to be to avert disaster, as we, in turn, released our nuclear stockpile on the aggressor. After that we would have time to go on to win.

These views received varying degrees of concurrence. Admiral [Robert B.] Carney [Chief of Naval Operations] for one, reported that the Navy was tailoring its forces to follow these policies, increasing its early striking power and cutting back amphibious forces, not so necessary as formerly, in the early stages of hostilities. General [Matthew B.] Ridgeway [Chief of Staff], however, recently returned from Europe, was deeply troubled about the security of United States forces then overseas. In event of war it would not be possible to support them quickly unless reinforcements of large size (perhaps ten divisions he felt) were constantly ready to sail at a moment's notice. In his opinion our deployed strength was inadequate, and our ready reserve units at hand too small.

I could not help being sympathetic. The safety of United States troops and their dependents in Europe was my concern as well. I stressed to General Ridgway that I had no intention of allowing Europe to be overrun, as it had been in 1940. But we knew that the Soviets maintained something in the neighborhood of 175 divisions active in Europe at all times. The United States had twenty divisions, only five of which were in Europe. Therefore, in view of the disparity in the strengths of the opposing ground forces, it seemed clear that only by the interposition of our nuclear weapons could we promptly stop a major Communist aggression in that area. Two more divisions or ten more divisions, on our side, would not make very much difference against this Soviet ground force.

But I was not pessimistic. My intention was firm: to launch the Strategic Air Command immediately upon trustworthy evidence of a general attack against the West. So I repeated that first priority must be given to the task of meeting the atomic threat, the only kind of attack that could, without notice, endanger our very existence.

I pointed out that no commander—no nation—ever had, when conflict threatened, all the forces of all kinds that might be considered desirable. Therefore it was the responsibility of leadership —civil and military—to decide upon priorities. This done, the next task was to assure maximum efficiency in the forces calculated to be permanently necessary.

As time went on this doctrine came to be largely accepted in principle. But then there was raised another argument, based on the assumption that as a nuclear balance between the West and the East became foreseeable, the danger of atomic war would recede and our real problem would be to provide more ground forces and conventional support types to win small, brush-fire conflicts. In a climate of mutual deterrence, several of these "small wars" *could* conceivably occur simultaneously; therefore, it was asserted, we must greatly reinforce our conventional forces. The argument was based upon the premise that we would never, under any kind of circumstance, provocation, or aggression, employ our nuclear strength.

In my opinion this kind of solution was the product of timidity —a solution that began by seeing danger behind every tree or bush. This was also an unrealistic solution, one that required massive defense units of such size and capacity that no matter how universal and threatening the danger or how many the local "disturbances," we could quickly defeat them by conventional means. I refused to turn the United States into an armed camp.

To emphasize my convictions, I stressed that the United States would not employ the same policies and resources to fight another war as were used in the Korean conflict. I saw no sense in wasting manpower in costly small wars that could not achieve decisive results under the political and military circumstances then existing. I felt that this kind of military policy would play into the hands of a potential enemy whose superiority in available military manpower was obvious. We should refuse to permit our adversary to enjoy a sanctuary from which he could operate without danger to himself; we would not allow him to blackmail us into placing limitations upon the types of weapons we would employ. Moreover, in the matter of brush-fire wars I pointed out that we would not try to maintain the conventional power to police the whole world, even though we would cooperate with our allies on the spot. The Communists would have to be made to realize that should they be guilty of major aggression, we would strike with means of our own choosing at the head of the Communist power.

If we were wise enough, and sufficiently self-confident to concentrate on making our defense establishment effective, flexible, and economical, rather than heavy, clumsy, and costly, I believed we could be both secure and prosperous.

When it came time to prepare budgets, it was particularly difficult to get the Joint Chiefs of Staff, collectively, to be guided by these policies. Each believed that although the sums allocated to the others were quite sufficient for national safety, the amounts approved for his own particular service were inadequate. The result was that budgetary decisions had to be made, rather than approved, at the civilian echelon. Thus the internal differences in our highest military mechanism tended to neutralize the advisory influence they should have enjoyed as a body.

Strategic deployment of forces, coordination among services, and manpower and budgetary problems, however, are not the only military matters of concern to a President. Equally important is the matter of how the research and development efforts of the Department of Defense are managed, for in the process of establishing sensible priorities for high-cost programs of this kind, the nature of the entire military posture is determined.

The most dramatic action in this field during the early years of my administration was, for all practical purposes, the beginning of research and development on ballistic missiles of intermediate and intercontinental ranges. These vehicles, with their nuclear warheads, were destined to make previous concepts of warfare obsolete and could possibly reduce the duration of a modern war to a matter of hours. Our problem in the development of long-range ballistic weapons was complicated by prior neglect of their potential capabilities. For example, in fiscal year 1953, the United States spent only a million dollars on long-range ballistic missiles, less than it was spending to support the price of peanuts.

This lack of concern with the ballistic missile was undoubtedly partly the result of preoccupation with the aerodynamic missile, or pilotless aircraft. Development of the aerodynamic weapon could be expected to be quicker—and at that time it was thought to be more practical than the ballistic type, which had to leave and re-enter the earth's atmosphere. On two aerodynamic projects, the Snark and the Navajo, a great deal of time and money had already been used.

But then, through the conclusions and recommendations of the scientists, presented to me in 1954 and early 1955, it became clear that the matter of developing ballistic missiles was urgent. Indications were that the Soviets had been working on this type of weapon for a number of years, and our development programs were promptly accorded the highest priorities.

While it was easy to direct the Defense Department to go full speed ahead, it was not so easy to devise the best organization of the missile program itself. It might have been best, had it been feasible, to remove the whole missile program from the hands of the regular military services and to establish another "Manhattan Project," similar to that through which the atomic bomb was developed during World War II. This scheme would have had the advantage of concentrating the best scientific minds on one set of programs and eliminating duplication and rivalry among the various service activities. However, by the time the urgency of the program became apparent, each of the services had already organized and was using experimental teams of scientists and engineers for missile development. To tear up all of these organizations and to transplant the scientists, engineers, and officers already engaged in the business, seemed to me, to Secretary Wilson, and to my military-scientific advisers to promise more delay than would continuation of existing procedures.

This was a close decision. The problems of achieving coordination among services were severe. However, the urgent need for quick results dictated that this disadvantage be accepted. The decision was, I believe, the right one, although interservice rivalries in this field were by no means eliminated.

Another question was whether the priority to be accorded the IRBM[1] deserved to be as high as the more glamorous ICBM.[2] For the immediate military problem, I thought it was. I realized that the political and psychological impact on the world of the early development of a reliable IRBM would be enormous, while its military value would, for the time being, be practically equal to that of the ICBM, since the former, located on bases on foreign soil, could strike any target in Communist areas as well as could an ICBM fired from the United States. However, since in the long term the ICBM promised great advantages over the IRBM, I directed that both phases of the missile program should have the highest possible priority in the use of talent, money, and materials.

In early 1955 it came to my attention that the Navy, by combining techniques all of which had already been proven, could now begin development of a new weapon system which would enable them eventually to fire a ballistic missile from a submerged nuclear submarine. The missiles would carry nuclear warheads and be of sufficient range to hit critical targets in the Sino-Soviet land mass. Thus it would constitute an almost invulnerable re-

[1] Intermediate range ballistic missile [Ed.].
[2] Intercontinental ballistic missile [Ed.].

taliatory capability, separate and apart from the missiles and planes located in the United States and on foreign bases. The project was undertaken at once, and before the end of my years in the White House, some of these highly valuable "Polaris" submarines were on station as a growing part of our nuclear deterrent.

I have pondered, on occasion, the evolution of the military art during the mid-fifties. The Army in which I was commissioned a second lieutenant in 1915 underwent phenomenal changes in the thirty years from then until the German surrender in 1945. Auto-firing guns, motor transport, fighter and bomber airplanes, tanks, and many types of rockets all came into common use. But those changes, startling as they were, faded into insignificance when compared to those of the postwar period, particularly during my first three years in the Presidency.

New military developments, therefore, brought about important changes in the duties that absorbed the urgent and continuous attention of the President. The title of Commander-in-Chief of the armed forces had become something real and critical even in peace. I was incessantly involved in basic decisions, planning, and meeting with Defense and Atomic Energy Commission officials to approve annual increments in the national atomic stockpile and its dispersal in far-flung posts around the globe. My every footstep was followed by a courier carrying a satchel filled with draft war orders to be issued by code number in case of emergency.

Our military structure and equipment were changing so rapidly that even the comforting old slogan "Tried and true" was gone. In its place had sprung up a disquieting new one: "If it works, it's obsolete."

45. Dwight D. Eisenhower Looks to a Complex Future

IN HIS FAREWELL ADDRESS, JANUARY 18, 1961, PRESIDENT EISENHOWER reviewed the whole problem of war and defense in its broadest terms. It is arresting to compare this with Washington's Farewell in 1796

(Document 8) or Jackson's in 1837 (Document 15); these were three of our four primarily military Presidents. And there is no better way of showing how greatly both the military problem and the focus of military thought had been transformed by the 165 years they span. Eisenhower not only pointed to the potential dangers to democracy inherent in the new giant "military-industrial complex," but saw as well the ultimate necessity for disarmament and the infeasibility of the war system itself as the governing element in international relations. He regretted his failure to accomplish more toward the resolution of these great issues; but few earlier American soldiers would have even recognized their existence.

This evening I come to you with a message of leave-taking and farewell, and to share a few final thoughts with you, my countrymen.

Like every other citizen, I wish the new President, and all who will labor with him, Godspeed. I pray that the coming years will be blessed with peace and prosperity for all.

I.

Our people expect their President and the Congress to find essential agreement on issues of great moment, the wise resolution of which will better shape the future of the Nation.

My own relations with the Congress, which began on a remote and tenuous basis when, long ago, a member of the Senate appointed me to West Point, have since ranged to the intimate during the war and immediate post-war period, and, finally, to the mutually interdependent during these past eight years.

In this final relationship, the Congress and the Administration have, on most vital issues, cooperated well, to serve the national good rather than mere partisanship, and so have assured that the business of the Nation should go forward. So, my official relation-

From *Public Papers of the Presidents of the United States, Dwight D. Eisenhower, 1960–1961* (Washington, D.C.: Government Printing Office, 1961), pp. 1036–1040.

ship with the Congress ends in a feeling, on my part, of gratitude that we have been able to do so much together.

II.

We now stand ten years past the midpoint of a century that has witnessed four major wars among great nations. Three of these involved our own country. Despite these holocausts America is today the strongest, the most influential and most productive nation in the world. Understandably proud of this pre-eminence, we yet realize that America's leadership and prestige depend, not merely upon our unmatched material progress, riches and military strength, but on how we use our power in the interests of world peace and human betterment.

III.

Throughout America's adventure in free government, our basic purposes have been to keep the peace; to foster progress in human achievement, and to enhance liberty, dignity and integrity among people and among nations. To strive for less would be unworthy of a free and religious people. Any failure traceable to arrogance, or for lack of comprehension or readiness to sacrifice would inflict upon us grievous hurt both at home and abroad.

Progress toward these noble goals is persistently threatened by the conflict now engulfing the world. It commands our whole attention, absorbs our very beings. We face a hostile ideology—global in scope, atheistic in character, ruthless in purpose, and insidious in method. Unhappily the danger it poses promises to be of indefinite duration. To meet it successfully, there is called for, not so much the emotional and transitory sacrifices of crisis, but rather those which enable us to carry forward steadily, surely, and without complaint the burdens of a prolonged and complex struggle—with liberty the stake. Only thus shall we remain, despite every provocation, on our charted course toward permanent peace and human betterment.

Crises there will continue to be. In meeting them, whether

foreign or domestic, great or small, there is a recurring temptation to feel that some spectacular and costly action could become
the miraculous solution to all current difficulties. A huge increase
in newer elements of our defense; development of unrealistic
programs to cure every ill in agriculture; a dramatic expansion in
basic and applied research—these and many other possibilities,
each possibly promising in itself, may be suggested as the only
way to the road we wish to travel.

But each proposal must be weighed in the light of a broader
consideration: the need to maintain balance in and among national programs—balance between the private and the public
economy, balance between cost and hoped for advantage—balance between the clearly necessary and the comfortably desirable;
balance between our essential requirements as a nation and the
duties imposed by the nation upon the individual; balance between actions of the moment and the national welfare of the
future. Good judgment seeks balance and progress; lack of it
eventually finds imbalance and frustration.

The record of many decades stands as proof that our people
and their government have, in the main, understood these truths
and have responded to them well, in the face of stress and threat.
But threats, new in kind or degree, constantly arise. I mention
two only.

IV.

A vital element in keeping the peace is our military establishment. Our arms must be mighty, ready for instant action, so that
no potential aggressor may be tempted to risk his own destruction.

Our military organization today bears little relation to that
known by any of my predecessors in peacetime, or indeed by the
fighting men of World War II or Korea.

Until the latest of our world conflicts, the United States had no
armaments industry. American makers of plowshares could, with
time and as required, make swords as well. But now we can no
longer risk emergency improvisation of national defense; we have

been compelled to create a permanent armaments industry of vast proportions. Added to this, three and a half million men and women are directly engaged in the defense establishment. We annually spend on military security more than the net income of all United States corporations.

This conjunction of an immense military establishment and a large arms industry is new in the American experience. The total influence—economic, political, even spiritual—is felt in every city, every State house, every office of the Federal government. We recognize the imperative need for this development. Yet we must not fail to comprehend its grave implications. Our toil, resources and livelihood are all involved; so is the very structure of our society.

In the councils of government, we must guard against the acquisition of unwarranted influence, whether sought or unsought, by the military-industrial complex. The potential for the disastrous rise of misplaced power exists and will persist.

We must never let the weight of this combination endanger our liberties or democratic processes. We should take nothing for granted. Only an alert and knowledgeable citizenry can compel the proper meshing of the huge industrial and military machinery of defense with our peaceful methods and goals, so that security and liberty may prosper together.

Akin to, and largely responsible for the sweeping changes in our industrial-military posture, has been the technological revolution during recent decades.

In this revolution, research has become central; it also becomes more formalized, complex, and costly. A steadily increasing share is conducted for, by, or at the direction of, the Federal government.

Today, the solitary inventor, tinkering in his shop, has been overshadowed by task forces of scientists in laboratories and testing fields. In the same fashion, the free university, historically the fountainhead of free ideas and scientific discovery, has experienced a revolution in the conduct of research. Partly because of the huge costs involved, a government contract becomes virtually a substitute for intellectual curiosity. For every old blackboard there are now hundreds of new electronic computers.

The prospect of domination of the nation's scholars by Federal employment, project allocations, and the power of money is ever present—and is gravely to be regarded.

Yet, in holding scientific research and discovery in respect, as we should, we must also be alert to the equal and opposite danger that public policy could itself become the captive of a scientific-technological elite.

It is the task of statesmanship to mold, to balance, and to integrate these and other forces, new and old, within the principles of our democratic system—ever aiming toward the supreme goals of our free society.

V.

Another factor in maintaining balance involves the element of time. As we peer into society's future, we—you and I, and our government—must avoid the impulse to live only for today, plundering, for our own ease and convenience, the precious resources of tomorrow. We cannot mortgage the material assets of our grandchildren without risking the loss also of their political and spiritual heritage. We want democracy to survive for all generations to come, not to become the insolvent phantom of tomorrow.

VI.

Down the long lane of the history yet to be written America knows that this world of ours, ever growing smaller, must avoid becoming a community of dreadful fear and hate, and be, instead, a proud confederation of mutual trust and respect.

Such a confederation must be one of equals. The weakest must come to the conference table with the same confidence as do we, protected as we are by our moral, economic, and military strength. That table, though scarred by many past frustrations, cannot be abandoned for the certain agony of the battlefield.

Disarmament, with mutual honor and confidence, is a continuing imperative. Together we must learn how to compose differences, not with arms, but with intellect and decent purpose. Because this need is so sharp and apparent I confess that I lay down my official responsibilities in this field with a definite sense of disappointment. As one who has witnessed the horror and the lingering sadness of war—as one who knows that another war could utterly destroy this civilization which has been so slowly and painfully built over thousands of years—I wish I could say tonight that a lasting peace is in sight.

Happily, I can say that war has been avoided. Steady progress toward our ultimate goal has been made. But, so much remains to be done. As a private citizen, I shall never cease to do what little I can to help the world advance along that road.

VII.

So—in this my last night to you as your President—I thank you for the many opportunities you have given me for public service in war and peace. I trust that in that service you find some things worthy; as for the rest of it, I know you will find ways to improve performance in the future.

You and I—my fellow citizens—need to be strong in our faith that all nations, under God, will reach the goal of peace with justice. May we be ever unswerving in devotion to principle, confident but humble with power, diligent in pursuit of the Nation's great goals.

To all the peoples of the world, I once more give expression to America's prayerful and continuing aspiration:

We pray that peoples of all faiths, all races, all nations, may have their great human needs satisfied; that those now denied opportunity shall come to enjoy it to the full; that all who yearn for freedom may experience its spiritual blessings; that those who have freedom will understand, also, its heavy responsibilities; that all who are insensitive to the needs of others will learn charity; that the scourges of poverty, disease and ignorance will be made to disappear from the earth, and that, in the goodness of time, all peoples will come to live together in a peace guaranteed by the binding force of mutual respect and love.

46. John F. Kennedy Moves Away from the Cold War Concept

THE KENNEDY ADMINISTRATION MADE NO BASIC CHANGES IN THE MILITARY policies of its predecessor, but it did try to put them in a new context. In his Farewell Address, Eisenhower still saw the military problem as one of defense against a "hostile ideology . . . ruthless in purpose and insidious in method" posing a danger that promised to be "of indefinite duration." President Kennedy, in his address at the American University on June 10, 1963, saw more clearly the community as well as the diversity of interests between the United States and the Soviet Union, the possibility of a peaceful co-existence, and the impossibility of any purely military solution for world problems. The address moved American and possibly Russian military thought into a new perspective. It was, at least, influential in the negotiation of the nuclear test-ban treaty, the only significant step toward the limitation of armaments since 1922; and it helped lay the foundations of the new attitudes that by the end of 1963 were producing a new synthesis of foreign, military, and defense policy.

. . . I have . . . chosen this time and this place to discuss a topic on which ignorance too often abounds and the truth is too rarely perceived—yet it is the most important topic on earth: world peace.

What kind of peace do I mean? What kind of peace do we seek? Not a Pax Americana enforced on the world by American weapons of war. Not the peace of the grave or the security of the slave. I am talking about genuine peace, the kind of peace that makes life on earth worth living, the kind that enables men and nations to grow and to hope and to build a better life for their children—not merely peace for Americans but peace for all

From *Public Papers of the Presidents, John F. Kennedy, 1963* (Washington, D.C.: Government Printing Office, 1964) pp. 460–464.

men and women—not merely peace in our time but peace for all time.

I speak of peace because of the new face of war. Total war makes no sense in an age when great powers can maintain large and relatively invulnerable nuclear forces and refuse to surrender without resort to those forces. It makes no sense in an age when a single nuclear weapon contains almost ten times the explosive force delivered by all of the allied air forces in the Second World War. It makes no sense in an age when the deadly poisons produced by a nuclear exchange would be carried by wind and water and soil and seed to the far corners of the globe and to generations yet unborn.

Today the expenditure of billions of dollars every year on weapons acquired for the purpose of making sure we never need to use them is essential to keeping the peace. But surely the acquisition of such idle stockpiles—which can only destroy and never create—is not the only, much less the most efficient, means of assuring peace.

I speak of peace, therefore, as the necessary rational end of rational men. I realize that the pursuit of peace is not as dramatic as the pursuit of war—and frequently the words of the pursuer fall on deaf ears. But we have no more urgent task.

Some say that it is useless to speak of world peace or world law or world disarmament—and that it will be useless until the leaders of the Soviet Union adopt a more enlightened attitude. I hope they do. I believe we can help them do it. But I also believe that we must reexamine our own attitude—as individuals and as a Nation—for our attitude is as essential as theirs. And every graduate of this school, every thoughtful citizen who despairs of war and wishes to bring peace, should begin by looking inward—by examining his own attitude toward the possibilities of peace, toward the Soviet Union, toward the course of the cold war and toward freedom and peace here at home.

First: Let us examine our attitude toward peace itself. Too many of us think it is impossible. Too many think it unreal. But that is a dangerous, defeatist belief. It leads to the conclusion that war is inevitable—that mankind is doomed—that we are gripped by forces we cannot control.

We need not accept that view. Our problems are manmade—therefore, they can be solved by man. And man can be as big as he wants. No problem of human destiny is beyond human beings. Man's reason and spirit have often solved the seemingly unsolvable—and we believe they can do it again.

I am not referring to the absolute, infinite concept of universal peace and good will of which some fantasies and fanatics dream. I do not deny the value of hopes and dreams but we merely invite discouragement and incredulity by making that our only and immediate goal.

Let us focus instead on a more practical, more attainable peace—based not on a sudden revolution in human nature but on a gradual evolution in human institutions—on a series of concrete actions and effective agreements which are in the interest of all concerned. There is no single, simple key to this peace—no grand or magic formula to be adopted by one or two powers. Genuine peace must be the product of many nations, the sum of many acts. It must be dynamic, not static, changing to meet the challenge of each new generation. For peace is a process—a way of solving problems.

With such a peace, there will still be quarrels and conflicting interests, as there are within families and nations. World peace, like community peace, does not require that each man love his neighbor—it requires only that they live together in mutual tolerance, submitting their disputes to a just and peaceful settlement. And history teaches us that enmities between nations, as between individuals, do not last forever. However fixed our likes and dislikes may seem, the tide of time and events will often bring surprising changes in the relations between nations and neighbors.

So let us persevere. Peace need not be impracticable, and war need not be inevitable. By defining our goal more clearly, by making it seem more manageable and less remote, we can help all peoples to see it, to draw hope from it, and to move irresistibly toward it.

Second: Let us reexamine our attitude toward the Soviet Union. It is discouraging to think that their leaders may actually believe what their propagandists write. It is discouraging to read a recent authoritative Soviet text on *Military Strategy* and find, on page after page, wholly baseless and incredible claims—such as the allegation that "American imperialist circles are preparing to unleash different types of wars . . . that there is a very real threat of a preventive war being unleashed by American imperialists against the Soviet Union . . . [and that] the political aims of the American imperialists are to enslave economically and politically the European and other capitalist countries . . . [and] to achieve world domination . . . by means of aggressive wars."

Truly, as it was written long ago: "The wicked flee when no man pursueth." Yet it is sad to read these Soviet statements—to realize the extent of the gulf between us. But it is also a warning —a warning to the American people not to fall into the same trap as the Soviets, not to see only a distorted and desperate view of the other side, not to see conflict as inevitable, accommodation as impossible, and communication as nothing more than an exchange of threats.

No government or social system is so evil that its people must be considered as lacking in virtue. As Americans, we find communism profoundly repugnant as a negation of personal freedom and dignity. But we can still hail the Russian people for their many achievements—in science and space, in economic and industrial growth, in culture and in acts of courage.

Among the many traits the peoples of our two countries have in common, none is stronger than our mutual abhorrence of war. Almost unique, among the major world powers, we have never been at war with each other. And no nation in the history of battle ever suffered more than the Soviet Union suffered in the course of the Second World War. At least 20 million lost their lives. Countless millions of homes and farms were burned or sacked. A third of the nation's territory, including nearly two thirds of its industrial base, was turned into a wasteland—a loss equivalent to the devastation of this country east of Chicago.

Today, should total war ever break out again—no matter how

—our two countries would become the primary targets. It is an ironic but accurate fact that the two strongest powers are the two in the most danger of devastation. All we have built, all we have worked for, would be destroyed in the first 24 hours. And even in the cold war, which brings burdens and dangers to so many countries, including this Nation's closest allies—our two countries bear the heaviest burdens. For we are both devoting massive sums of money to weapons that could be better devoted to combating ignorance, poverty, and disease. We are both caught up in a vicious and dangerous cycle in which suspicion on one side breeds suspicion on the other, and new weapons beget counterweapons.

In short, both the United States and its allies, and the Soviet Union and its allies, have a mutually deep interest in a just and genuine peace and in halting the arms race. Agreements to this end are in the interests of the Soviet Union as well as ours—and even the most hostile nations can be relied upon to accept and keep those treaty obligations, and only those treaty obligations, which are in their own interest.

So, let us not be blind to our differences—but let us also direct attention to our common interests and to the means by which those differences can be resolved. And if we cannot end now our differences, at least we can help make the world safe for diversity. For, in the final analysis, our most basic common link is that we all inhabit this small planet. We all breathe the same air. We all cherish our children's future. And we are all mortal.

Third: Let us reexamine our attitude toward the cold war, remembering that we are not engaged in a debate, seeking to pile up debating points. We are not here distributing blame or pointing the finger of judgment. We must deal with the world as it is, and not as it might have been had the history of the last 18 years been different.

We must, therefore, persevere in the search for peace in the hope that constructive changes within the Communist bloc might bring within reach solutions which now seem beyond us. We must conduct our affairs in such a way that it becomes in the Communists' interest to agree on a genuine peace. Above all, while defending our own vital interests, nuclear powers must avert those confrontations which bring an adversary to a choice of either a humiliating retreat or a nuclear war. To adopt that kind of course in the nuclear age would be evidence only of the bankruptcy of our policy—or of a collective death-wish for the world.

To secure these ends, America's weapons are nonprovocative, carefully controlled, designed to deter, and capable of selective use. Our military forces are committed to peace and disciplined in self-restraint. Our diplomats are instructed to avoid unnecessary irritants and purely rhetorical hostility.

For we can seek a relaxation of tensions without relaxing our guard. And, for our part, we do not need to use threats to prove that we are resolute. We do not need to jam foreign broadcasts out of fear our faith will be eroded. We are unwilling to impose our system on any unwilling people—but we are willing and able to engage in peaceful competition with any people on earth.

Meanwhile, we seek to strengthen the United Nations, to help solve its financial problems, to make it a more effective instrument for peace, to develop it into a genuine world security system—a system capable of resolving disputes on the basis of law, of insuring the security of the large and the small, and of creating conditions under which arms can finally be abolished. . . .

. . . The United States will make no deal with the Soviet Union at the expense of other nations and other peoples, not merely because they are our partners, but also because their interests and ours converge.

Our interests converge, however, not only in defending the frontiers of freedom, but in pursuing the paths of peace. It is our hope —and the purpose of allied policies—to convince the Soviet Union that she, too, should let each nation choose its own future, so long as that choice does not interfere with the choices of others. The Communist drive to impose their political and economic system on others is the primary cause of world tension today. For there can be no doubt that, if all nations could refrain from interfering in the self-determination of others, the peace would be much more assured.

This will require a new effort to achieve world law—a new context for world discussions. It will require increased understanding between the Soviets and ourselves. And increased understanding will require increased contact and communication. One step in this direction is the proposed arrangement for a direct line between Moscow and Washington, to avoid on each side the dangerous delays, misunderstandings, and misreadings of the other's actions which might occur at a time of crisis.

We have also been talking in Geneva about other first-step measures of arms control, designed to limit the intensity of the arms race and to reduce the risks of accidental war. Our primary long-range interest in Geneva, however, is general and complete disarmament—designed to take place by stages, permitting parallel political developments to build the new institutions of peace which would take the place of arms. The pursuit of disarmament has been an effort of this Government since the 1920's. It has been urgently sought by the past three administrations. And however dim the prospects may be today, we intend to continue this effort —to continue it in order that all countries, including our own, can better grasp what the problems and possibilities of disarmament are.

The one major area of these negotiations where the end is in sight, yet where a fresh start is badly needed, is in a treaty to outlaw nuclear tests. The conclusion of such a treaty, so near and yet so far, would check the spiraling arms race in one of its most dangerous areas. It would place the nuclear powers in a position to deal more effectively with one of the greatest hazards which man faces in 1963, the further spread of nuclear arms. It would increase our security—it would decrease the prospects of war. Surely this goal is sufficiently important to require our steady pursuit, yielding neither to the temptation to give up the whole effort nor the temptation to give up our insistence on vital and responsible safeguards.

I am taking this opportunity, therefore, to announce two important decisions in this regard.

First: Chairman Khrushchev, Prime Minister Macmillan, and I

have agreed that high-level discussions will shortly begin in Moscow looking toward early agreement on a comprehensive test ban treaty. Our hopes must be tempered with the caution of history—but with our hopes go the hopes of all mankind.

Second: To make clear our good faith and solemn convictions on the matter, I now declare that the United States does not propose to conduct nuclear tests in the atmosphere so long as other states do not do so. We will not be the first to resume. Such a declaration is no substitute for a formal binding treaty, but I hope it will help us achieve one. Nor would such a treaty be a substitute for disarmament, but I hope it will help us achieve it. . . .

. . . The United States, as the world knows, will never start a war. We do not want a war. We do not now expect a war. This generation of Americans has already had enough—more than enough—of war and hate and oppression. We shall be prepared if others wish it. We shall be alert to try to stop it. But we shall also do our part to build a world of peace where the weak are safe and the strong are just. We are not helpless before that task or hopeless of its success. Confident and unafraid, we labor on—not toward a strategy of annihilation but toward a strategy of peace.

47. Robert S. McNamara: Defense Policy of the 1960's

BENEATH THE SEVERAL IMMEDIATE CRISES CONFRONTED BY THE KENnedy administration, the great, underlying problems of war and defense policy remained as before—to adjust both military and political strategy to the existence of thermo-nuclear weapons and their missile-carriers; to combine the various arms of national policy, including the armed services, into a coherent military-political instrument capable of serving the true interests of one hundred and ninety million human beings, rather than destroying them; to relate the requirements of defense to those of the domestic polity and economy of a free society. Obviously, these problems can never be finally answered in a fast-changing world; but at the time of President Kennedy's death, American military thought was converging upon a reasonably self-consistent structure of military policy and preparation that summarized today's best answers.

In a speech in November 1963, Robert S. McNamara, the unusually able Secretary of Defense, reviewed something of the history of the military problem, indicated the force levels of all kinds maintained by the United States, and expounded a good deal of the political-strategic reasoning on which they are based. Because this talk in effect represents the outcome of a great deal of American military thought over the past twenty complicated and difficult years, it is used to conclude the present volume.

Before long this Administration will be presenting, once again, the details of a proposed national defense budget for the consideration of the Congress and the public. Given the importance of these matters, their complexities and uncertainties and the existence of real differences of opinion, a degree of controversy is inevitable, and even desirable.

Some controversies, however, reveal underlying differences in perspective that scarcely suggest the participants are living in the same world. Within the past few weeks, some critics have suggested that we have literally hundreds of times more strength than we need; others have accused us of risking the whole future of the nation by engaging in unilateral disarmament. I would like to believe that criticisms bracketing our policy in that fashion prove it to be rational and sound. But a discrepancy of that order cannot be reassuring. . . .

. . . As a prelude, then, to the coming season of debate, I should like to identify and discuss some basic matters on which a considerable degree of consensus seems to me both possible and desirable, although by no means assured.

These include those over-all comparative strengths and weaknesses of the opposing military alliances that form the bold relief in the strategic environment. In short, they are the considerations that seem to have relatively long-term significance compared to the annual budget cycle.

Matters of that degree of permanence tend to be stamped on our minds as being unchanging and unchangeable, the unques-

From Robert S. McNamara, "Remarks Before the Economic Club of New York," November 18, 1963, Department of Defense News Release 1486-63.

tioned framework of daily and yearly policy-making. Yet these factors of which I shall speak do change: more swiftly and more profoundly than our picture of them tends to change. Indeed, I believe it is just the fact that over the last decade this topography has changed—while many maps have not—that accounts for some apparently irreconcilable controversies.

Let me recall the earlier period briefly, for comparison. The strategic landscape at the outset of the 'Fifties was dominated by two outstanding features. One was the practical U.S. monopoly of deliverable, strategic nuclear weapons. The other was the Soviet Union and Communist China's virtual monopoly of ground force on the continents of Europe and Asia.

Both of these determinants of Western military policy had changed considerably by the end of the Korean War. The Soviets had produced atomic explosions and had created a sizable nuclear delivery capability against Europe, while NATO ground forces had expanded rapidly, and military operations in Korea had greatly tarnished the significance of Chinese Communist superiority in numbers. But the old notions of monopoly persisted as short-cut aids to thinking on policy matters. And they were not so misleading as they came later to be. Soviet armed forces approaching five million men still heavily outweighed the NATO forces in Europe; and Soviet delivery capability against the U.S. was dwarfed by that of SAC. Moreover, tactical nuclear weapons were being heralded as a new nuclear monopoly for the West.

Even as these earlier notions of monopolies grew obsolete, ideas about the feasibility of alternative policies continued to reflect them. So did ideas about how wars might be fought. Nuclear operations, both strategic and tactical, by the U.S. in response to Soviet aggression against our allies were considered to be virtually unilateral. Hence it was supposed the problem of credibility of the U.S. response would scarcely arise, even in the case of relatively limited Soviet aggressions. Western reliance upon nuclear weapons, in particular strategic systems, both to deter and to oppose non-nuclear attack of any size seemed not only adequate but also unique in its adequacy.

That sort of situation is convenient for policy-makers. It makes policy easy to choose and easy to explain. Perhaps that is why throughout most of the 'Fifties, while the Soviets under various pressures decreased their ground forces and the NATO allies built theirs up, and while the Soviets acquired a massive nuclear threat against Europe and laid the groundwork for a sizable threat against the U.S., the picture underlying most policy debate remained that appropriate to 1949. It was a picture of a Communist Goliath in conventional strength facing a Western David, almost naked of conventional arms but alone possessed of a nuclear sling.

Toward the end of that decade, the prospect that the Soviets would acquire intercontinental ballistic missiles at a time when our strategic forces consisted almost entirely of bombers focused our attention and our budget even more sharply than before upon our strategic forces. The urgency of the problem of deterring the most massive of attacks was a new reason for thinking that the West could spare neither resources nor thought to deal more specifically with lesser threats. The most urgent task was to provide for deterrence of massive aggression by assuring the survival under any attack of forces at least adequate, in the calculations of a potential attacker, to destroy his society in retaliation. It was now not the assurance of continued nuclear superiority that preempted the attention of policy-makers but, on the contrary, the struggle to maintain it.

But it is time for the maps to change by which policy is charted and justified. The old ones, which assumed a U.S. nuclear monopoly, both strategic and tactical, and a Communist monopoly of ground combat strength, are too far removed from reality to serve as even rough guides. Neither we nor our allies can afford the crudities of maps that tell us that old policies are still forced upon us, when a true picture would show important new avenues of necessity and choice.

What most needs changing is a picture of ourselves and of the Western Alliance as essentially at bay, outmanned and outgunned except for nuclear arms no longer exclusively ours. We should not think of ourselves as forced by limitations of resources to rely upon strategies of desperation and threats of vast mutual destruction, compelled to deal only with the most massive and immediate challenges, letting lesser ones go by default. It would be a striking historical phenomenon if that self-image should be justified. We are the largest member of an Alliance with a population of almost 450 million people, an aggregate annual product which is fast approaching a trillion dollars, and a modern and diverse technological base without parallel, facing the Soviet Union and its European satellites with their hundred million fewer people and an aggregate output no more than half that of the West.

And quite apart from ignoring the underlying strengths of the West, the outdated picture I have described takes no account of the military capabilities in being that our investment over the last decade, and specifically in the last few years, have bought for us. If new problems put strong claims on our attention and our resources today, it is very largely because we have come a large part of the way that is feasible toward solving some old ones.

Let me summarize the current status of the balance of strategic nuclear forces, that part of the military environment that has preoccupied our attention for so long. In strictly relative numerical terms, the situation is the familiar one. The U.S. force now contains more than 500 operational long-range ballistic missiles—ATLAS, TITAN, MINUTEMAN, POLARIS—and is planned to increase to over 1700 by 1966. There is no doubt in our minds and none in the minds of the Soviets that these missiles can penetrate to their targets. In addition, the U.S. has Strategic Air Command bombers on air alert and over 500 bombers on quick reaction ground alert. By comparison, the consensus is that today the Soviets could place about half as many bombers over North America on a first strike. The Soviets are estimated to have today only a fraction as many intercontinental missiles as we do. Furthermore, their submarine-launched ballistic missiles are short range, and generally are not comparable to our POLARIS force. The Soviets pose a very large threat against Europe, including hundreds of intermediate and medium-range ballistic missiles. This threat is today and will continue to be covered by the clear superiority of our strategic forces.

The most wishful of Soviet planners would have to calculate as a certainty that the most effective surprise attack they could launch would still leave us with the capability to destroy the attacker's society. What is equally pertinent is that the relative numbers and survivability of U.S. strategic forces would permit us to retaliate against all the urgent Soviet military targets that are subject to attack, thus contributing to the limitation of damage to ourselves and our allies.

Deterrence of deliberate, calculated attack seems as well assured as it can be, and the damage-limiting capability of our numerically superior forces is, I believe, well worth its incremental cost. It is a capability to which the smaller forces of the Soviet Union could not realistically aspire. That is one reason, among others, why I would not trade our strategic posture for that of the Soviets at any point during the coming decade.

But given the kind of force that the Soviets are building, including submarine-launched missiles beyond the reach of our offensive forces, the damage which the Soviets could inflict on us and our allies, no matter what we do to limit it, remains extremely high.

That has been true for our allies ever since the middle and late 'Fifties. Soviet acquisition of a sizable delivery capability against the U.S., and more significantly their acquisition of relatively protected forces, submarine-launched or hardened,[1] has been long and often prematurely heralded. Its arrival at last merely dramatizes the need to recognize that strategic nuclear war would under all foreseeable circumstances be bilateral—and highly destructive to both sides.

Larger budgets for U.S. strategic forces would not change that fact. They could have only a decreasing incremental effect in limiting somewhat the damage that the U.S. and its allies could suffer in a general nuclear war. In short, we cannot buy the capability to make a strategic bombing campaign once again a unilateral prospect.

[1] Ground installations protected against direct nuclear hits or near misses [Ed.].

That must, I suggest, be accepted as one of the determinants affecting policy. Another is that the same situation confronts the Soviet leaders, in a way that is even more intensely confining. In fact, enormous increases in Soviet budgets would be required for them to achieve any significant degree of damage-limiting capability. The present Soviet leaders show no tendency to challenge the basis of the U.S. strategic deterrent posture by such expenditures.

In the last two years alone, we have increased the number of nuclear warheads in the strategic alert forces by 100%. During that period we have more than doubled the megatonnage of the strategic alert forces. The fact that further increases in strategic force size will at last encounter rapidly diminishing returns—which is largely an effect of the very large investments the U.S. has made in this area—should be reflected in future budgets. The funding for the initial introduction of missiles into our forces is nearing completion. We can anticipate that the annual expenditure on strategic forces will drop substantially, and level off well below the present rate of spending. This is not to rule out the possibility that research now in progress on possible new technological developments, including the possibility of useful ballistic missile defenses, will require major new expenditures. In any event, there will be recurring costs of modernization.

In the field of tactical nuclear weapons, the picture is in important respects similar. The U.S. at present has in stockpile or planned for stockpile tens of thousands of nuclear explosives for tactical use on the battlefield, in anti-submarine warfare and against aircraft. They include warheads for artillery, battlefield missiles, demolition munitions, bombs, depth charges, air-to-air missiles and surface-to-air missiles. The consensus is that the U.S. is presently substantially superior in design, diversity and numbers in this class of weapons.

This is an indispensable superiority, as we can readily understand if we consider how our problems of strategic choice would be altered if the tables were reversed and it were the Soviet Union which held a commanding lead in this field. Nevertheless, what we have is superiority, not monopoly, and even if tactical nuclear warfare can be limited, below some ill-defined threshold of strategic exchange, the key fact is that if the West initiates such warfare in the future, it must be expected to be bilateral, in any theater which engaged the Soviet Union. Again, we cannot buy back a monopoly, or the assurance of unilateral use.

Finally, there is the area of what we call our general purpose forces. Within the last two years, we have increased the number of our combat-ready Army divisions by about 45%, from 11 to 16. There has been a 30% increase in the number of tactical air squadrons; a 75% increase in airlift capabilities; and a 100% increase in ship construction and conversion to modernize the fleet.

But it is not only force size that matters. The key to the effective utilization of these forces is combat readiness and mobility.

The most recent demonstration of our ability to reinforce our troops presently stationed in Europe occurred last month in Operation BIG LIFT, the first of a series of planned large-scale, world-wide exercises. For the first time in military history, an entire division was airlifted from one continent to another. That movement could never have been accomplished without a massive increase in our airlift capability, which is still being expanded. (It will have risen 400% between 1961 and 1967.) It required the development of new techniques to preposition combat equipment, of which we have two extra division sets now in Europe. It called for new techniques in military training and administration to make sure that units are really ready to move out on a moment's notice. This exercise, in which some 16,000 airmen and soldiers and more than 350 planes took part, is directly relevant to the needs of Europe, where it brought a seventh division to join the six that are to remain in place. It is also relevant to the ability of the U.S. to fulfill its policy commitments world-wide, swiftly and in effective strength.

But, it might be asked, what is the significance of all this for the realistic security problems of the United States and its allies? To what contingencies are these forces expected to contribute, and how effective might they be, measured against the strength of opposing forces? How meaningful is it to talk of 16 or 20 or 30 divisions in opposing the ground armies of the Soviet Union and Communist China?

Such questions are often meant to be merely rhetorical, in view of the supposed masses of Communist troops. The fact is that they are serious, difficult questions, to which I shall suggest some tentative answers. But it is difficult to encourage realistic discussions of specific contingencies so long as the shadow of the Communist horde hangs unchallenged over the debate. The actual contingencies that seem to be to me most likely and most significant are not those which would involve all, or even a major part, of the Soviet Bloc or Chinese Communist armed forces, nor do they all involve Europe. Hence, aggregate figures of armed strength of NATO and the Warsaw Pact nations are not immediately relevant to them. But it is useful to make these over-all comparisons precisely because misleading or obsolete notions of these very aggregates often produce an attitude of hopelessness toward any attempt to prepare to meet Communist forces in ground combat, however limited in scope.

The announced total of Soviet armed forces for 1955 was indeed a formidable 5.75 million men. Today that figure has been cut to about 3.3 million; the Warsaw Pact total including the Soviets is only about 4.5 million. Against that, it is today the members of NATO whose active armed forces number over five million. The ground forces of NATO nations total 3.2 million, of which 2.2 million men are in Europe, as against the Soviet ground combat forces total of about 2 million men, and a Warsaw Pact total of about 3 million. Both the Soviet Union and the U.S. forces of course include units stationed in the Far East. In Central Europe, NATO has more men, and more combat troops, on the ground than does the Bloc. It has more men on the ground in West Germany than the Bloc does in East Germany. It has more and better tactical aircraft, and these planes on the average can carry twice the payload twice as far as the Soviet counterparts.

These facts are hard to reconcile with the familiar picture of the Russian Army as incomparably massive. The usual index cited to support that picture is numbers of total active divisions, and the specific number familiar from the past is 175 divisions in the Soviet Army.

This total, if true, would indeed present a paradox. The Soviet ground forces are reliably estimated to be very close to two million men, compared to about one million for the U.S. How is it that the Soviets can muster ten times the number of active, combat-ready, fully-manned divisions that the United States has manned, with only twice as many men on active duty? The answer is simply that they do not. Recent intensive investigation has shown that the number of active Soviet divisions that are maintained at manning levels anywhere close to combat readiness is less than half of the 160–175 figure.

What remains is a large number, but even that is misleading. For one thing, U.S. divisions have about twice as many men in the division unit and its immediate combat supporting units as comparable Soviet divisions. A U.S. mechanized division has far more personnel in maneuvering units, far more in armored cavalry, far more engineers, far more signals, far more light armored personnel carriers, and far more aircraft available in support than Soviet divisions. In addition to longer staying power, much of the U.S. manpower and equipment margin is muscle that would make itself felt on D-Day. If, on the other hand, we were to reorganize along Soviet lines, we could display far greater numbers of divisions comparable to those of the Soviets.

The Soviet combat-ready force remains a formidable one. Moreover, the Russians do have a powerful mobilization capability; in particular, they have a large number of lightly manned or cadre divisions to be filled out on mobilization. Still, this reality remains strikingly different from our accustomed maps of it.

I do not wish to suggest that such aggregate comparisons are by themselves a valid index to military capabilities. But they are enough to suggest the absurdity, as a picture of the prevailing military strengths on which new efforts might build, of David and Goliath notions borrowed from 1949.

None of this is to say that NATO strength on the ground in Europe is adequate to turn back without nuclear weapons an all-out surprise non-nuclear attack.

But that is not in any case the contingency toward which the recent and future improvements in the mobility and capabilities of U.S. general purpose forces are primarily oriented. Aggression on that scale would mean a war about the future of Europe and, as a consequence, the future of the U.S. and the USSR. In the face of threats of that magnitude, our nuclear superiority remains highly relevant to deterrence. The Soviets know that even non-nuclear aggression at that high end of the spectrum of conflict so threatens our most vital interests that we and our allies are prepared to make whatever response may be required to defeat it, no matter how terrible the consequences for our own society.

The probability that the Soviet leaders would choose to invoke that exchange seems to me very low indeed. They know well what even the Chinese Communist leaders must recognize upon further reflection, that a nuclear war would mean destruction of everything they have built up for themselves during the last 50 years.

If we were to consider a spectrum of the possible cases of Communist aggression, then, ranging from harassment, covert aggression and indirect challenge at one end of the scale to the massive invasion of Western Europe or a full scale nuclear strike against the West at the other end, it is clear that our nuclear superiority has been and should continue to be an effective deterrent to aggression at the high end of the spectrum. It is equally clear, on the other hand, that at the very low end of the spectrum a nuclear response may not be fully credible, and that nuclear power alone cannot be an effective deterrent at this level in the future any more than it has been in the past.

The fact is that at every level of force, the Alliance in general, and the U.S. Armed Forces in particular, have greater and more effective strength than we are in the habit of thinking we have— and with reasonable continued effort we can have whatever strength we need. I have spoken already of strategic weapons, where the great superiority of the United States is the superiority also of the Alliance. In tactical nuclear weapons a parallel superiority exists—and while many of our Allies share with us in manning the systems which would use these tactical warheads in the hour of need, it is not unfair to point out that, even more than in the strategic field, the tactical nuclear strength of the Alliance is a contribution of the United States. That strength has been increased, on the ground in Europe by more than 60% in the last two years. Today the thousands of U.S. warheads deployed on the continent for the immediate defense of Europe have a combined explosive strength more than 10,000 times the force of the nuclear weapons used to end the Second War. Tactical nuclear strength the Alliance has today, and we have provided it.

But neither we nor our Allies can find the detonation of such weapons—and their inevitable bilateral exchange—an easy first choice. At the lower end of the spectrum, therefore, we also need strong and ready conventional forces. We have done our part here and we continue to believe it just—and practicable—for our partners to do theirs.

The most difficult questions arise over the best means for meeting a variety of dangerous intermediate challenges in many parts of the world: those which threaten the possibility of sizable conflict while still not raising the immediate issue of the national survival of ourselves or of any member of our alliances. Conflicts might arise out of Soviet subversion and political aggression backed up by military measures in non-NATO areas in Europe, Latin America, the Middle East and Africa. There is a range of challenges that could arise from Communist China and its satellites in the Far East and in Southeast Asia. Most dangerously, approaching the upper end of the spectrum, there is the possibility of limited Soviet pressures on NATO territory itself, along the vast front running from Norway to Greece and Turkey. Both the flanks and the center contain potential targets. And always, of course, there are the contingencies that could arise in relation to Berlin.

It is difficult to say just how probable any of these circumstances might be, although they must be regarded as more likely than still larger aggressions. What one can say is that if any of these more likely contingencies should arise, they would be highly dangerous. Inaction, or weak action, could result in a serious setback, missed opportunity or even disaster. In fact, if either a nuclear exchange or a major Soviet attack should occur, it would most likely arise from a conflict on a lesser scale, which Western capabilities had failed to deter and which an inadequate Western response had failed to curb in time.

Since World War II, the expansionist impulse of the Communist Bloc is clear, but equally clear is its desire to avoid direct confrontation with the military forces of the free world. In Greece, in Berlin, and in Cuba, Communists have probed for military and political weakness but when they have encountered resistance, they have held back. Not only Communist doctrine has counselled this caution, but respect for the danger that any sizable, overt conflict would lead to nuclear war. It would follow that no deterrent would be more effective against these lesser and intermediate levels of challenge than the assurance that such moves would certainly meet prompt, effective military response by the West. That response could confront the Soviets with frustration of their purposes unless they chose themselves to escalate the conflict to a nuclear exchange, or to levels that made nuclear war highly probable—a choice they are unlikely to make in the face of our destructive power.

The basis for that particular assurance cannot be systems in development, or weapons in storage depots, or reserves that must be mobilized, trained and equipped, or troops without transport. We need the right combination of forward deployment and highly mobile combat-ready ground, sea and air units, capable of prompt and effective commitment to actual combat, in short, the sort of capability we are increasingly building in our forces.

This capability requires of us—as of our Allies—a military establishment that is, in the President's words, lean and fit. We must stop and ask ourselves before deciding whether to add a new and complex weapon system to our inventory, whether it is really the most effective way to do the job under the rigorous conditions of combat. We must examine constantly the possibilities for combining functions, particularly in weapons that could be used by two or more Services. Given this tough-minded sense of reality about the requirements of combat readiness, it should be possible for the United States not only to maintain but to expand this increased strength without overall increases in our defense budget. As our national productivity and our gross national product expand, the defense budget therefore need not keep pace. Indeed, it appears likely that measured in relative—and perhaps even absolute—terms, the defense budget will level off and perhaps decline a little. At the same time, we are continuing the essential effort to reduce the impact of Defense spending on our balance of payments. We have already brought this figure down from $2.7 billion in FY [fiscal year] 1961 to $1.7 billion for FY 1963, and we shall continue to reduce it, without reducing the combat ground forces deployed in Europe, and while strengthening our overall combat effectiveness.

And it must be our policy to continue to strengthen our combat effectiveness. I do not regard the present Communist leaders as wholly reckless in action. But recent experience, in Cuba and, on a lesser scale, in Berlin, has not persuaded me that I can predict with confidence the sorts of challenges that Communist leaders will come to think prudent and profitable. If they were again to miscalculate as dangerously as they did a year ago [in the Cuban missile crisis], it would be essential to confront them, wherever that might be, with the full consequences of their action: the certainty of meeting immediate, appropriate, and fully effective military action.

All of our strengths, including our strategic and tactical nuclear forces, contributed last year, and they would contribute in similar future situations to the effectiveness of our response, by providing a basis for assurance that the Soviets would not dangerously escalate or shift the locale of the conflict. But above all, in order to fashion that response, and to promise the Soviets local defeat in case of actual ground conflict, we had to use every element of the improvements in combat readiness and mobility that had been building over the preceding year and a half, including combat divisions, air transport, and tactical air. And the last ingredient was also there: the will to use those forces against Soviet troops and equipment.

Let us not delude ourselves with obsolete images into believing that our nuclear strength, great as it is, solves all of our problems of national security, or that we lack the strengths to meet those problems that it does not solve. In the contingencies that really threaten—the sort that have occurred and will occur again—we and our allies need no longer choose to live with the sense or the reality of inferiority to the Soviet Bloc in relevant, effective force. Let us be fully aware of the wide range of our military resources, and the freedom they can give us to pursue the peaceful objectives of the free world without fear of military aggression.

Index